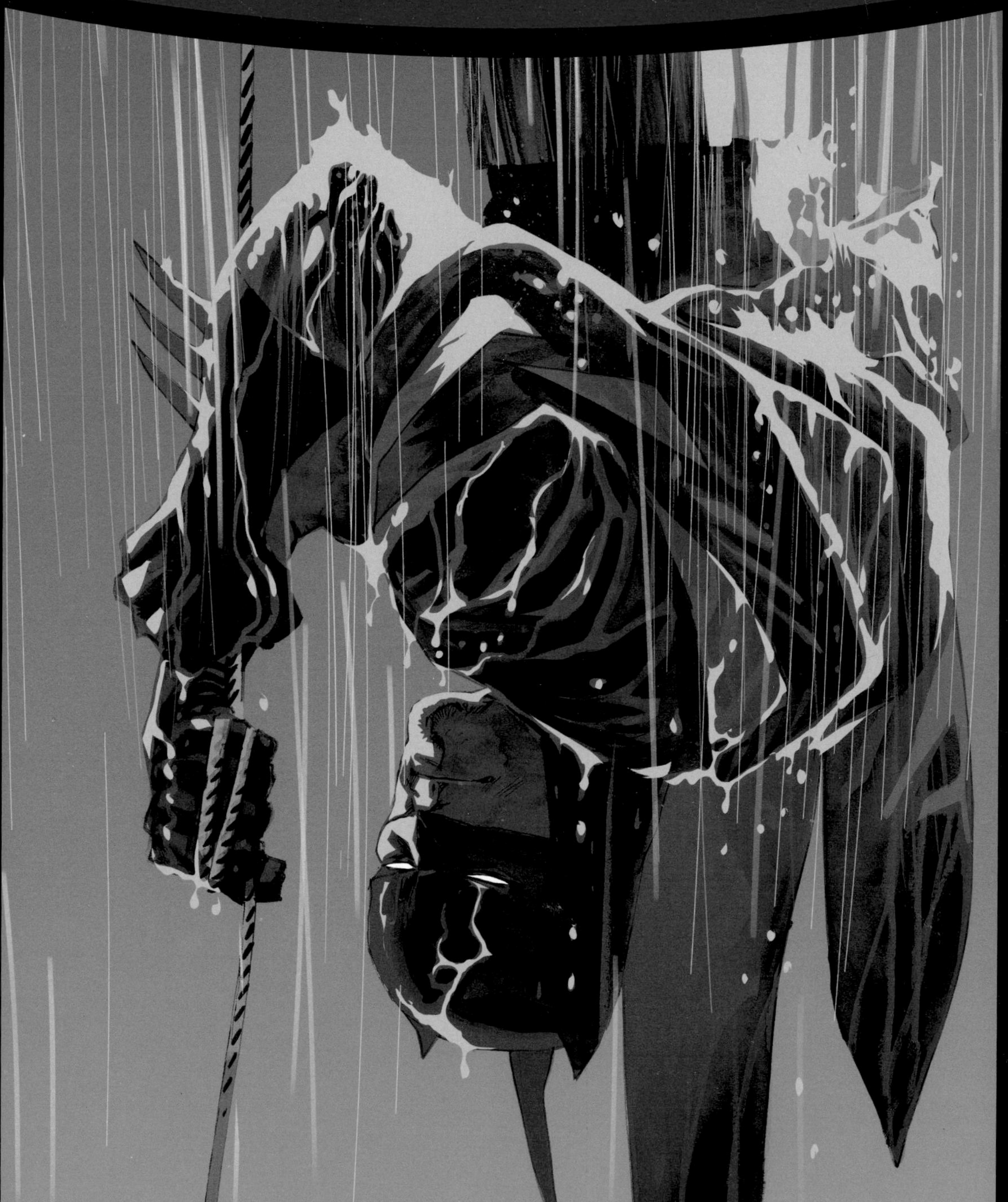

BATMAN: DETECTIVE COMICS

VOL. 6 FALL OF THE BATMEN

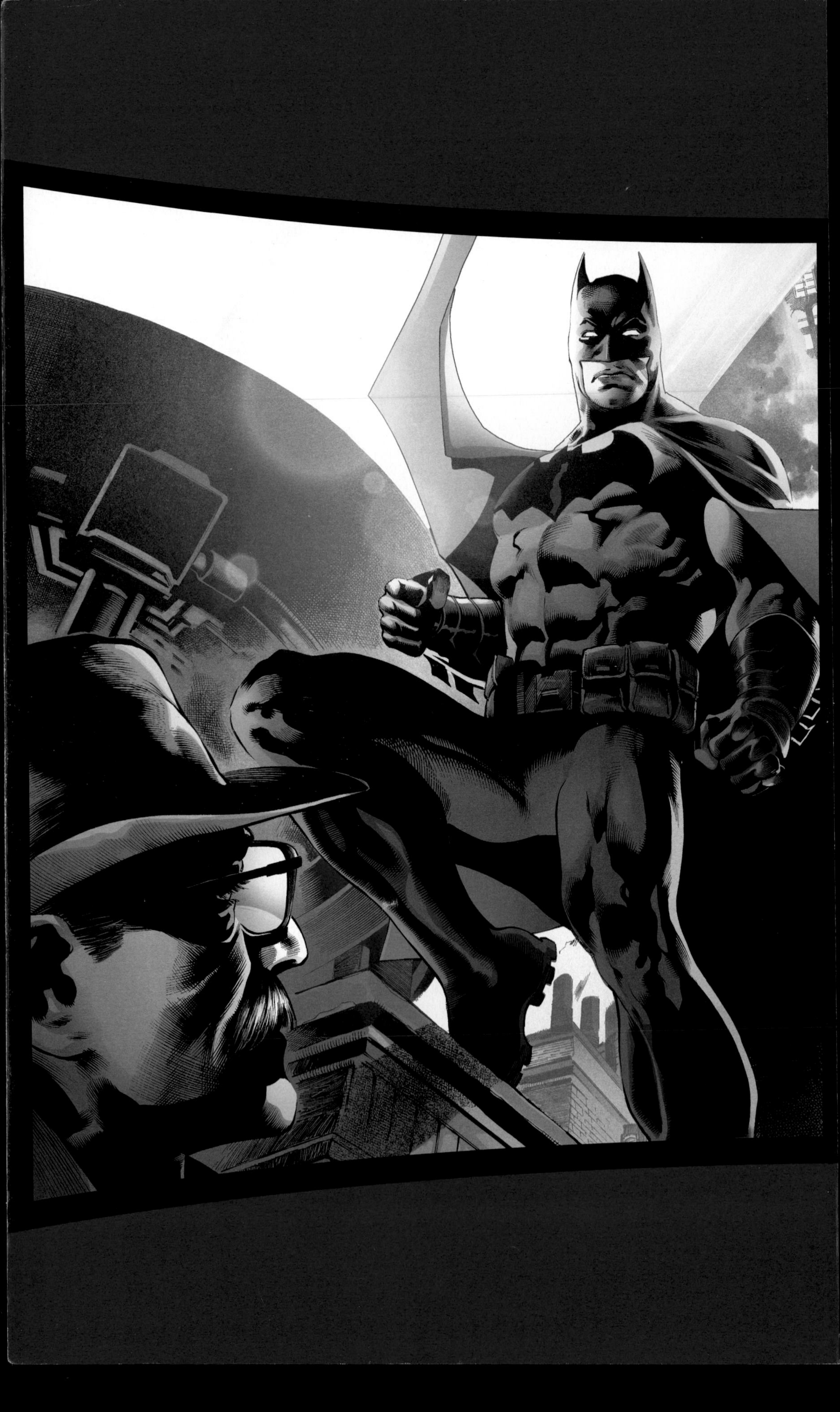

BATMAN: DETECTIVE COMICS

VOL.6 FALL OF THE BATMEN

JAMES TYNION IV
writer

**JOE BENNETT * MIGUEL MENDONÇA * JESUS MERINO
PHILIPPE BRIONES * EDDY BARROWS**
pencillers

**SAL REGLA * RICARDO JAIME * MARCIO LOERZER
DIANA EGEA * JESUS MERINO * PHILIPPE BRIONES * EBER FERREIRA**
inkers

JASON WRIGHT * ALLEN PASSALAQUA * ADRIANO LUCAS
colorists

SAL CIPRIANO
letterer

GUILLEM MARCH
collection cover artist

BATMAN created by BOB KANE with BILL FINGER

CHRIS CONROY Editor - Original Series ＊ **ANDREW MARINO DAVE WIELGOSZ** Assistant Editors - Original Series
JEB WOODARD Group Editor - Collected Editions ＊ **ROBIN WILDMAN** Editor - Collected Edition
STEVE COOK Design Director - Books ＊ **SHANNON STEWART** Publication Design

BOB HARRAS Senior VP - Editor-in-Chief, DC Comics ＊ **PAT McCALLUM** Executive Editor, DC Comics

DIANE NELSON President ＊ **DAN DiDIO** Publisher ＊ **JIM LEE** Publisher ＊ **GEOFF JOHNS** President & Chief Creative Officer
AMIT DESAI Executive VP - Business & Marketing Strategy, Direct to Consumer & Global Franchise Management
SAM ADES Senior VP & General Manager, Digital Services ＊ **BOBBIE CHASE** VP & Executive Editor, Young Reader & Talent Development
MARK CHIARELLO Senior VP - Art, Design & Collected Editions ＊ **JOHN CUNNINGHAM** Senior VP - Sales & Trade Marketing
ANNE DePIES Senior VP - Business Strategy, Finance & Administration ＊ **DON FALLETTI** VP - Manufacturing Operations
LAWRENCE GANEM VP - Editorial Administration & Talent Relations ＊ **ALISON GILL** Senior VP - Manufacturing & Operations
HANK KANALZ Senior VP - Editorial Strategy & Administration ＊ **JAY KOGAN** VP - Legal Affairs ＊ **JACK MAHAN** VP - Business Affairs
NICK J. NAPOLITANO VP - Manufacturing Administration ＊ **EDDIE SCANNELL** VP - Consumer Marketing
COURTNEY SIMMONS Senior VP - Publicity & Communications ＊ **JIM (SKI) SOKOLOWSKI** VP - Comic Book Specialty Sales & Trade Marketing
NANCY SPEARS VP - Mass, Book, Digital Sales & Trade Marketing ＊ **MICHELE R. WELLS** VP - Content Strategy

BATMAN: DETECTIVE COMICS VOL. 6—FALL OF THE BATMEN

DC Comics, 2900 West Alameda Ave., Burbank, CA 91505
Printed by LSC Communications, Kendallville, IN, USA. 5/18/18. First Printing.
ISBN: 978-1-4012-8145-8

Library of Congress Cataloging-in-Publication Data is available.

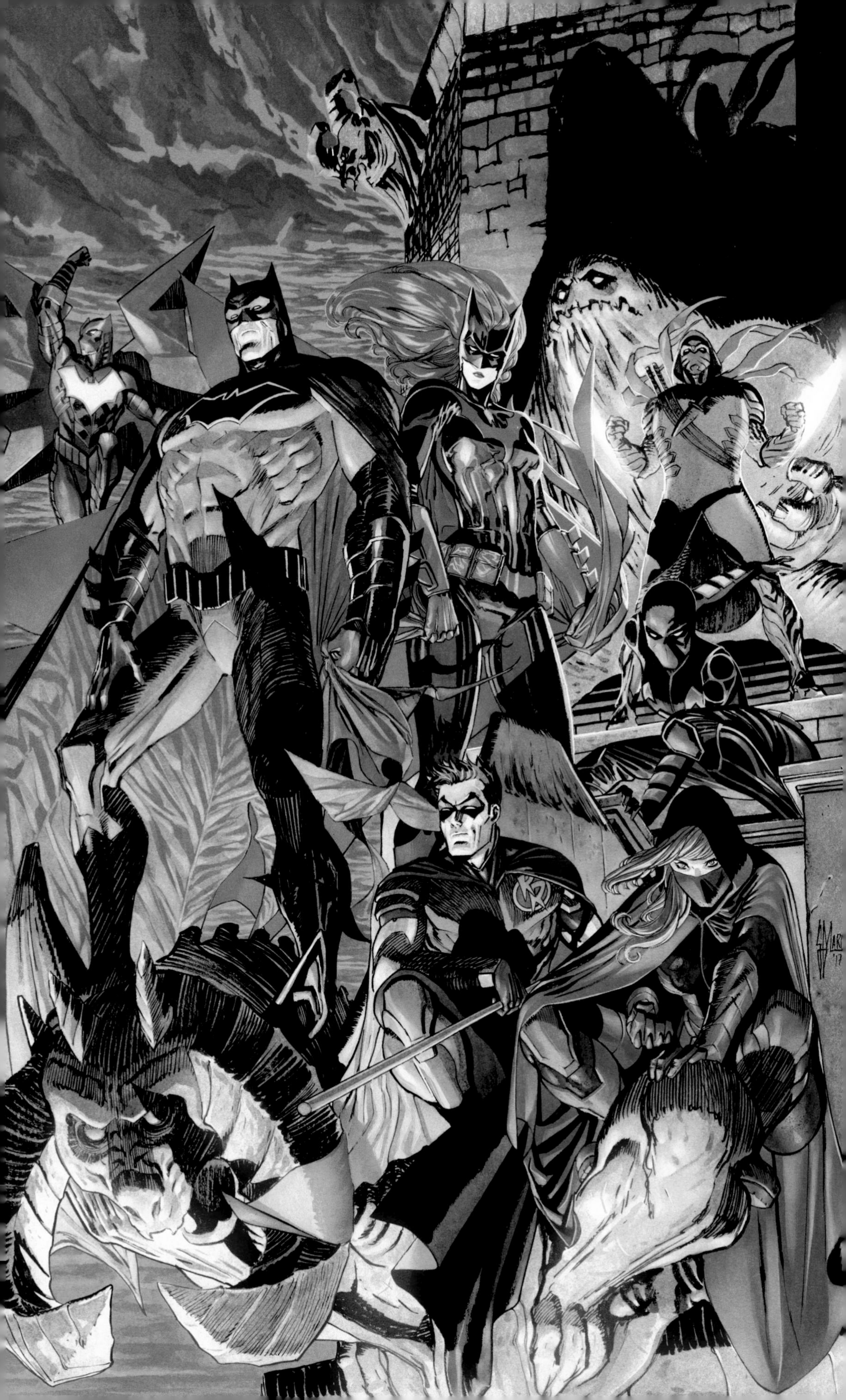

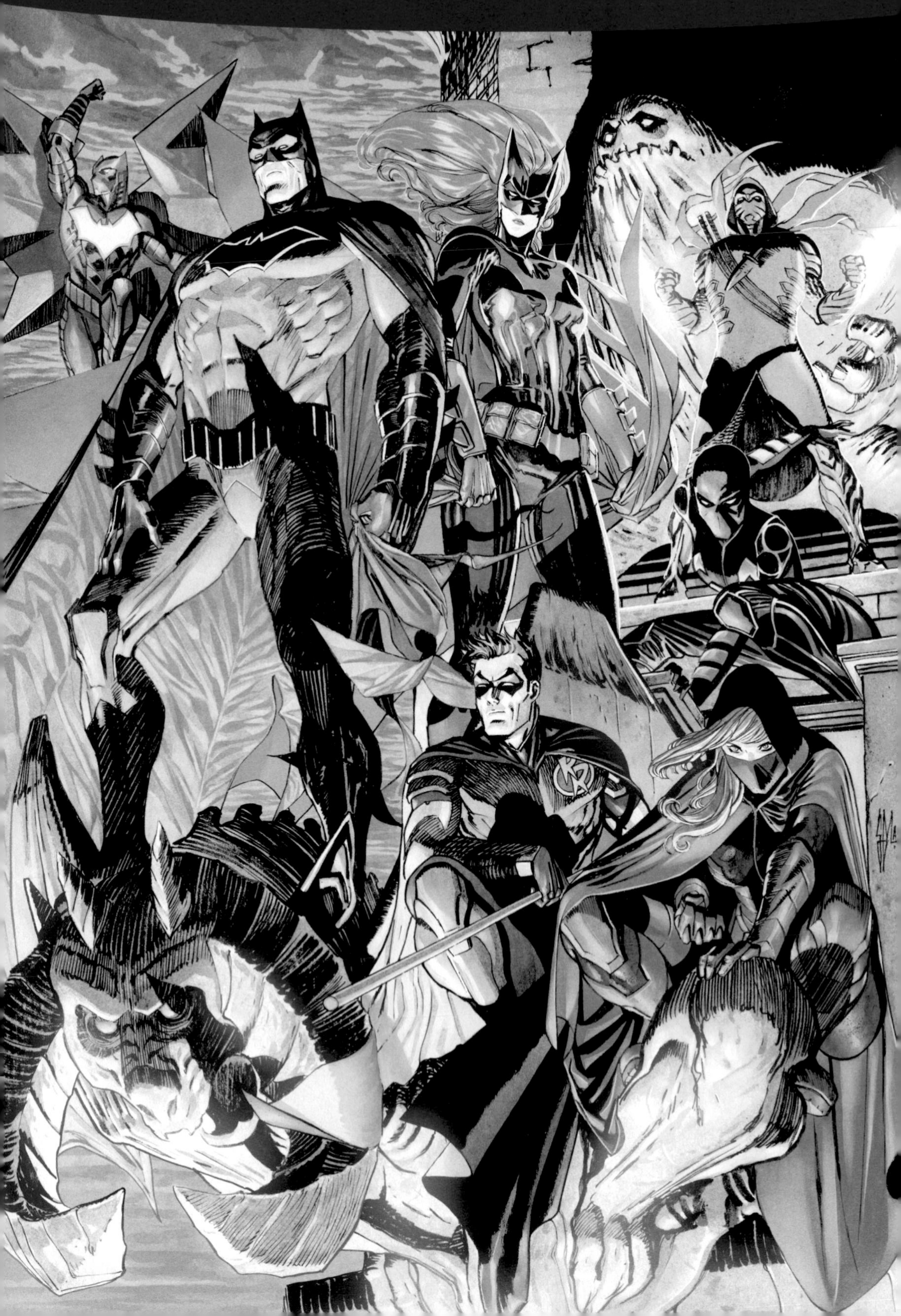

MR. MAYOR!

MR. MAYOR!

GCN BREAKING NEWS: MICHAEL AKINS APPOINTED NEW MAYOR OF GOTHAM • GCN SPORTS: KNIGHTS DROP GAME 7 TO DC B

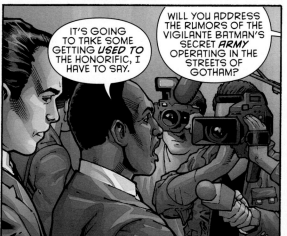

IT'S GOING TO TAKE SOME GETTING *USED TO* THE HONORIFIC, I HAVE TO SAY.

WILL YOU ADDRESS THE RUMORS OF THE VIGILANTE BATMAN'S SECRET *ARMY* OPERATING IN THE STREETS OF GOTHAM?

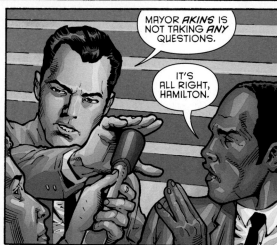

MAYOR *AKINS* IS NOT TAKING *ANY* QUESTIONS.

IT'S ALL RIGHT, HAMILTON.

PLEASE *FORGIVE* DEPUTY MAYOR *HILL.* OUR NEW ADMINISTRATION HASN'T HAD MUCH TIME TO DISCUSS THE PROVERBIAL *BAT* IN THE ROOM, BUT IT IS NOT MY INTENT TO SIT BACK AND IGNORE THE FACT THAT THERE *IS* A BATMAN IN THIS CITY.

I *ALSO* WILL NOT IGNORE THE FACT THAT OUR CITY SEES THREATS BEYOND THE ORDINARY, AND I RESPECT THAT IT MAY TAKE THE HELP OF EXTRAORDINARY PERSONS TO SUBDUE THOSE THREATS.

I WAS THE POLICE COMMISSIONER ONCE UPON A TIME, AND I HAD CAUSE TO LIGHT UP THE SIGNAL WHEN OUR CITY NEEDED A HERO.

AS MAYOR, I EXPECT I MAY CALL COMMISSIONER GORDON AND DIRECT HIM TO DO THE SAME FROM TIME TO TIME.

I HAVE NOT SEEN THE DIRECT EVIDENCE OF THE KIND OF *PARAMILITARY* BEHAVIOR THAT THE PRESS HAS STARTED TO SUGGEST-- HOWEVER, I CAN BE UNEQUIVOCAL IN MY RESPONSE TO IT.

GOTHAM CITY *HAS* A POLICE FORCE. IT DOES *NOT* NEED A SECOND.

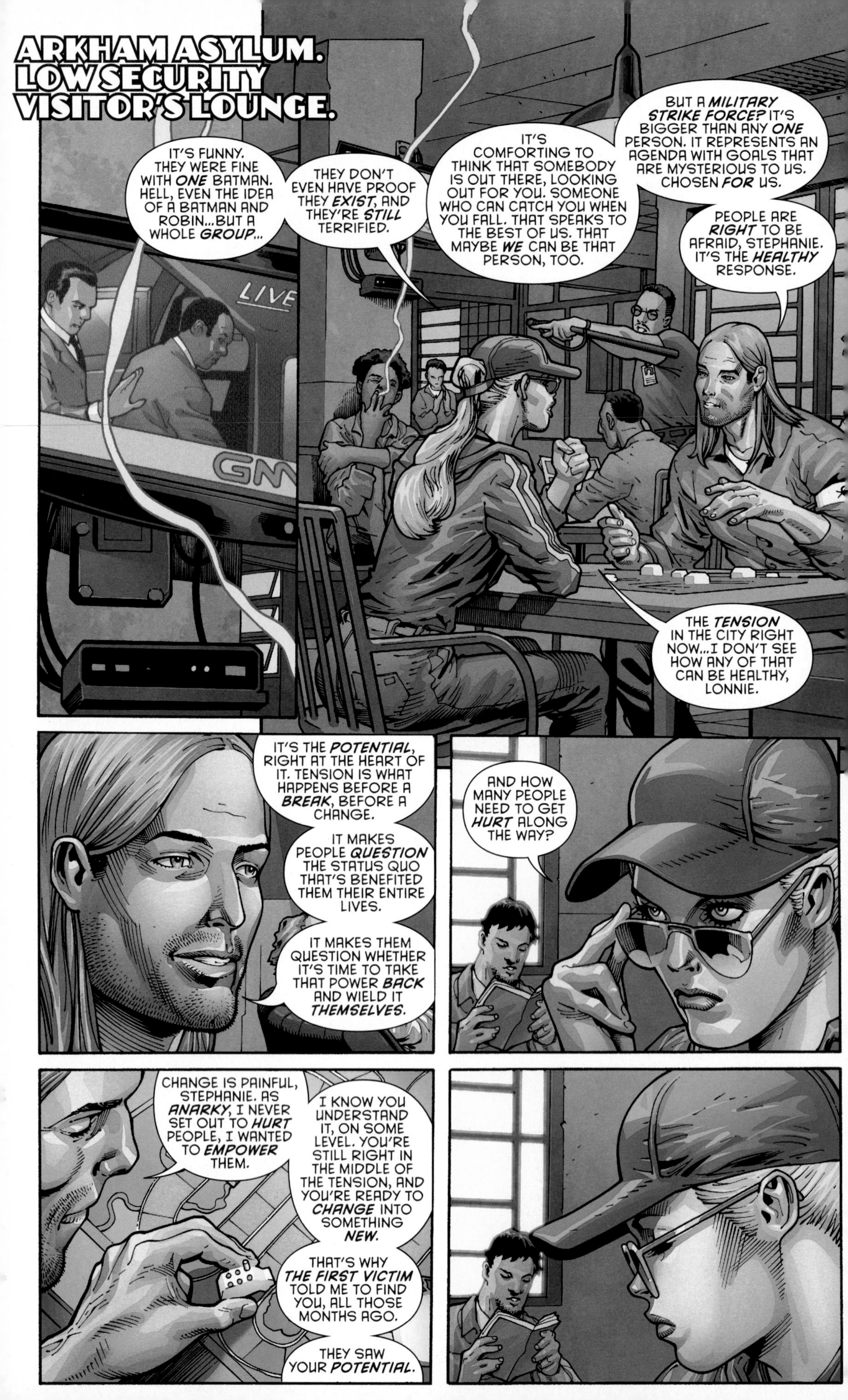
ARKHAM ASYLUM. LOW SECURITY VISITOR'S LOUNGE.
IT'S FUNNY. THEY WERE FINE WITH ONE BATMAN. HELL, EVEN THE IDEA OF A BATMAN AND ROBIN...BUT A WHOLE GROUP...
THEY DON'T EVEN HAVE PROOF THEY EXIST, AND THEY'RE STILL TERRIFIED.
IT'S COMFORTING TO THINK THAT SOMEBODY IS OUT THERE, LOOKING OUT FOR YOU. SOMEONE WHO CAN CATCH YOU WHEN YOU FALL. THAT SPEAKS TO THE BEST OF US. THAT MAYBE WE CAN BE THAT PERSON, TOO.
BUT A MILITARY STRIKE FORCE? IT'S BIGGER THAN ANY ONE PERSON. IT REPRESENTS AN AGENDA WITH GOALS THAT ARE MYSTERIOUS TO US. CHOSEN FOR US.
PEOPLE ARE RIGHT TO BE AFRAID, STEPHANIE. IT'S THE HEALTHY RESPONSE.
LIVE
GN
THE TENSION IN THE CITY RIGHT NOW...I DON'T SEE HOW ANY OF THAT CAN BE HEALTHY, LONNIE.
IT'S THE POTENTIAL, RIGHT AT THE HEART OF IT. TENSION IS WHAT HAPPENS BEFORE A BREAK, BEFORE A CHANGE.
IT MAKES PEOPLE QUESTION THE STATUS QUO THAT'S BENEFITED THEM THEIR ENTIRE LIVES.
IT MAKES THEM QUESTION WHETHER IT'S TIME TO TAKE THAT POWER BACK AND WIELD IT THEMSELVES.
AND HOW MANY PEOPLE NEED TO GET HURT ALONG THE WAY?
CHANGE IS PAINFUL, STEPHANIE. AS ANARKY, I NEVER SET OUT TO HURT PEOPLE, I WANTED TO EMPOWER THEM.
I KNOW YOU UNDERSTAND IT, ON SOME LEVEL. YOU'RE STILL RIGHT IN THE MIDDLE OF THE TENSION, AND YOU'RE READY TO CHANGE INTO SOMETHING NEW.
THAT'S WHY THE FIRST VICTIM TOLD ME TO FIND YOU, ALL THOSE MONTHS AGO.
THEY SAW YOUR POTENTIAL.

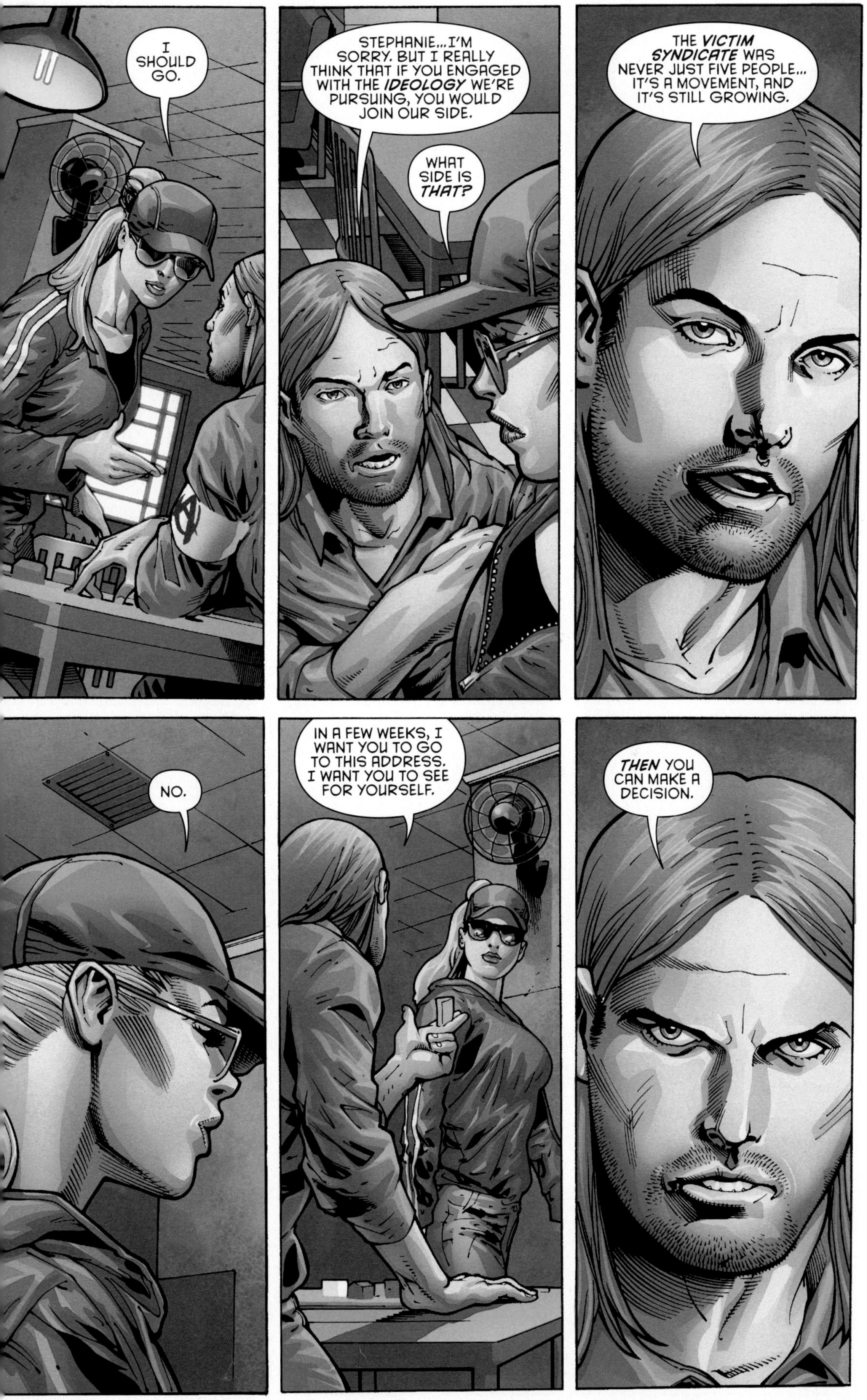
I SHOULD GO.
STEPHANIE...I'M SORRY. BUT I REALLY THINK THAT IF YOU ENGAGED WITH THE *IDEOLOGY* WE'RE PURSUING, YOU WOULD JOIN OUR SIDE.
WHAT SIDE IS *THAT?*
THE *VICTIM SYNDICATE* WAS NEVER JUST FIVE PEOPLE... IT'S A MOVEMENT, AND IT'S STILL GROWING.
NO.
IN A FEW WEEKS, I WANT YOU TO GO TO THIS ADDRESS. I WANT YOU TO SEE FOR YOURSELF.
THEN YOU CAN MAKE A DECISION.

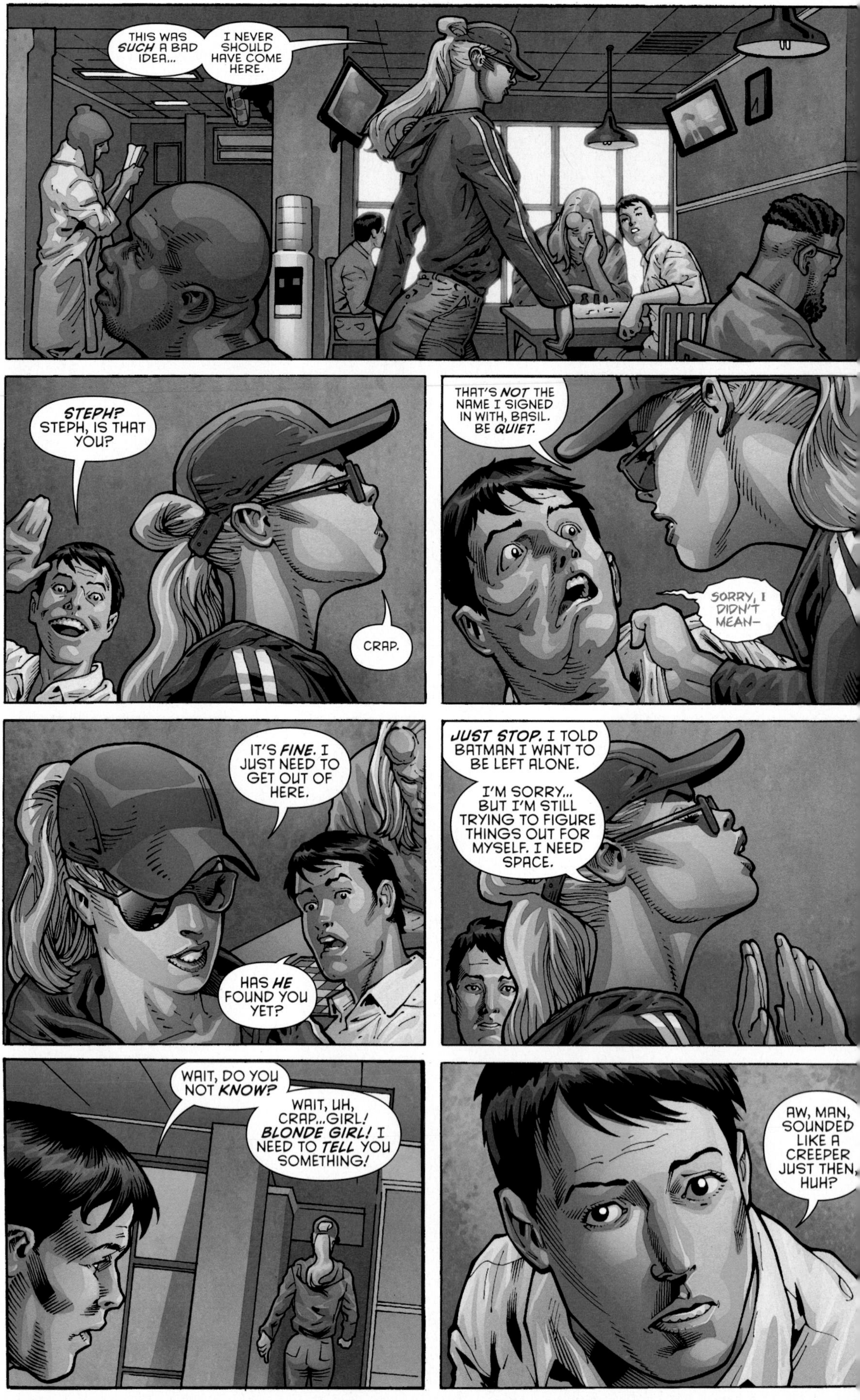
THIS WAS SUCH A BAD IDEA...
I NEVER SHOULD HAVE COME HERE.
STEPH? STEPH, IS THAT YOU?
CRAP.
THAT'S NOT THE NAME I SIGNED IN WITH, BASIL. BE QUIET.
SORRY, I DIDN'T MEAN—
IT'S FINE. I JUST NEED TO GET OUT OF HERE.
HAS HE FOUND YOU YET?
JUST STOP. I TOLD BATMAN I WANT TO BE LEFT ALONE.
I'M SORRY... BUT I'M STILL TRYING TO FIGURE THINGS OUT FOR MYSELF. I NEED SPACE.
WAIT, DO YOU NOT KNOW?
WAIT, UH, CRAP...GIRL! BLONDE GIRL! I NEED TO TELL YOU SOMETHING!
AW, MAN, SOUNDED LIKE A CREEPER JUST THEN, HUH?

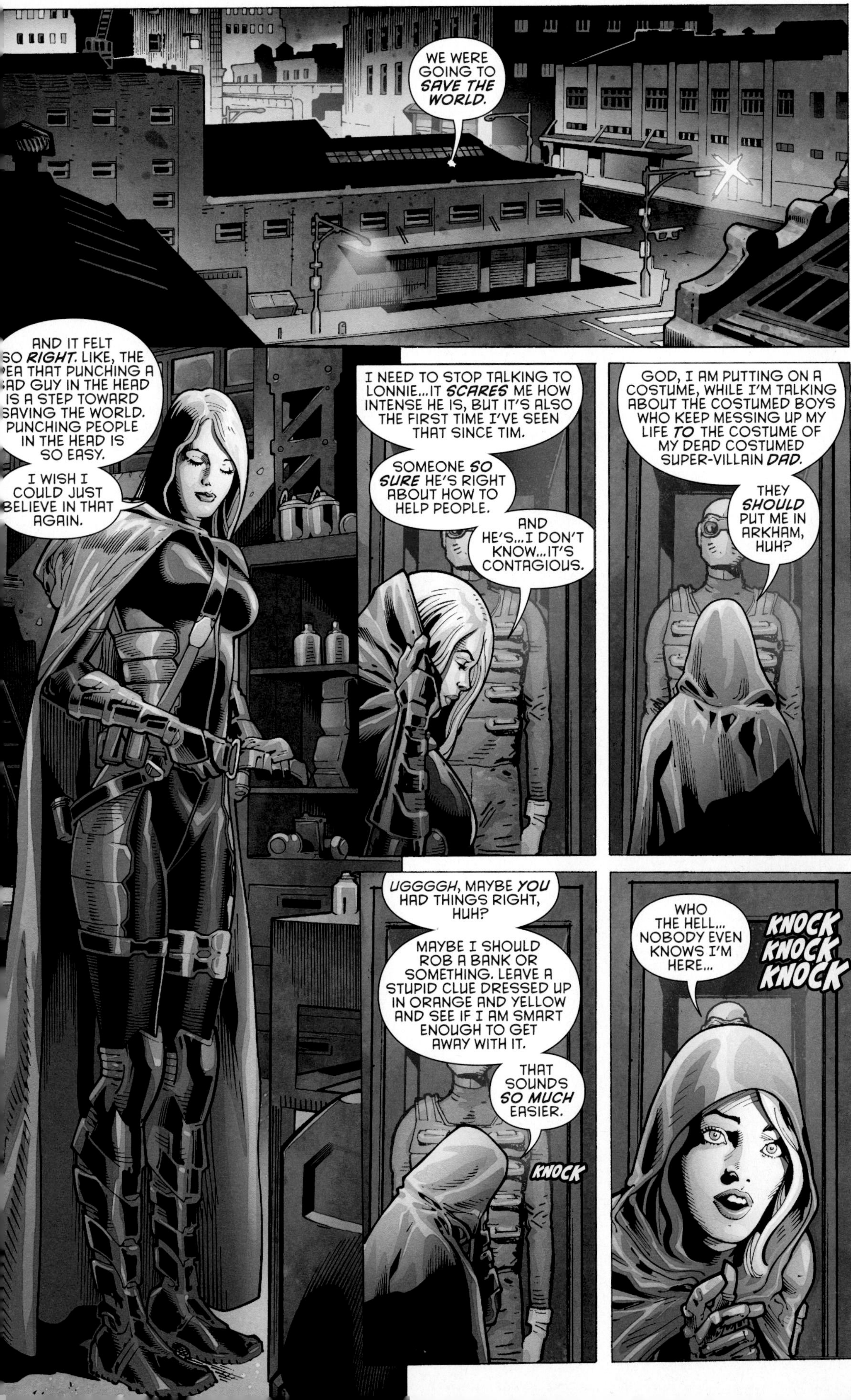

WE WERE GOING TO SAVE THE WORLD.
AND IT FELT SO RIGHT. LIKE, THE IDEA THAT PUNCHING A BAD GUY IN THE HEAD IS A STEP TOWARD SAVING THE WORLD. PUNCHING PEOPLE IN THE HEAD IS SO EASY.
I WISH I COULD JUST BELIEVE IN THAT AGAIN.
I NEED TO STOP TALKING TO LONNIE...IT SCARES ME HOW INTENSE HE IS, BUT IT'S ALSO THE FIRST TIME I'VE SEEN THAT SINCE TIM.
SOMEONE SO SURE HE'S RIGHT ABOUT HOW TO HELP PEOPLE.
AND HE'S...I DON'T KNOW...IT'S CONTAGIOUS.
GOD, I AM PUTTING ON A COSTUME, WHILE I'M TALKING ABOUT THE COSTUMED BOYS WHO KEEP MESSING UP MY LIFE TO THE COSTUME OF MY DEAD COSTUMED SUPER-VILLAIN DAD.
THEY SHOULD PUT ME IN ARKHAM, HUH?
UGGGGH, MAYBE YOU HAD THINGS RIGHT, HUH?
MAYBE I SHOULD ROB A BANK OR SOMETHING. LEAVE A STUPID CLUE DRESSED UP IN ORANGE AND YELLOW AND SEE IF I AM SMART ENOUGH TO GET AWAY WITH IT.
THAT SOUNDS SO MUCH EASIER.
KNOCK
WHO THE HELL... NOBODY EVEN KNOWS I'M HERE...
KNOCK KNOCK KNOCK

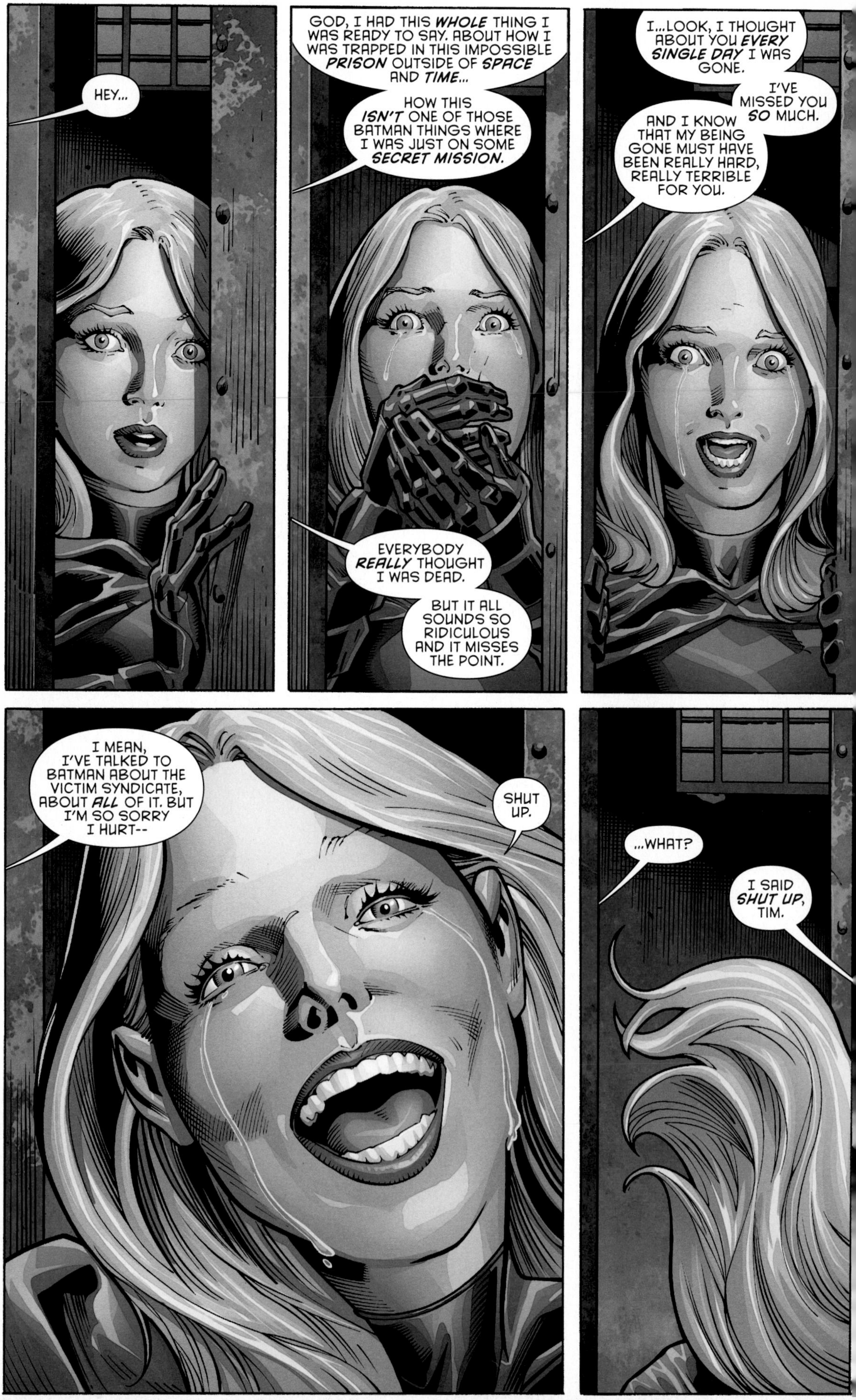
HEY...
GOD, I HAD THIS WHOLE THING I WAS READY TO SAY. ABOUT HOW I WAS TRAPPED IN THIS IMPOSSIBLE PRISON OUTSIDE OF SPACE AND TIME...
HOW THIS ISN'T ONE OF THOSE BATMAN THINGS WHERE I WAS JUST ON SOME SECRET MISSION.
EVERYBODY REALLY THOUGHT I WAS DEAD.
BUT IT ALL SOUNDS SO RIDICULOUS AND IT MISSES THE POINT.
I...LOOK, I THOUGHT ABOUT YOU EVERY SINGLE DAY I WAS GONE.
I'VE MISSED YOU SO MUCH.
AND I KNOW THAT MY BEING GONE MUST HAVE BEEN REALLY HARD, REALLY TERRIBLE FOR YOU.
I MEAN, I'VE TALKED TO BATMAN ABOUT THE VICTIM SYNDICATE, ABOUT ALL OF IT. BUT I'M SO SORRY I HURT--
SHUT UP.
...WHAT?
I SAID SHUT UP, TIM.

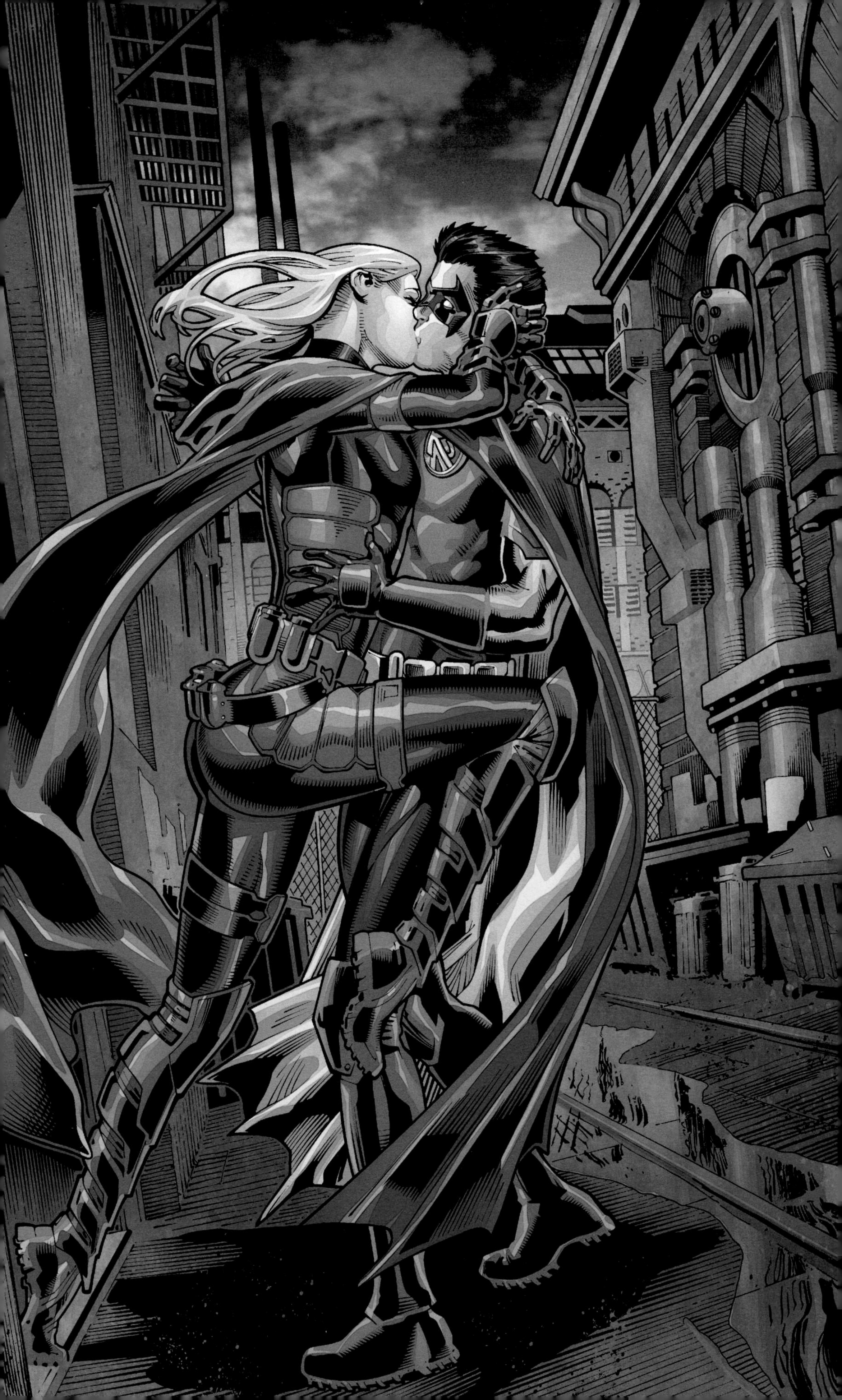

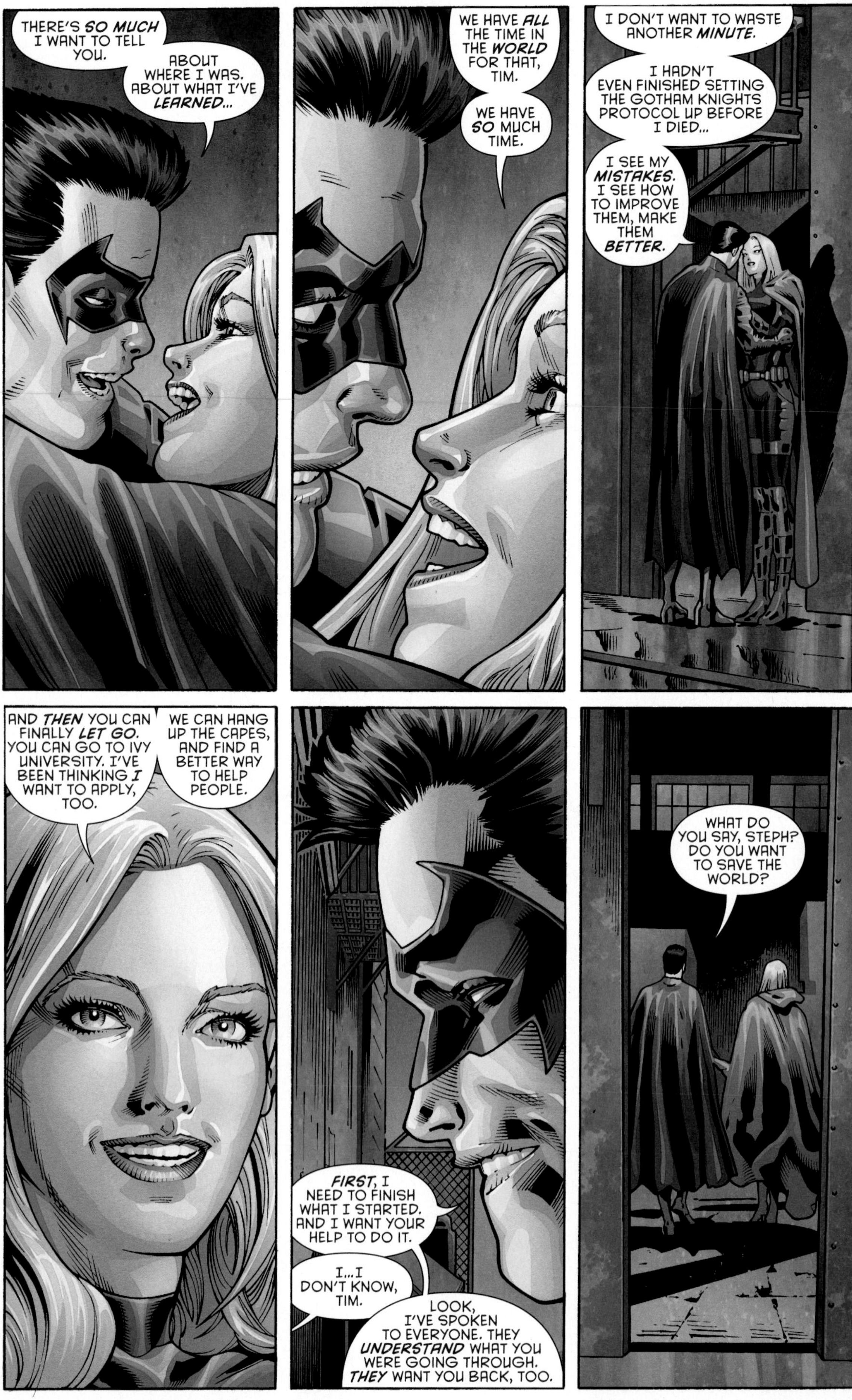
THERE'S SO MUCH I WANT TO TELL YOU.
ABOUT WHERE I WAS. ABOUT WHAT I'VE LEARNED...
WE HAVE ALL THE TIME IN THE WORLD FOR THAT, TIM.
WE HAVE SO MUCH TIME.
I DON'T WANT TO WASTE ANOTHER MINUTE.
I HADN'T EVEN FINISHED SETTING THE GOTHAM KNIGHTS PROTOCOL UP BEFORE I DIED...
I SEE MY MISTAKES. I SEE HOW TO IMPROVE THEM, MAKE THEM BETTER.
AND THEN YOU CAN FINALLY LET GO. YOU CAN GO TO IVY UNIVERSITY. I'VE BEEN THINKING I WANT TO APPLY, TOO.
WE CAN HANG UP THE CAPES, AND FIND A BETTER WAY TO HELP PEOPLE.
FIRST, I NEED TO FINISH WHAT I STARTED. AND I WANT YOUR HELP TO DO IT.
I...I DON'T KNOW, TIM.
LOOK, I'VE SPOKEN TO EVERYONE. THEY UNDERSTAND WHAT YOU WERE GOING THROUGH. THEY WANT YOU BACK, TOO.
WHAT DO YOU SAY, STEPH? DO YOU WANT TO SAVE THE WORLD?

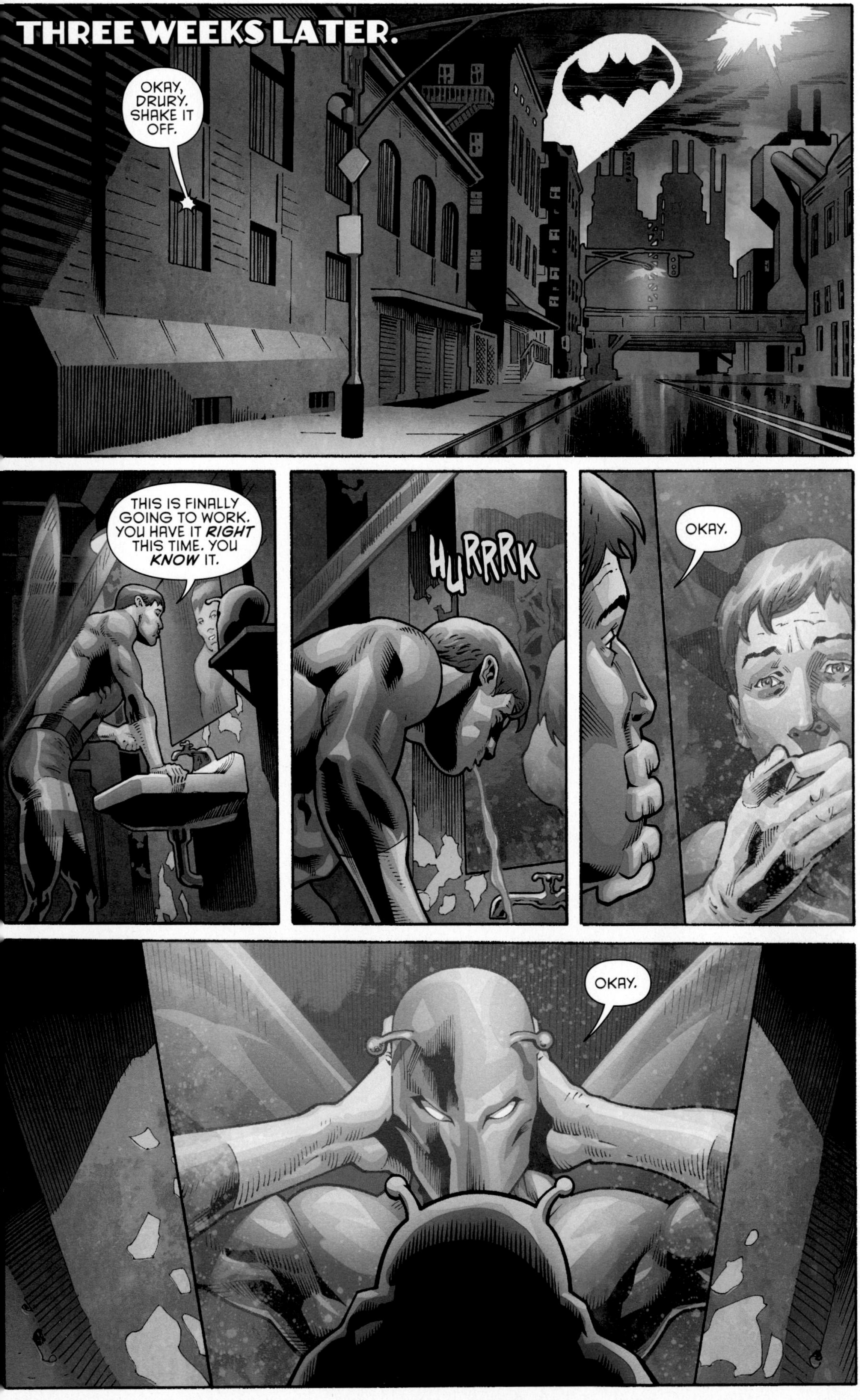
THREE WEEKS LATER.
OKAY, DRURY. SHAKE IT OFF.
THIS IS FINALLY GOING TO WORK. YOU HAVE IT RIGHT THIS TIME. YOU KNOW IT.
HURRRK
OKAY.
OKAY.

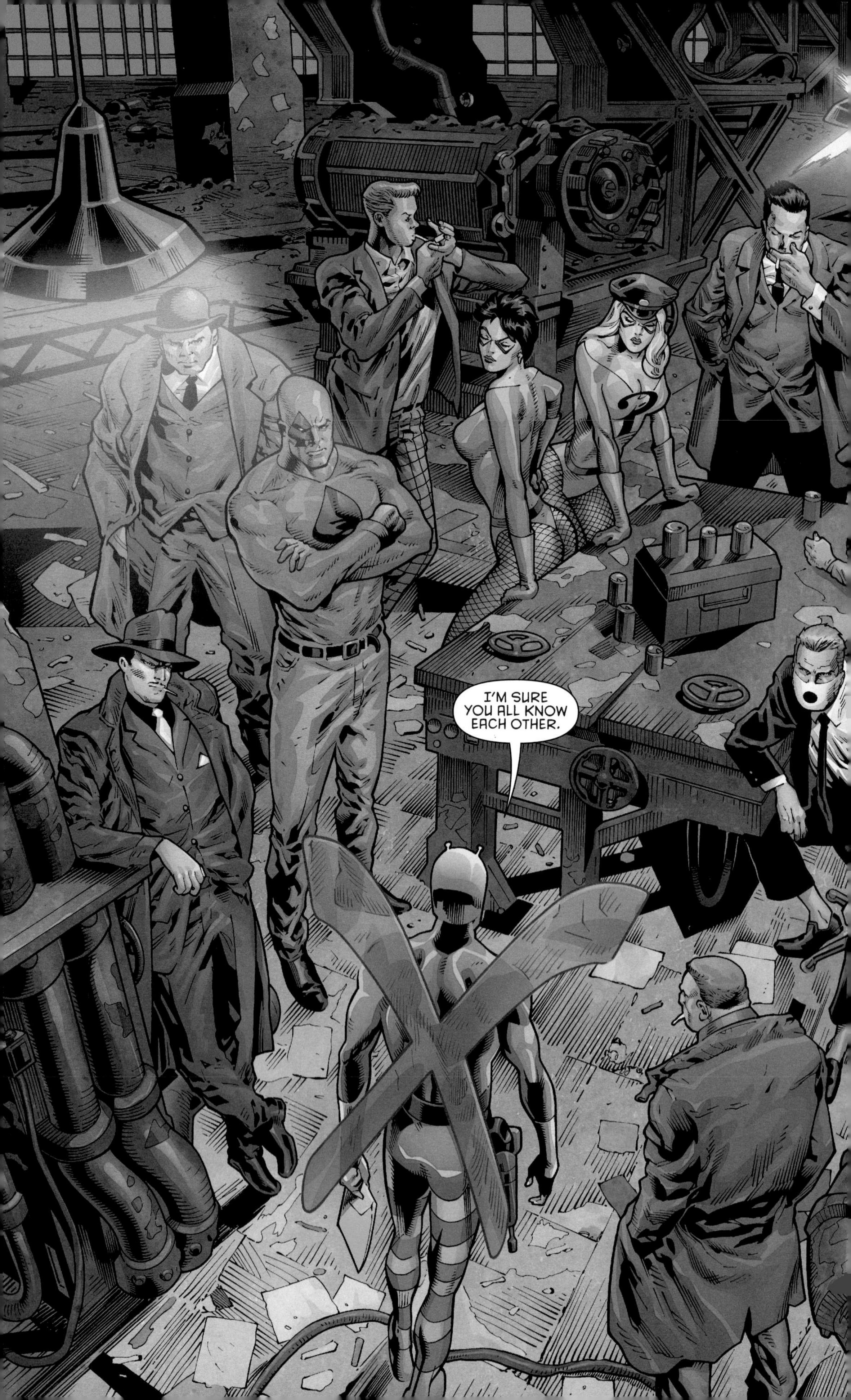
I'M SURE YOU ALL KNOW EACH OTHER.

EACH OF YOU ARE REPRESENTATIVES OF THE MOST *PROFITABLE* CRIMINAL ORGANIZATIONS IN GOTHAM CITY. I HAD *HOPED* YOUR BOSSES WOULD COME HERE, *DIRECTLY*...

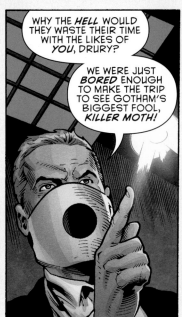

WHY THE *HELL* WOULD THEY WASTE THEIR TIME WITH THE LIKES OF *YOU*, DRURY?

WE WERE JUST *BORED* ENOUGH TO MAKE THE TRIP TO SEE GOTHAM'S BIGGEST FOOL, *KILLER MOTH!*

NO! THAT'S NOT *TRUE!* I'VE NEVER GOTTEN SO *MANY* OF YOU TO COME TO THE TABLE BEFORE.

YOU'RE NOT BORED. YOU'RE *SCARED.*

ALL OF YOUR OPERATIONS ARE GETTING *BUSTED* FROM ONE END OF THE CITY TO THE OTHER. NIGHT AFTER NIGHT, YOU'RE ALL LOSING *TERRITORY.*

HOW MUCH *REVENUE* HAVE YOUR BOSSES LOST IN THE LAST FEW WEEKS ALONE? MORE MONEY THAN ANY OF *YOU* SCHMUCKS HAVE SEEN IN A *LIFETIME.*

SO I AM *SICK* OF BEING TREATED LIKE A *JOKE.* YOUR BOSSES SENT YOU HERE TO HEAR ME OUT, SO I EXPECT YOU TO #@*$¢ LISTEN TO ME!

I KNOW WHAT'S CHANGED IN THIS CITY.

SOMEBODY SLIPPED ME THESE PHOTOS JUST THE OTHER DAY THAT CONFIRMED *ALL* MY FEARS. GOTHAM'S GOT ITS OWN LITTLE *JUSTICE LEAGUE* UP AND RUNNING.

THE *BATS* ARE MOVING LIKE TACTICAL *STRIKE FORCES*, IN AND OUT IN MINUTES.

YOUR BOSSES CAN'T JUST PAY OFF SOME SLOB IN THE GCPD SO THE SIGNAL DOESN'T GO UP. THE BATS DON'T *NEED* THE SIGNAL ANYMORE.

IN THE LAST THREE WEEKS, THEY'VE BASICALLY *ELIMINATED* ALL CRIMINAL ACTIVITY IN THE CITY.

AND THERE'S NO SIGN THAT IT'S GOING TO *STOP* ANY TIME SOON.

AND *WHAT?* YOU GOING TO TRY AND PITCH US ON THE SAME OLD THING? SOME KINDA *PROTECTION RACKET?*

HOW IS THE KILLER MOTH SUPPOSED TO STAND UP AGAINST AN *ARMY* OF BATMEN?

HOW, YOU ASK...?

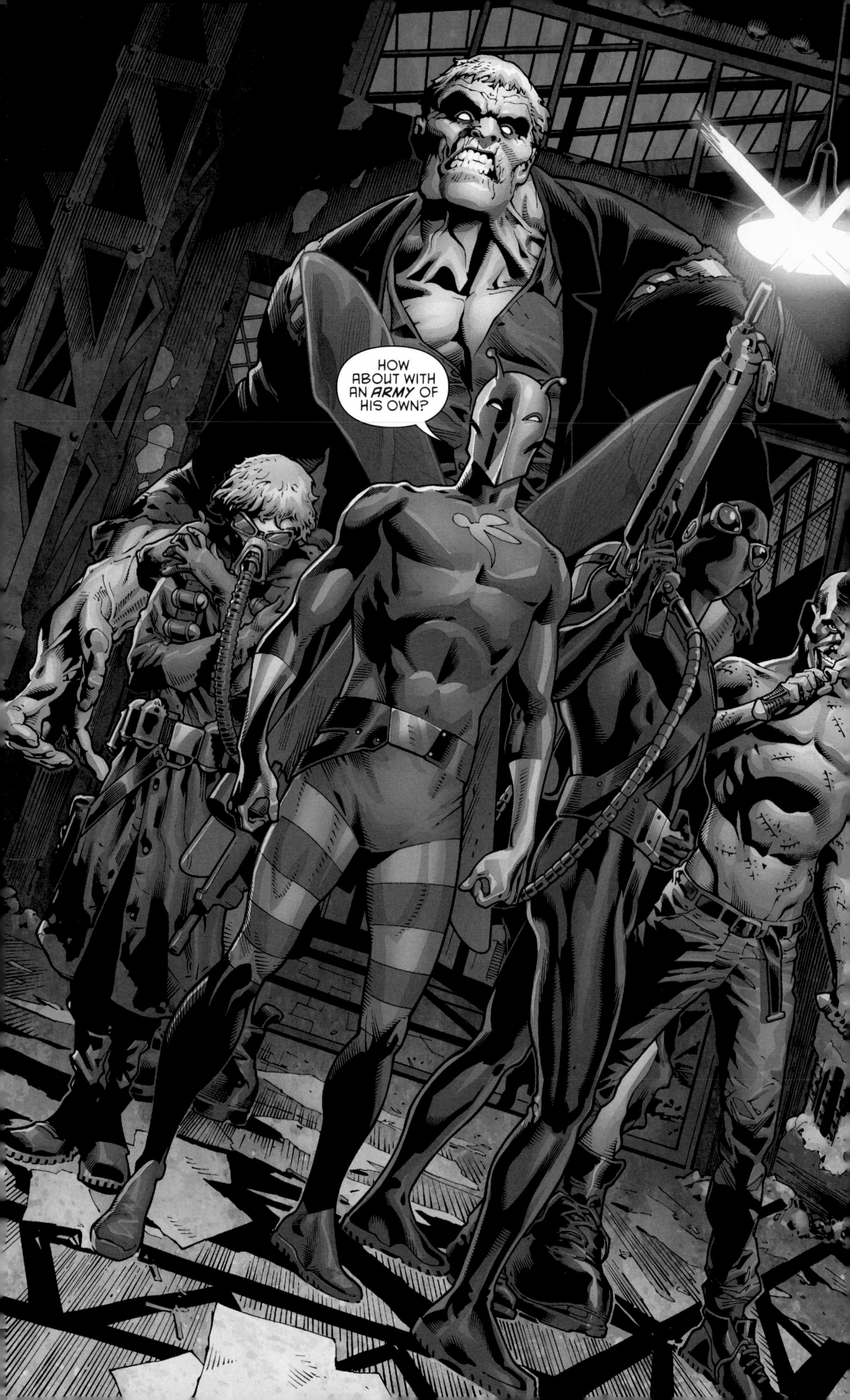
HOW ABOUT WITH AN ARMY OF HIS OWN?

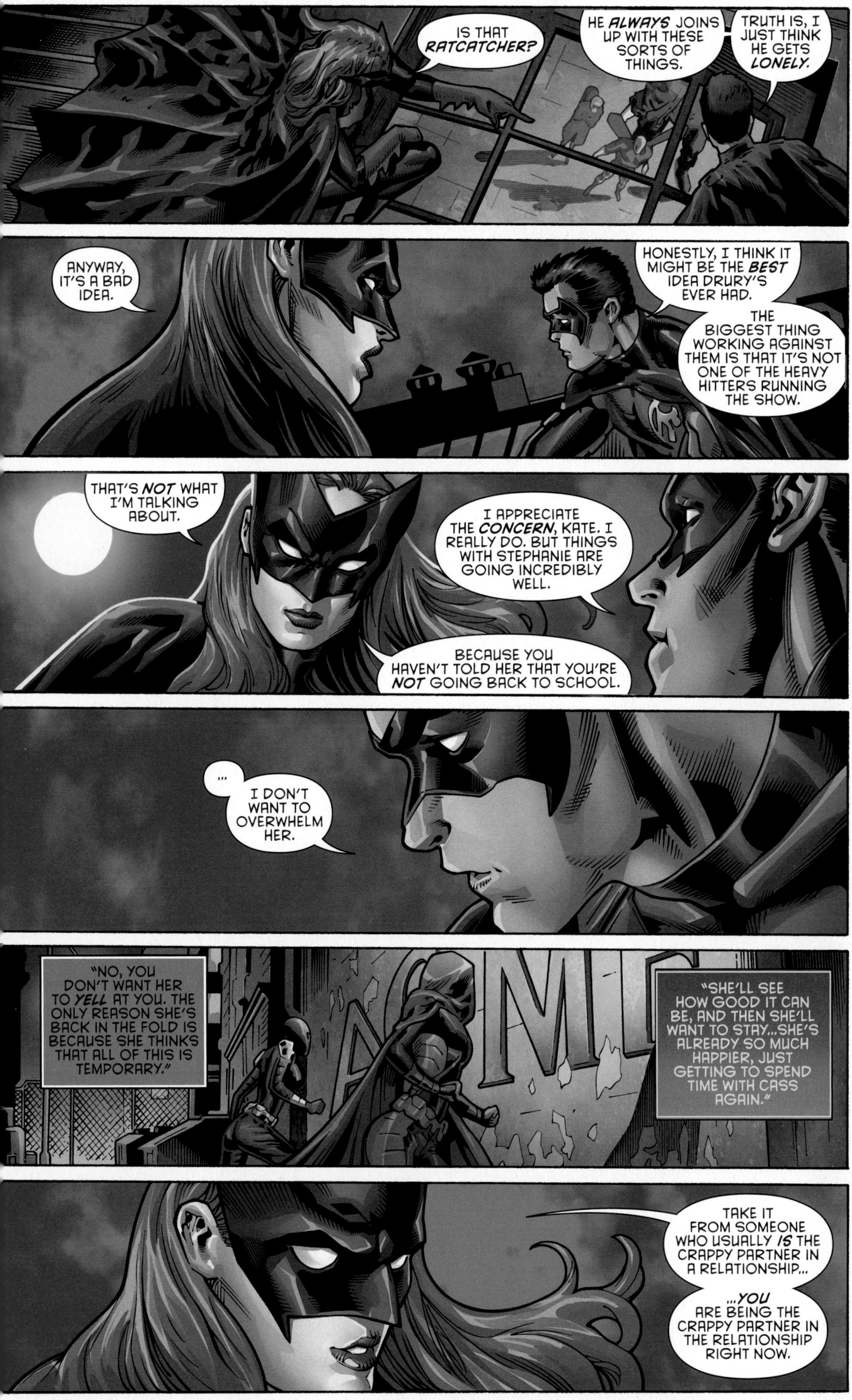

IS THAT RATCATCHER?
HE ALWAYS JOINS UP WITH THESE SORTS OF THINGS.
TRUTH IS, I JUST THINK HE GETS LONELY.
ANYWAY, IT'S A BAD IDEA.
HONESTLY, I THINK IT MIGHT BE THE BEST IDEA DRURY'S EVER HAD.
THE BIGGEST THING WORKING AGAINST THEM IS THAT IT'S NOT ONE OF THE HEAVY HITTERS RUNNING THE SHOW.
THAT'S NOT WHAT I'M TALKING ABOUT.
I APPRECIATE THE CONCERN, KATE. I REALLY DO. BUT THINGS WITH STEPHANIE ARE GOING INCREDIBLY WELL.
BECAUSE YOU HAVEN'T TOLD HER THAT YOU'RE NOT GOING BACK TO SCHOOL.
...
I DON'T WANT TO OVERWHELM HER.
"NO, YOU DON'T WANT HER TO YELL AT YOU. THE ONLY REASON SHE'S BACK IN THE FOLD IS BECAUSE SHE THINKS THAT ALL OF THIS IS TEMPORARY."
"SHE'LL SEE HOW GOOD IT CAN BE, AND THEN SHE'LL WANT TO STAY...SHE'S ALREADY SO MUCH HAPPIER, JUST GETTING TO SPEND TIME WITH CASS AGAIN."
TAKE IT FROM SOMEONE WHO USUALLY IS THE CRAPPY PARTNER IN A RELATIONSHIP...
...YOU ARE BEING THE CRAPPY PARTNER IN THE RELATIONSHIP RIGHT NOW.

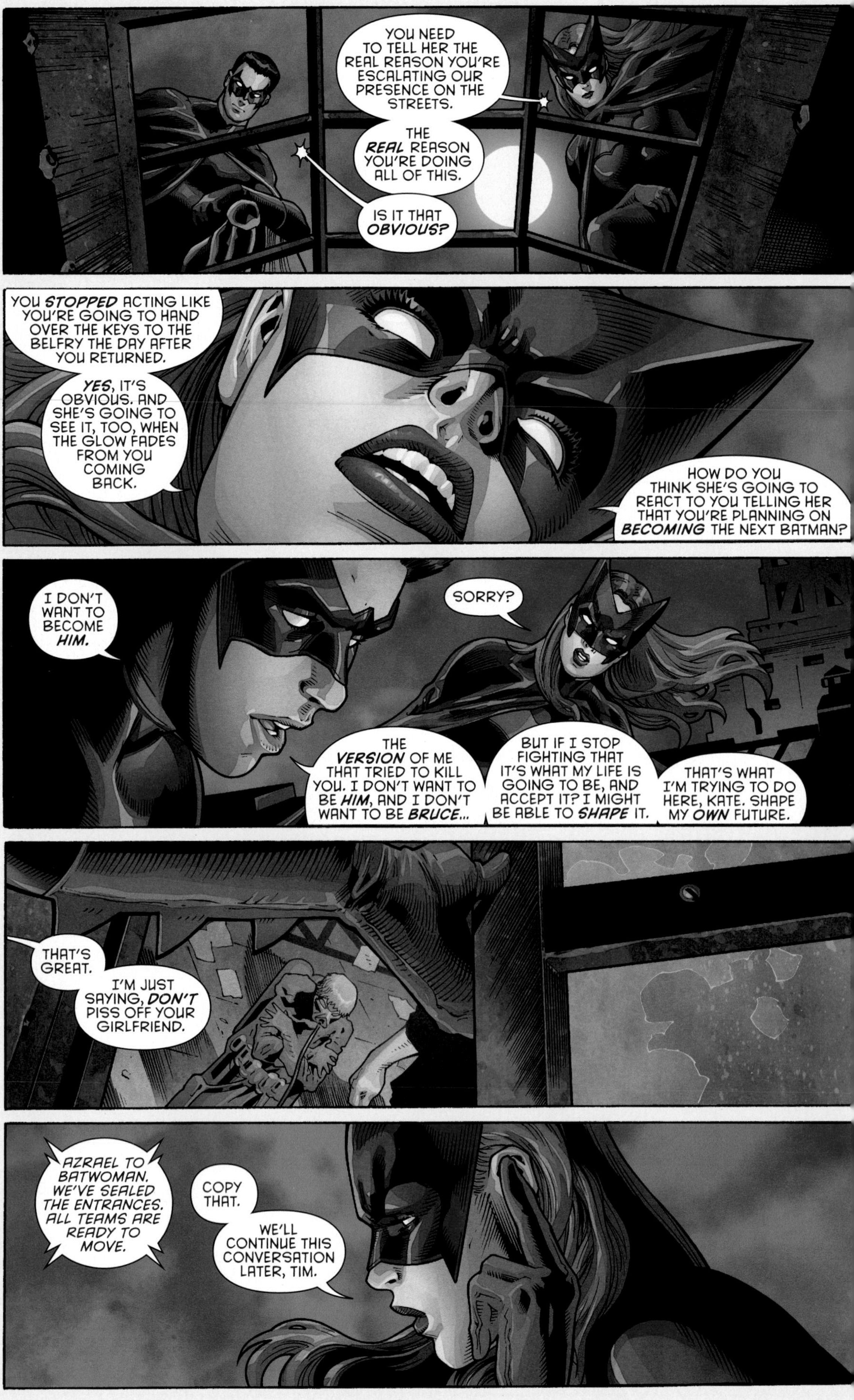

YOU NEED TO TELL HER THE REAL REASON YOU'RE ESCALATING OUR PRESENCE ON THE STREETS.
THE REAL REASON YOU'RE DOING ALL OF THIS.
IS IT THAT OBVIOUS?
YOU STOPPED ACTING LIKE YOU'RE GOING TO HAND OVER THE KEYS TO THE BELFRY THE DAY AFTER YOU RETURNED.
YES, IT'S OBVIOUS. AND SHE'S GOING TO SEE IT, TOO, WHEN THE GLOW FADES FROM YOU COMING BACK.
HOW DO YOU THINK SHE'S GOING TO REACT TO YOU TELLING HER THAT YOU'RE PLANNING ON BECOMING THE NEXT BATMAN?
I DON'T WANT TO BECOME HIM.
SORRY?
THE VERSION OF ME THAT TRIED TO KILL YOU. I DON'T WANT TO BE HIM, AND I DON'T WANT TO BE BRUCE...
BUT IF I STOP FIGHTING THAT IT'S WHAT MY LIFE IS GOING TO BE, AND ACCEPT IT? I MIGHT BE ABLE TO SHAPE IT.
THAT'S WHAT I'M TRYING TO DO HERE, KATE. SHAPE MY OWN FUTURE.
THAT'S GREAT.
I'M JUST SAYING, DON'T PISS OFF YOUR GIRLFRIEND.
AZRAEL TO BATWOMAN. WE'VE SEALED THE ENTRANCES. ALL TEAMS ARE READY TO MOVE.
COPY THAT.
WE'LL CONTINUE THIS CONVERSATION LATER, TIM.

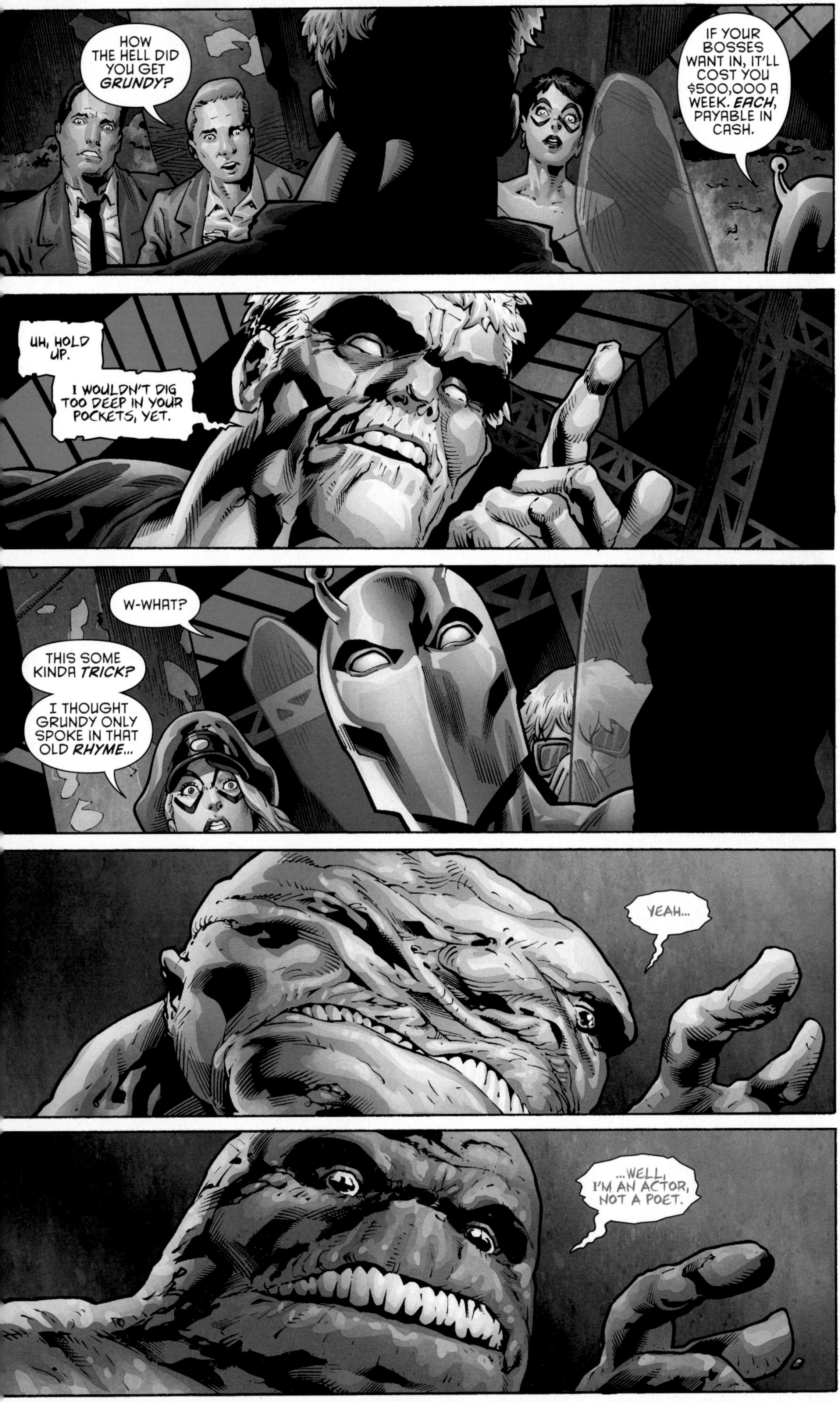

HOW THE HELL DID YOU GET *GRUNDY?*
IF YOUR BOSSES WANT IN, IT'LL COST YOU $500,000 A WEEK. *EACH*, PAYABLE IN CASH.
UH, HOLD UP.
I WOULDN'T DIG TOO DEEP IN YOUR POCKETS, YET.
W-WHAT?
THIS SOME KINDA *TRICK?*
I THOUGHT GRUNDY ONLY SPOKE IN THAT OLD *RHYME*...
YEAH...
...WELL, I'M AN ACTOR, NOT A POET.

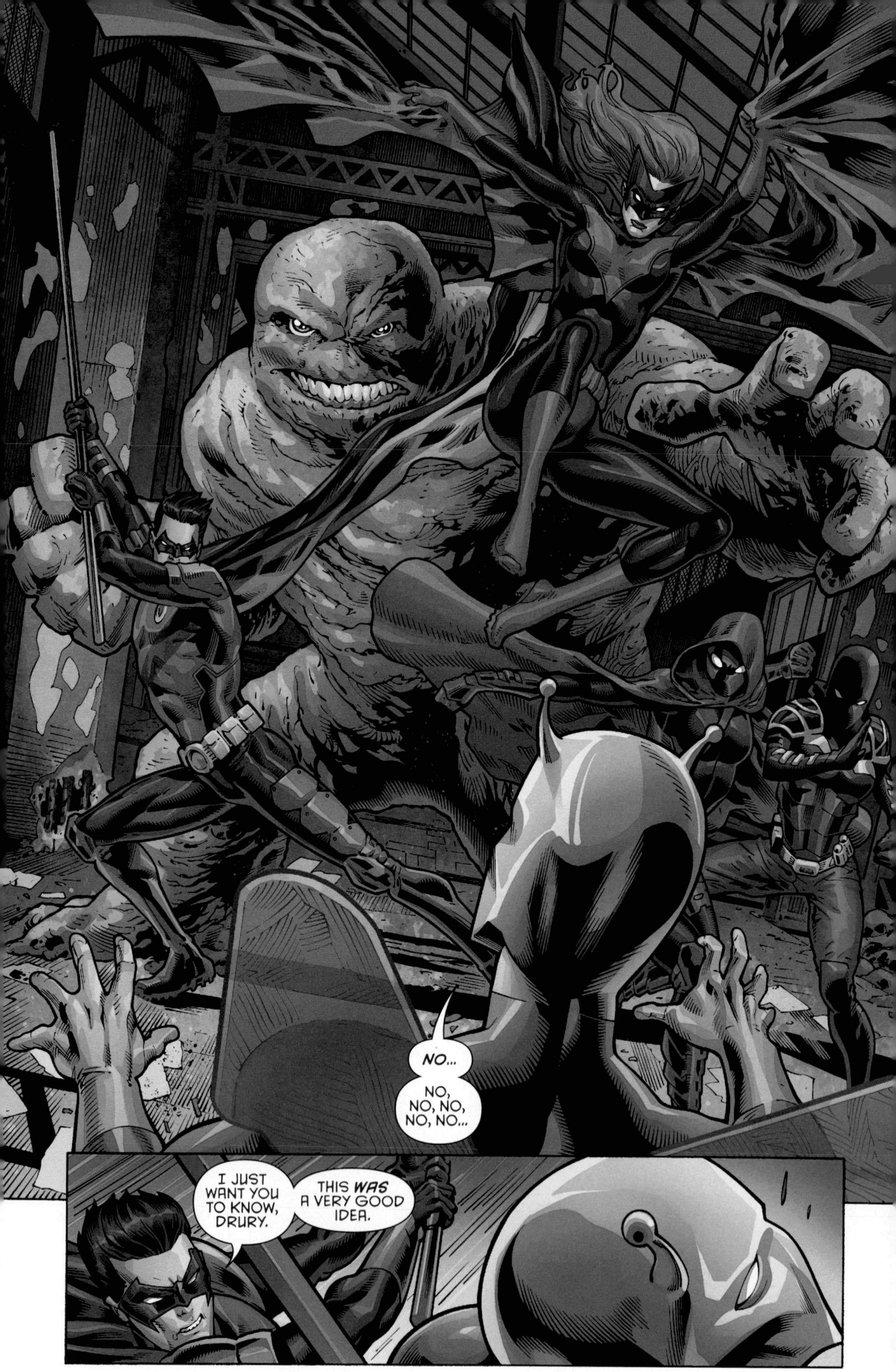
NO...
NO, NO, NO, NO, NO...
I JUST WANT YOU TO KNOW, DRURY.
THIS WAS A VERY GOOD IDEA.

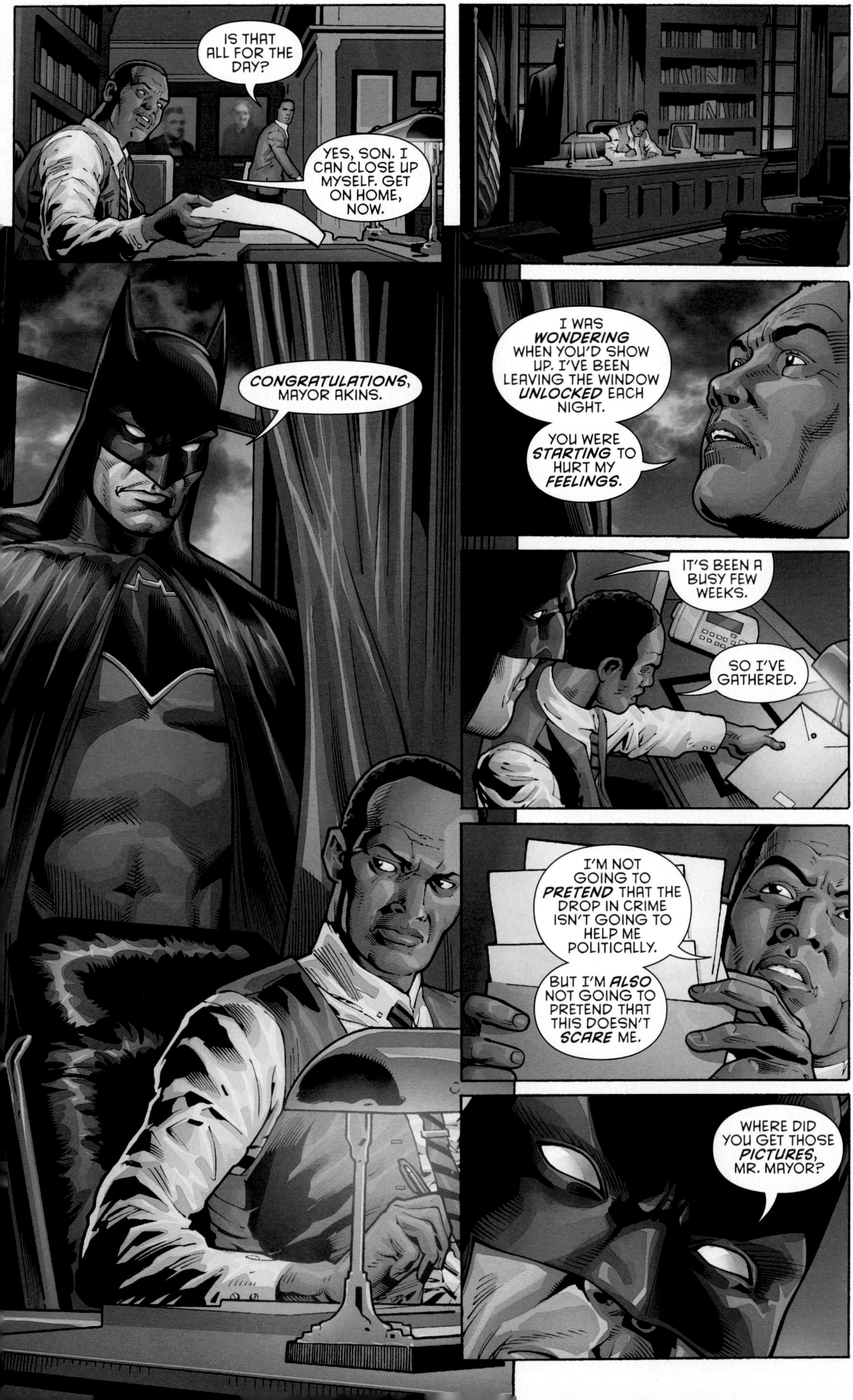
IS THAT ALL FOR THE DAY?
YES, SON. I CAN CLOSE UP MYSELF. GET ON HOME, NOW.
CONGRATULATIONS, MAYOR AKINS.
I WAS WONDERING WHEN YOU'D SHOW UP. I'VE BEEN LEAVING THE WINDOW UNLOCKED EACH NIGHT.
YOU WERE STARTING TO HURT MY FEELINGS.
IT'S BEEN A BUSY FEW WEEKS.
SO I'VE GATHERED.
I'M NOT GOING TO PRETEND THAT THE DROP IN CRIME ISN'T GOING TO HELP ME POLITICALLY.
BUT I'M ALSO NOT GOING TO PRETEND THAT THIS DOESN'T SCARE ME.
WHERE DID YOU GET THOSE PICTURES, MR. MAYOR?

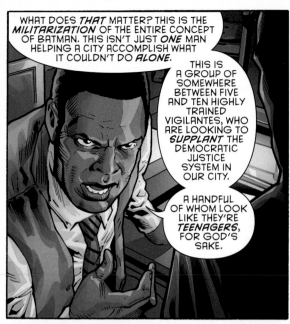

WHAT DOES *THAT* MATTER? THIS IS THE *MILITARIZATION* OF THE ENTIRE CONCEPT OF BATMAN. THIS ISN'T JUST *ONE* MAN HELPING A CITY ACCOMPLISH WHAT IT COULDN'T DO *ALONE*.

THIS IS A GROUP OF SOMEWHERE BETWEEN FIVE AND TEN HIGHLY TRAINED VIGILANTES, WHO ARE LOOKING TO *SUPPLANT* THE DEMOCRATIC JUSTICE SYSTEM IN OUR CITY.

A HANDFUL OF WHOM LOOK LIKE THEY'RE *TEENAGERS*, FOR GOD'S SAKE.

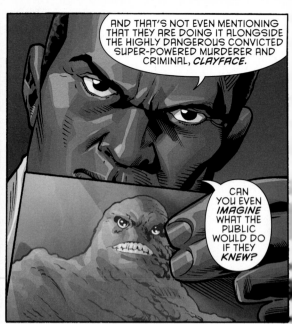

AND THAT'S NOT EVEN MENTIONING THAT THEY ARE DOING IT ALONGSIDE THE HIGHLY DANGEROUS CONVICTED SUPER-POWERED MURDERER AND CRIMINAL, *CLAYFACE*.

CAN YOU EVEN *IMAGINE* WHAT THE PUBLIC WOULD DO IF THEY *KNEW*?

SAYS THE MAN WHO ACCEPTED *HAMILTON HILL JR.* AS HIS DEPUTY MAYOR IN ORDER TO GET APPOINTED TO THIS OFFICE.

YES, BATMAN. SAYS *THAT* MAN. SAYS THE *MAYOR* OF GOTHAM CITY.

I WANT TO ASK YOU A *QUESTION*, BATMAN. I'M GOING TO ASK IT BLUNTLY, AND I WANT YOU TO *ANSWER* ME HONESTLY.

WHERE DOES THIS *END*?

THE CITY IS BOILING OVER, AND THEY'RE TOO STUPID TO SEE IT. IT SCREAMS FOR CHANGE, BUT THEY WON'T ANSWER THE CALL.

STEPHANIE WAS *SO CLOSE* TO SEEING THROUGH THEIR LIES. WHY SHE WOULD TURN BACK NOW...

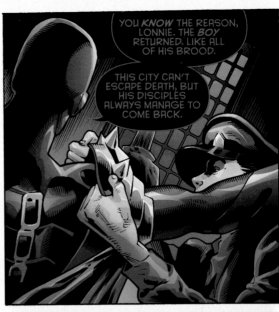

YOU *KNOW* THE REASON, LONNIE. THE *BOY* RETURNED. LIKE ALL OF HIS BROOD.

THIS CITY CAN'T ESCAPE DEATH, BUT HIS DISCIPLES ALWAYS MANAGE TO COME BACK.

RED ROBIN. FILLING HER HEAD WITH *LIES* ALL OVER AGAIN.

YOU MUSTN'T BLAME HER, LONNIE. SHE'S BEEN DAMAGED BY THIS WAR, LIKE SO MANY OF US HAVE.

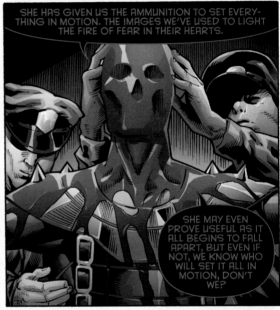

SHE HAS GIVEN US THE AMMUNITION TO SET EVERYTHING IN MOTION. THE IMAGES WE'VE USED TO LIGHT THE FIRE OF FEAR IN THEIR HEARTS.

SHE MAY EVEN PROVE USEFUL AS IT ALL BEGINS TO FALL APART, BUT EVEN IF NOT, WE KNOW WHO WILL SET IT ALL IN MOTION, DON'T WE?

YES, YES OF COURSE.

THE CITY TREMBLES IN FEAR, ANARKY. WE NEED ONLY STOKE THE FLAME.

AND IN THE END, BATMAN'S ENTIRE FAMILY WILL *FALL* AT THE HANDS OF ONE OF THEIR OWN.

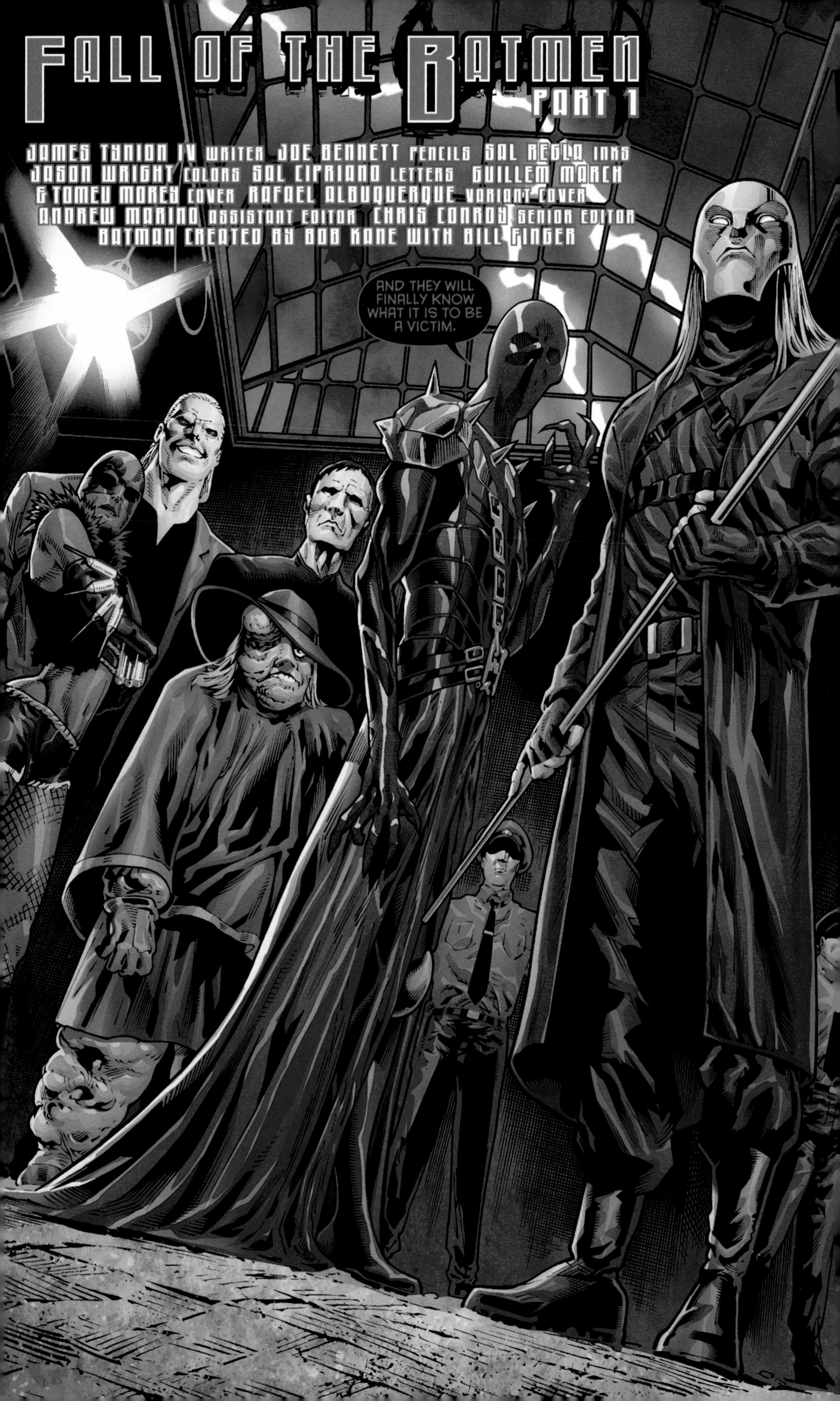
FALL OF THE BATMEN
PART 1
JAMES TYNION IV WRITER JOE BENNETT PENCILS SAL REGLA INKS
JASON WRIGHT COLORS SAL CIPRIANO LETTERS GUILLEM MARCH
& TOMEU MOREY COVER RAFAEL ALBUQUERQUE VARIANT COVER
ANDREW MARINO ASSISTANT EDITOR CHRIS CONROY SENIOR EDITOR
BATMAN CREATED BY BOB KANE WITH BILL FINGER
AND THEY WILL FINALLY KNOW WHAT IT IS TO BE A VICTIM.

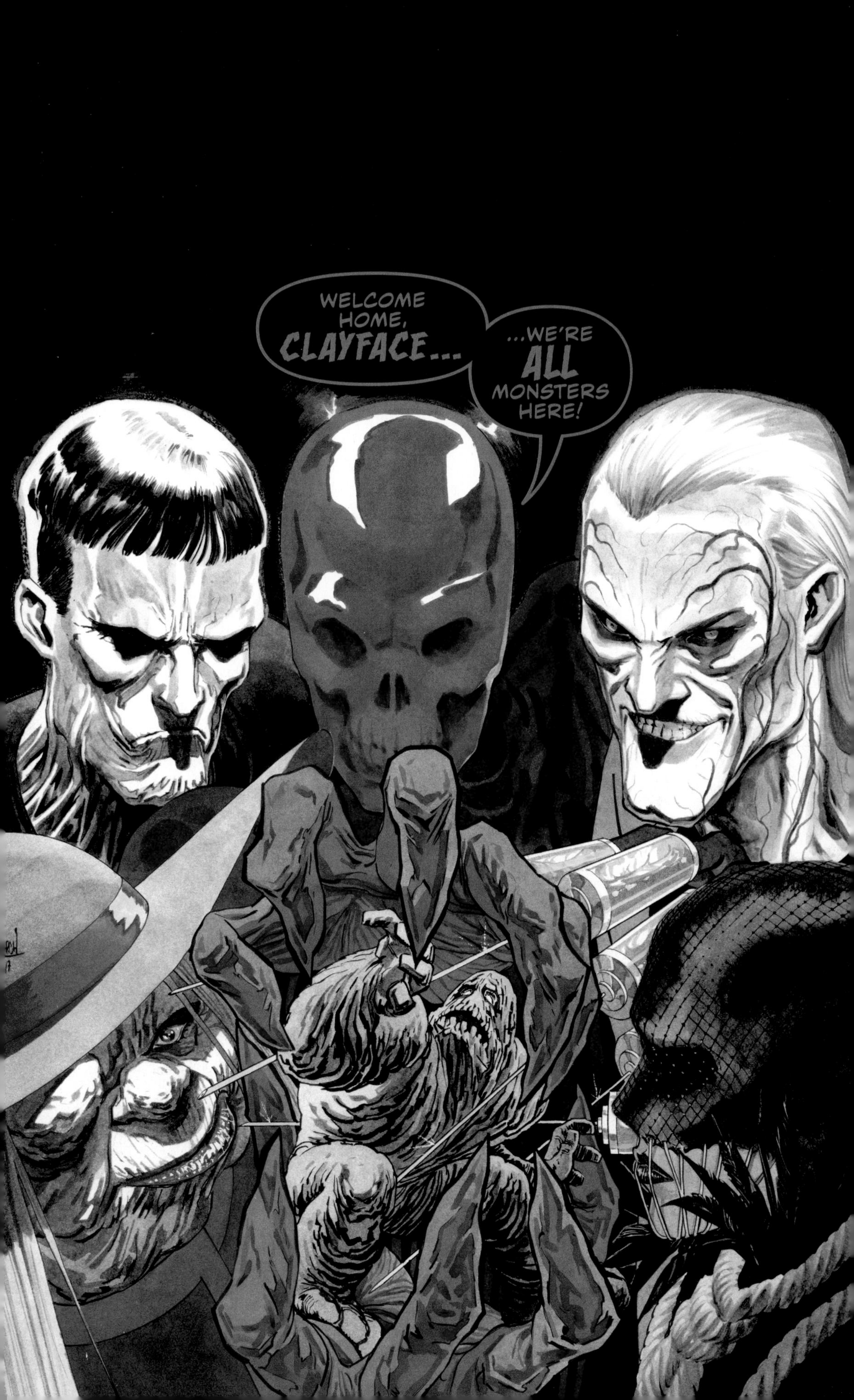
WELCOME HOME, CLAYFACE...
...WE'RE ALL MONSTERS HERE!

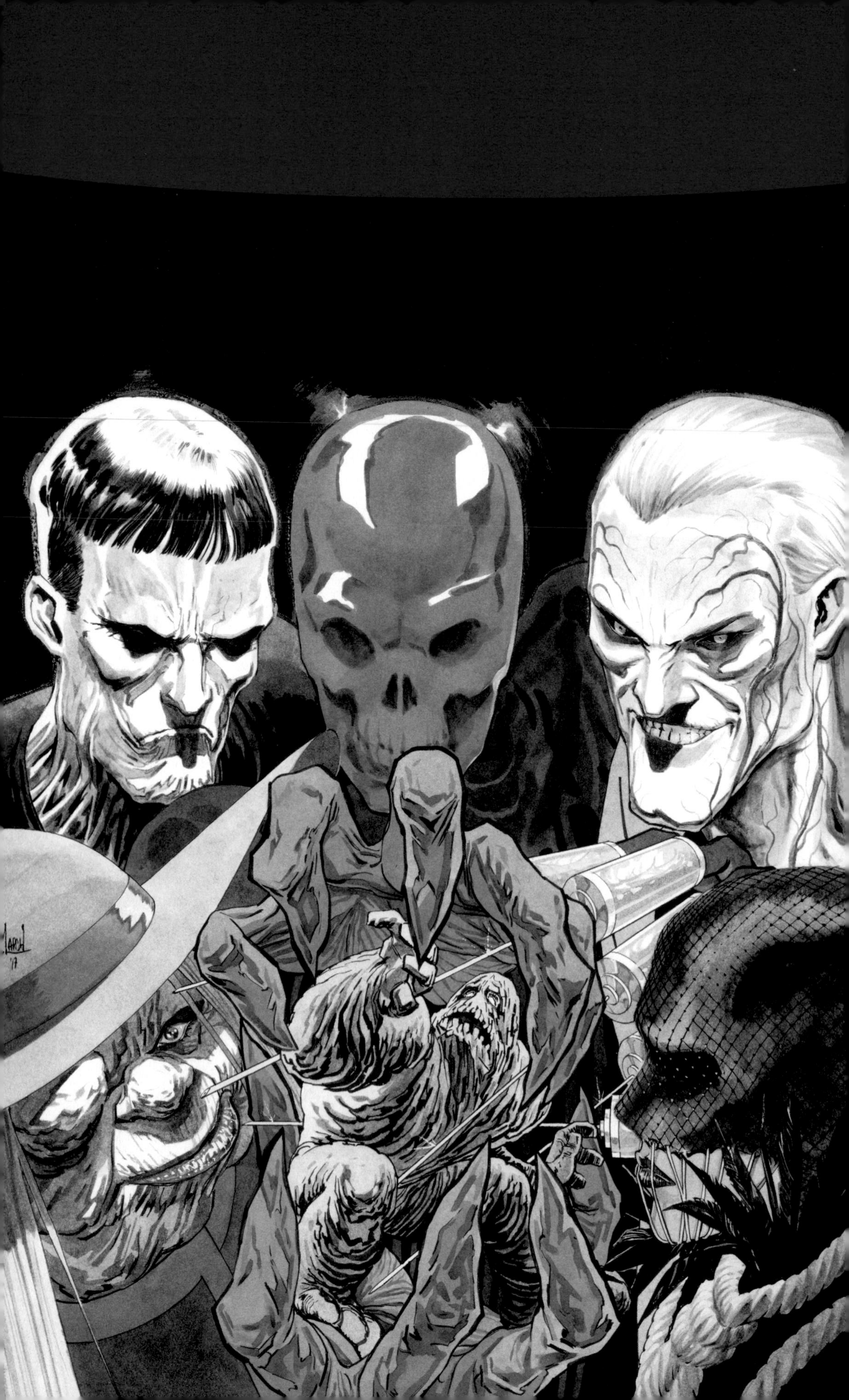

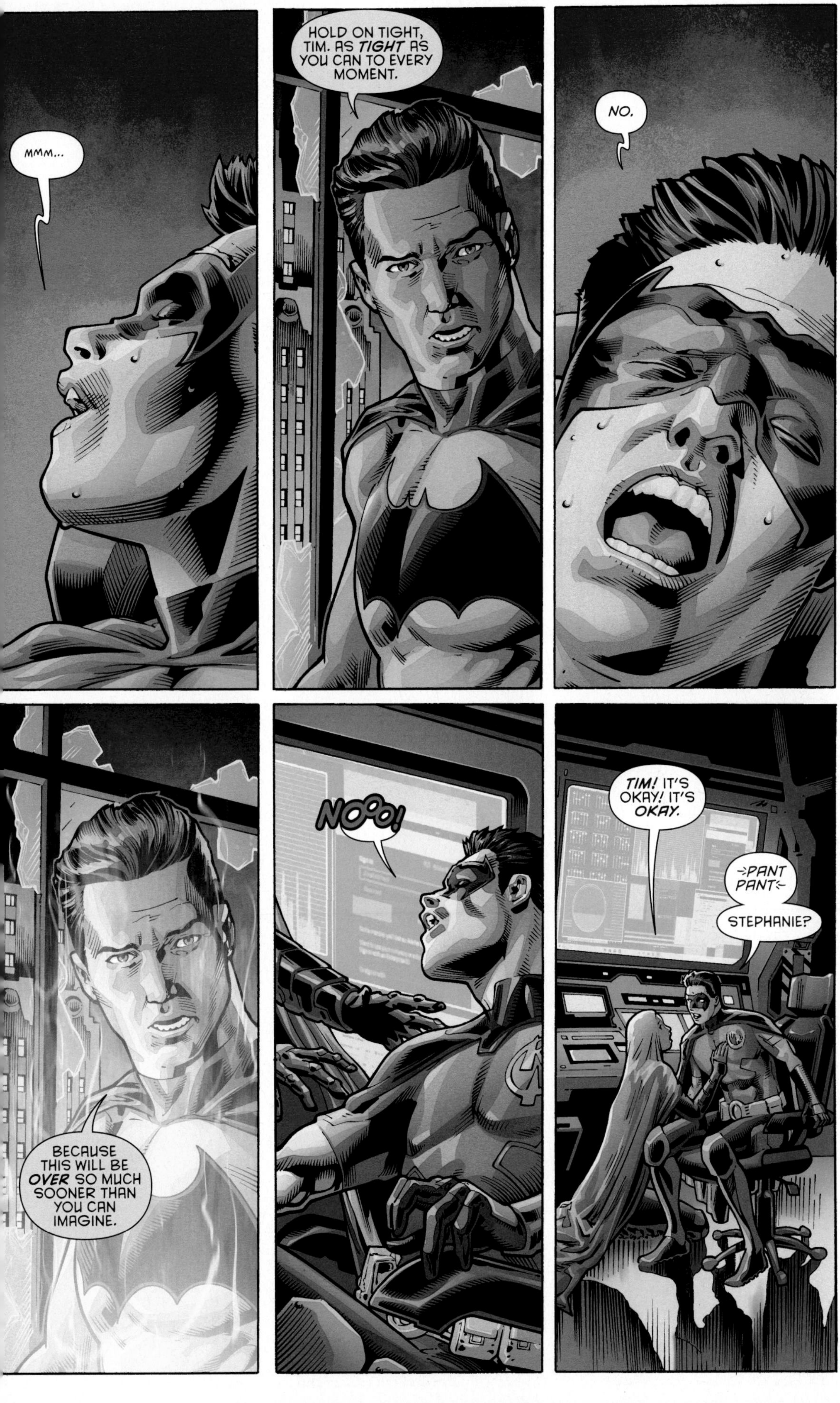

MMM...
HOLD ON TIGHT, TIM. AS *TIGHT* AS YOU CAN TO EVERY MOMENT.
NO.
BECAUSE THIS WILL BE *OVER* SO MUCH SOONER THAN YOU CAN IMAGINE.
NOOO!
TIM! IT'S OKAY! IT'S *OKAY.*
PANT PANT
STEPHANIE?

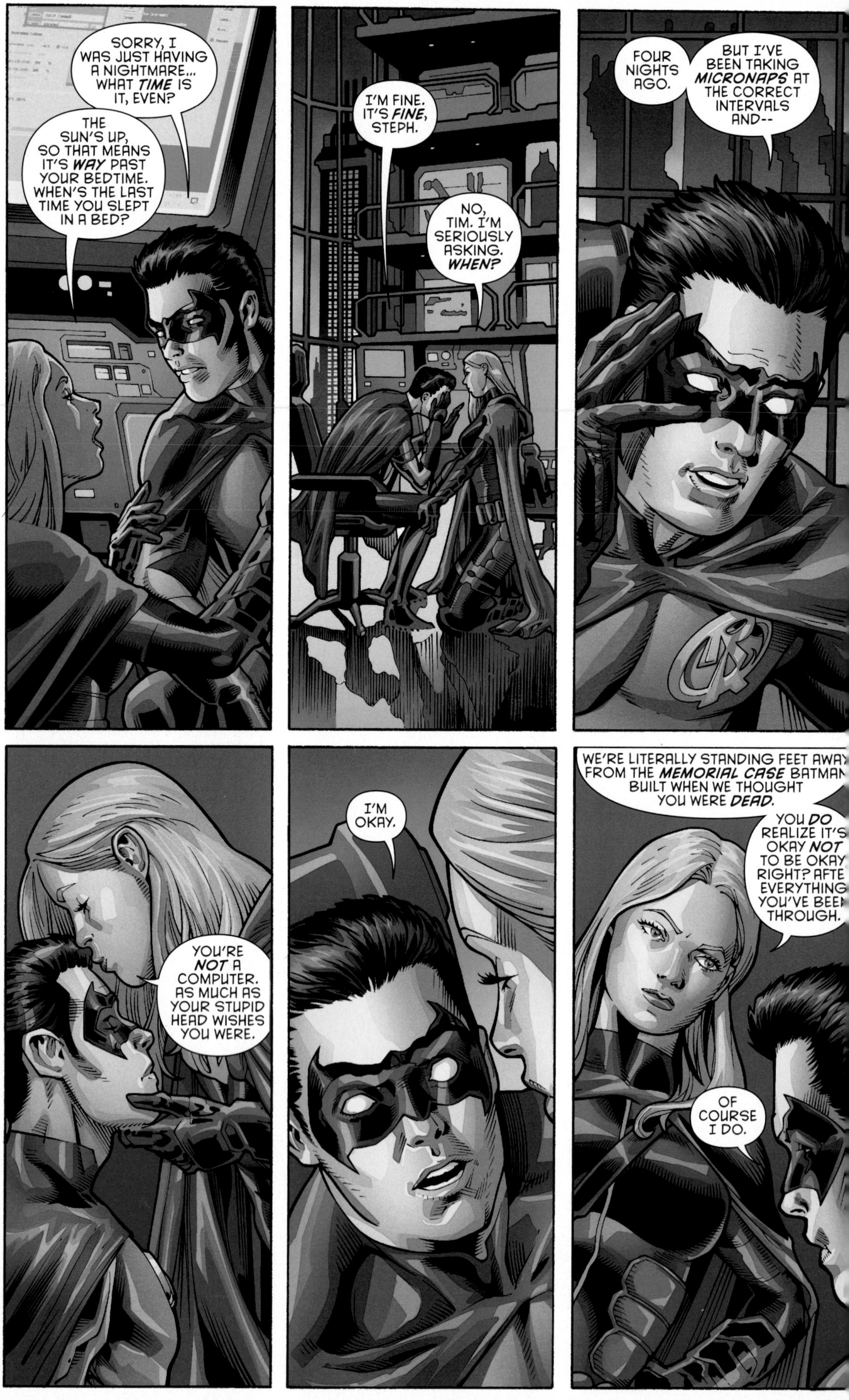

SORRY, I WAS JUST HAVING A NIGHTMARE... WHAT *TIME* IS IT, EVEN?
THE SUN'S UP, SO THAT MEANS IT'S *WAY* PAST YOUR BEDTIME. WHEN'S THE LAST TIME YOU SLEPT IN A BED?
I'M FINE. IT'S *FINE*, STEPH.
NO, TIM. I'M SERIOUSLY ASKING. *WHEN?*
FOUR NIGHTS AGO.
BUT I'VE BEEN TAKING *MICRONAPS* AT THE CORRECT INTERVALS AND--
YOU'RE *NOT* A COMPUTER. AS MUCH AS YOUR STUPID HEAD WISHES YOU WERE.
I'M OKAY.
WE'RE LITERALLY STANDING FEET AWAY FROM THE *MEMORIAL CASE* BATMAN BUILT WHEN WE THOUGHT YOU WERE *DEAD*.
YOU *DO* REALIZE IT'S OKAY *NOT* TO BE OKAY, RIGHT? AFTER EVERYTHING YOU'VE BEEN THROUGH.
OF COURSE I DO.

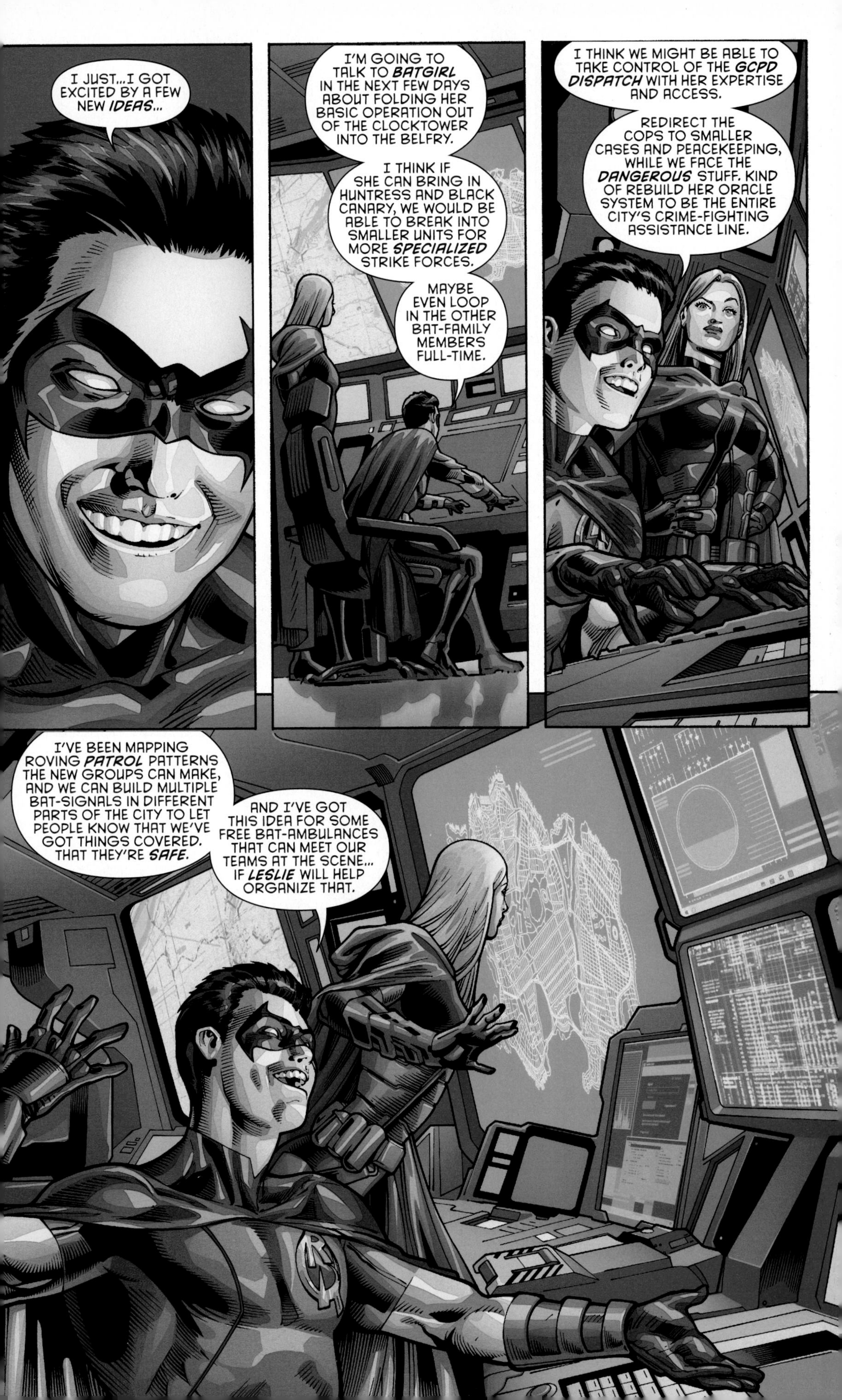
I JUST...I GOT EXCITED BY A FEW NEW *IDEAS*...
I'M GOING TO TALK TO *BATGIRL* IN THE NEXT FEW DAYS ABOUT FOLDING HER BASIC OPERATION OUT OF THE CLOCKTOWER INTO THE BELFRY.
I THINK IF SHE CAN BRING IN HUNTRESS AND BLACK CANARY, WE WOULD BE ABLE TO BREAK INTO SMALLER UNITS FOR MORE *SPECIALIZED* STRIKE FORCES.
MAYBE EVEN LOOP IN THE OTHER BAT-FAMILY MEMBERS FULL-TIME.
I THINK WE MIGHT BE ABLE TO TAKE CONTROL OF THE *GCPD DISPATCH* WITH HER EXPERTISE AND ACCESS.
REDIRECT THE COPS TO SMALLER CASES AND PEACEKEEPING, WHILE WE FACE THE *DANGEROUS* STUFF. KIND OF REBUILD HER ORACLE SYSTEM TO BE THE ENTIRE CITY'S CRIME-FIGHTING ASSISTANCE LINE.
I'VE BEEN MAPPING ROVING *PATROL* PATTERNS THE NEW GROUPS CAN MAKE, AND WE CAN BUILD MULTIPLE BAT-SIGNALS IN DIFFERENT PARTS OF THE CITY TO LET PEOPLE KNOW THAT WE'VE GOT THINGS COVERED. THAT THEY'RE *SAFE*.
AND I'VE GOT THIS IDEA FOR SOME FREE BAT-AMBULANCES THAT CAN MEET OUR TEAMS AT THE SCENE... IF *LESLIE* WILL HELP ORGANIZE THAT.

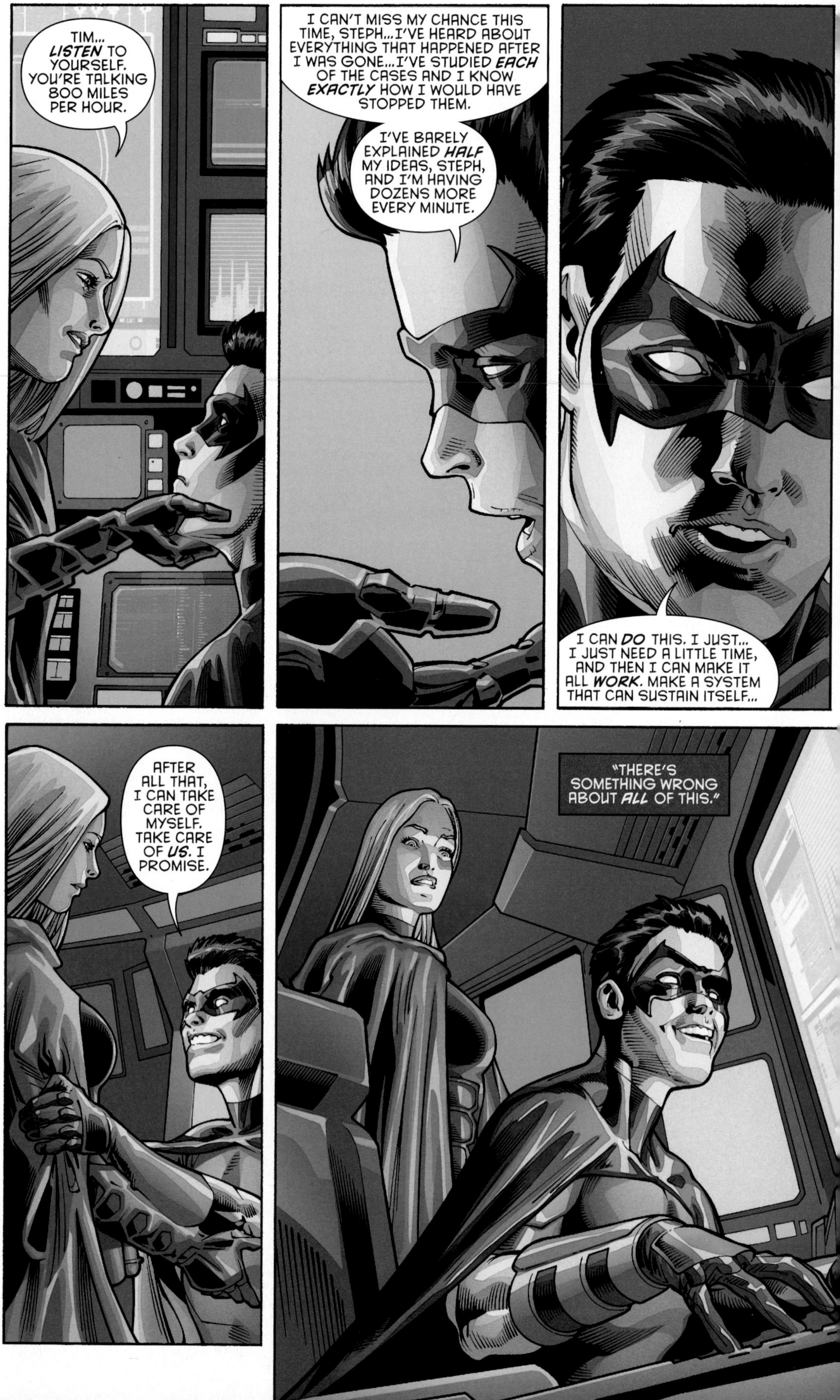

TIM... LISTEN TO YOURSELF. YOU'RE TALKING 800 MILES PER HOUR.
I CAN'T MISS MY CHANCE THIS TIME, STEPH...I'VE HEARD ABOUT EVERYTHING THAT HAPPENED AFTER I WAS GONE...I'VE STUDIED EACH OF THE CASES AND I KNOW EXACTLY HOW I WOULD HAVE STOPPED THEM.
I'VE BARELY EXPLAINED HALF MY IDEAS, STEPH, AND I'M HAVING DOZENS MORE EVERY MINUTE.
I CAN DO THIS. I JUST... I JUST NEED A LITTLE TIME, AND THEN I CAN MAKE IT ALL WORK. MAKE A SYSTEM THAT CAN SUSTAIN ITSELF...
AFTER ALL THAT, I CAN TAKE CARE OF MYSELF. TAKE CARE OF US. I PROMISE.
"THERE'S SOMETHING WRONG ABOUT ALL OF THIS."

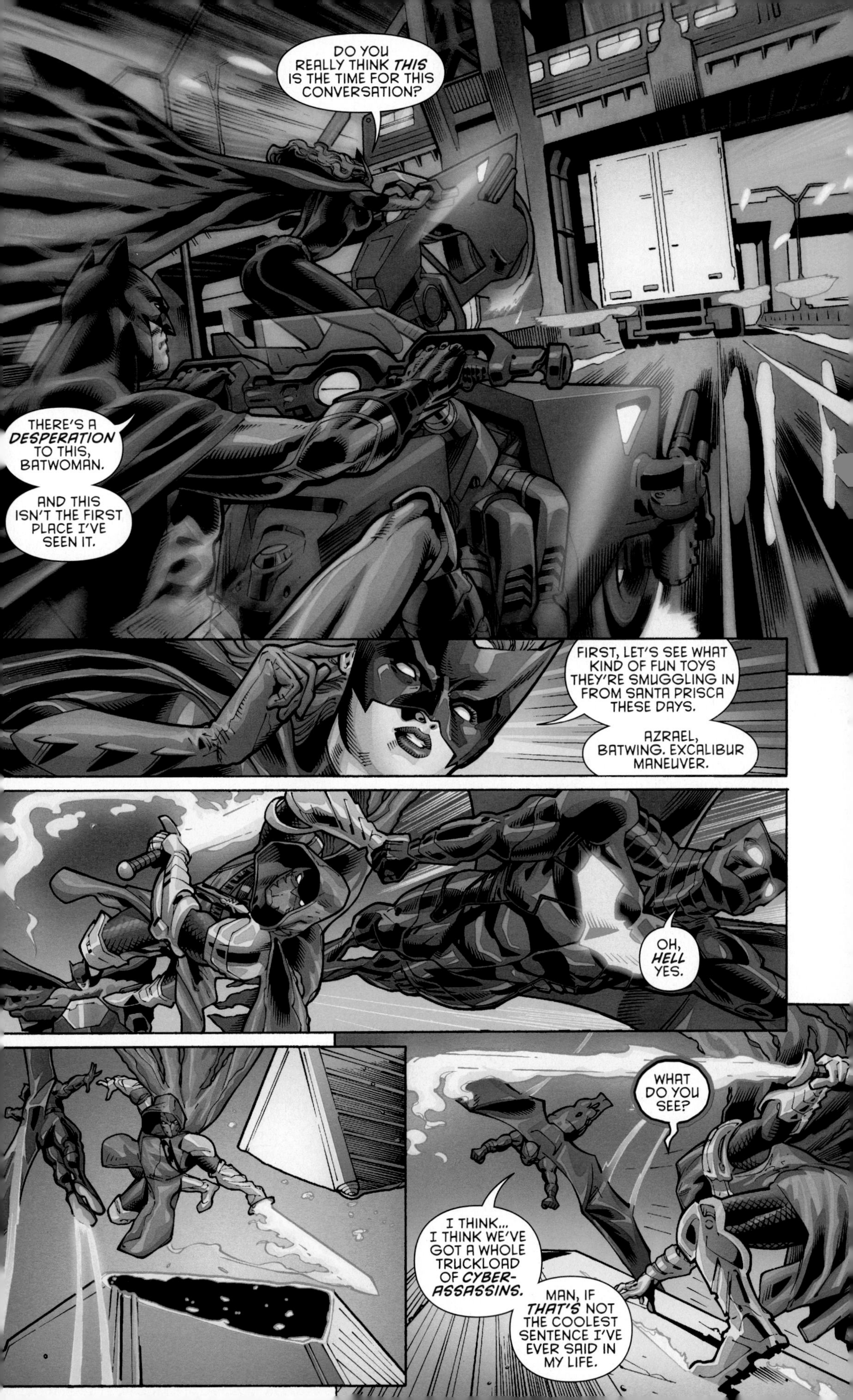
DO YOU REALLY THINK *THIS* IS THE TIME FOR THIS CONVERSATION?
THERE'S A *DESPERATION* TO THIS, BATWOMAN.
AND THIS ISN'T THE FIRST PLACE I'VE SEEN IT.
FIRST, LET'S SEE WHAT KIND OF FUN TOYS THEY'RE SMUGGLING IN FROM SANTA PRISCA THESE DAYS.
AZRAEL, BATWING. EXCALIBUR MANEUVER.
OH, *HELL* YES.
WHAT DO YOU SEE?
I THINK... I THINK WE'VE GOT A WHOLE TRUCKLOAD OF *CYBER-ASSASSINS.*
MAN, IF *THAT'S* NOT THE COOLEST SENTENCE I'VE EVER SAID IN MY LIFE.

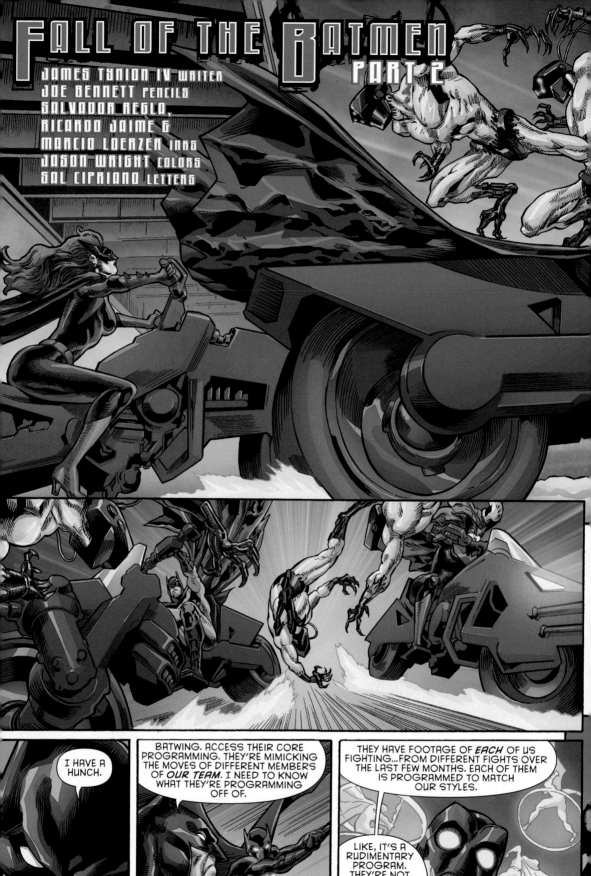

FALL OF THE BATMEN
PART 2

JAMES TYNION IV WRITER
JOE BENNETT PENCILS
SALVADOR REGLA,
RICARDO JAIME &
MARCIO LOERZER INKS
JASON WRIGHT COLORS
SAL CIPRIANO LETTERS

I HAVE A HUNCH.

BATWING. ACCESS THEIR CORE PROGRAMMING. THEY'RE MIMICKING THE MOVES OF DIFFERENT MEMBERS OF *OUR TEAM*. I NEED TO KNOW WHAT THEY'RE PROGRAMMING OFF OF.

THEY HAVE FOOTAGE OF *EACH* OF US FIGHTING...FROM DIFFERENT FIGHTS OVER THE LAST FEW MONTHS. EACH OF THEM IS PROGRAMMED TO MATCH OUR STYLES.

LIKE, IT'S A RUDIMENTARY PROGRAM. THEY'RE NOT DOING IT *WELL*. BUT THEY'RE USING OUR OWN METHODS AGAINST US.

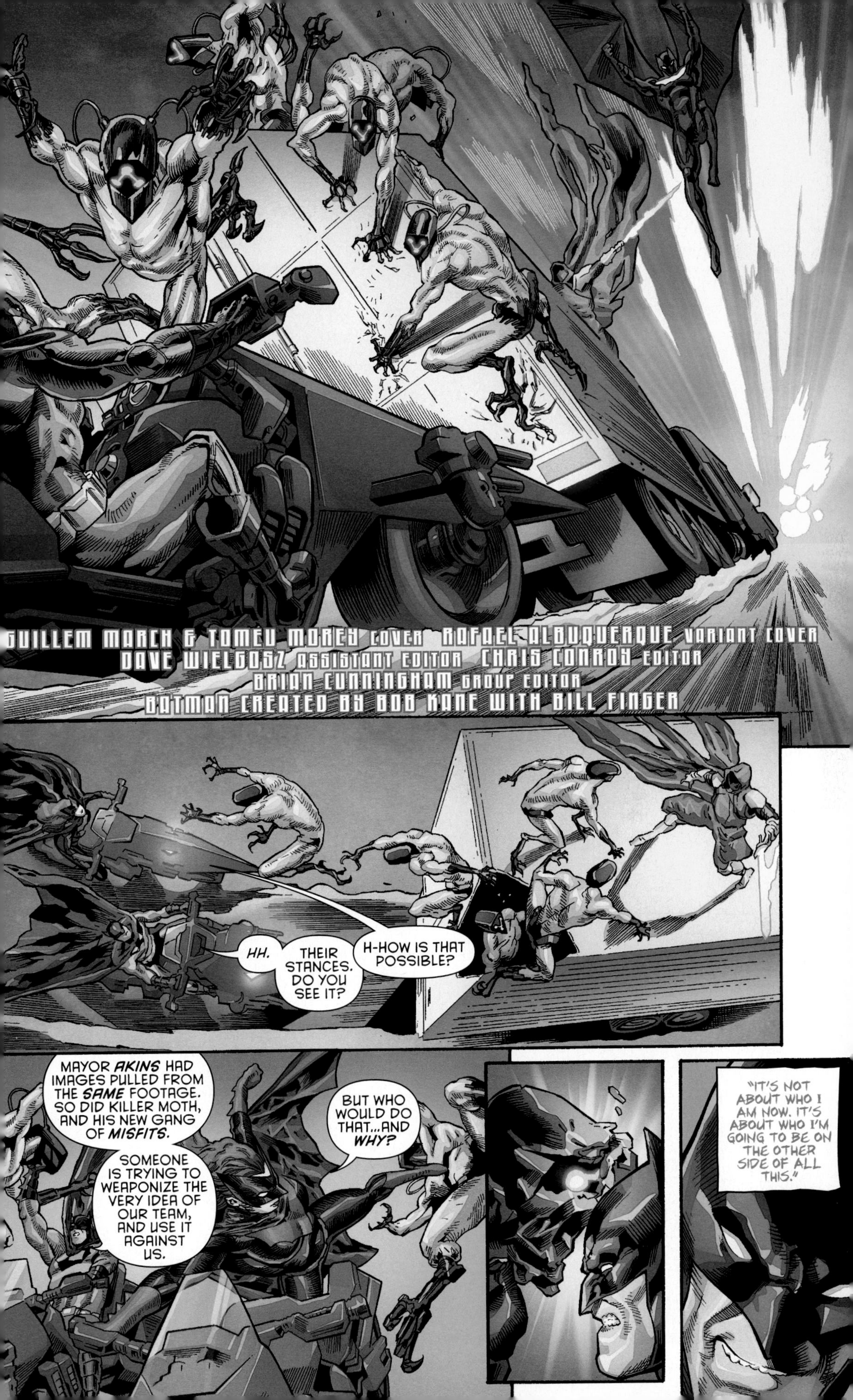
GUILLEM MARCH & TOMEU MOREY COVER RAFAEL ALBUQUERQUE VARIANT COVER
DAVE WIELGOSZ ASSISTANT EDITOR CHRIS CONROY EDITOR
BRIAN CUNNINGHAM GROUP EDITOR
BATMAN CREATED BY BOB KANE WITH BILL FINGER
HH.
THEIR STANCES. DO YOU SEE IT?
H-HOW IS THAT POSSIBLE?
MAYOR *AKINS* HAD IMAGES PULLED FROM THE *SAME* FOOTAGE. SO DID KILLER MOTH, AND HIS NEW GANG OF *MISFITS*.
SOMEONE IS TRYING TO WEAPONIZE THE VERY IDEA OF OUR TEAM, AND USE IT AGAINST US.
BUT WHO WOULD DO THAT...AND *WHY?*
"IT'S NOT ABOUT WHO I AM NOW. IT'S ABOUT WHO I'M GOING TO BE ON THE OTHER SIDE OF ALL THIS."

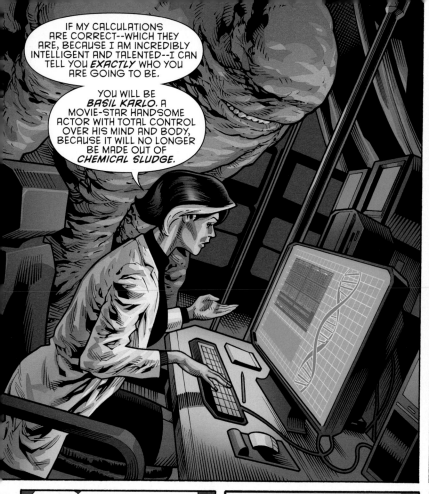

IF MY CALCULATIONS ARE CORRECT--WHICH THEY ARE, BECAUSE I AM INCREDIBLY INTELLIGENT AND TALENTED--I CAN TELL YOU *EXACTLY* WHO YOU ARE GOING TO BE.

YOU WILL BE *BASIL KARLO.* A MOVIE-STAR HANDSOME ACTOR WITH TOTAL CONTROL OVER HIS MIND AND BODY, BECAUSE IT WILL NO LONGER BE MADE OUT OF *CHEMICAL SLUDGE.*

LET'S JUST CALL THAT CLAY, OR MUD. "SLUDGE" JUST MAKES ME FEEL DIRTY.

YOU WON'T HAVE TO CALL IT *ANYTHING* FOR MUCH LONGER.

HELL... WHY ARE YOU EVEN DOIN' THIS FOR ME, DOC? YOU'VE SEEN HOW BAD I CAN GET. THE KIND OF DAMAGE I'VE CAUSED...

I KNOW THAT WHATEVER THIS CURE DOES, I'LL *ALWAYS* FEEL THE PAIN I'VE CAUSED ALL THOSE PEOPLE. I'LL ALWAYS HAVE TO LIVE WITH THAT...

BUT I'M WORRIED IT GOES FURTHER THAN THAT, DEEPER...WHAT IF YOU'RE ALL WRONG, AND THAT DARKNESS IS STILL THERE. WHAT IF DEEP DOWN I *AM* JUST THAT DANGEROUS MONSTER?

WHAT IF THAT FEELING *NEVER* GOES AWAY?

THEN YOU'LL KNOW FOR SURE. AND THAT KIND OF KNOWLEDGE *TREMENDOUS* POWERFUL, BASIL.

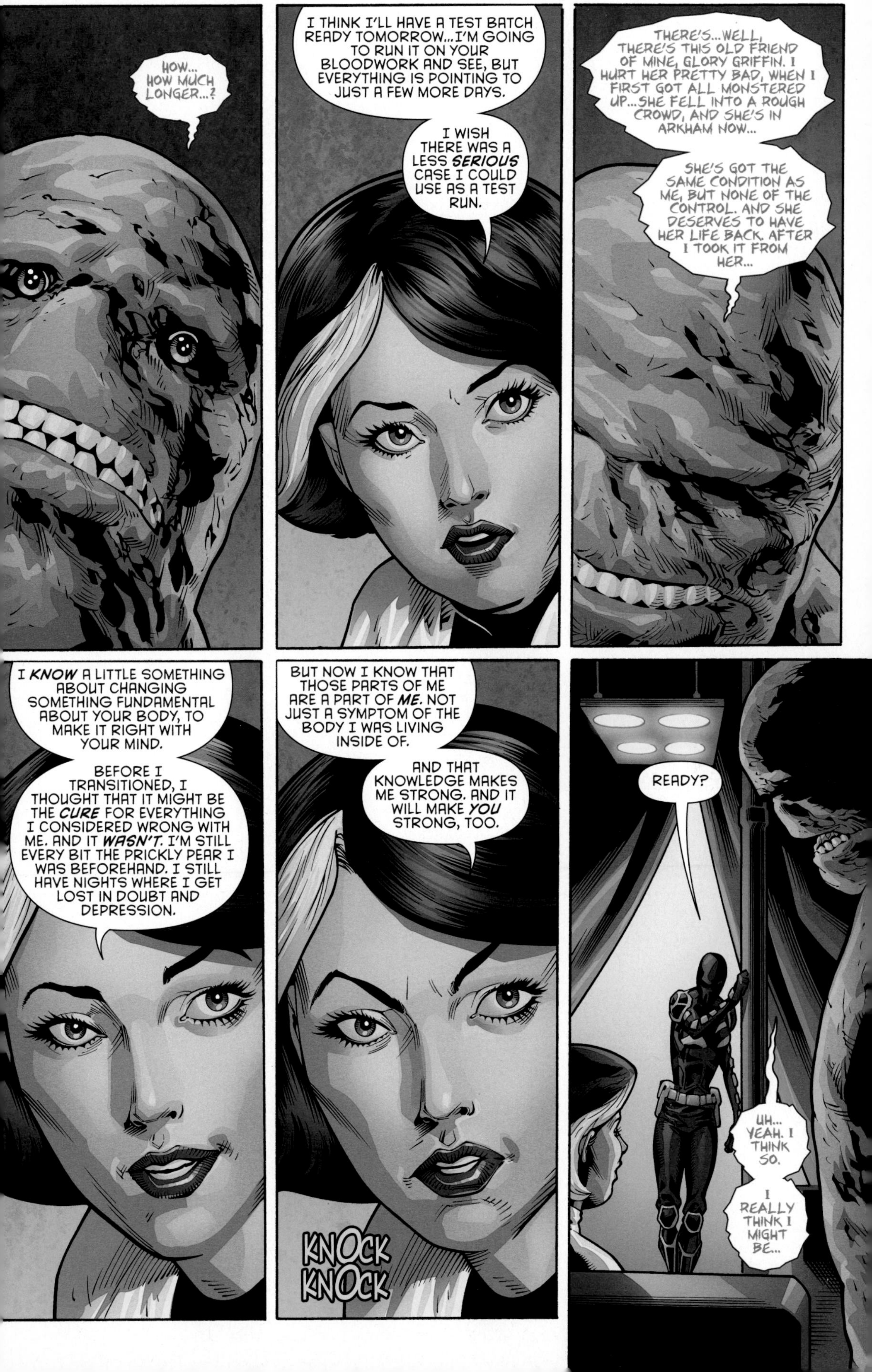
HOW... HOW MUCH LONGER...?
I THINK I'LL HAVE A TEST BATCH READY TOMORROW...I'M GOING TO RUN IT ON YOUR BLOODWORK AND SEE, BUT EVERYTHING IS POINTING TO JUST A FEW MORE DAYS.
I WISH THERE WAS A LESS SERIOUS CASE I COULD USE AS A TEST RUN.
THERE'S...WELL, THERE'S THIS OLD FRIEND OF MINE, GLORY GRIFFIN. I HURT HER PRETTY BAD, WHEN I FIRST GOT ALL MONSTERED UP...SHE FELL INTO A ROUGH CROWD, AND SHE'S IN ARKHAM NOW...
SHE'S GOT THE SAME CONDITION AS ME, BUT NONE OF THE CONTROL. AND SHE DESERVES TO HAVE HER LIFE BACK. AFTER I TOOK IT FROM HER...
I KNOW A LITTLE SOMETHING ABOUT CHANGING SOMETHING FUNDAMENTAL ABOUT YOUR BODY, TO MAKE IT RIGHT WITH YOUR MIND.
BEFORE I TRANSITIONED, I THOUGHT THAT IT MIGHT BE THE CURE FOR EVERYTHING I CONSIDERED WRONG WITH ME. AND IT WASN'T. I'M STILL EVERY BIT THE PRICKLY PEAR I WAS BEFOREHAND. I STILL HAVE NIGHTS WHERE I GET LOST IN DOUBT AND DEPRESSION.
BUT NOW I KNOW THAT THOSE PARTS OF ME ARE A PART OF ME. NOT JUST A SYMPTOM OF THE BODY I WAS LIVING INSIDE OF.
AND THAT KNOWLEDGE MAKES ME STRONG. AND IT WILL MAKE YOU STRONG, TOO.
KNOCK KNOCK
READY?
UH... YEAH. I THINK SO.
I REALLY THINK I MIGHT BE...

SHOULD NEVER HAVE LET JULIA GO TO RIO...

DAMN CYBER-ASSASSIN...

BATWOMAN'S HQ.

LOOKS LIKE YOU NEED A *HAND*, SOLDIER.

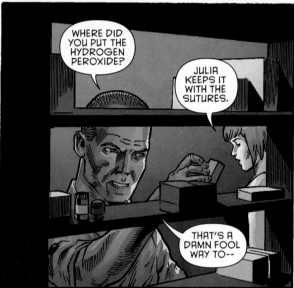

WHERE DID YOU PUT THE HYDROGEN PEROXIDE?

JULIA KEEPS IT WITH THE SUTURES.

THAT'S A DAMN FOOL WAY TO--

DAD. *STOP.* WHY ARE YOU HERE?

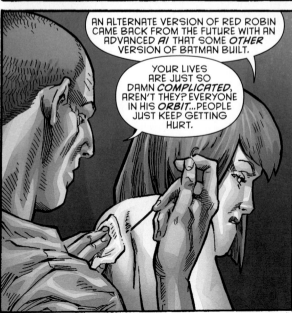

AN ALTERNATE VERSION OF RED ROBIN CAME BACK FROM THE FUTURE WITH AN ADVANCED *AI* THAT SOME *OTHER* VERSION OF BATMAN BUILT.

YOUR LIVES ARE JUST SO DAMN *COMPLICATED*, AREN'T THEY? EVERYONE IN HIS *ORBIT*...PEOPLE JUST KEEP GETTING HURT.

YOU *WOULD* KNOW ALL ABOUT HURTING PEOPLE.

YES, I WOULD. ALL PATCHED UP.

DAD...

I WAS WAITING IN THE NEXT ROOM, BUT IT LOOKS LIKE THIS MIGHT TAKE A WHILE. I CAN STITCH YOU UP. I'VE DONE IT BEFORE.

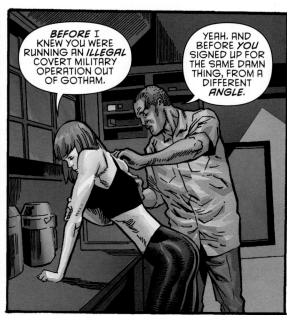

BEFORE I KNEW YOU WERE RUNNING AN *ILLEGAL* COVERT MILITARY OPERATION OUT OF GOTHAM.

YEAH. AND BEFORE *YOU* SIGNED UP FOR THE SAME DAMN THING, FROM A DIFFERENT *ANGLE.*

A FEW WEEKS BACK, THE LAST OF OUR WAR DRONES ACTIVATED ON THEIR OWN ACCORD AND TRIED TO *KILL* YOU. THIS INFORMATION WAS *KEPT* FROM ME UNTIL IT WAS TOO LATE TO RESPOND.

WE TOOK CARE OF THEM OURSELVES. AND *YOU* WEREN'T A SUSPECT.

EITHER WAY, I'VE *EXPELLED* OUR WEAPONS DEVELOPER, *ULYSSES ARMSTRONG,* FROM THE COLONY. HIS CREATIONS WON'T HURT YOUR PEOPLE ANY LONGER.

IF YOU DON'T MIND MY ASKING, WHO *WAS* BEHIND THE HACK?

OKAY. WE'RE *DONE* HERE.

DAMMIT. THAT'S NOT... KATE. I NEED YOU TO *LISTEN.*

ONE OF MY MILITARY CONTACTS PASSED A DOSSIER ALONG TO ME THE OTHER DAY. IT HAS *DETAILED IMAGES* OF EACH MEMBER OF YOUR TEAM.

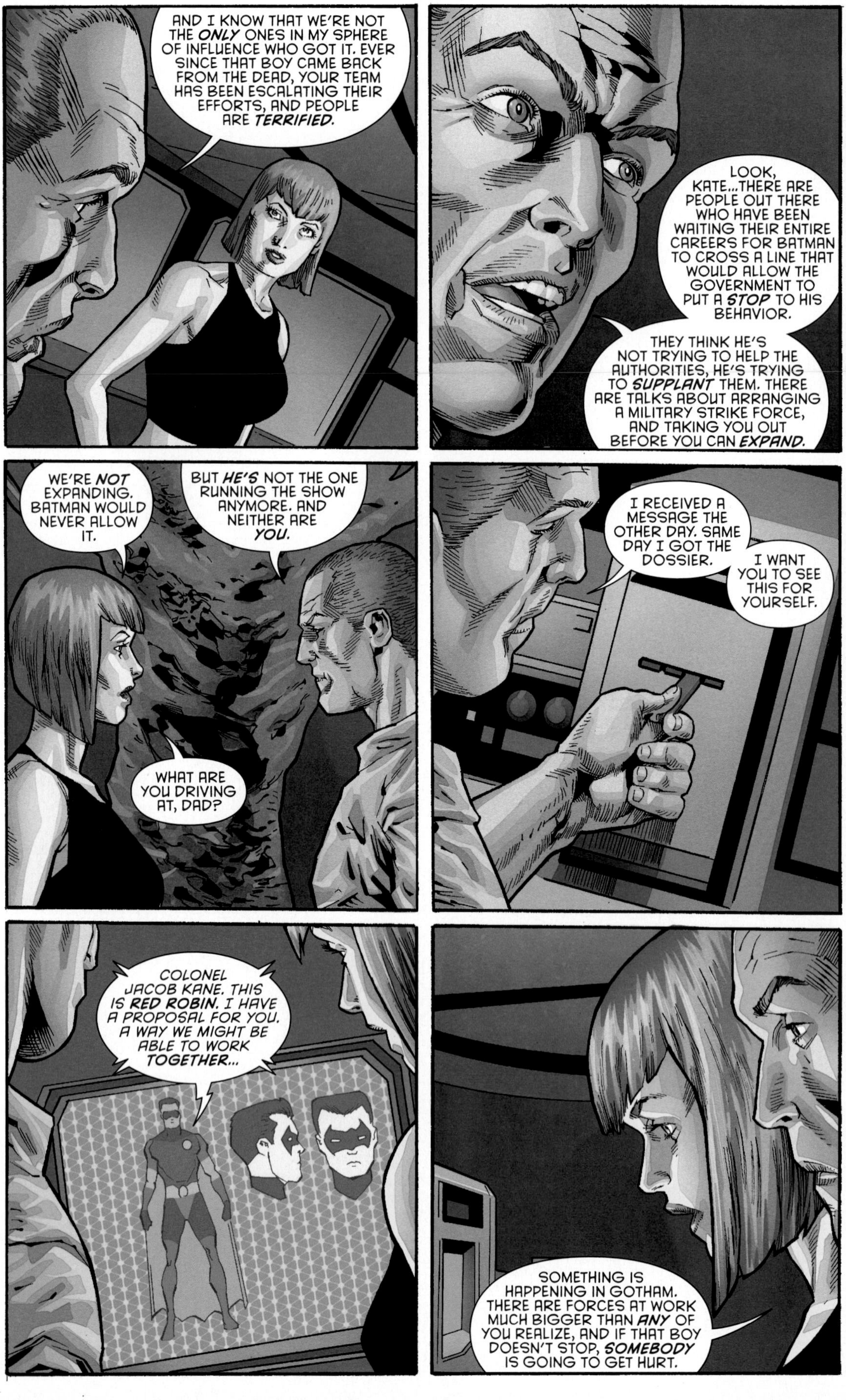
AND I KNOW THAT WE'RE NOT THE *ONLY* ONES IN MY SPHERE OF INFLUENCE WHO GOT IT. EVER SINCE THAT BOY CAME BACK FROM THE DEAD, YOUR TEAM HAS BEEN ESCALATING THEIR EFFORTS, AND PEOPLE ARE *TERRIFIED*.
LOOK, KATE...THERE ARE PEOPLE OUT THERE WHO HAVE BEEN WAITING THEIR ENTIRE CAREERS FOR BATMAN TO CROSS A LINE THAT WOULD ALLOW THE GOVERNMENT TO PUT A *STOP* TO HIS BEHAVIOR.
THEY THINK HE'S NOT TRYING TO HELP THE AUTHORITIES, HE'S TRYING TO *SUPPLANT* THEM. THERE ARE TALKS ABOUT ARRANGING A MILITARY STRIKE FORCE, AND TAKING YOU OUT BEFORE YOU CAN *EXPAND*.
WE'RE *NOT* EXPANDING. BATMAN WOULD NEVER ALLOW IT.
BUT *HE'S* NOT THE ONE RUNNING THE SHOW ANYMORE. AND NEITHER ARE *YOU*.
WHAT ARE YOU DRIVING AT, DAD?
I RECEIVED A MESSAGE THE OTHER DAY. SAME DAY I GOT THE DOSSIER.
I WANT YOU TO SEE THIS FOR YOURSELF.
COLONEL JACOB KANE. THIS IS **RED ROBIN**. I HAVE A PROPOSAL FOR YOU. A WAY WE MIGHT BE ABLE TO WORK **TOGETHER**...
SOMETHING IS HAPPENING IN GOTHAM. THERE ARE FORCES AT WORK MUCH BIGGER THAN *ANY* OF YOU REALIZE, AND IF THAT BOY DOESN'T STOP, *SOMEBODY* IS GOING TO GET HURT.

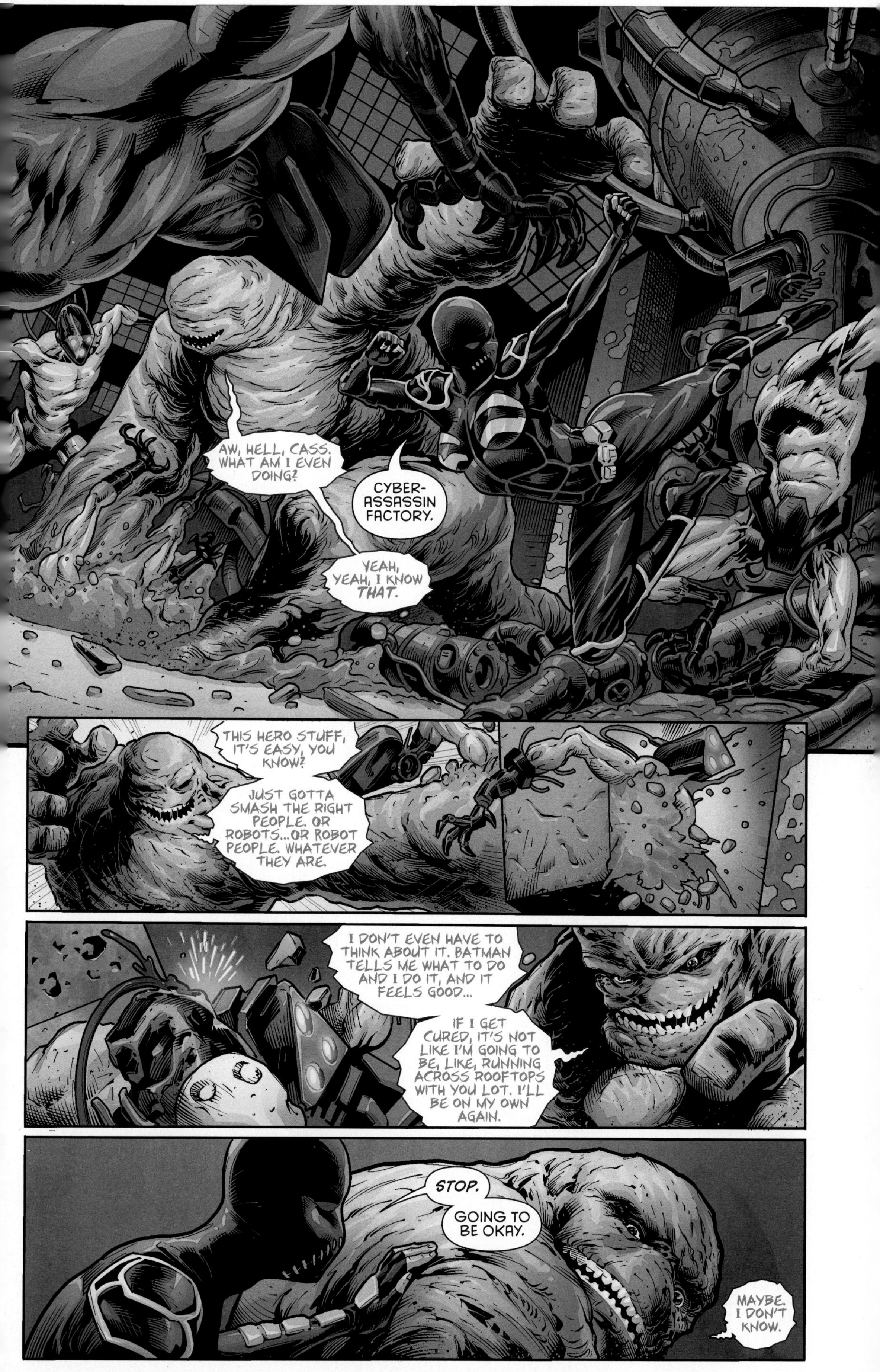
AW, HELL, CASS. WHAT AM I EVEN DOING?
CYBER-ASSASSIN FACTORY.
YEAH, YEAH, I KNOW THAT.
THIS HERO STUFF, IT'S EASY, YOU KNOW?
JUST GOTTA SMASH THE RIGHT PEOPLE. OR ROBOTS...OR ROBOT PEOPLE. WHATEVER THEY ARE.
I DON'T EVEN HAVE TO THINK ABOUT IT. BATMAN TELLS ME WHAT TO DO AND I DO IT, AND IT FEELS GOOD...
IF I GET CURED, IT'S NOT LIKE I'M GOING TO BE, LIKE, RUNNING ACROSS ROOFTOPS WITH YOU LOT. I'LL BE ON MY OWN AGAIN.
STOP.
GOING TO BE OKAY.
MAYBE. I DON'T KNOW.

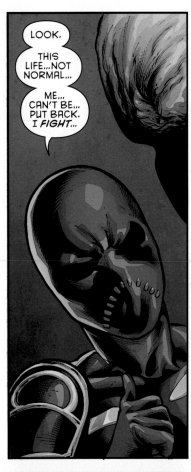

LOOK.

THIS LIFE...NOT NORMAL...

ME... CAN'T BE... PUT BACK. I *FIGHT*...

YOU GET... *LIFE*.

I SCREWED IT ALL UP ONCE BEFORE. WHAT'S TO SAY I WON'T JUST DO IT AGAIN? MESS MY WHOLE LIFE UP, TOP TO BOTTOM.

HURT PEOPLE AGAIN.

I'LL HIT YOU.

NOW THERE'S A SCARY THOUGHT.

THANKS, CASS...NOBODY ELSE REALLY UNDERSTANDS. THINK WE CAN STILL RUN SHAKESPEARE LINES WHEN I'M NOT A BIG SCARY CLAY MONSTER ANYMORE?

YES.

OKAY...THEN THERE'S JUST ONE LAST THING I NEED TO DO.

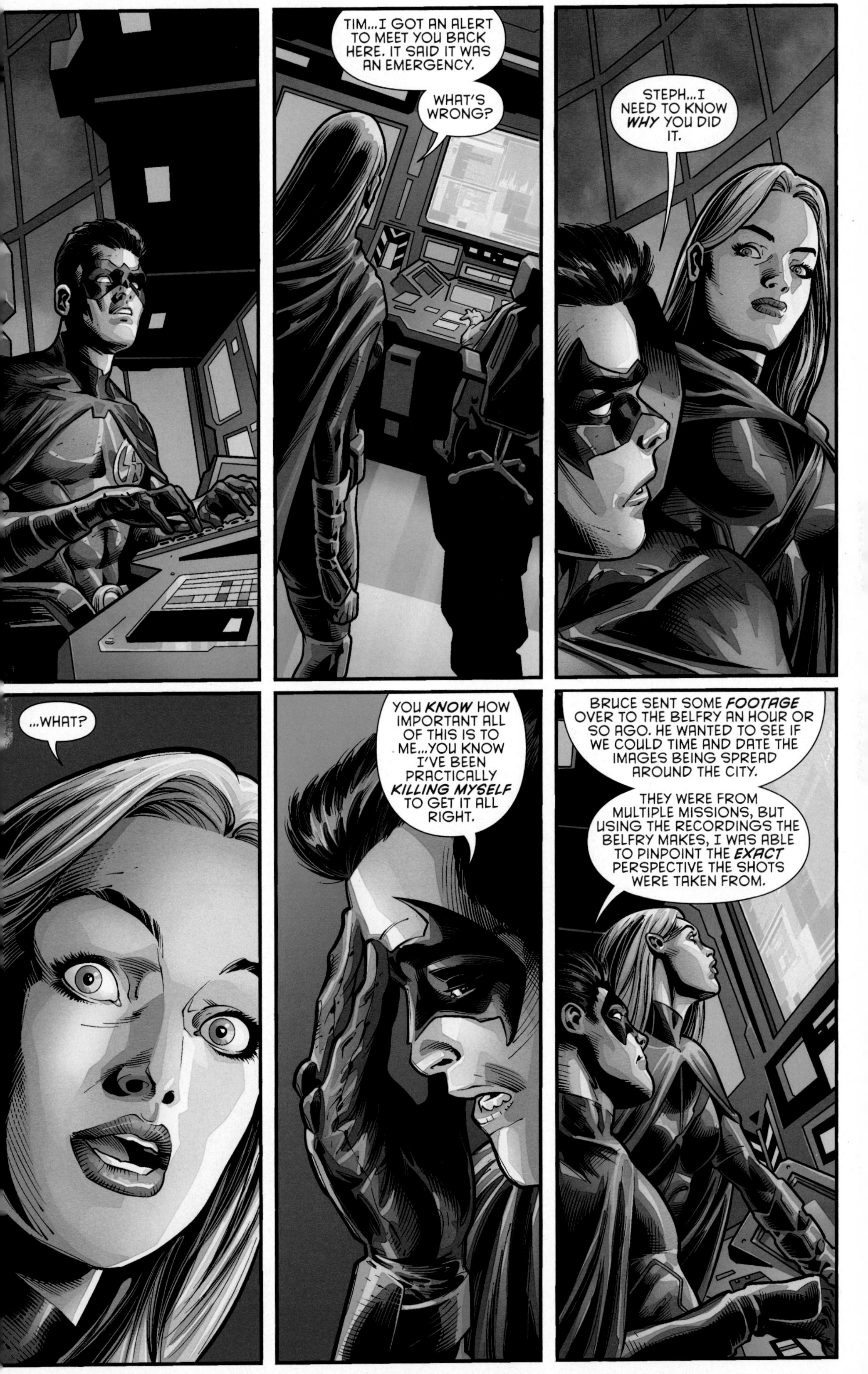
TIM...I GOT AN ALERT TO MEET YOU BACK HERE. IT SAID IT WAS AN EMERGENCY.
WHAT'S WRONG?
STEPH...I NEED TO KNOW *WHY* YOU DID IT.
...WHAT?
YOU *KNOW* HOW IMPORTANT ALL OF THIS IS TO ME...YOU KNOW I'VE BEEN PRACTICALLY *KILLING MYSELF* TO GET IT ALL RIGHT.
BRUCE SENT SOME *FOOTAGE* OVER TO THE BELFRY AN HOUR OR SO AGO. HE WANTED TO SEE IF WE COULD TIME AND DATE THE IMAGES BEING SPREAD AROUND THE CITY.
THEY WERE FROM MULTIPLE MISSIONS, BUT USING THE RECORDINGS THE BELFRY MAKES, I WAS ABLE TO PINPOINT THE *EXACT* PERSPECTIVE THE SHOTS WERE TAKEN FROM.

AND IT WAS YOU. *YOUR PHONE.*

EXCUSE ME?

PLEASE DON'T LIE TO ME.

YOU'RE NOT EVEN GIVING ME A *CHANCE* TO LIE, TIM. YOU'RE JUST BARRELING TOWARD A CONVICTION, BECAUSE YOU'RE MISTER TEN-STEPS-AHEAD.

BUT YOU'RE *WRONG.* AND IT *SUCKS* THAT YOU DIDN'T COME AT THIS ASSUMING THAT *FIRST.*

IT MATCHES YOUR M.O. EXACTLY. IT'S WHAT YOU *TOLD* BATMAN YOU WOULD DO TO GET BACK AT HIM DURING THE VICTIM SYNDICATE ATTACKS...

WHO ELSE WOULD KNOW HOW PERFECTLY TO FRAME YOU, HERE? WHOEVER IT IS WOULD HAVE TO KNOW THE *EXACT* FAULT LINES OF THE TEAM.

PULL UP THE PHONE'S CORE PROGRAMMING.

I'VE ALREADY--

DO IT.

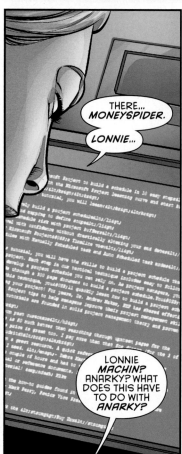

THERE... *MONEYSPIDER.*

LONNIE...

LONNIE *MACHIN?* ANARKY? WHAT DOES THIS HAVE TO DO WITH *ANARKY?*

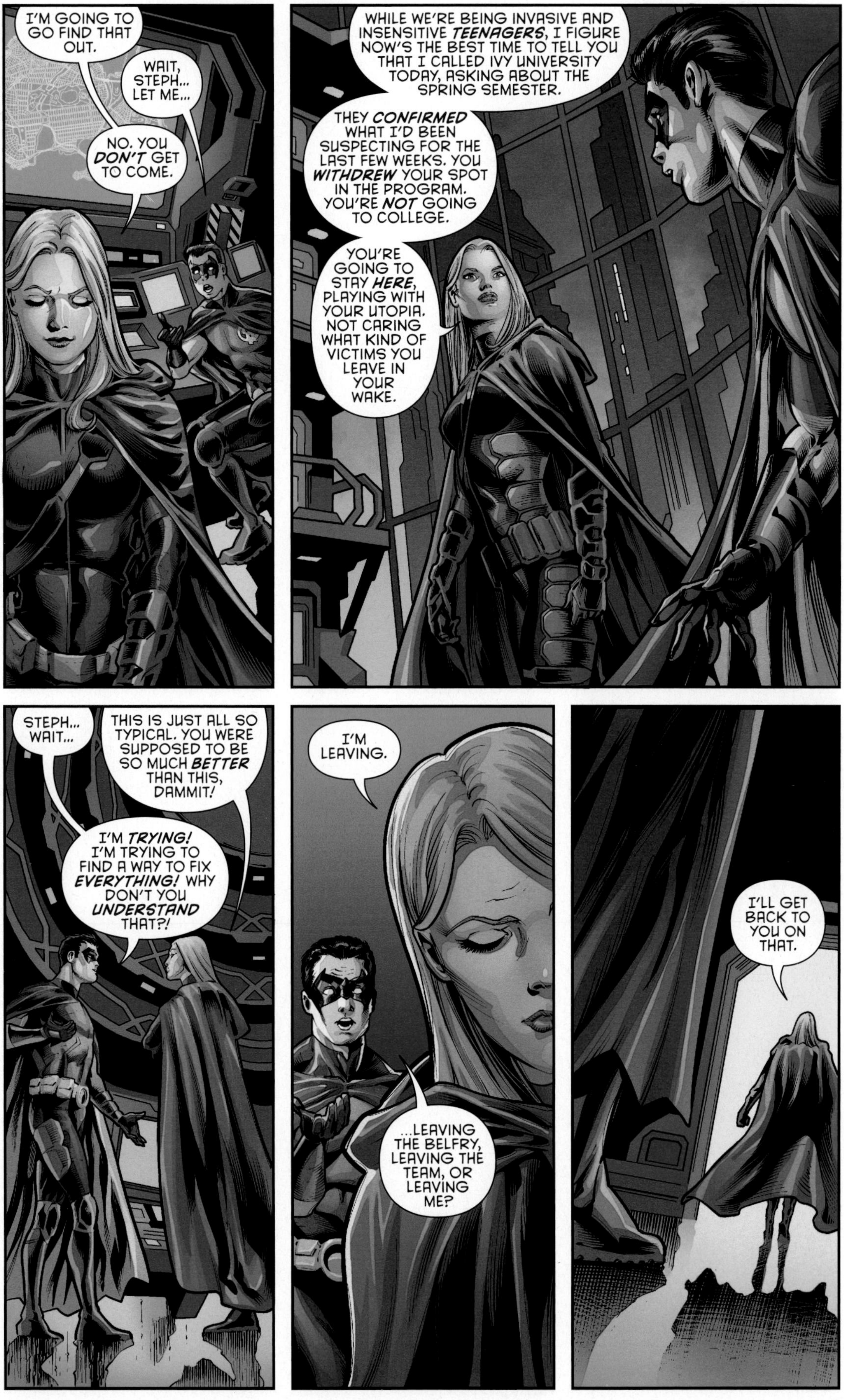
I'M GOING TO GO FIND THAT OUT.
WAIT, STEPH... LET ME...
NO. YOU *DON'T* GET TO COME.
WHILE WE'RE BEING INVASIVE AND INSENSITIVE *TEENAGERS*, I FIGURE NOW'S THE BEST TIME TO TELL YOU THAT I CALLED IVY UNIVERSITY TODAY, ASKING ABOUT THE SPRING SEMESTER.
THEY *CONFIRMED* WHAT I'D BEEN SUSPECTING FOR THE LAST FEW WEEKS. YOU *WITHDREW* YOUR SPOT IN THE PROGRAM. YOU'RE *NOT* GOING TO COLLEGE.
YOU'RE GOING TO STAY *HERE*, PLAYING WITH YOUR UTOPIA. NOT CARING WHAT KIND OF VICTIMS YOU LEAVE IN YOUR WAKE.
STEPH... WAIT...
THIS IS JUST ALL SO TYPICAL. YOU WERE SUPPOSED TO BE SO MUCH *BETTER* THAN THIS, DAMMIT!
I'M *TRYING!* I'M TRYING TO FIND A WAY TO FIX *EVERYTHING!* WHY DON'T YOU *UNDERSTAND* THAT?!
I'M LEAVING.
...LEAVING THE BELFRY, LEAVING THE TEAM, OR LEAVING ME?
I'LL GET BACK TO YOU ON THAT.

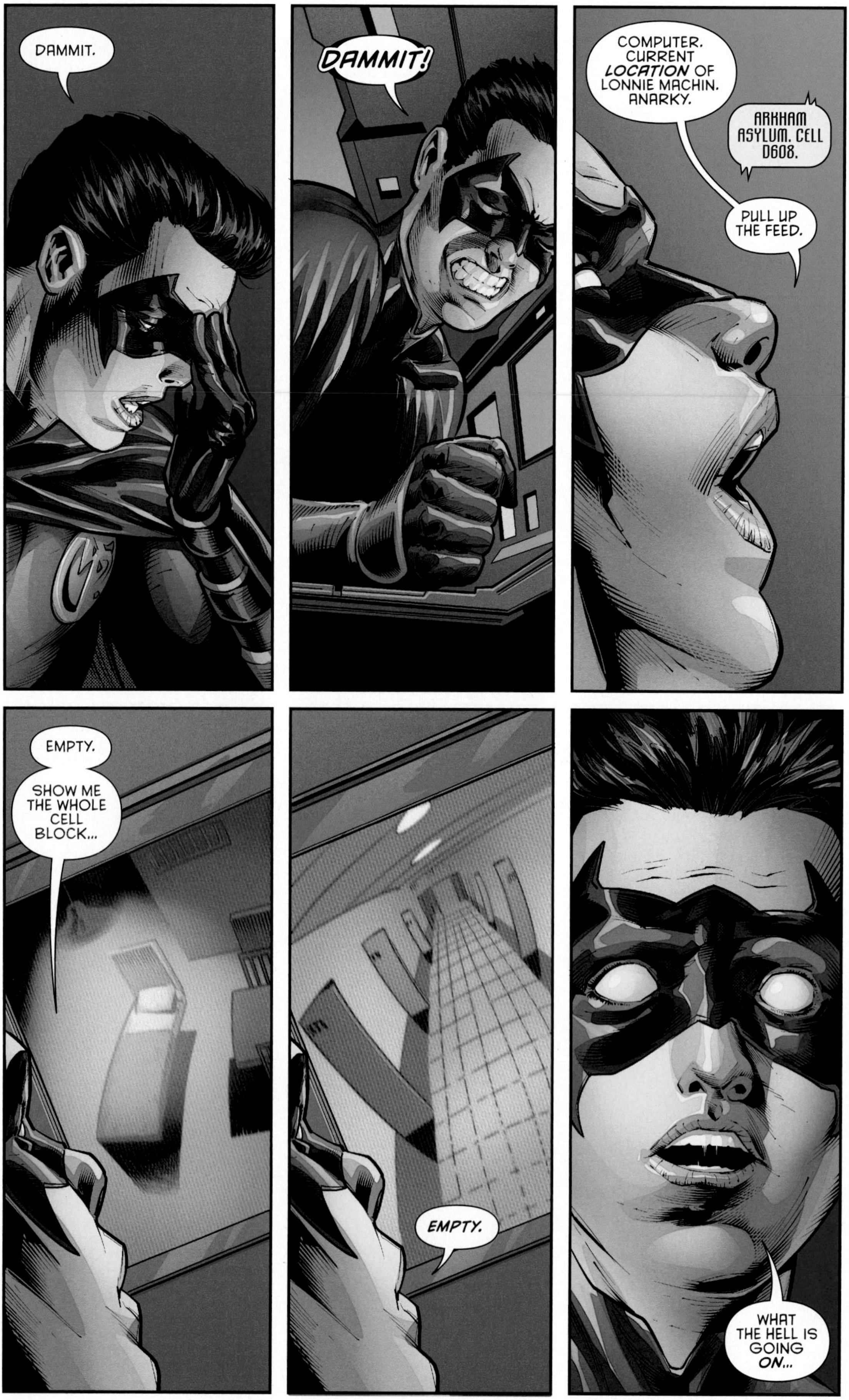
DAMMIT.
DAMMIT!
COMPUTER. CURRENT *LOCATION* OF LONNIE MACHIN. ANARKY.
ARKHAM ASYLUM. CELL D608.
PULL UP THE FEED.
EMPTY.
SHOW ME THE WHOLE CELL BLOCK...
EMPTY.
WHAT THE HELL IS GOING *ON*...

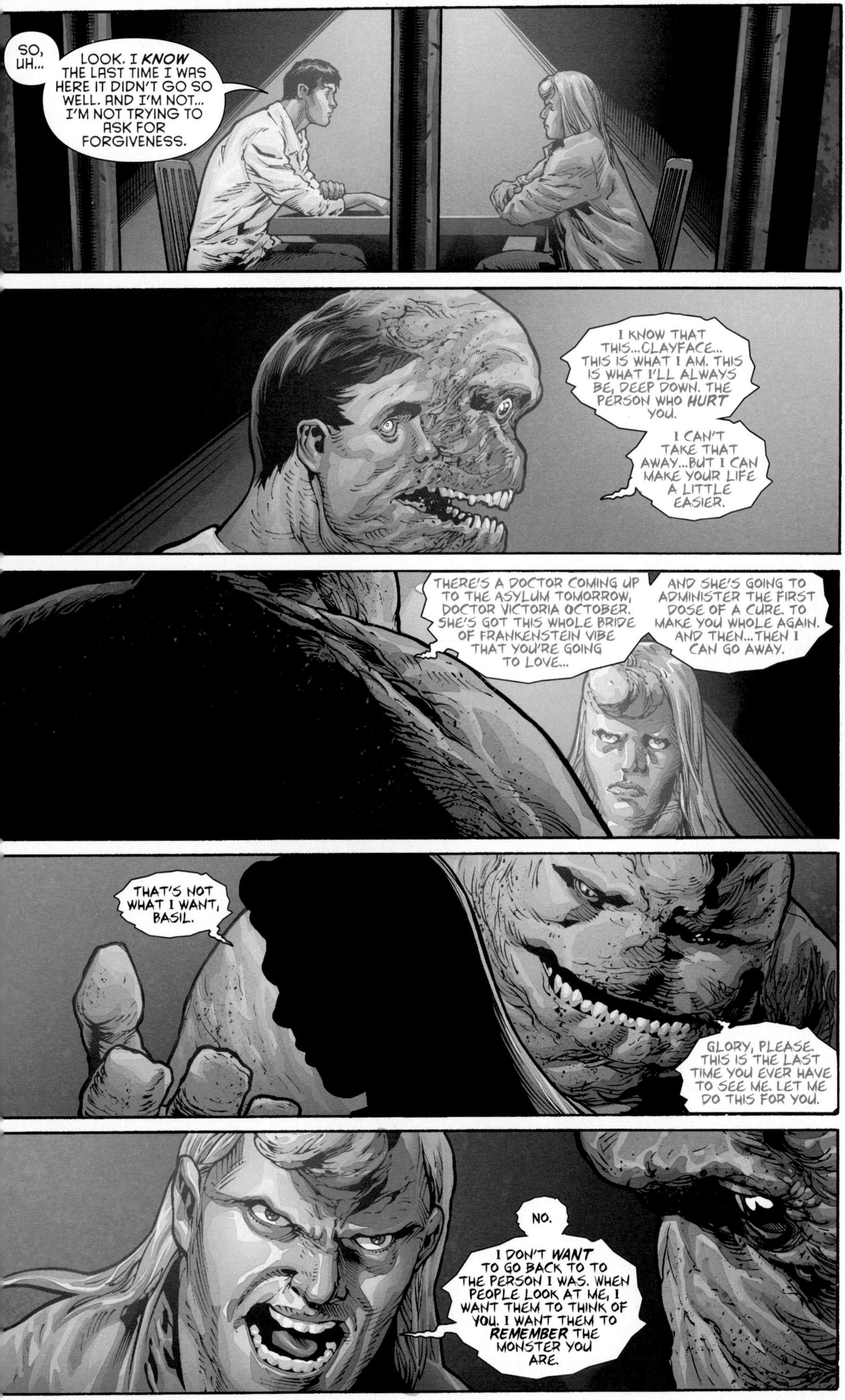

SO, UH...
LOOK. I KNOW THE LAST TIME I WAS HERE IT DIDN'T GO SO WELL. AND I'M NOT... I'M NOT TRYING TO ASK FOR FORGIVENESS.
I KNOW THAT THIS...CLAYFACE... THIS IS WHAT I AM. THIS IS WHAT I'LL ALWAYS BE, DEEP DOWN. THE PERSON WHO HURT YOU.
I CAN'T TAKE THAT AWAY...BUT I CAN MAKE YOUR LIFE A LITTLE EASIER.
THERE'S A DOCTOR COMING UP TO THE ASYLUM TOMORROW, DOCTOR VICTORIA OCTOBER. SHE'S GOT THIS WHOLE BRIDE OF FRANKENSTEIN VIBE THAT YOU'RE GOING TO LOVE...
AND SHE'S GOING TO ADMINISTER THE FIRST DOSE OF A CURE. TO MAKE YOU WHOLE AGAIN. AND THEN...THEN I CAN GO AWAY.
THAT'S NOT WHAT I WANT, BASIL.
GLORY, PLEASE. THIS IS THE LAST TIME YOU EVER HAVE TO SEE ME. LET ME DO THIS FOR YOU.
NO.
I DON'T WANT TO GO BACK TO TO THE PERSON I WAS. WHEN PEOPLE LOOK AT ME, I WANT THEM TO THINK OF YOU. I WANT THEM TO REMEMBER THE MONSTER YOU ARE.

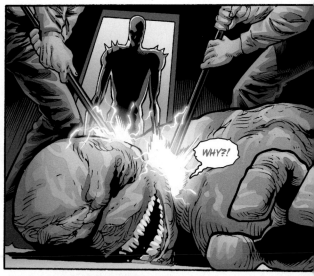

A FEW MINUTES AGO, EVERY NEWS AGENCY IN GOTHAM CITY RECEIVED A DOSSIER WITH UNEQUIVOCAL PROOF THAT THE *WANTED CRIMINAL CLAYFACE* IS WORKING WITH BATMAN.

AND THE PEOPLE WILL FINALLY UNDERSTAND WHAT THE VICTIM SYNDICATE HAS BEEN SAYING FROM THE BEGINNING...

WHY?!

WHY ARE YOU DOING THIS?

BECAUSE THE IDEA THAT YOU JUST GET TO WALK FREE FROM ALL OF THIS AND START OVER? I CAN'T ALLOW THAT TO HAPPEN, BASIL.

HOLD HIM DOWN.

THE CITY NEEDS TO *KNOW* WHAT YOU REALLY ARE.

NO... NO!

AND THEY *WILL*, SOON ENOUGH.

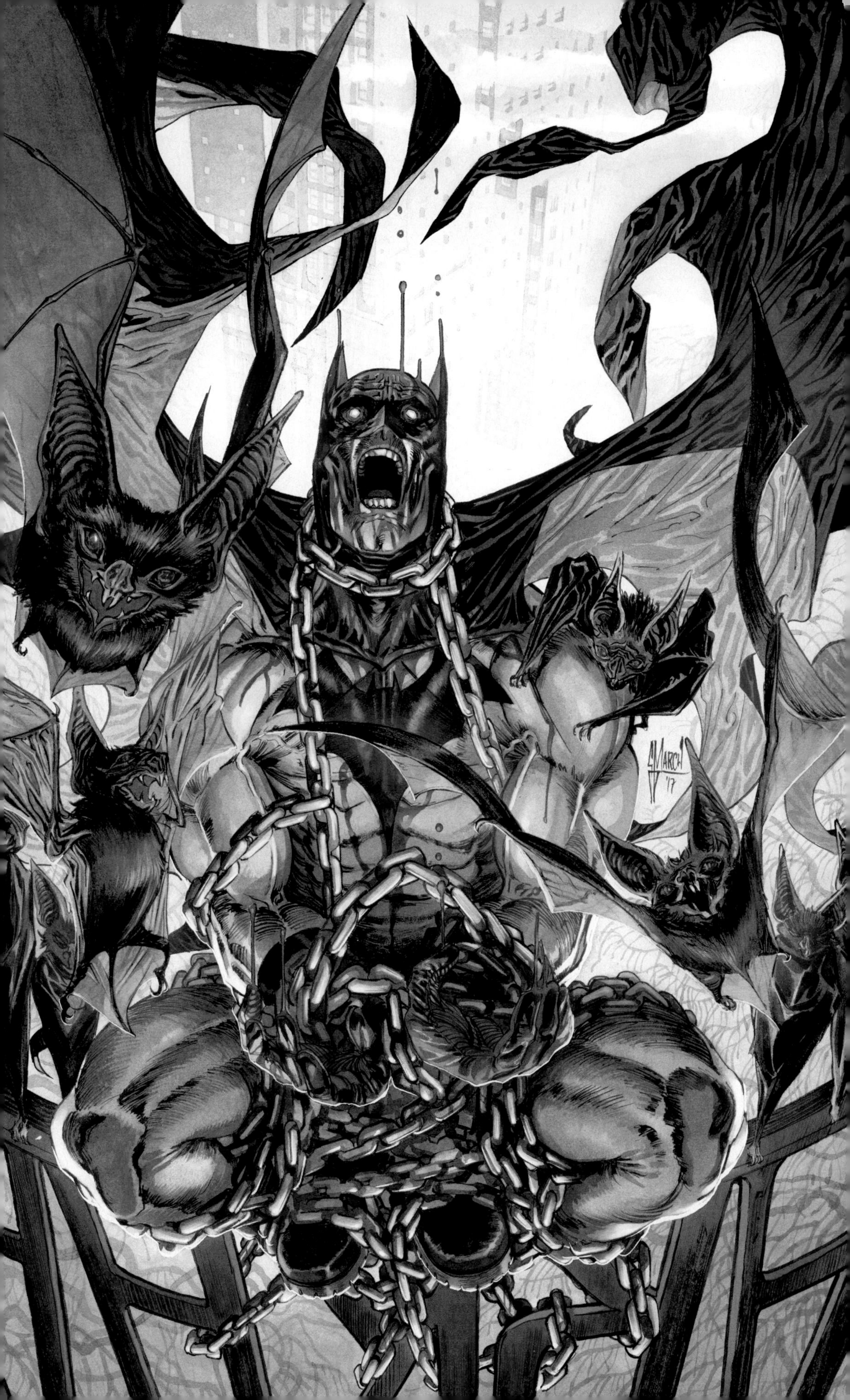

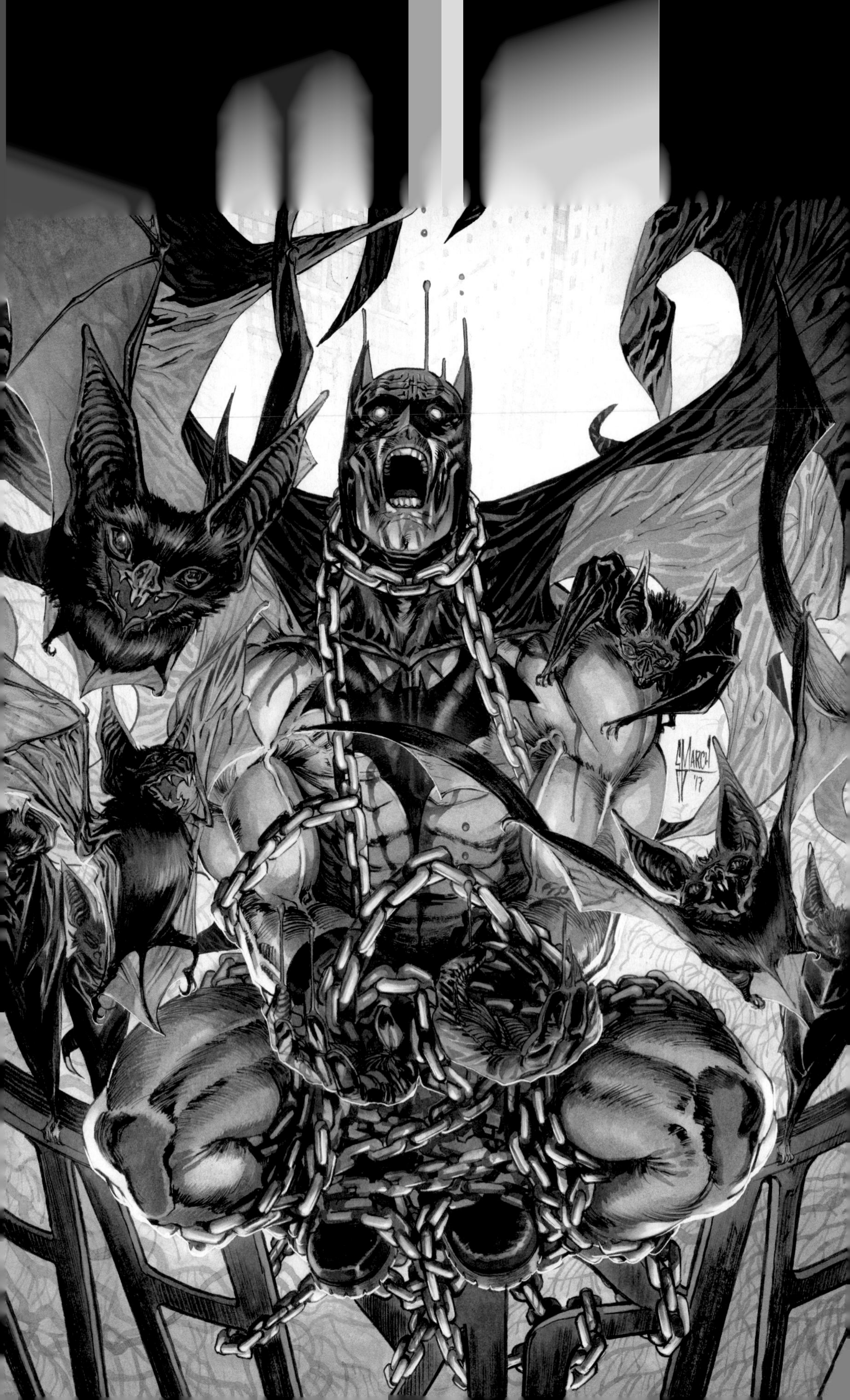

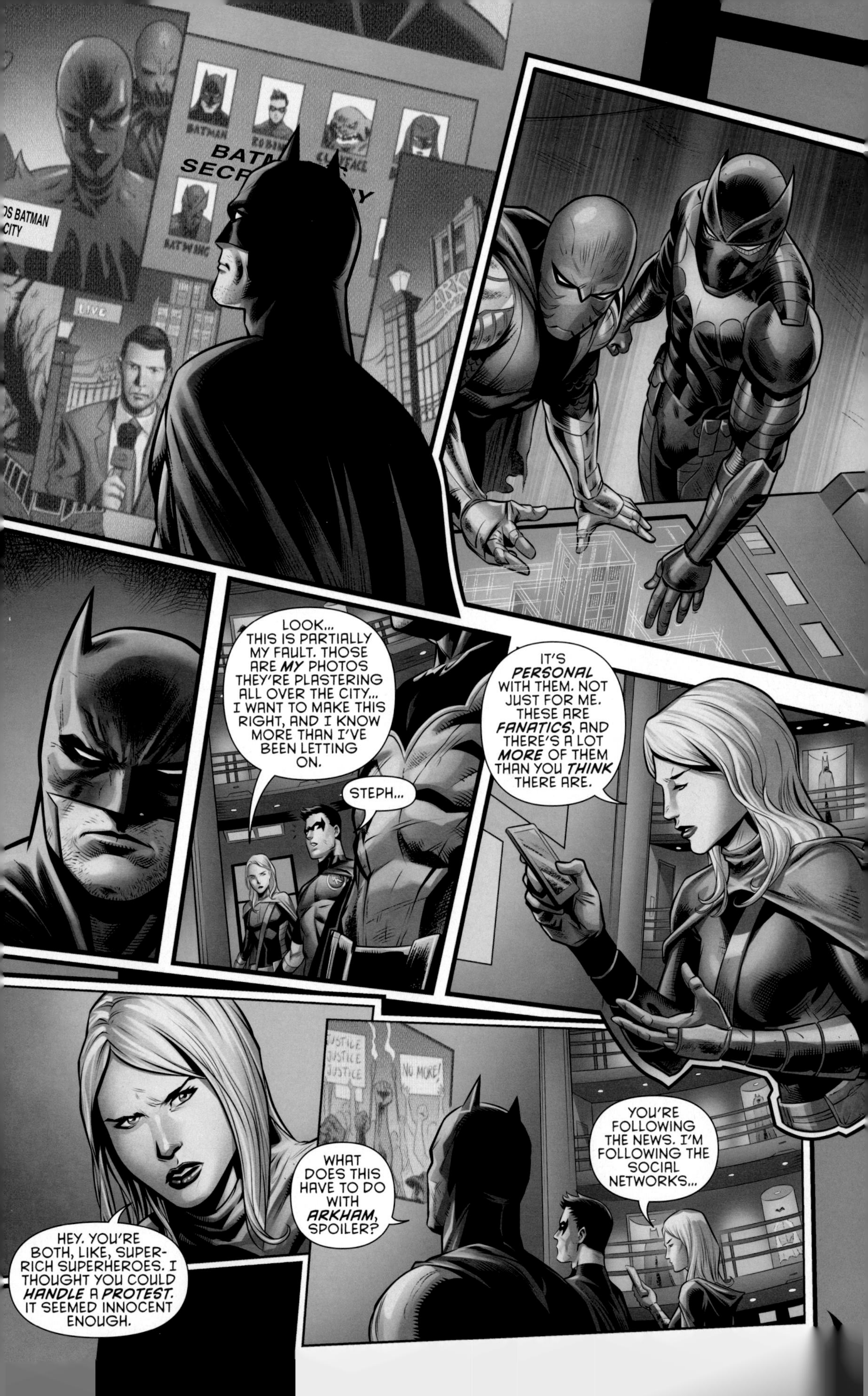
BATMAN
ROBIN
CLAYFACE
BATWING
BATM
SECR
OS BATMAN
CITY
LIVE
LOOK... THIS IS PARTIALLY MY FAULT. THOSE ARE *MY* PHOTOS THEY'RE PLASTERING ALL OVER THE CITY... I WANT TO MAKE THIS RIGHT, AND I KNOW MORE THAN I'VE BEEN LETTING ON.
STEPH...
IT'S *PERSONAL* WITH THEM. NOT JUST FOR ME. THESE ARE *FANATICS*, AND THERE'S A LOT *MORE* OF THEM THAN YOU *THINK* THERE ARE.
JUSTICE
JUSTICE
JUSTICE
NO MORE!
HEY. YOU'RE BOTH, LIKE, SUPER-RICH SUPERHEROES. I THOUGHT YOU COULD *HANDLE* A *PROTEST*. IT SEEMED INNOCENT ENOUGH.
WHAT DOES THIS HAVE TO DO WITH *ARKHAM*, SPOILER?
YOU'RE FOLLOWING THE NEWS. I'M FOLLOWING THE SOCIAL NETWORKS...

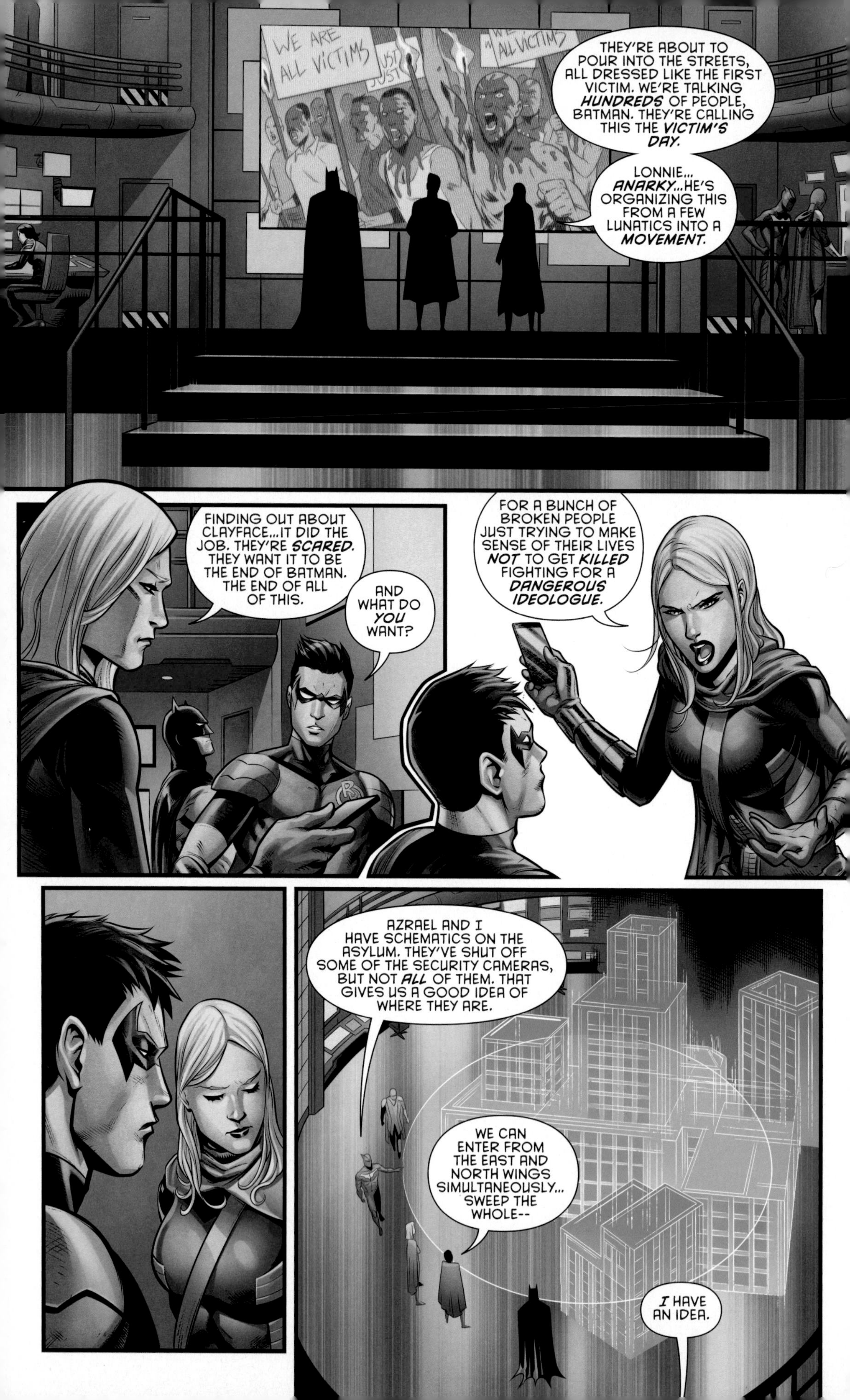

WE ARE ALL VICTIMS
JUST
WE ALL VICTIMS
THEY'RE ABOUT TO POUR INTO THE STREETS, ALL DRESSED LIKE THE FIRST VICTIM. WE'RE TALKING *HUNDREDS* OF PEOPLE, BATMAN. THEY'RE CALLING THIS THE *VICTIM'S DAY.*
LONNIE... *ANARKY*...HE'S ORGANIZING THIS FROM A FEW LUNATICS INTO A *MOVEMENT.*
FINDING OUT ABOUT CLAYFACE...IT DID THE JOB. THEY'RE *SCARED.* THEY WANT IT TO BE THE END OF BATMAN. THE END OF ALL OF THIS.
AND WHAT DO *YOU* WANT?
FOR A BUNCH OF BROKEN PEOPLE JUST TRYING TO MAKE SENSE OF THEIR LIVES *NOT* TO GET *KILLED* FIGHTING FOR A *DANGEROUS IDEOLOGUE.*
AZRAEL AND I HAVE SCHEMATICS ON THE ASYLUM. THEY'VE SHUT OFF SOME OF THE SECURITY CAMERAS, BUT NOT *ALL* OF THEM. THAT GIVES US A GOOD IDEA OF WHERE THEY ARE.
WE CAN ENTER FROM THE EAST AND NORTH WINGS SIMULTANEOUSLY... SWEEP THE WHOLE--
I HAVE AN IDEA.

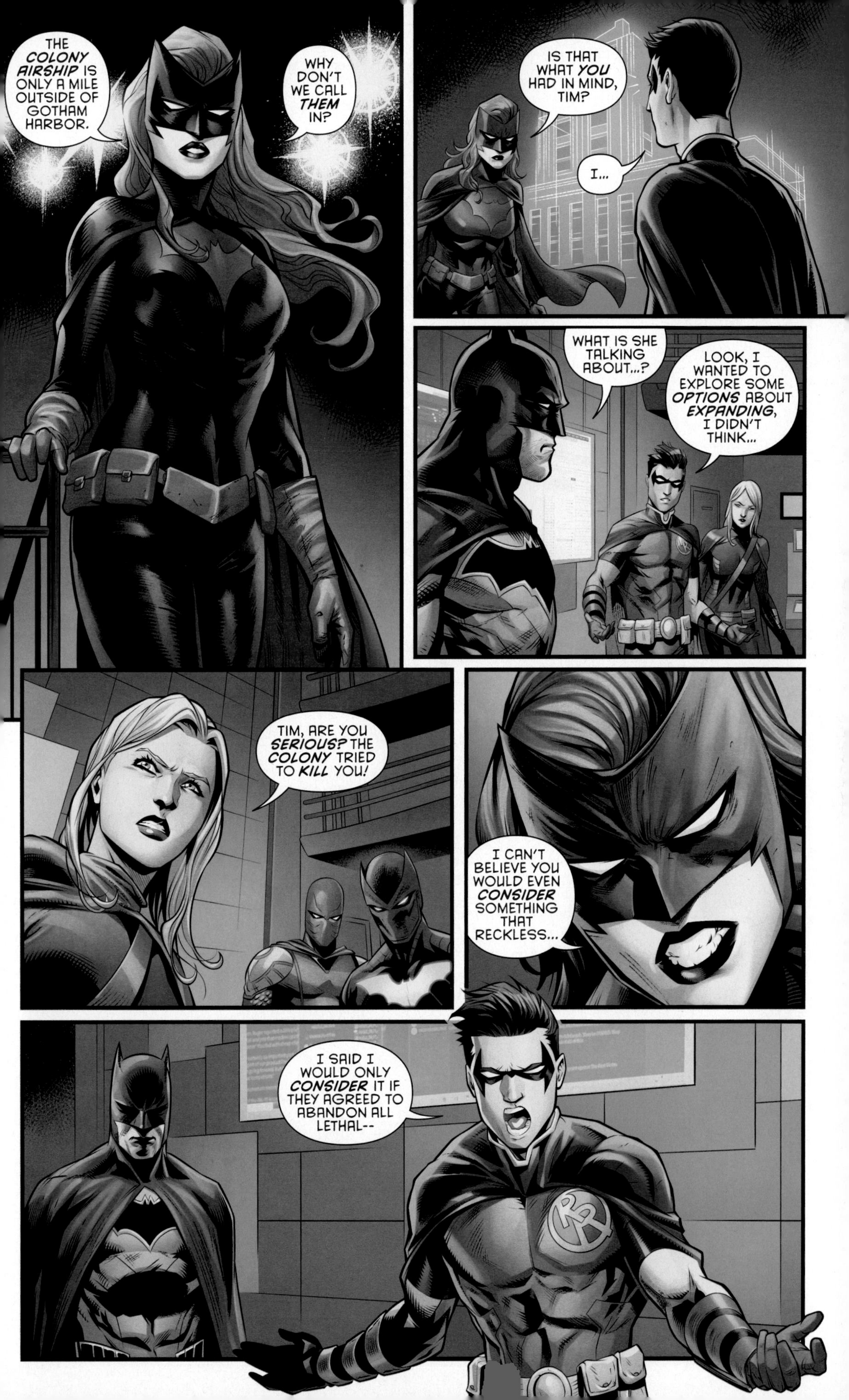
THE COLONY AIRSHIP IS ONLY A MILE OUTSIDE OF GOTHAM HARBOR.
WHY DON'T WE CALL THEM IN?
IS THAT WHAT YOU HAD IN MIND, TIM?
I...
WHAT IS SHE TALKING ABOUT...?
LOOK, I WANTED TO EXPLORE SOME OPTIONS ABOUT EXPANDING, I DIDN'T THINK...
TIM, ARE YOU SERIOUS? THE COLONY TRIED TO KILL YOU!
I CAN'T BELIEVE YOU WOULD EVEN CONSIDER SOMETHING THAT RECKLESS...
I SAID I WOULD ONLY CONSIDER IT IF THEY AGREED TO ABANDON ALL LETHAL--

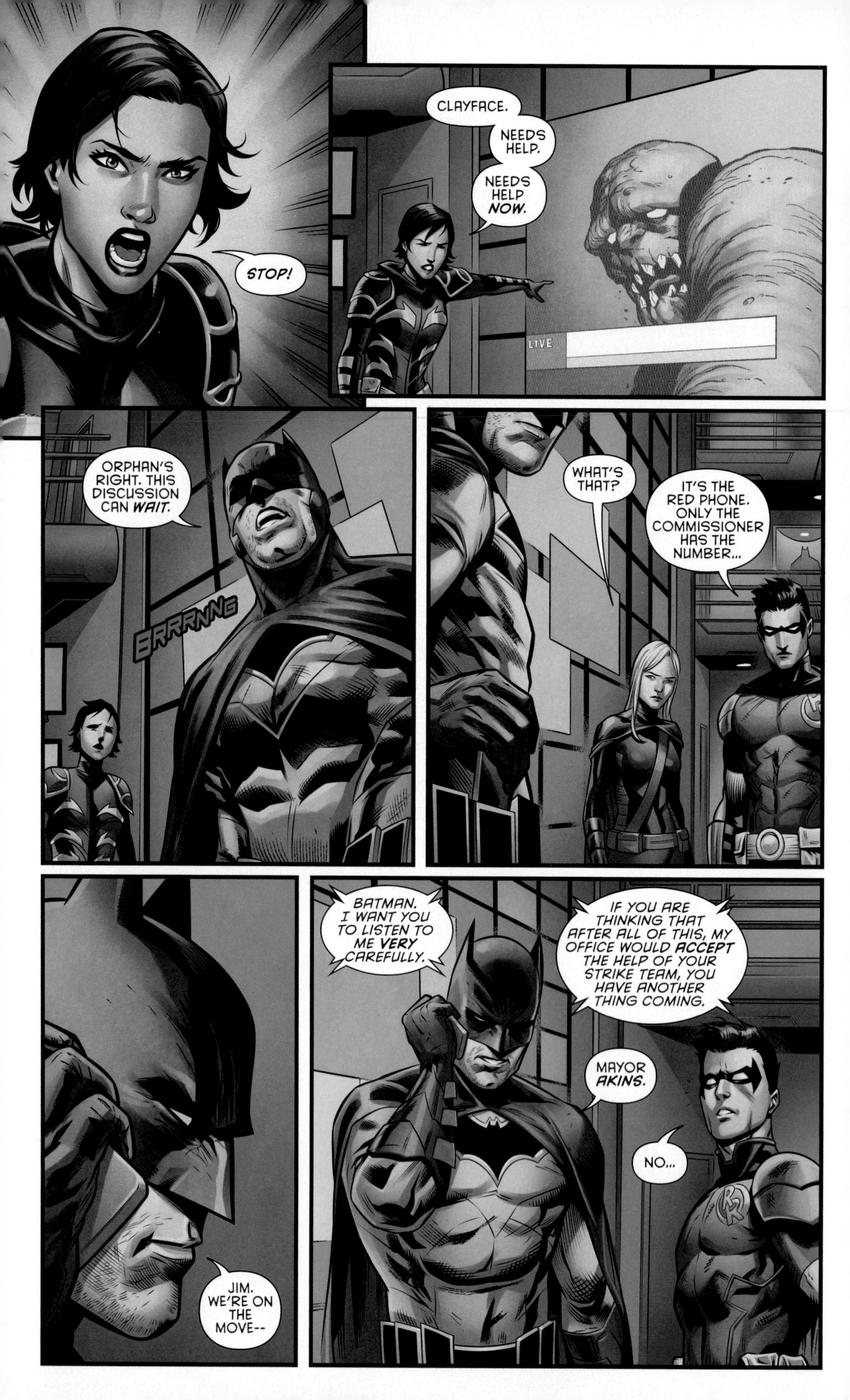
STOP!
CLAYFACE.
NEEDS HELP.
NEEDS HELP NOW.
LIVE
ORPHAN'S RIGHT. THIS DISCUSSION CAN WAIT.
BRRRNNG
WHAT'S THAT?
IT'S THE RED PHONE. ONLY THE COMMISSIONER HAS THE NUMBER...
JIM. WE'RE ON THE MOVE--
BATMAN. I WANT YOU TO LISTEN TO ME VERY CAREFULLY.
IF YOU ARE THINKING THAT AFTER ALL OF THIS, MY OFFICE WOULD ACCEPT THE HELP OF YOUR STRIKE TEAM, YOU HAVE ANOTHER THING COMING.
MAYOR AKINS.
NO...

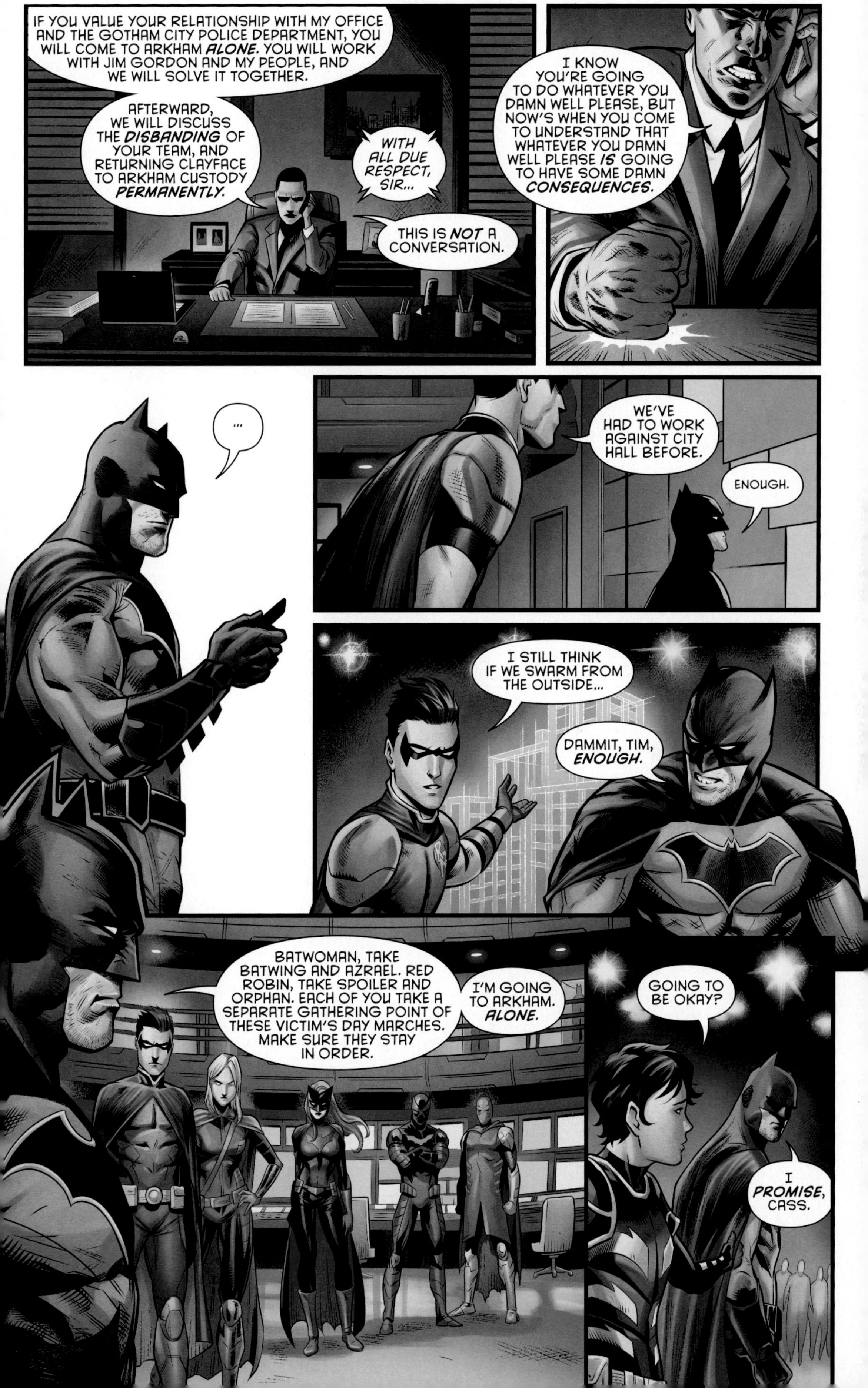
IF YOU VALUE YOUR RELATIONSHIP WITH MY OFFICE AND THE GOTHAM CITY POLICE DEPARTMENT, YOU WILL COME TO ARKHAM ALONE. YOU WILL WORK WITH JIM GORDON AND MY PEOPLE, AND WE WILL SOLVE IT TOGETHER.
AFTERWARD, WE WILL DISCUSS THE DISBANDING OF YOUR TEAM, AND RETURNING CLAYFACE TO ARKHAM CUSTODY PERMANENTLY.
WITH ALL DUE RESPECT, SIR...
THIS IS NOT A CONVERSATION.
I KNOW YOU'RE GOING TO DO WHATEVER YOU DAMN WELL PLEASE, BUT NOW'S WHEN YOU COME TO UNDERSTAND THAT WHATEVER YOU DAMN WELL PLEASE IS GOING TO HAVE SOME DAMN CONSEQUENCES.
...
WE'VE HAD TO WORK AGAINST CITY HALL BEFORE.
ENOUGH.
I STILL THINK IF WE SWARM FROM THE OUTSIDE...
DAMMIT, TIM, ENOUGH.
BATWOMAN, TAKE BATWING AND AZRAEL. RED ROBIN, TAKE SPOILER AND ORPHAN. EACH OF YOU TAKE A SEPARATE GATHERING POINT OF THESE VICTIM'S DAY MARCHES. MAKE SURE THEY STAY IN ORDER.
I'M GOING TO ARKHAM. ALONE.
GOING TO BE OKAY?
I PROMISE, CASS.

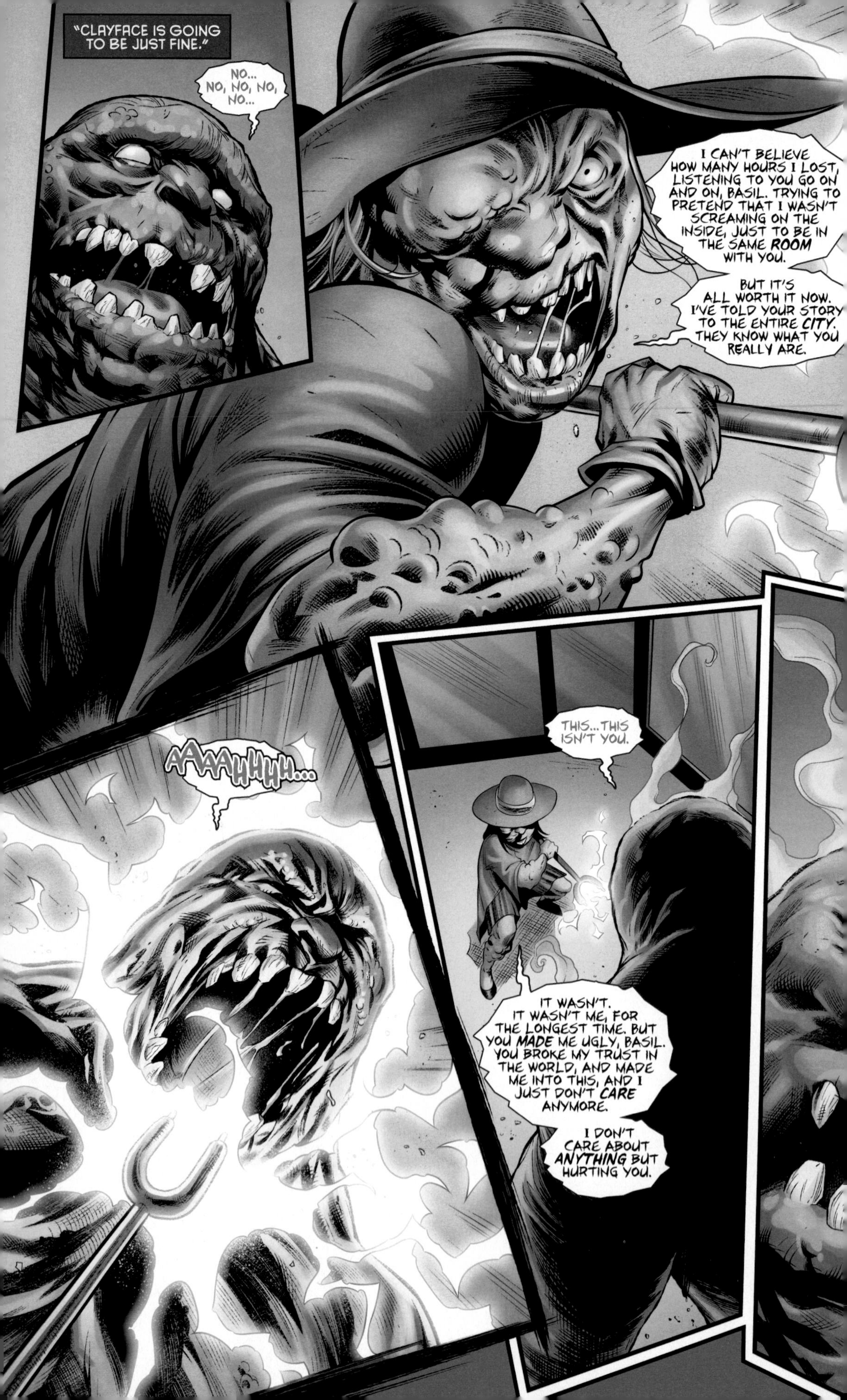
"CLAYFACE IS GOING TO BE JUST FINE."
NO... NO, NO, NO, NO...
I CAN'T BELIEVE HOW MANY HOURS I LOST, LISTENING TO YOU GO ON AND ON, BASIL. TRYING TO PRETEND THAT I WASN'T SCREAMING ON THE INSIDE, JUST TO BE IN THE SAME ROOM WITH YOU.
BUT IT'S ALL WORTH IT NOW. I'VE TOLD YOUR STORY TO THE ENTIRE CITY. THEY KNOW WHAT YOU REALLY ARE.
AAAAHHHH...
THIS... THIS ISN'T YOU.
IT WASN'T. IT WASN'T ME, FOR THE LONGEST TIME. BUT YOU MADE ME UGLY, BASIL. YOU BROKE MY TRUST IN THE WORLD, AND MADE ME INTO THIS, AND I JUST DON'T CARE ANYMORE.
I DON'T CARE ABOUT ANYTHING BUT HURTING YOU.

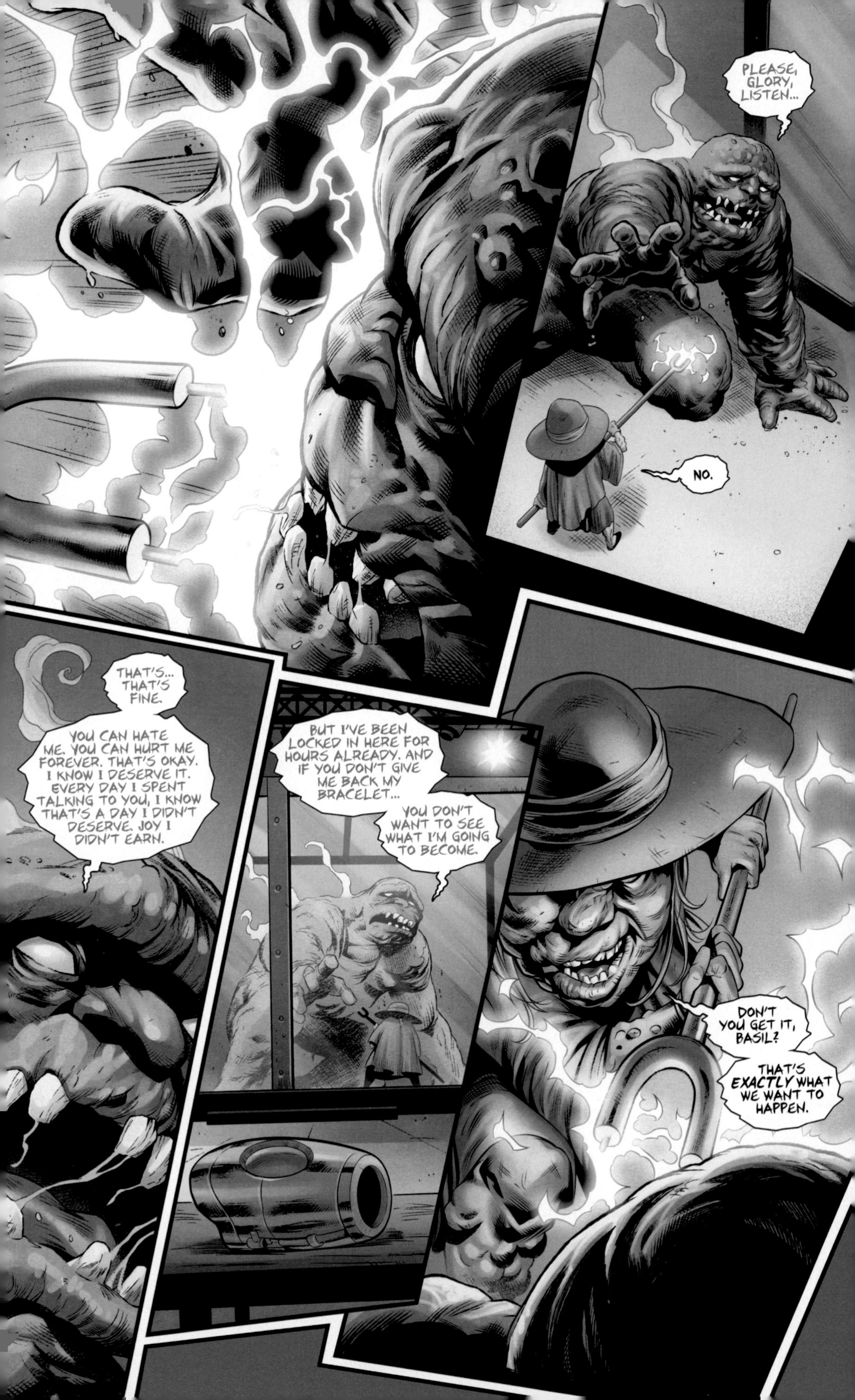
PLEASE, GLORY, LISTEN...
NO.
THAT'S... THAT'S FINE.
YOU CAN HATE ME. YOU CAN HURT ME FOREVER. THAT'S OKAY. I KNOW I DESERVE IT. EVERY DAY I SPENT TALKING TO YOU, I KNOW THAT'S A DAY I DIDN'T DESERVE. JOY I DIDN'T EARN.
BUT I'VE BEEN LOCKED IN HERE FOR HOURS ALREADY. AND IF YOU DON'T GIVE ME BACK MY BRACELET...
YOU DON'T WANT TO SEE WHAT I'M GOING TO BECOME.
DON'T YOU GET IT, BASIL?
THAT'S *EXACTLY* WHAT WE WANT TO HAPPEN.

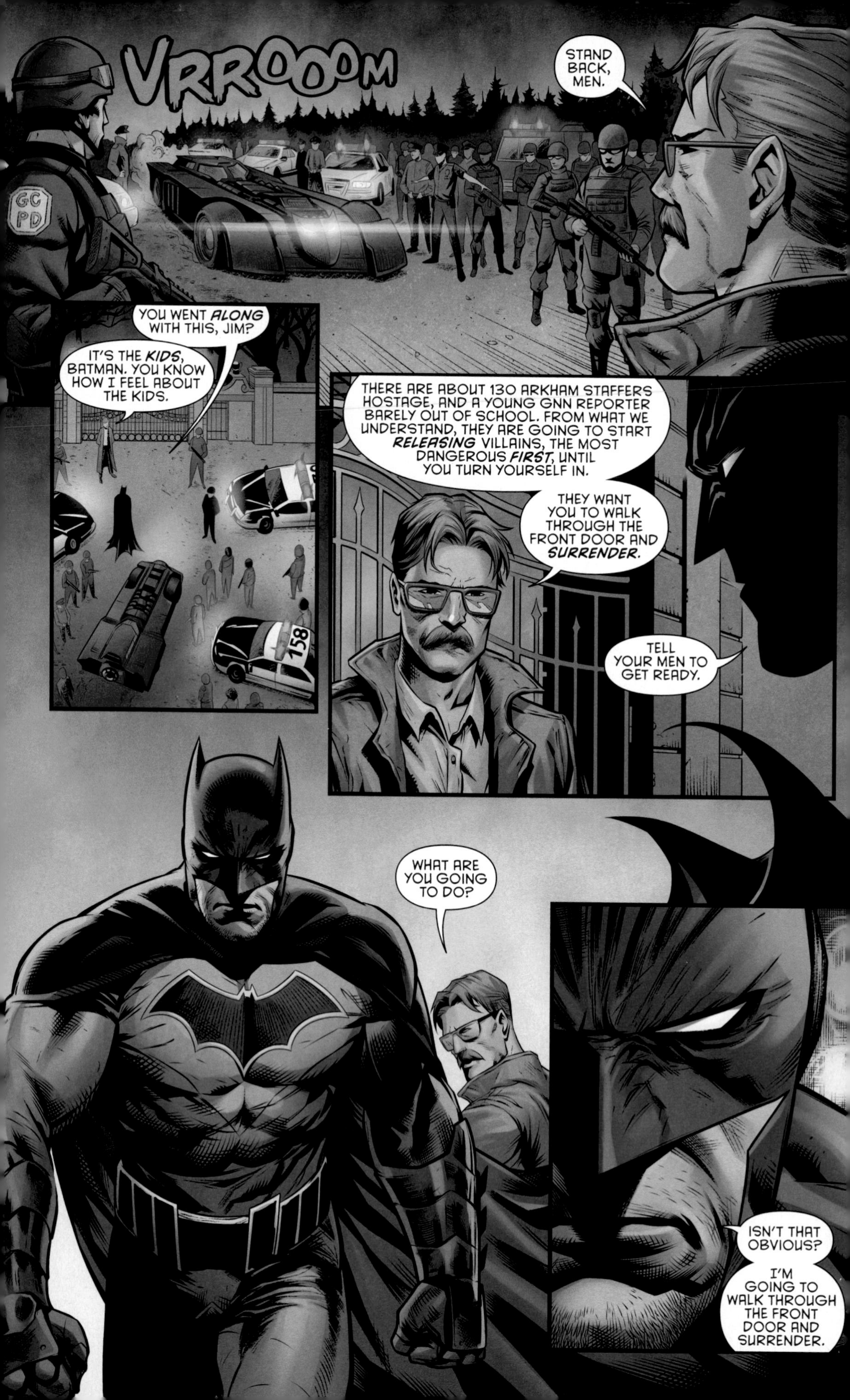
VRROOOM
STAND BACK, MEN.
YOU WENT ALONG WITH THIS, JIM?
IT'S THE KIDS, BATMAN. YOU KNOW HOW I FEEL ABOUT THE KIDS.
THERE ARE ABOUT 130 ARKHAM STAFFERS HOSTAGE, AND A YOUNG GNN REPORTER BARELY OUT OF SCHOOL. FROM WHAT WE UNDERSTAND, THEY ARE GOING TO START RELEASING VILLAINS, THE MOST DANGEROUS FIRST, UNTIL YOU TURN YOURSELF IN.
THEY WANT YOU TO WALK THROUGH THE FRONT DOOR AND SURRENDER.
TELL YOUR MEN TO GET READY.
WHAT ARE YOU GOING TO DO?
ISN'T THAT OBVIOUS?
I'M GOING TO WALK THROUGH THE FRONT DOOR AND SURRENDER.

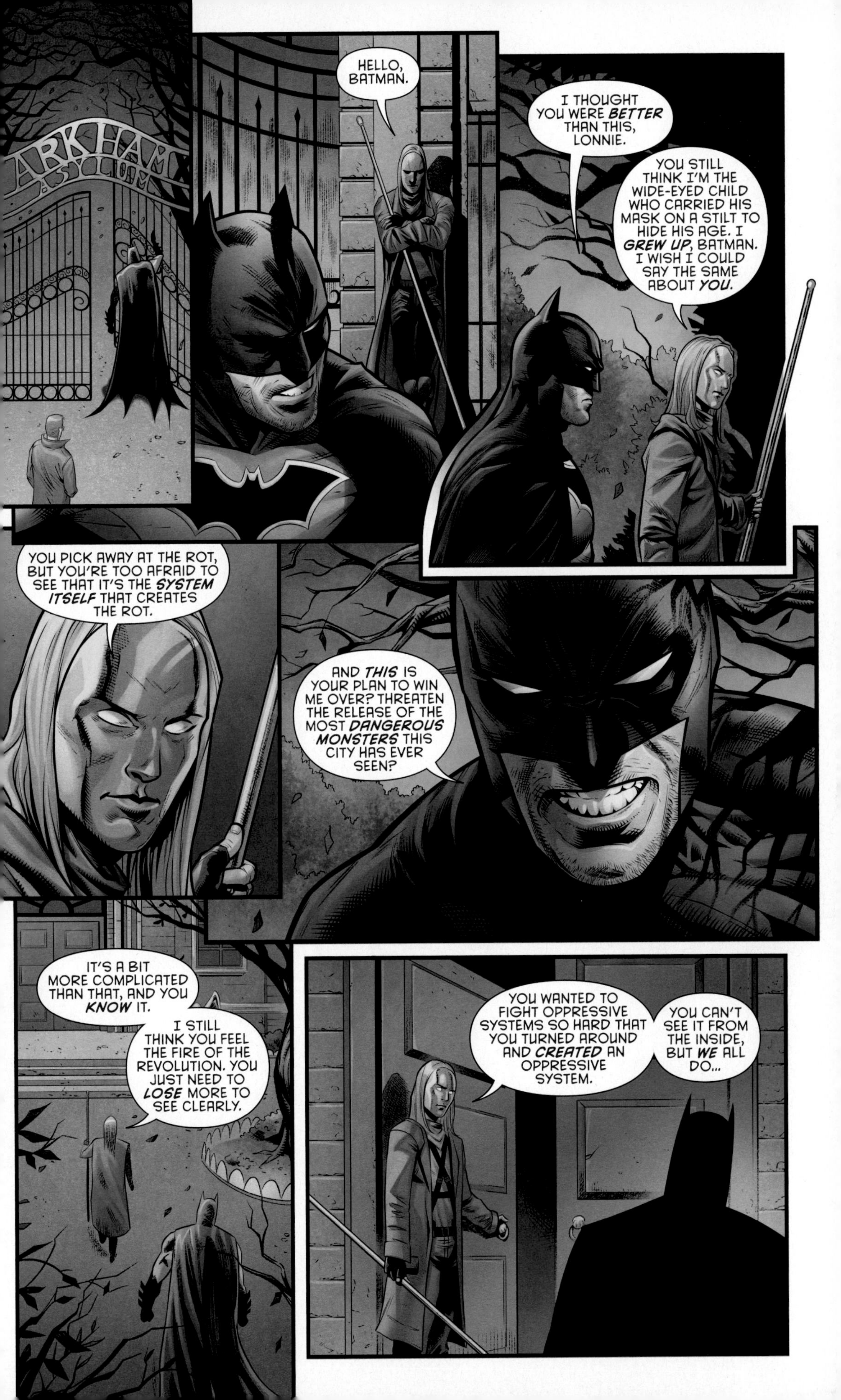
ARKHAM ASYLUM
HELLO, BATMAN.
I THOUGHT YOU WERE BETTER THAN THIS, LONNIE.
YOU STILL THINK I'M THE WIDE-EYED CHILD WHO CARRIED HIS MASK ON A STILT TO HIDE HIS AGE. I GREW UP, BATMAN. I WISH I COULD SAY THE SAME ABOUT YOU.
YOU PICK AWAY AT THE ROT, BUT YOU'RE TOO AFRAID TO SEE THAT IT'S THE SYSTEM ITSELF THAT CREATES THE ROT.
AND THIS IS YOUR PLAN TO WIN ME OVER? THREATEN THE RELEASE OF THE MOST DANGEROUS MONSTERS THIS CITY HAS EVER SEEN?
IT'S A BIT MORE COMPLICATED THAN THAT, AND YOU KNOW IT.
I STILL THINK YOU FEEL THE FIRE OF THE REVOLUTION. YOU JUST NEED TO LOSE MORE TO SEE CLEARLY.
YOU WANTED TO FIGHT OPPRESSIVE SYSTEMS SO HARD THAT YOU TURNED AROUND AND CREATED AN OPPRESSIVE SYSTEM.
YOU CAN'T SEE IT FROM THE INSIDE, BUT WE ALL DO...

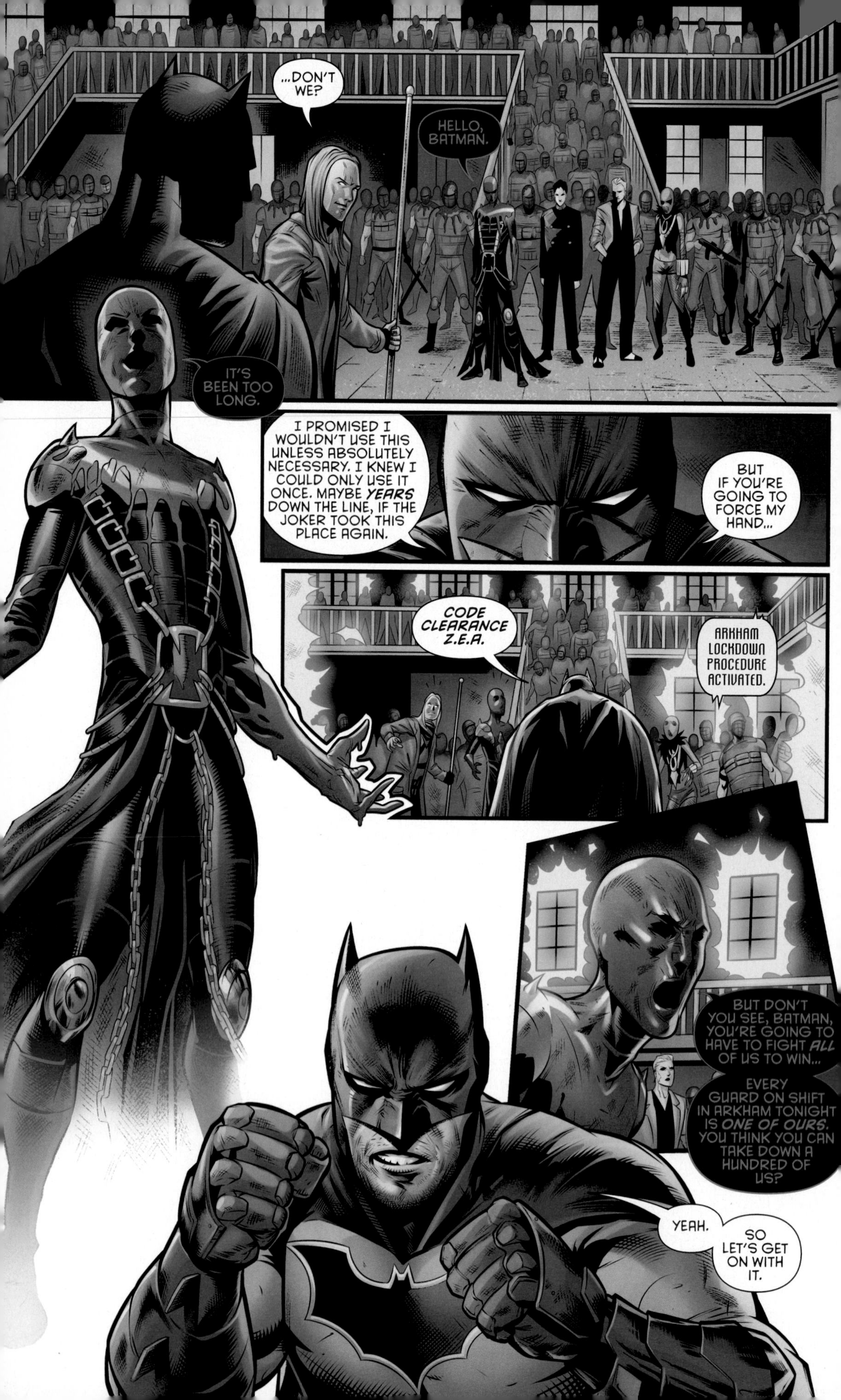

...DON'T WE?
HELLO, BATMAN.
IT'S BEEN TOO LONG.
I PROMISED I WOULDN'T USE THIS UNLESS ABSOLUTELY NECESSARY. I KNEW I COULD ONLY USE IT ONCE. MAYBE YEARS DOWN THE LINE, IF THE JOKER TOOK THIS PLACE AGAIN.
BUT IF YOU'RE GOING TO FORCE MY HAND...
CODE CLEARANCE Z.E.A.
ARKHAM LOCKDOWN PROCEDURE ACTIVATED.
BUT DON'T YOU SEE, BATMAN, YOU'RE GOING TO HAVE TO FIGHT ALL OF US TO WIN...
EVERY GUARD ON SHIFT IN ARKHAM TONIGHT IS ONE OF OURS. YOU THINK YOU CAN TAKE DOWN A HUNDRED OF US?
YEAH.
SO LET'S GET ON WITH IT.

WE ARE ALL VICTIMS

THIS DOESN'T MAKE ANY *SENSE.*

VICTMS

TIM, YOU NEED TO STOP TRYING TO CONTROL EVERYTHING AND *SLOW DOWN.* I CAN HEAR THE ANXIETY IN YOUR VOICE. YOU'RE JUST WORRIED THAT BATMAN'S LOSING FAITH IN THE PLAN.

NO, STEPH. IT'S *MORE* THAN THAT.

WHY THESE LOCATIONS? WE'RE NOWHERE NEAR ANY OF THE CITY GOVERNMENT OR POLICE STATIONS. HELL, THEY'RE NOT EVEN NEAR WAYNE LANDMARKS...

WHY *PUT* THESE PEOPLE HERE...?

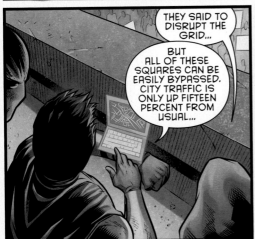

THEY SAID TO DISRUPT THE GRID...

BUT ALL OF THESE SQUARES CAN BE EASILY BYPASSED. CITY TRAFFIC IS ONLY UP FIFTEEN PERCENT FROM USUAL...

IT'S LIKE THEY WANTED THEM TO *SEE* SOMETHING...

SEWER.

SHE'S RIGHT. THEY'RE ALL SEWER HUBS...

THEY'RE ALL DIRECTLY DOWN PIPELINE FROM ARKHAM...

NO.

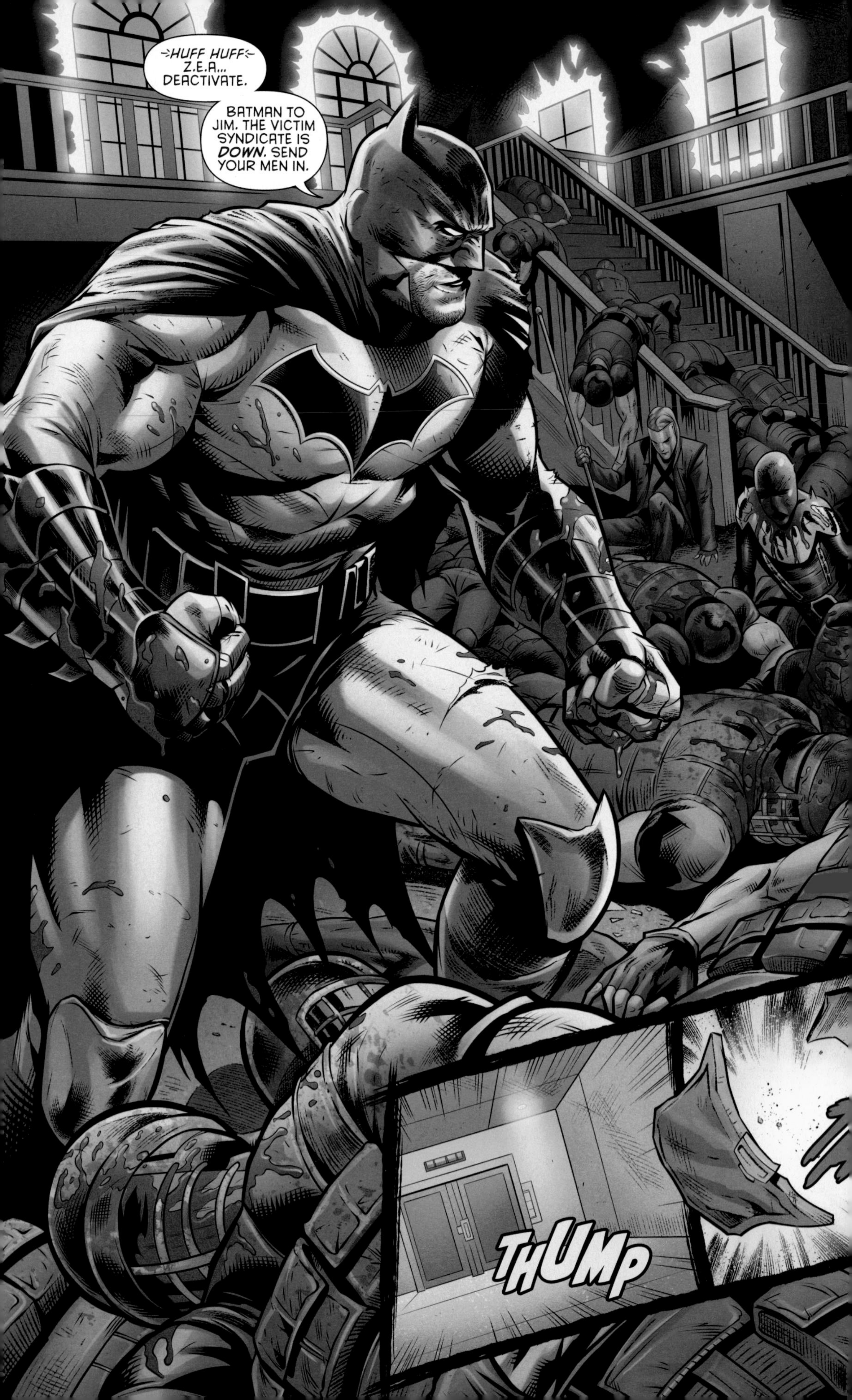

-HUFF HUFF-
Z.E.A... DEACTIVATE.
BATMAN TO JIM. THE VICTIM SYNDICATE IS DOWN. SEND YOUR MEN IN.
THUMP

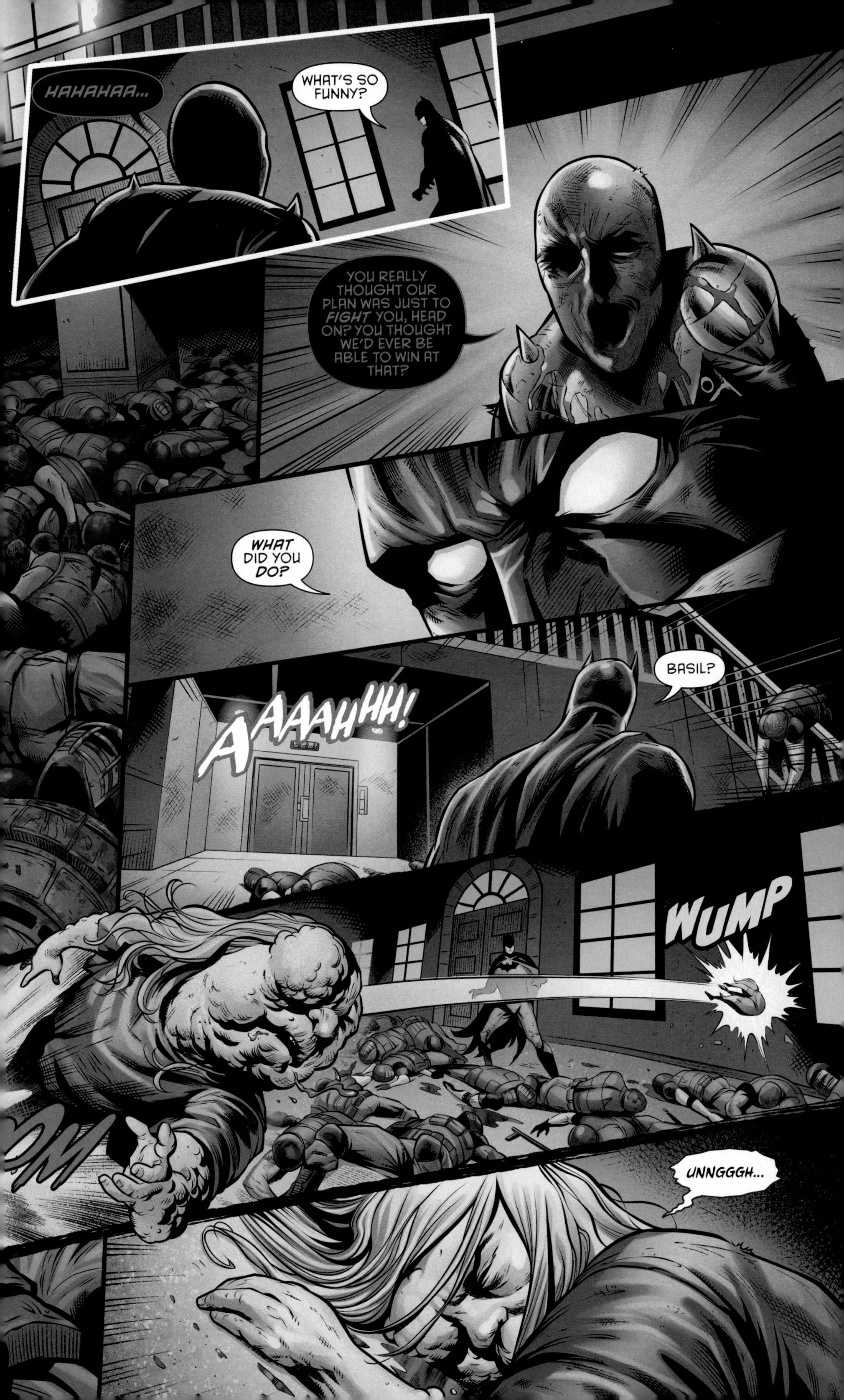
HAHAHAA...
WHAT'S SO FUNNY?
YOU REALLY THOUGHT OUR PLAN WAS JUST TO FIGHT YOU, HEAD ON? YOU THOUGHT WE'D EVER BE ABLE TO WIN AT THAT?
WHAT DID YOU DO?
AAAAHHH!
BASIL?
WUMP
UNNGGGH...

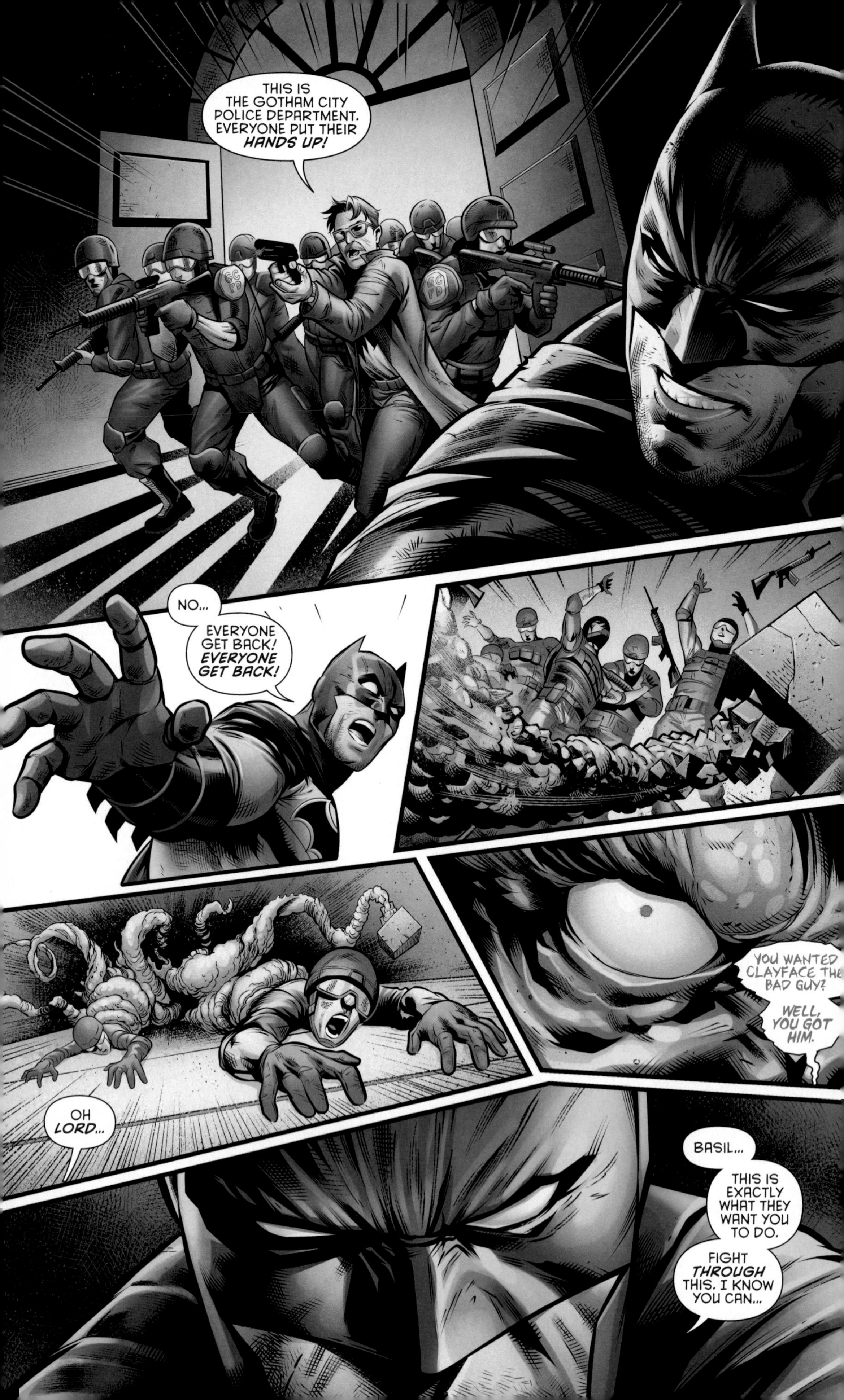
THIS IS THE GOTHAM CITY POLICE DEPARTMENT. EVERYONE PUT THEIR *HANDS UP!*
NO...
EVERYONE GET BACK! *EVERYONE GET BACK!*
OH *LORD...*
YOU WANTED CLAYFACE THE BAD GUY?
WELL, YOU GOT HIM.
BASIL...
THIS IS EXACTLY WHAT THEY WANT YOU TO DO.
FIGHT *THROUGH* THIS. I KNOW YOU CAN...

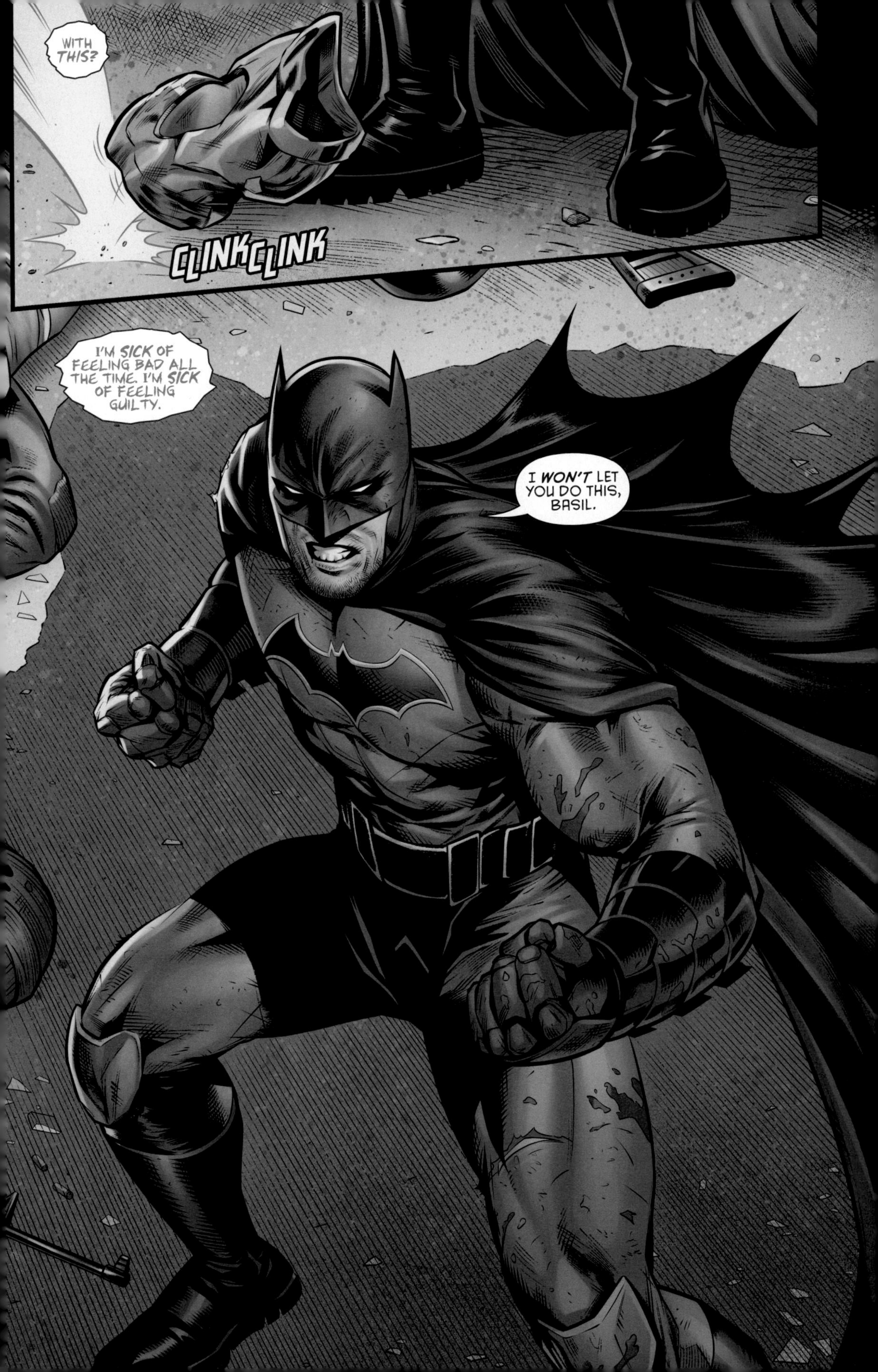
WITH THIS?
CLINKCLINK
I'M SICK OF FEELING BAD ALL THE TIME. I'M SICK OF FEELING GUILTY.
I WON'T LET YOU DO THIS, BASIL.

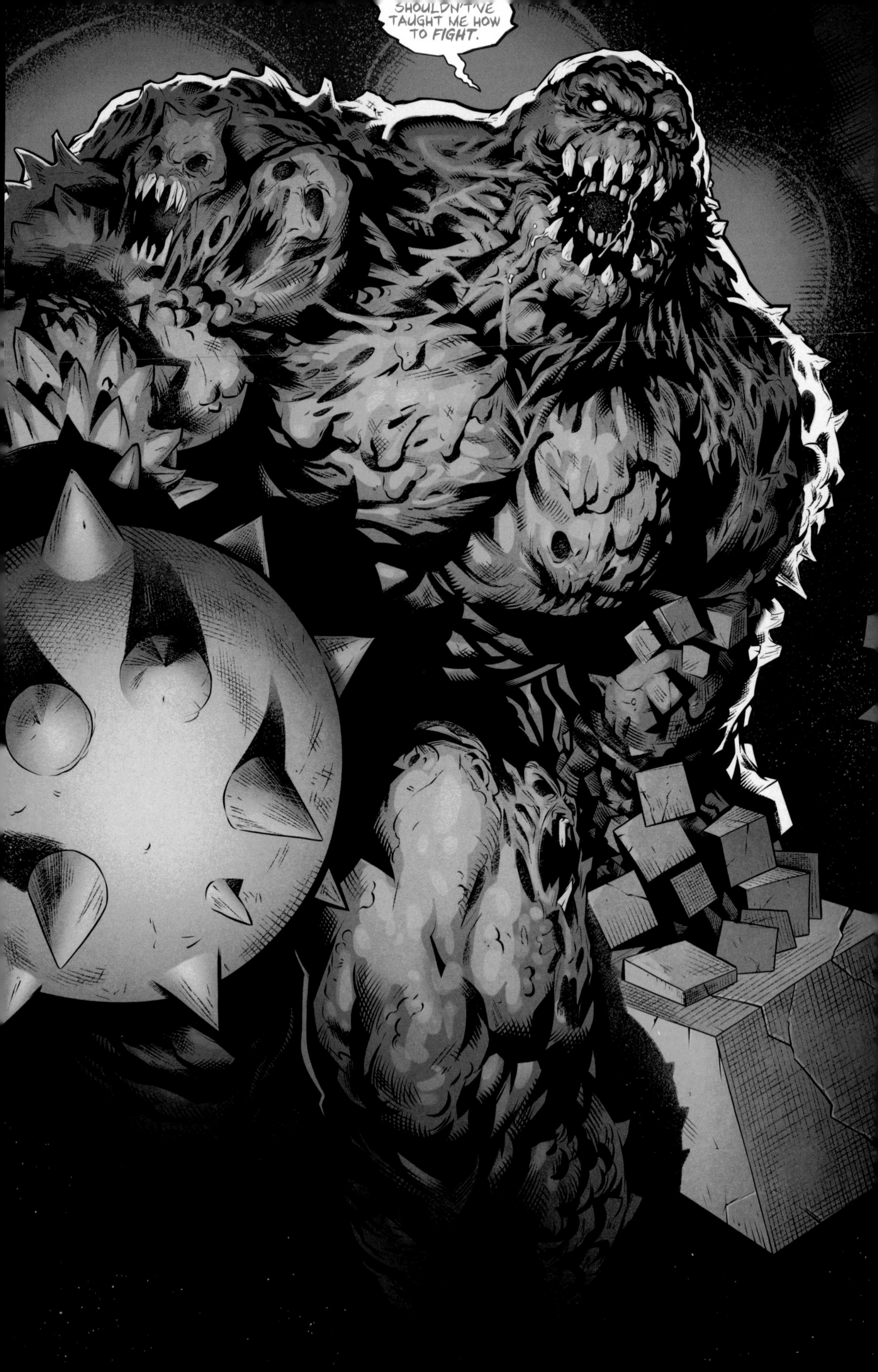
SHOULDN'T'VE TAUGHT ME HOW TO FIGHT.

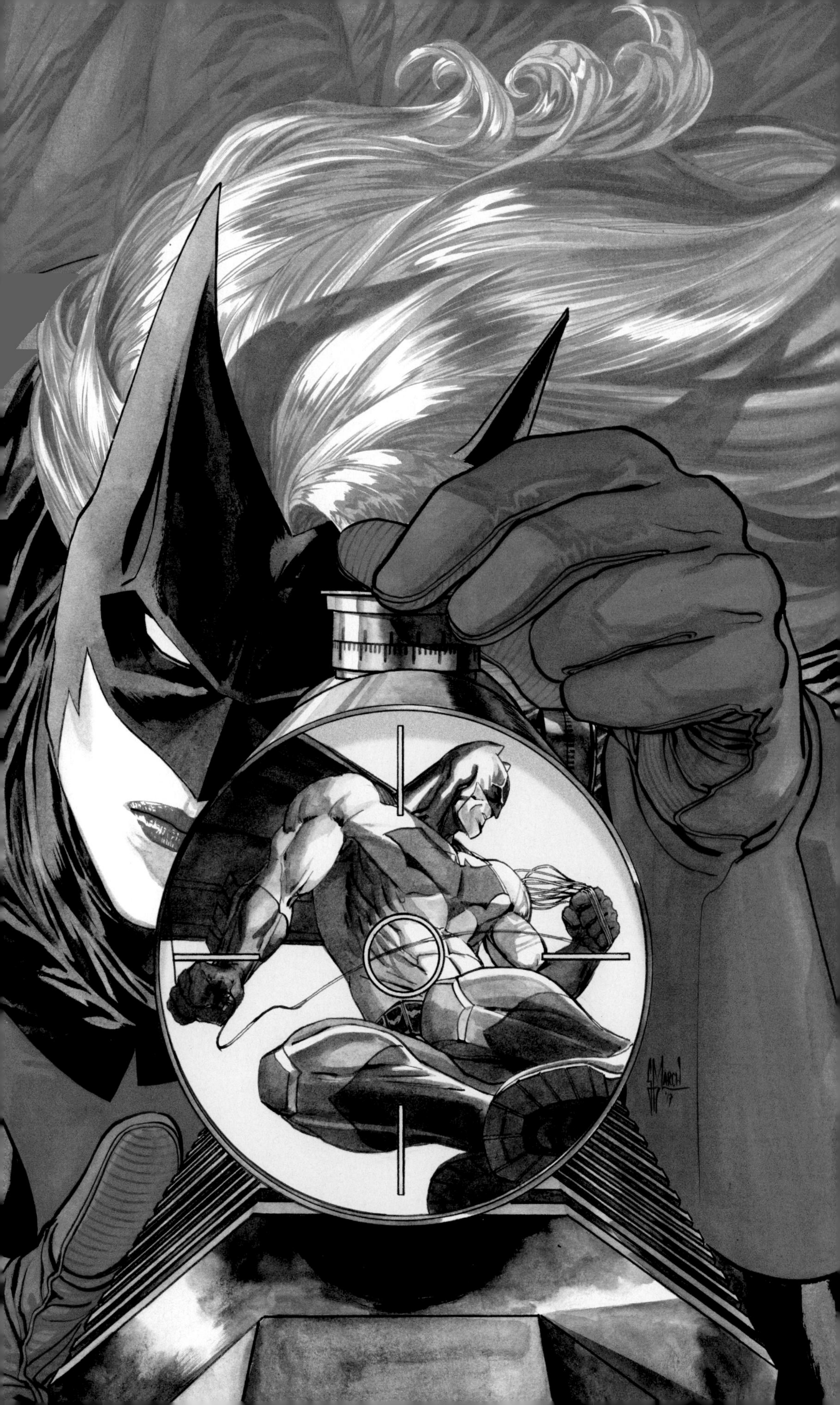

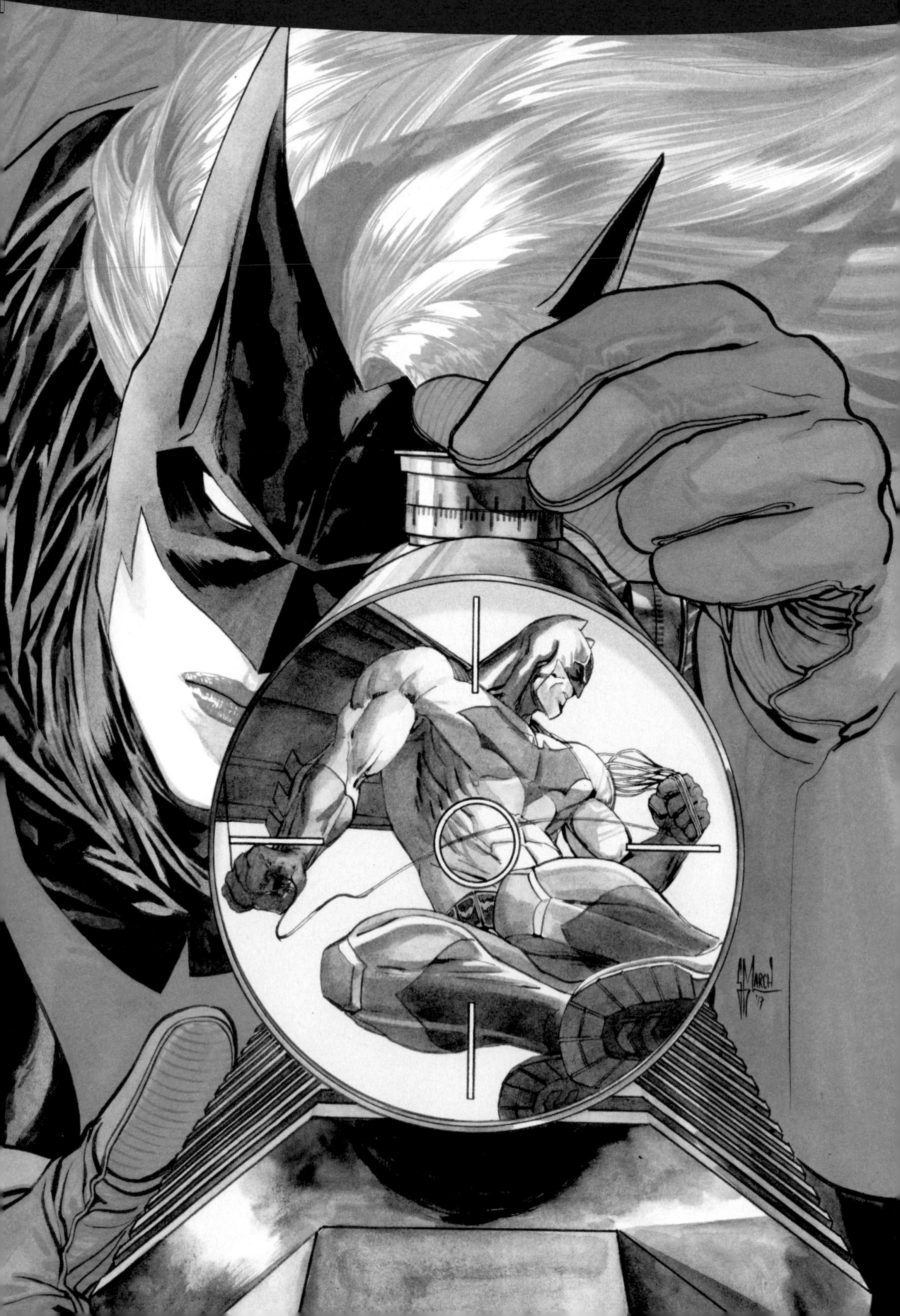

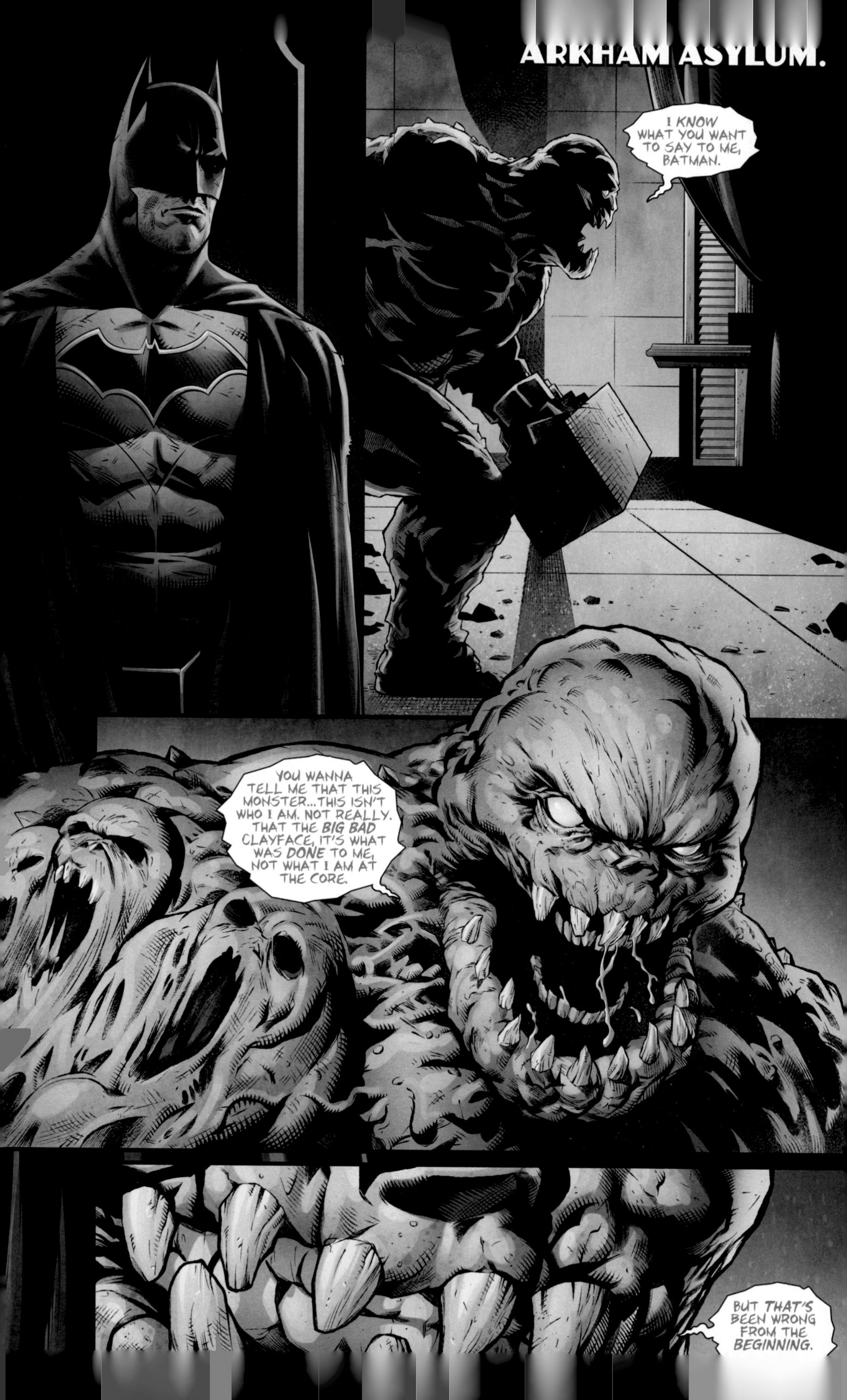
ARKHAM ASYLUM.
I KNOW WHAT YOU WANT TO SAY TO ME, BATMAN.
YOU WANNA TELL ME THAT THIS MONSTER...THIS ISN'T WHO I AM. NOT REALLY. THAT THE BIG BAD CLAYFACE, IT'S WHAT WAS DONE TO ME, NOT WHAT I AM AT THE CORE.
BUT THAT'S BEEN WRONG FROM THE BEGINNING.

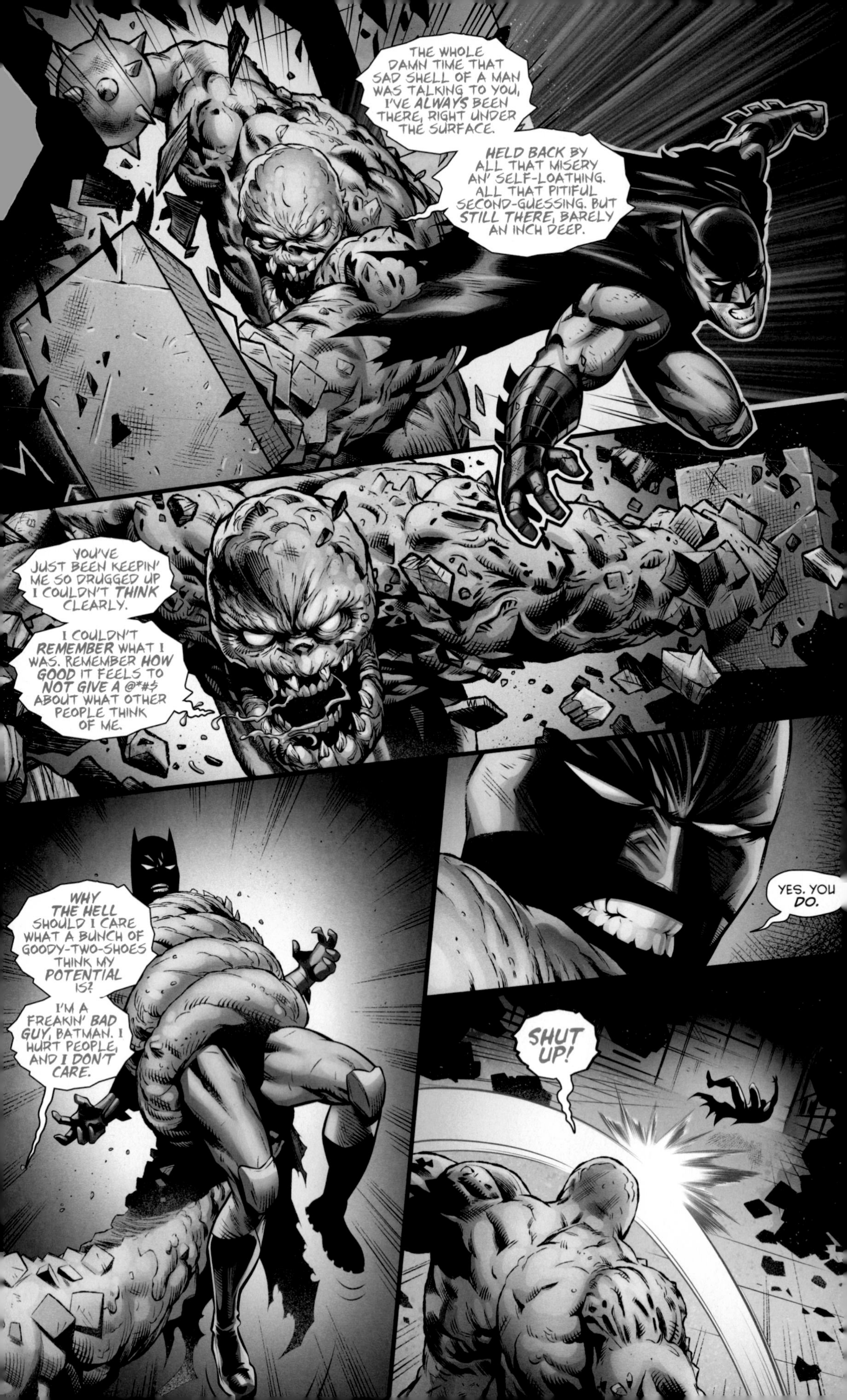
THE WHOLE DAMN TIME THAT SAD SHELL OF A MAN WAS TALKING TO YOU, I'VE ALWAYS BEEN THERE, RIGHT UNDER THE SURFACE.
HELD BACK BY ALL THAT MISERY AN' SELF-LOATHING. ALL THAT PITIFUL SECOND-GUESSING. BUT STILL THERE, BARELY AN INCH DEEP.
YOU'VE JUST BEEN KEEPIN' ME SO DRUGGED UP I COULDN'T THINK CLEARLY.
I COULDN'T REMEMBER WHAT I WAS. REMEMBER HOW GOOD IT FEELS TO NOT GIVE A @*#$ ABOUT WHAT OTHER PEOPLE THINK OF ME.
WHY THE HELL SHOULD I CARE WHAT A BUNCH OF GOODY-TWO-SHOES THINK MY POTENTIAL IS?
I'M A FREAKIN' BAD GUY, BATMAN. I HURT PEOPLE, AND I DON'T CARE.
YES. YOU DO.
SHUT UP!

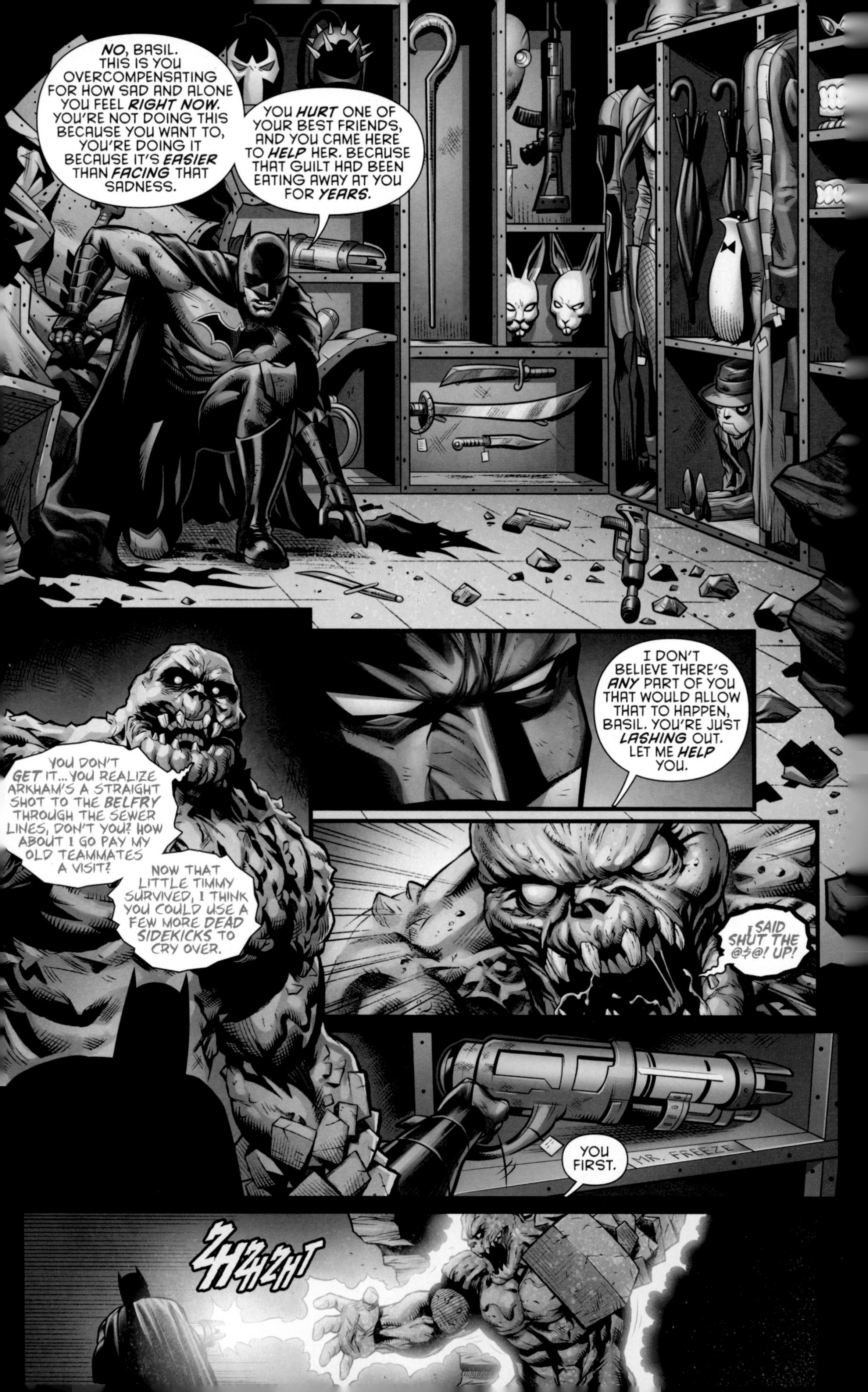
NO, BASIL. THIS IS YOU OVERCOMPENSATING FOR HOW SAD AND ALONE YOU FEEL RIGHT NOW. YOU'RE NOT DOING THIS BECAUSE YOU WANT TO, YOU'RE DOING IT BECAUSE IT'S EASIER THAN FACING THAT SADNESS.
YOU HURT ONE OF YOUR BEST FRIENDS, AND YOU CAME HERE TO HELP HER. BECAUSE THAT GUILT HAD BEEN EATING AWAY AT YOU FOR YEARS.
YOU DON'T GET IT...YOU REALIZE ARKHAM'S A STRAIGHT SHOT TO THE BELFRY THROUGH THE SEWER LINES, DON'T YOU? HOW ABOUT I GO PAY MY OLD TEAMMATES A VISIT?
NOW THAT LITTLE TIMMY SURVIVED, I THINK YOU COULD USE A FEW MORE DEAD SIDEKICKS TO CRY OVER.
I DON'T BELIEVE THERE'S ANY PART OF YOU THAT WOULD ALLOW THAT TO HAPPEN, BASIL. YOU'RE JUST LASHING OUT. LET ME HELP YOU.
I SAID SHUT THE @$@! UP!
MR. FREEZE
YOU FIRST.
ZHZHZHT

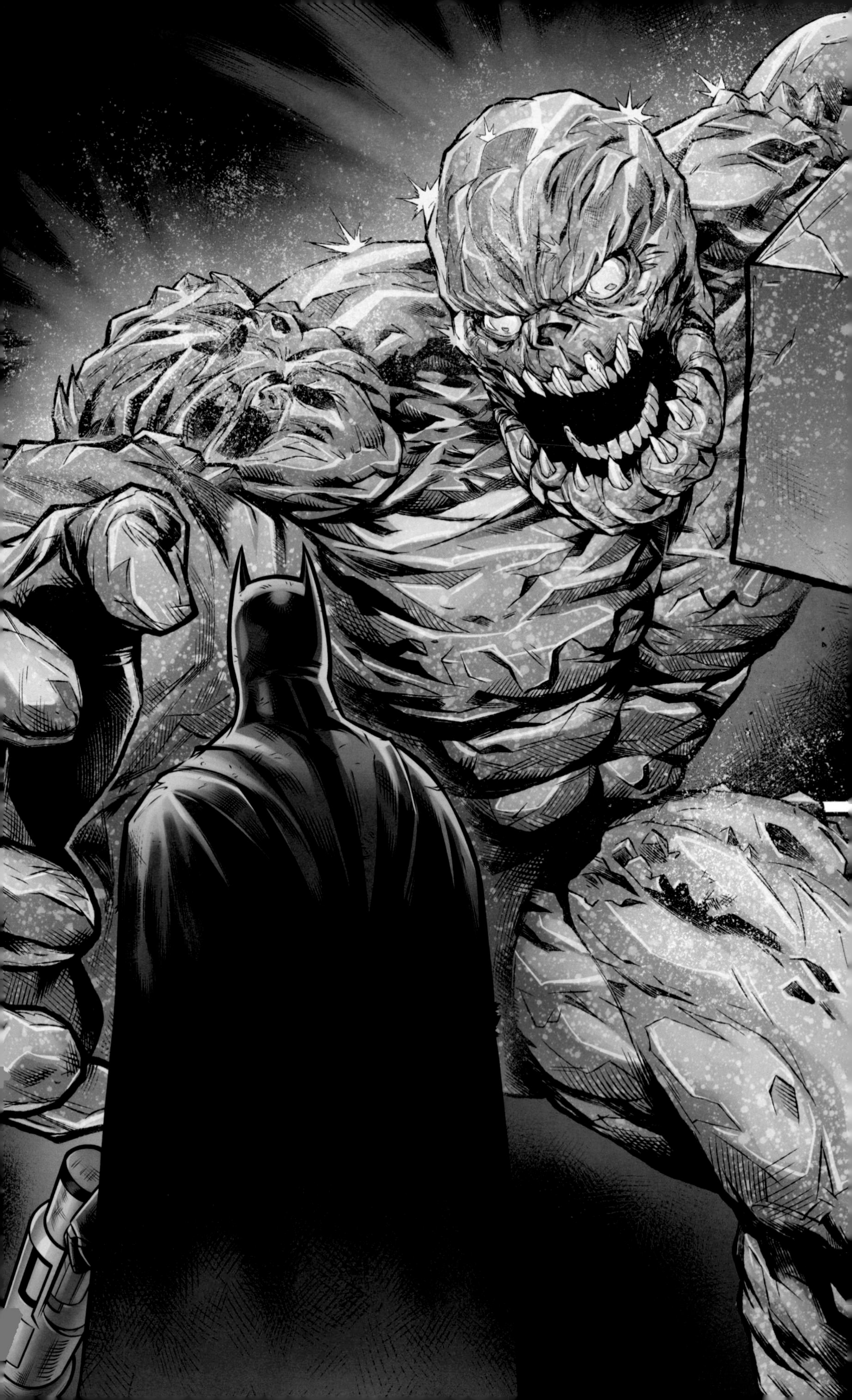

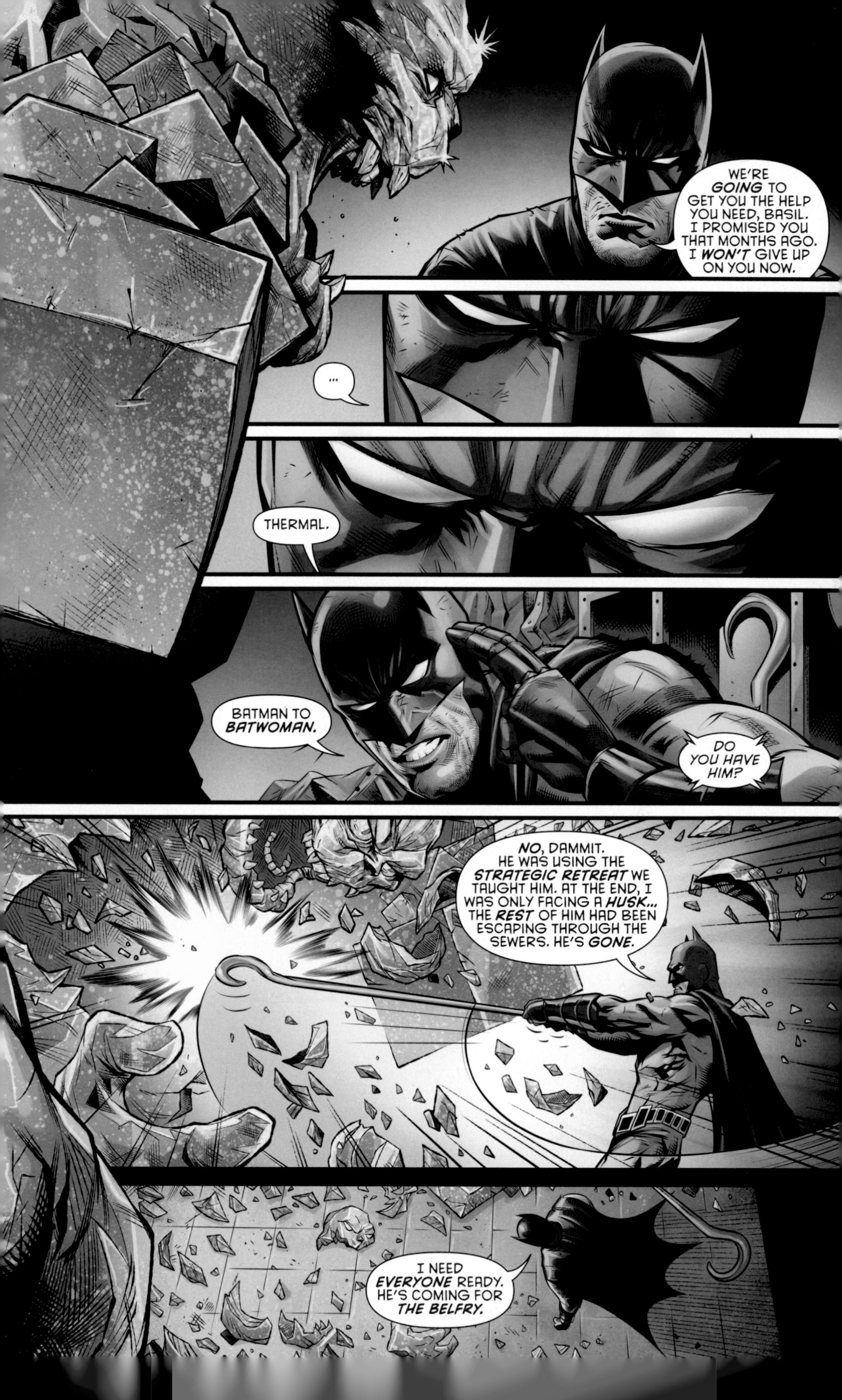

WE'RE *GOING* TO GET YOU THE HELP YOU NEED, BASIL. I PROMISED YOU THAT MONTHS AGO. I *WON'T* GIVE UP ON YOU NOW.
...
THERMAL.
BATMAN TO *BATWOMAN.*
DO YOU HAVE HIM?
NO, DAMMIT. HE WAS USING THE *STRATEGIC RETREAT* WE TAUGHT HIM. AT THE END, I WAS ONLY FACING A *HUSK*... THE *REST* OF HIM HAD BEEN ESCAPING THROUGH THE SEWERS. HE'S *GONE.*
I NEED *EVERYONE* READY. HE'S COMING FOR *THE BELFRY.*

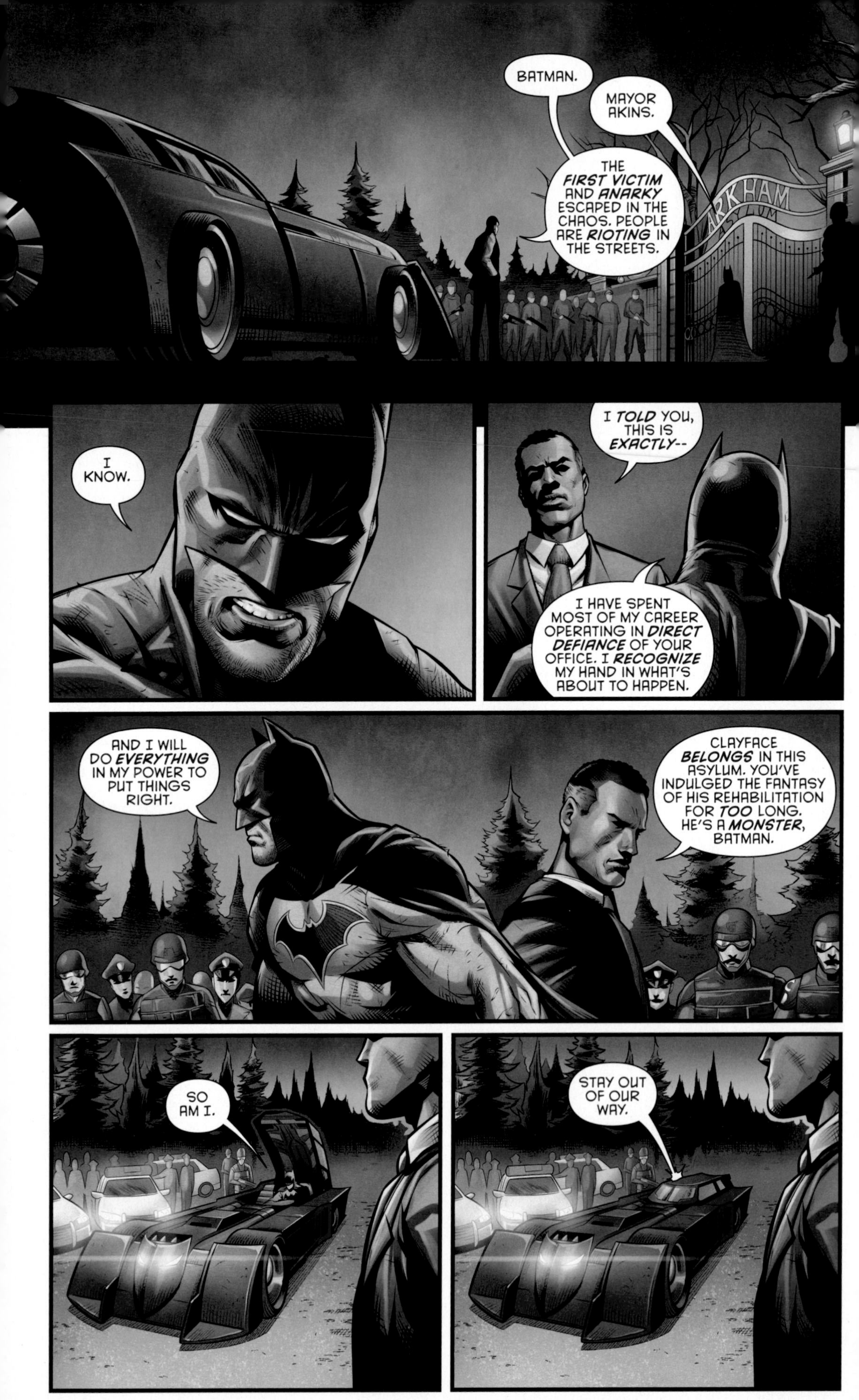

BATMAN.
MAYOR AKINS.
THE FIRST VICTIM AND ANARKY ESCAPED IN THE CHAOS. PEOPLE ARE RIOTING IN THE STREETS.
ARKHAM ASYLUM
I KNOW.
I TOLD YOU, THIS IS EXACTLY--
I HAVE SPENT MOST OF MY CAREER OPERATING IN DIRECT DEFIANCE OF YOUR OFFICE. I RECOGNIZE MY HAND IN WHAT'S ABOUT TO HAPPEN.
AND I WILL DO EVERYTHING IN MY POWER TO PUT THINGS RIGHT.
CLAYFACE BELONGS IN THIS ASYLUM. YOU'VE INDULGED THE FANTASY OF HIS REHABILITATION FOR TOO LONG. HE'S A MONSTER, BATMAN.
SO AM I.
STAY OUT OF OUR WAY.

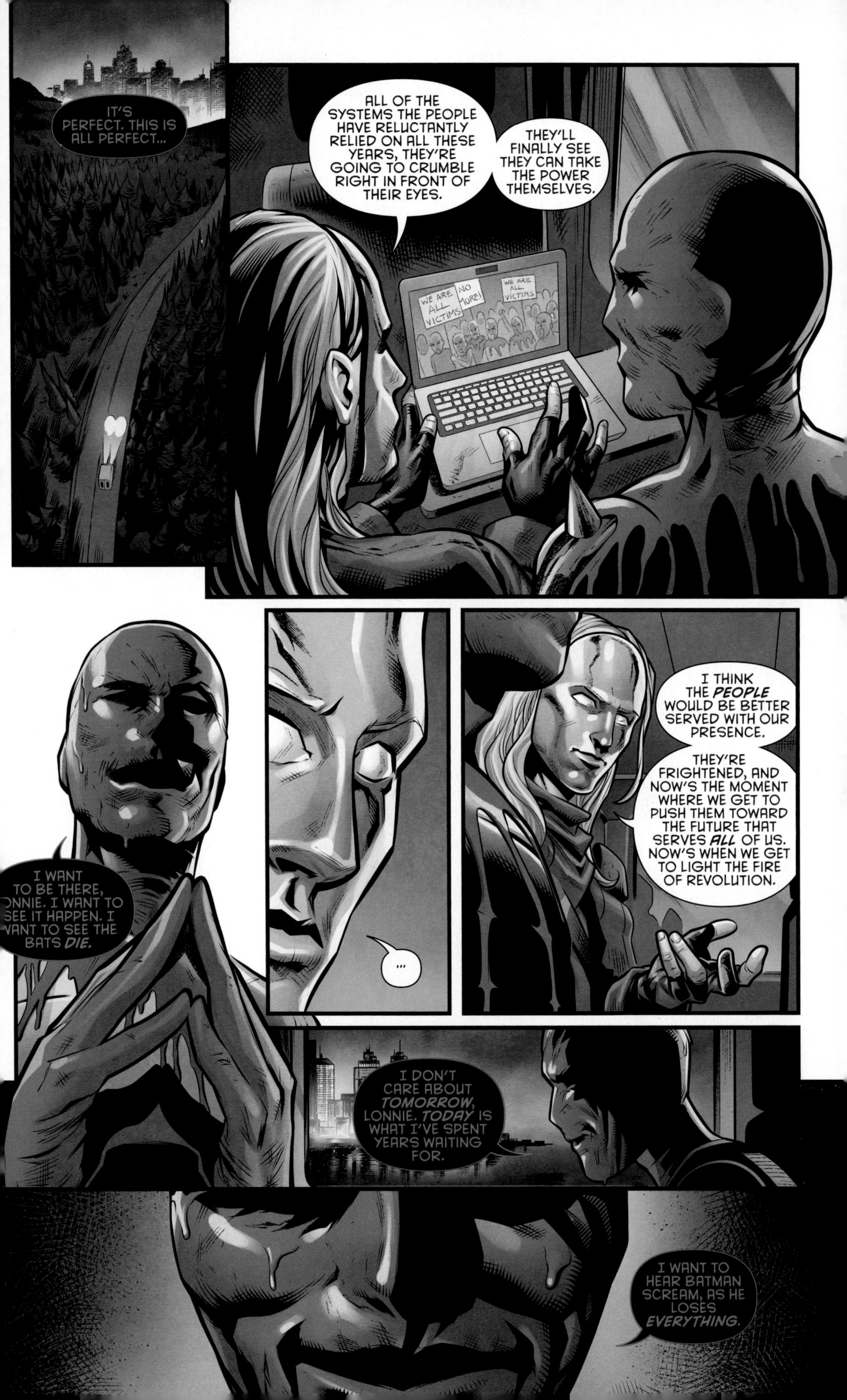
IT'S PERFECT. THIS IS ALL PERFECT...
ALL OF THE SYSTEMS THE PEOPLE HAVE RELUCTANTLY RELIED ON ALL THESE YEARS, THEY'RE GOING TO CRUMBLE RIGHT IN FRONT OF THEIR EYES.
THEY'LL FINALLY SEE THEY CAN TAKE THE POWER THEMSELVES.
WE ARE ALL VICTIMS
NO MORE!
WE ARE ALL VICTIMS
I WANT TO BE THERE, ONNIE. I WANT TO SEE IT HAPPEN. I WANT TO SEE THE BATS DIE.
...
I THINK THE PEOPLE WOULD BE BETTER SERVED WITH OUR PRESENCE.
THEY'RE FRIGHTENED, AND NOW'S THE MOMENT WHERE WE GET TO PUSH THEM TOWARD THE FUTURE THAT SERVES ALL OF US. NOW'S WHEN WE GET TO LIGHT THE FIRE OF REVOLUTION.
I DON'T CARE ABOUT TOMORROW, LONNIE. TODAY IS WHAT I'VE SPENT YEARS WAITING FOR.
I WANT TO HEAR BATMAN SCREAM, AS HE LOSES EVERYTHING.

HE MUST BE SO *FRIGHTENED* RIGHT NOW...I CAN HARDLY IMAGINE.

LIVE

WHEN HE LOST CONTROL BEFORE, WHEN I SAW IT HAPPEN...IT WAS A *FEAR* RESPONSE. THE FEAR AND FRUSTRATION OF NOT BEING ABLE TO *STOP* HIMSELF.

G T.V

WHAT THIS *VICTIM SYNDICATE* HAS DONE TO HIM, IT'S DRAWN OUT ALL OF HIS WORST FEARS ABOUT HIMSELF AND MADE THEM SO REAL THAT HE'S RETREATED INTO HIMSELF.

WHAT WE'RE FACING IS A KIND OF PROTECTIVE SHELL.

WELL, DR. OCTOBER, THAT PROTECTIVE SHELL IS GOING TO *HURT PEOPLE.*

THEY OFTEN DO, YOUNG MAN.

MAKE HIM... *BETTER?*

PLEASE?

THE *CURE*...IT WORKED ON A FEW CELLS HERE IN A LABORATORY SETTING, BUT THE FINAL DOSE WILL BE READY WITHIN THE NEXT HOUR OR TWO.

IT WOULDN'T *SET* HIM LIKE THIS, WOULD IT? KEEP HIM *LOCKED* IN HIS MORE VIOLENT STATE?

I HAVE DEVELOPED A HIGHLY EXPERIMENTAL SERUM TO CURE AN ANOMALOUS CONDITION STRAIGHT OUT OF SCIENCE FICTION. THERE'S *LITTLE* I CAN SAY FOR SURE.

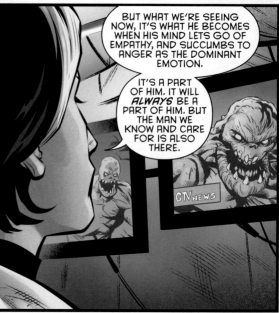

BUT WHAT WE'RE SEEING NOW, IT'S WHAT HE BECOMES WHEN HIS MIND LETS GO OF EMPATHY, AND SUCCUMBS TO ANGER AS THE DOMINANT EMOTION.

IT'S A PART OF HIM. IT WILL *ALWAYS* BE A PART OF HIM. BUT THE MAN WE KNOW AND CARE FOR IS ALSO THERE.

GTV NEWS

AND THE VERSION OF HIM THAT BREAKS THROUGH? IT'LL BE HIM, *ENTIRELY*. WITH ALL THE EMOTIONAL POTENTIAL HE HAS TO HURT NOW, BUT ALL OF THE *HUMANITY* THERE, THE PARTS OF HIM THAT WANT TO HELP PEOPLE. THAT FEEL *GOOD* HELPING PEOPLE.

AND THE PEOPLE WILL *STILL* WANT HIS HEAD ON A PIKE.

I CAN'T BELIEVE THEY'D BE SO STUPID AS TO BE MANIPULATED LIKE THIS...

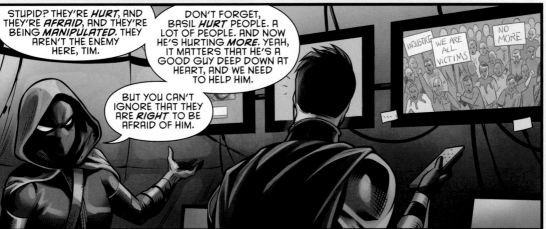

STUPID? THEY'RE *HURT*, AND THEY'RE *AFRAID*, AND THEY'RE BEING *MANIPULATED*. THEY AREN'T THE ENEMY HERE, TIM.

BUT YOU CAN'T IGNORE THAT THEY ARE *RIGHT* TO BE AFRAID OF HIM.

DON'T FORGET, BASIL *HURT* PEOPLE. A LOT OF PEOPLE. AND NOW HE'S HURTING *MORE*. YEAH, IT MATTERS THAT HE'S A GOOD GUY DEEP DOWN AT HEART, AND WE NEED TO HELP HIM.

INJUSTICE — WE ARE ALL VICTIMS — NO MORE

YOU'RE STARTING TO *SCARE* ME. BASED ON EVERYTHING YOU TOLD ME, THAT'S THE KIND OF THING *HE* WOULD SAY. THAT *FUTURE* TIM.

...

WHAT HE WOULD SAY...

WHY DO YOU HAVE THAT LOOK ON YOUR FACE?

HE SAID IT WOULD HAPPEN *SOON*, STEPH. THE THING THAT MADE IT ALL FALL APART...

THAT *SHE* WOULD DO IT...

RED ROBIN TO BATWOMAN. WHERE *ARE* YOU?

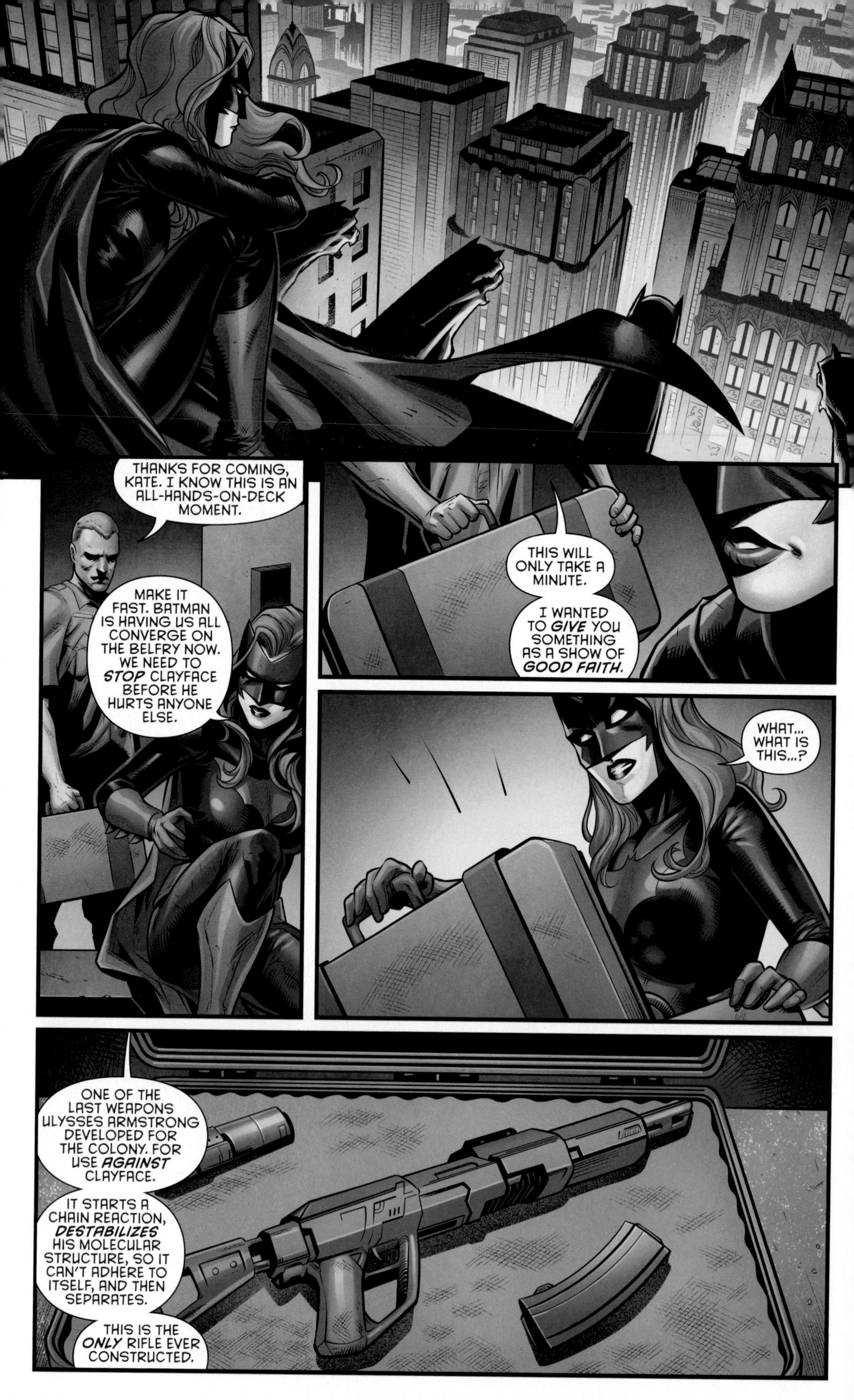
THANKS FOR COMING, KATE. I KNOW THIS IS AN ALL-HANDS-ON-DECK MOMENT.
MAKE IT FAST. BATMAN IS HAVING US ALL CONVERGE ON THE BELFRY NOW. WE NEED TO STOP CLAYFACE BEFORE HE HURTS ANYONE ELSE.
THIS WILL ONLY TAKE A MINUTE.
I WANTED TO GIVE YOU SOMETHING AS A SHOW OF GOOD FAITH.
WHAT... WHAT IS THIS...?
ONE OF THE LAST WEAPONS ULYSSES ARMSTRONG DEVELOPED FOR THE COLONY. FOR USE AGAINST CLAYFACE.
IT STARTS A CHAIN REACTION, DESTABILIZES HIS MOLECULAR STRUCTURE, SO IT CAN'T ADHERE TO ITSELF, AND THEN SEPARATES.
THIS IS THE ONLY RIFLE EVER CONSTRUCTED.

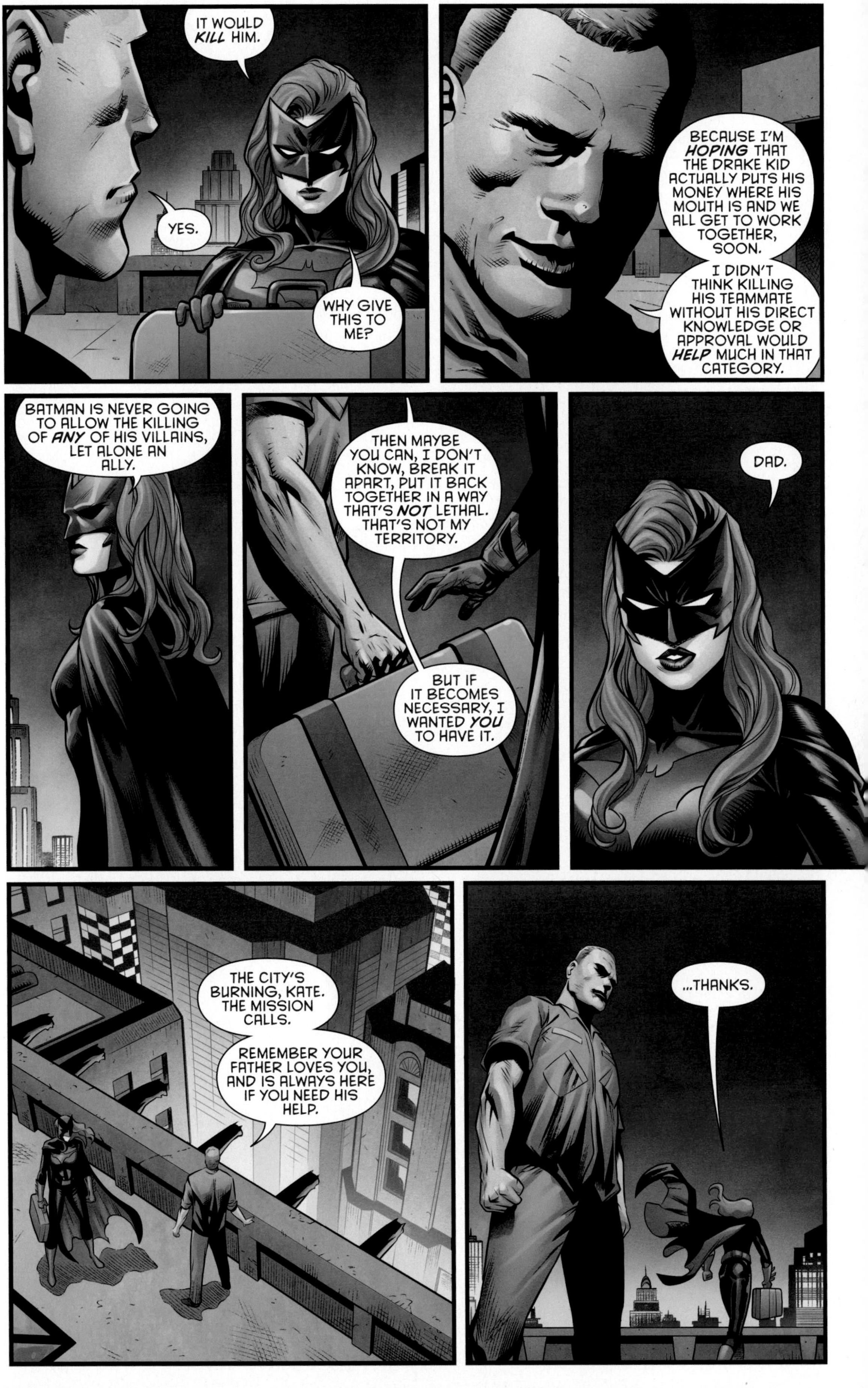
IT WOULD *KILL* HIM.
YES.
WHY GIVE THIS TO ME?
BECAUSE I'M *HOPING* THAT THE DRAKE KID ACTUALLY PUTS HIS MONEY WHERE HIS MOUTH IS AND WE ALL GET TO WORK TOGETHER, SOON.
I DIDN'T THINK KILLING HIS TEAMMATE WITHOUT HIS DIRECT KNOWLEDGE OR APPROVAL WOULD *HELP* MUCH IN THAT CATEGORY.
BATMAN IS NEVER GOING TO ALLOW THE KILLING OF *ANY* OF HIS VILLAINS, LET ALONE AN ALLY.
THEN MAYBE YOU CAN, I DON'T KNOW, BREAK IT APART, PUT IT BACK TOGETHER IN A WAY THAT'S *NOT* LETHAL. THAT'S NOT MY TERRITORY.
BUT IF IT BECOMES NECESSARY, I WANTED *YOU* TO HAVE IT.
DAD.
THE CITY'S BURNING, KATE. THE MISSION CALLS.
REMEMBER YOUR FATHER LOVES YOU, AND IS ALWAYS HERE IF YOU NEED HIS HELP.
...THANKS.

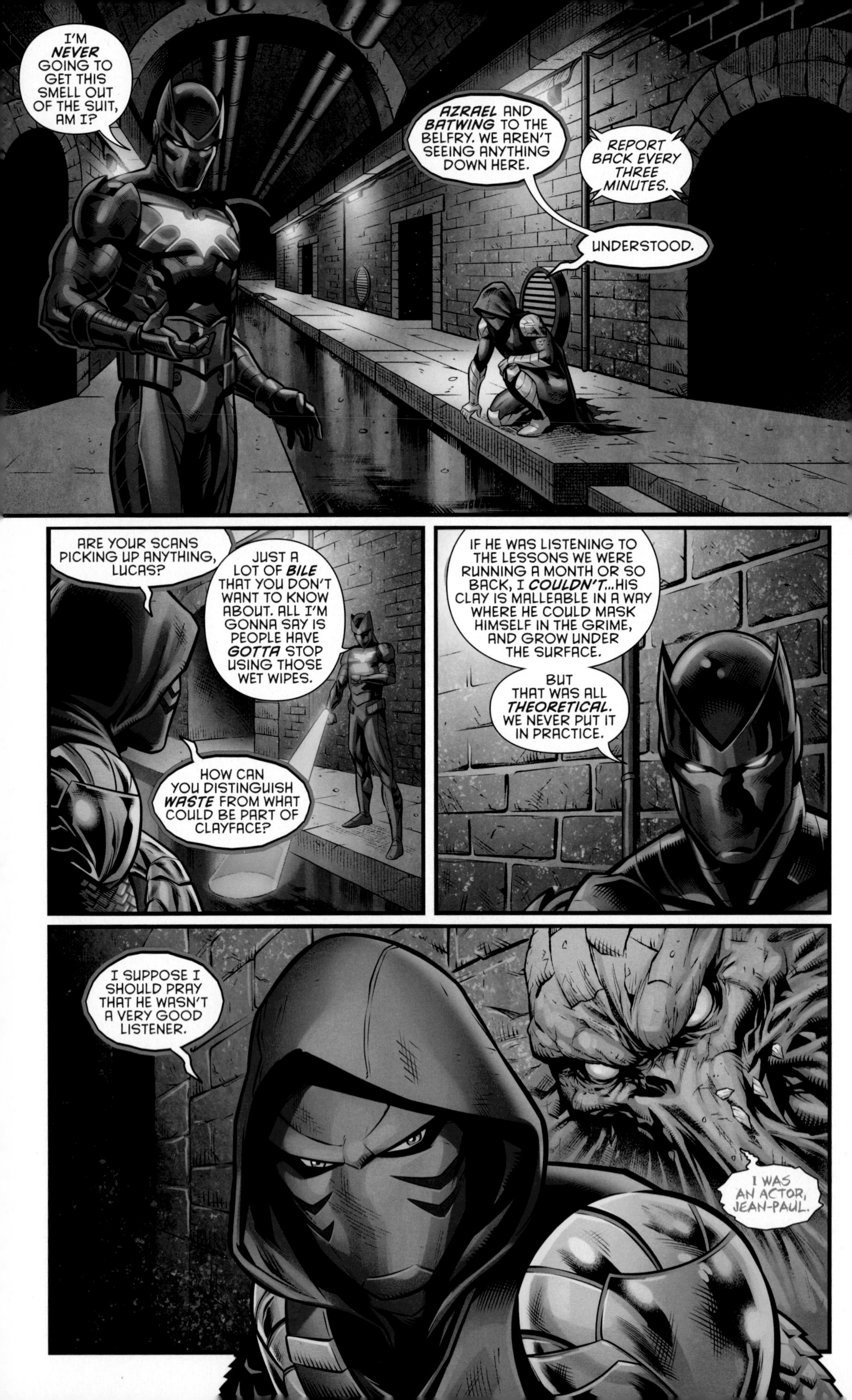
I'M NEVER GOING TO GET THIS SMELL OUT OF THE SUIT, AM I?
AZRAEL AND BATWING TO THE BELFRY. WE AREN'T SEEING ANYTHING DOWN HERE.
REPORT BACK EVERY THREE MINUTES.
UNDERSTOOD.
ARE YOUR SCANS PICKING UP ANYTHING, LUCAS?
JUST A LOT OF BILE THAT YOU DON'T WANT TO KNOW ABOUT. ALL I'M GONNA SAY IS PEOPLE HAVE GOTTA STOP USING THOSE WET WIPES.
HOW CAN YOU DISTINGUISH WASTE FROM WHAT COULD BE PART OF CLAYFACE?
IF HE WAS LISTENING TO THE LESSONS WE WERE RUNNING A MONTH OR SO BACK, I COULDN'T...HIS CLAY IS MALLEABLE IN A WAY WHERE HE COULD MASK HIMSELF IN THE GRIME, AND GROW UNDER THE SURFACE.
BUT THAT WAS ALL THEORETICAL. WE NEVER PUT IT IN PRACTICE.
I SUPPOSE I SHOULD PRAY THAT HE WASN'T A VERY GOOD LISTENER.
I WAS AN ACTOR, JEAN-PAUL.

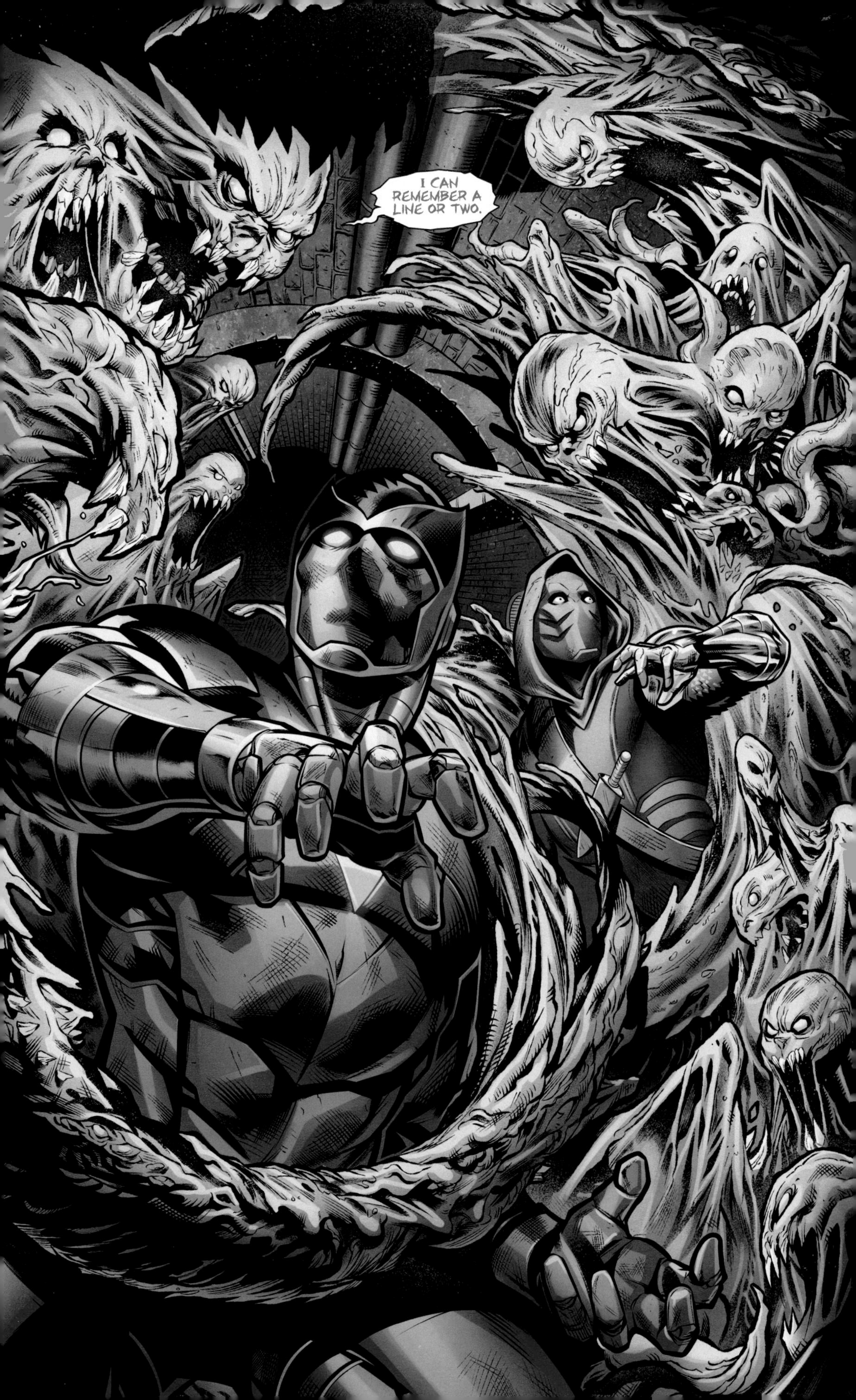
I CAN REMEMBER A LINE OR TWO.

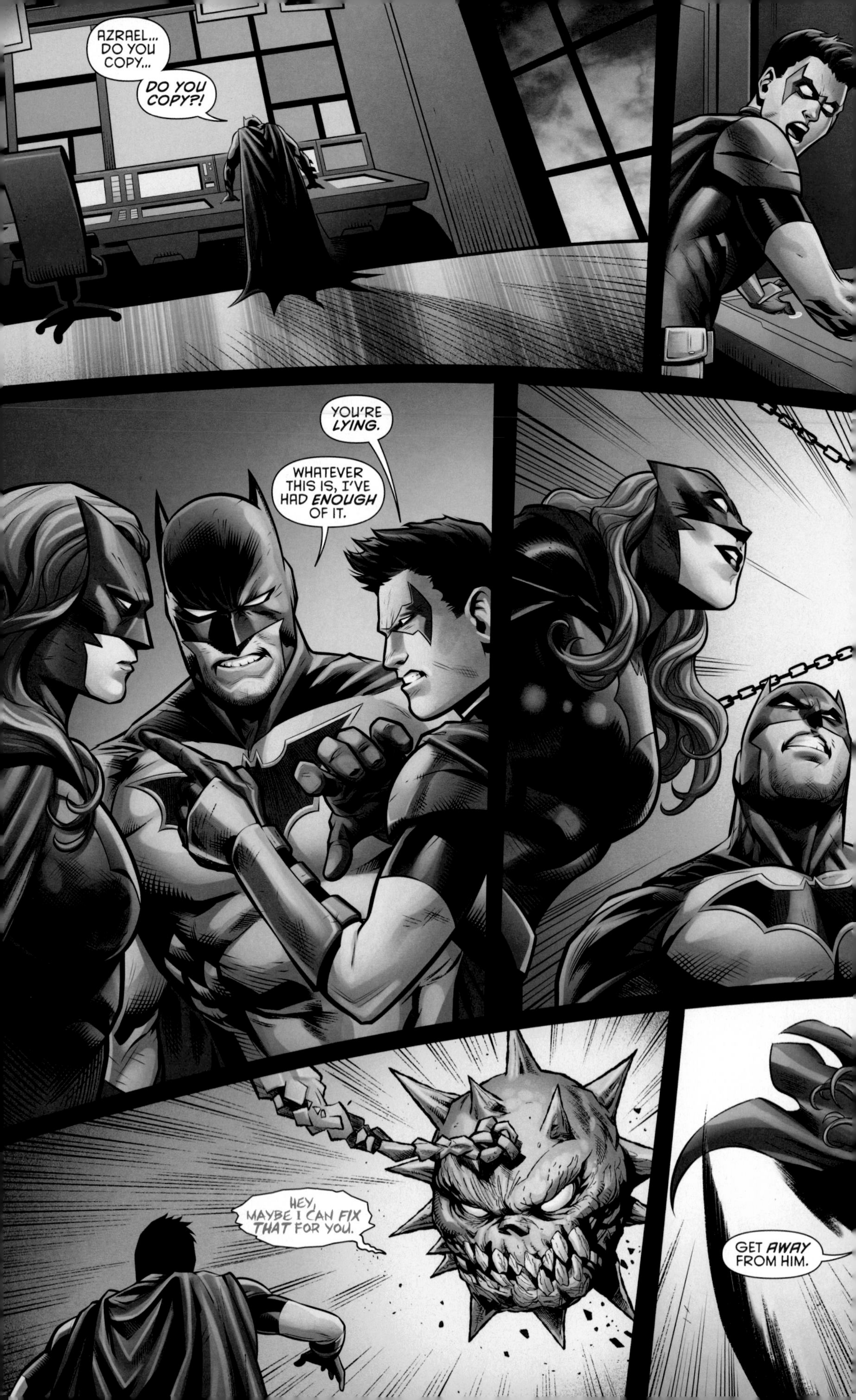
AZRAEL... DO YOU COPY...
DO YOU COPY?!
YOU'RE LYING.
WHATEVER THIS IS, I'VE HAD ENOUGH OF IT.
HEY, MAYBE I CAN FIX THAT FOR YOU.
GET AWAY FROM HIM.

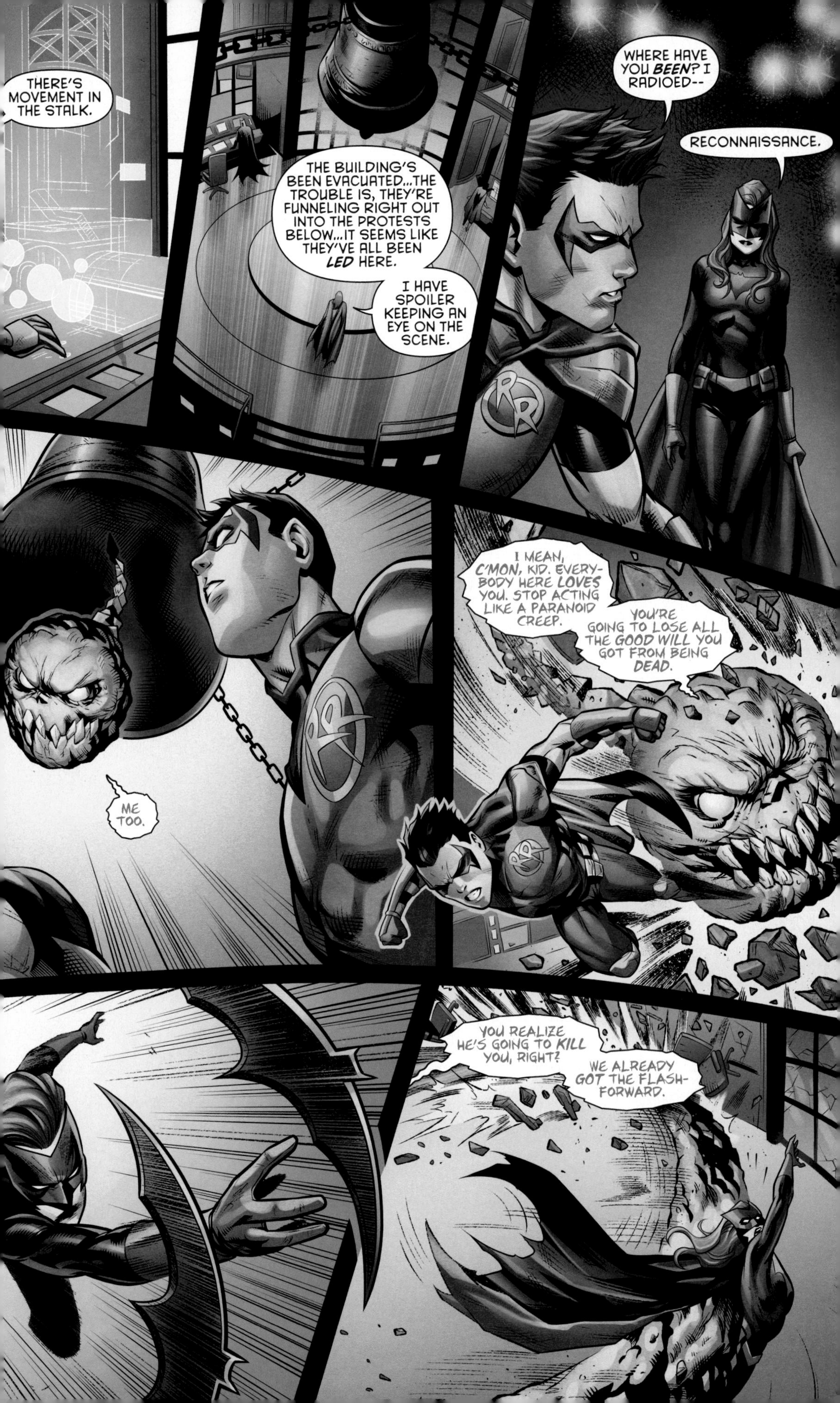
THERE'S MOVEMENT IN THE STALK.
THE BUILDING'S BEEN EVACUATED...THE TROUBLE IS, THEY'RE FUNNELING RIGHT OUT INTO THE PROTESTS BELOW...IT SEEMS LIKE THEY'VE ALL BEEN *LED* HERE.
I HAVE SPOILER KEEPING AN EYE ON THE SCENE.
WHERE HAVE YOU *BEEN*? I RADIOED--
RECONNAISSANCE.
ME TOO.
I MEAN, *C'MON*, KID. EVERYBODY HERE *LOVES* YOU. STOP ACTING LIKE A PARANOID CREEP.
YOU'RE GOING TO LOSE ALL THE *GOOD WILL* YOU GOT FROM BEING *DEAD*.
YOU REALIZE HE'S GOING TO *KILL* YOU, RIGHT?
WE ALREADY *GOT* THE FLASH-FORWARD.

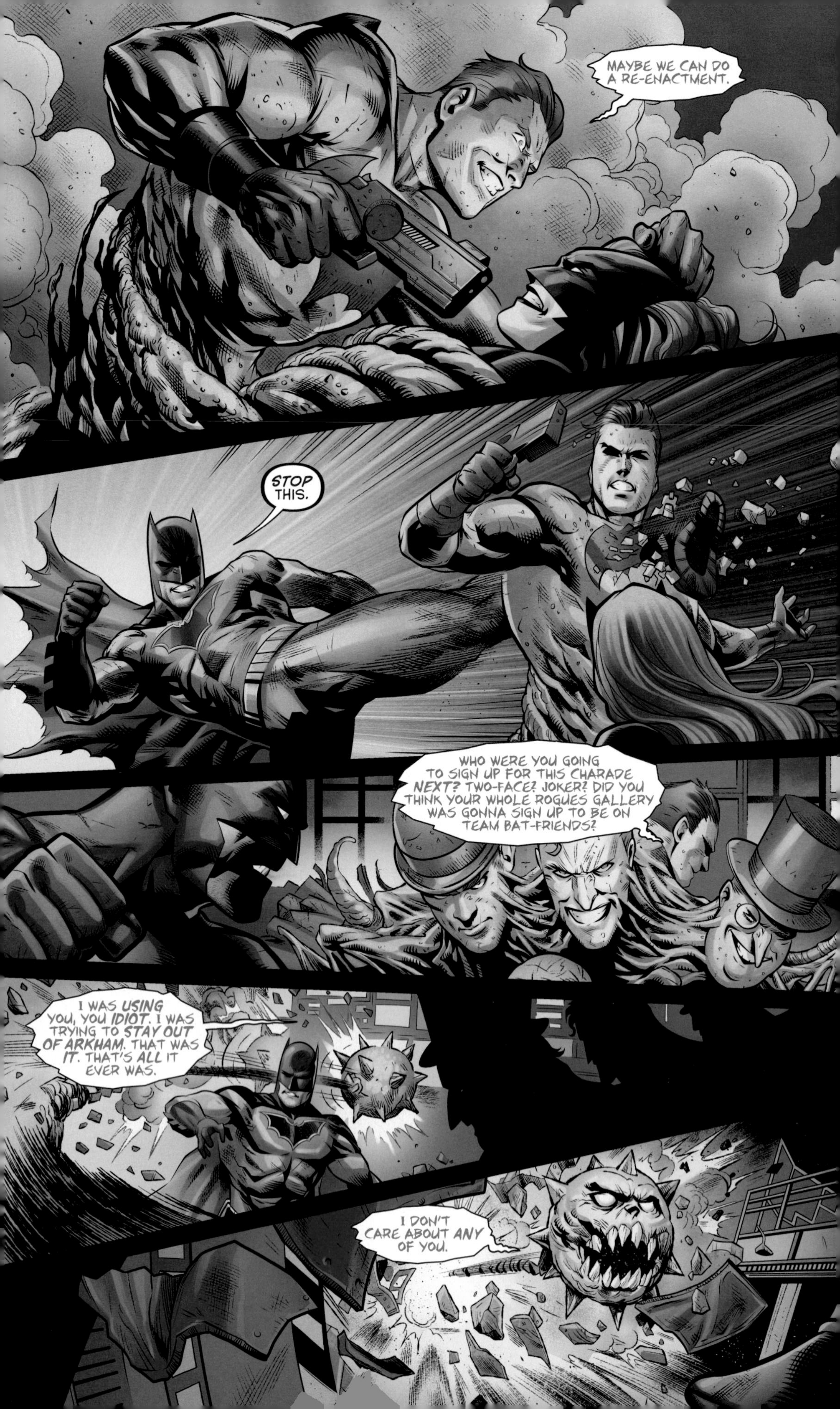
MAYBE WE CAN DO A RE-ENACTMENT.
STOP THIS.
WHO WERE YOU GOING TO SIGN UP FOR THIS CHARADE NEXT? TWO-FACE? JOKER? DID YOU THINK YOUR WHOLE ROGUES GALLERY WAS GONNA SIGN UP TO BE ON TEAM BAT-FRIENDS?
I WAS USING YOU, YOU IDIOT. I WAS TRYING TO STAY OUT OF ARKHAM. THAT WAS IT. THAT'S ALL IT EVER WAS.
I DON'T CARE ABOUT ANY OF YOU.

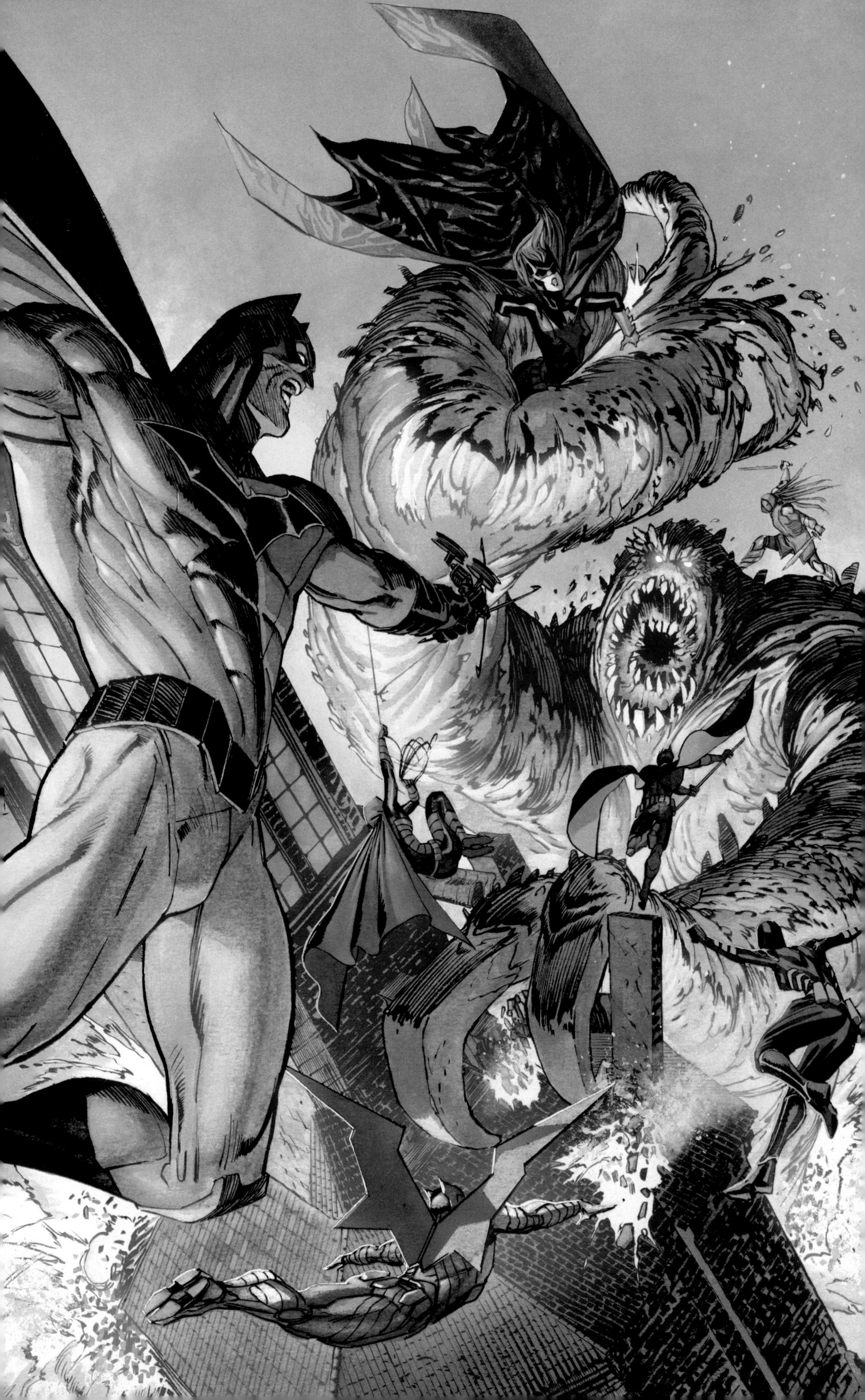

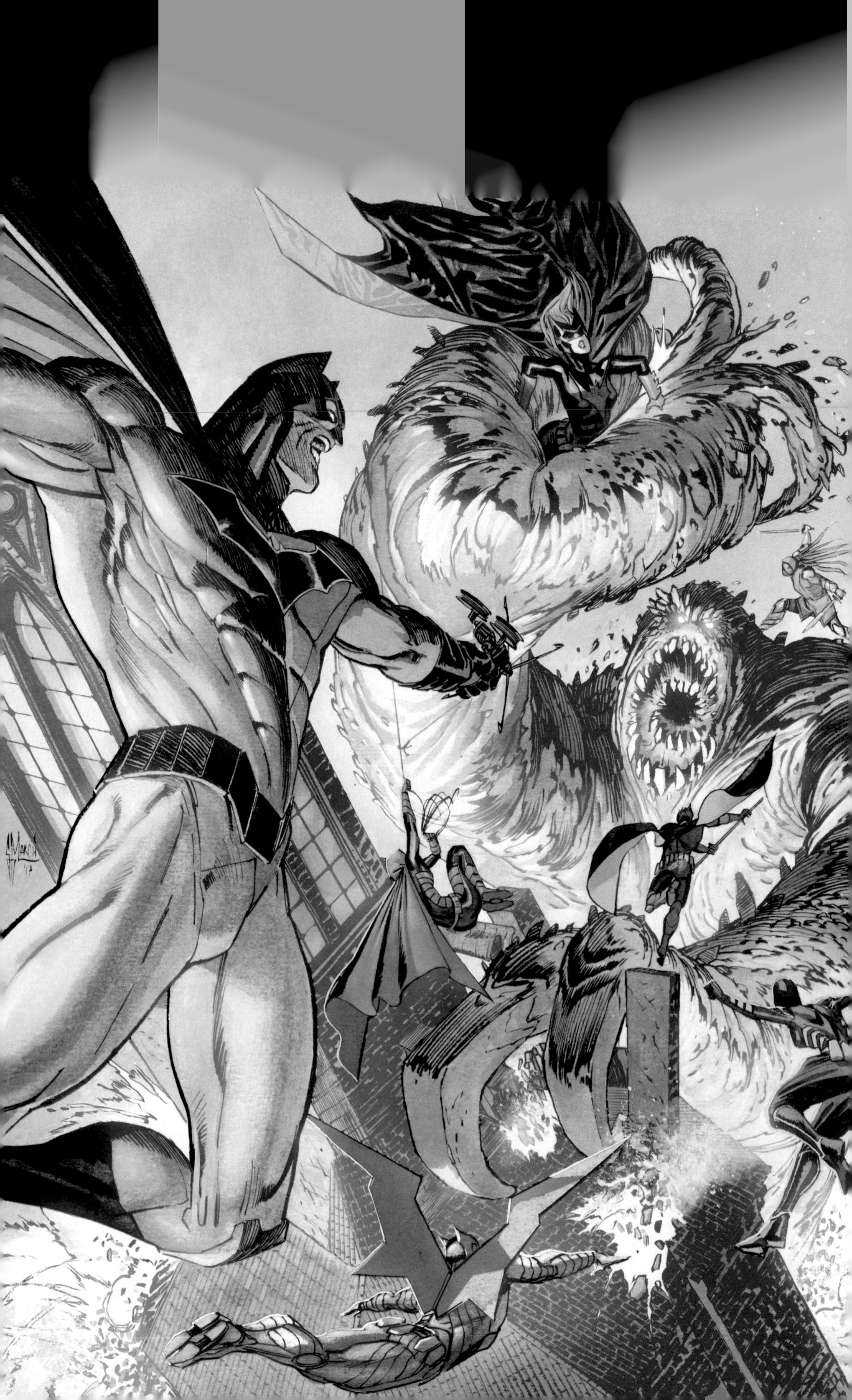

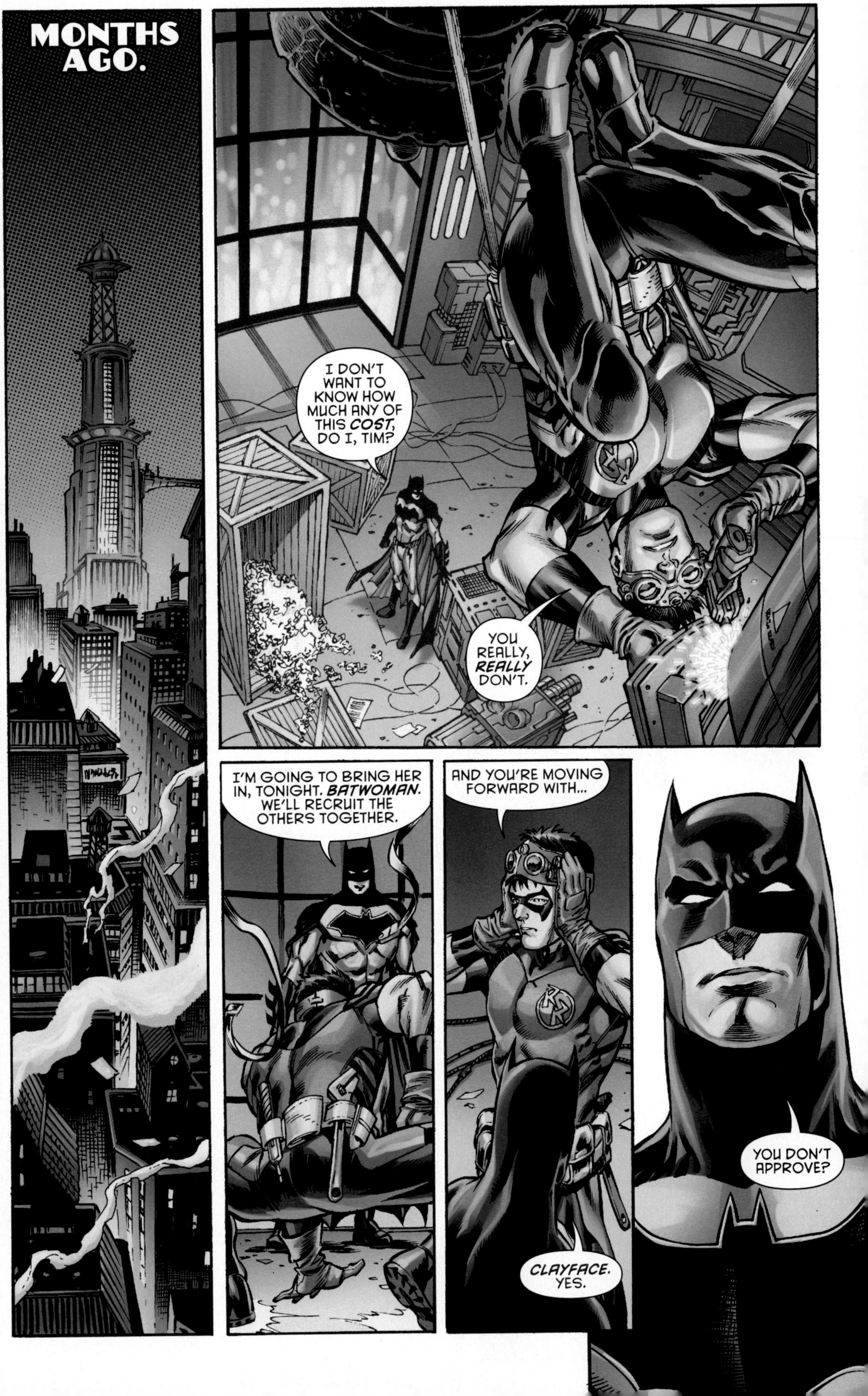
MONTHS AGO.
I DON'T WANT TO KNOW HOW MUCH ANY OF THIS COST, DO I, TIM?
YOU REALLY, REALLY DON'T.
I'M GOING TO BRING HER IN, TONIGHT. BATWOMAN. WE'LL RECRUIT THE OTHERS TOGETHER.
AND YOU'RE MOVING FORWARD WITH...
CLAYFACE. YES.
YOU DON'T APPROVE?

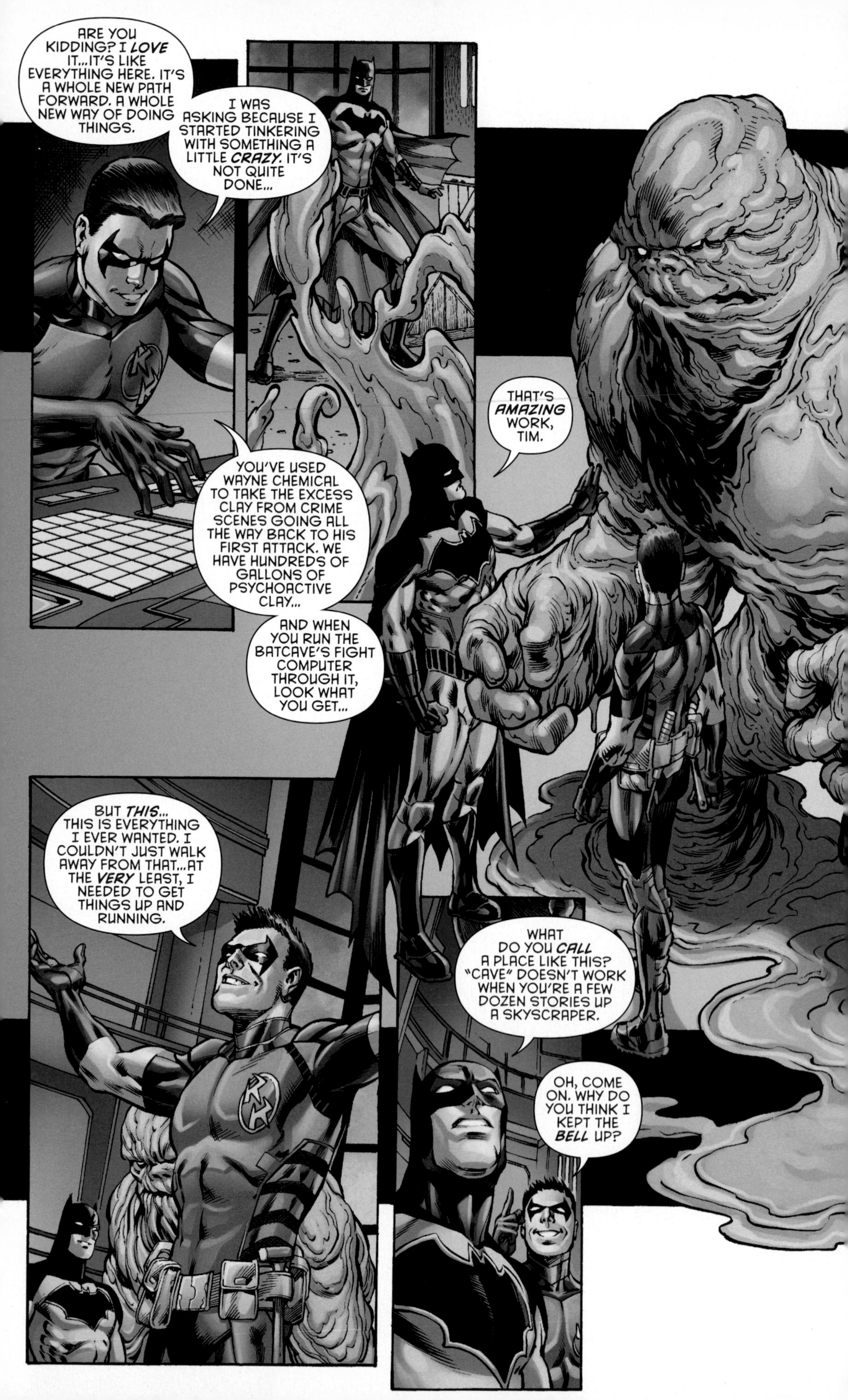
ARE YOU KIDDING? I LOVE IT...IT'S LIKE EVERYTHING HERE. IT'S A WHOLE NEW PATH FORWARD. A WHOLE NEW WAY OF DOING THINGS.
I WAS ASKING BECAUSE I STARTED TINKERING WITH SOMETHING A LITTLE CRAZY. IT'S NOT QUITE DONE...
YOU'VE USED WAYNE CHEMICAL TO TAKE THE EXCESS CLAY FROM CRIME SCENES GOING ALL THE WAY BACK TO HIS FIRST ATTACK. WE HAVE HUNDREDS OF GALLONS OF PSYCHOACTIVE CLAY...
AND WHEN YOU RUN THE BATCAVE'S FIGHT COMPUTER THROUGH IT, LOOK WHAT YOU GET...
THAT'S AMAZING WORK, TIM.
BUT THIS... THIS IS EVERYTHING I EVER WANTED. I COULDN'T JUST WALK AWAY FROM THAT...AT THE VERY LEAST, I NEEDED TO GET THINGS UP AND RUNNING.
WHAT DO YOU CALL A PLACE LIKE THIS? "CAVE" DOESN'T WORK WHEN YOU'RE A FEW DOZEN STORIES UP A SKYSCRAPER.
OH, COME ON. WHY DO YOU THINK I KEPT THE BELL UP?

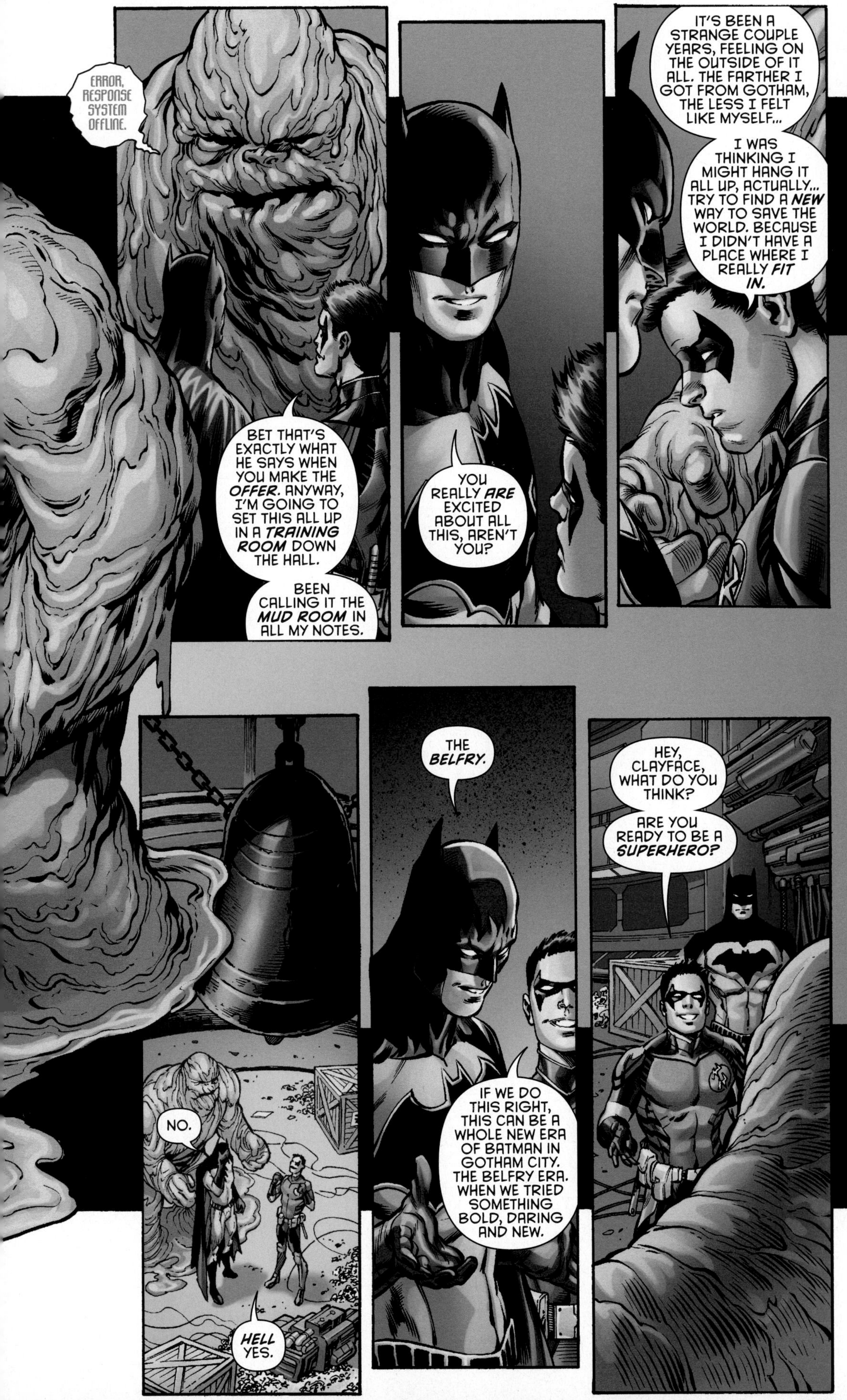

ERROR, RESPONSE SYSTEM OFFLINE.
BET THAT'S EXACTLY WHAT HE SAYS WHEN YOU MAKE THE *OFFER*. ANYWAY, I'M GOING TO SET THIS ALL UP IN A *TRAINING ROOM* DOWN THE HALL.
BEEN CALLING IT THE *MUD ROOM* IN ALL MY NOTES.
YOU REALLY *ARE* EXCITED ABOUT ALL THIS, AREN'T YOU?
IT'S BEEN A STRANGE COUPLE YEARS, FEELING ON THE OUTSIDE OF IT ALL. THE FARTHER I GOT FROM GOTHAM, THE LESS I FELT LIKE MYSELF...
I WAS THINKING I MIGHT HANG IT ALL UP, ACTUALLY... TRY TO FIND A *NEW* WAY TO SAVE THE WORLD. BECAUSE I DIDN'T HAVE A PLACE WHERE I REALLY *FIT IN.*
THE *BELFRY.*
IF WE DO THIS RIGHT, THIS CAN BE A WHOLE NEW ERA OF BATMAN IN GOTHAM CITY. THE BELFRY ERA. WHEN WE TRIED SOMETHING BOLD, DARING AND NEW.
HEY, CLAYFACE, WHAT DO YOU THINK?
ARE YOU READY TO BE A *SUPERHERO?*
NO.
HELL YES.

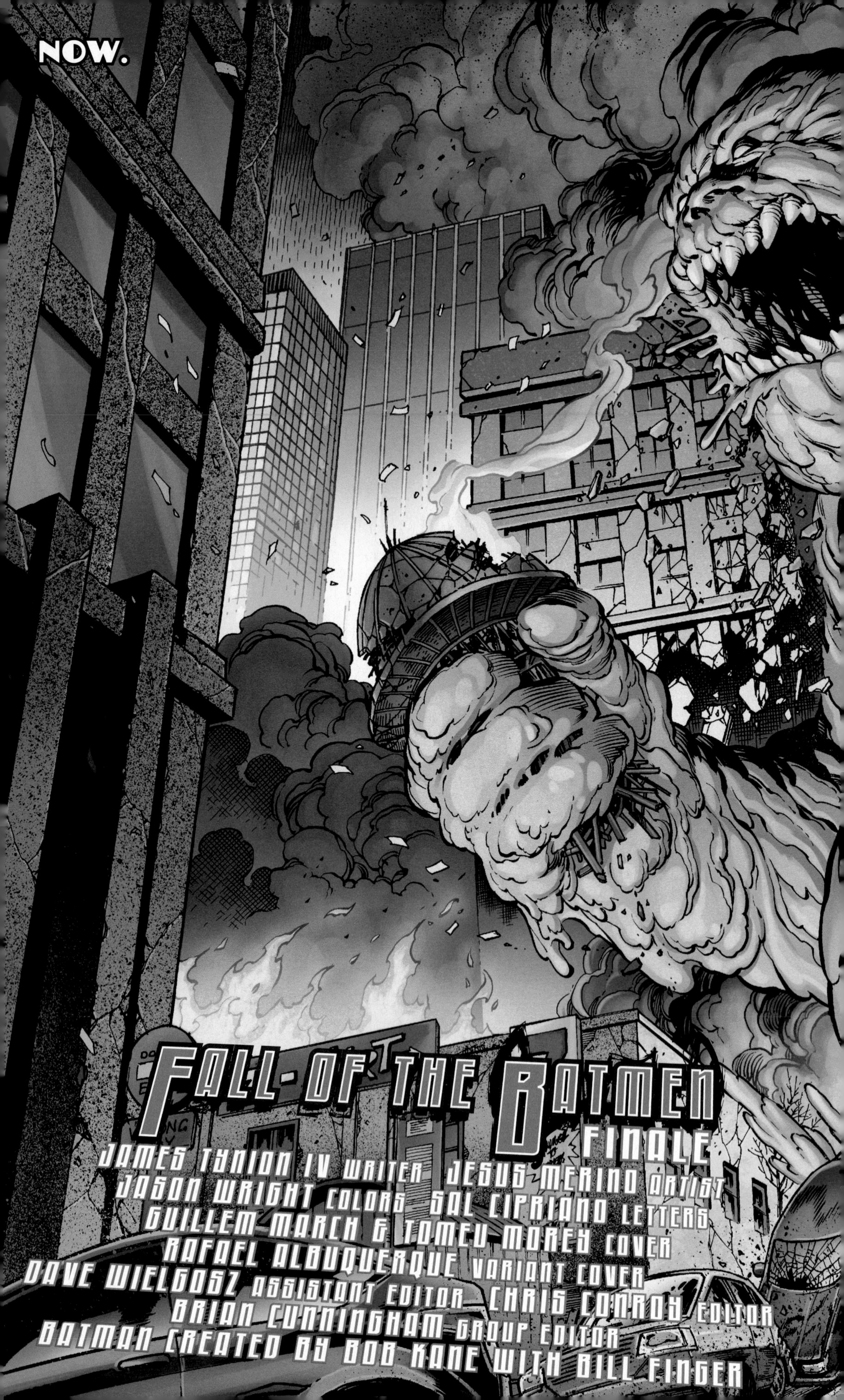
NOW.
FALL OF THE BATMEN
FINALE
JAMES TYNION IV WRITER JESUS MERINO ARTIST
JASON WRIGHT COLORS SOL CIPRIANO LETTERS
GUILLEM MARCH & TOMEU MOREY COVER
RAFAEL ALBUQUERQUE VARIANT COVER
DAVE WIELGOSZ ASSISTANT EDITOR CHRIS CONROY EDITOR
BRIAN CUNNINGHAM GROUP EDITOR
BATMAN CREATED BY BOB KANE WITH BILL FINGER

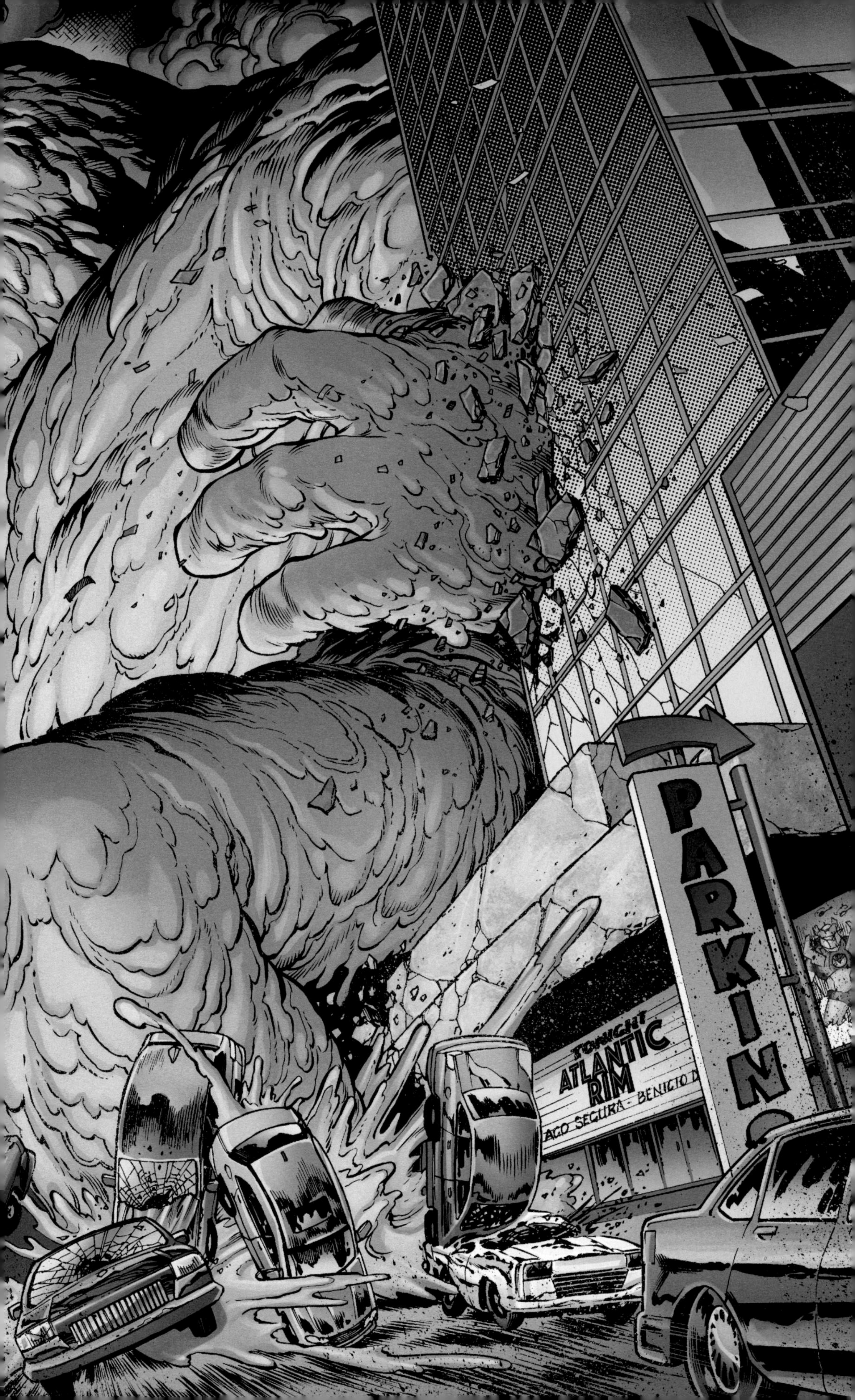
PARKIN
TONIGHT
ATLANTIC RIM
AGO SEGURA · BENICIO D

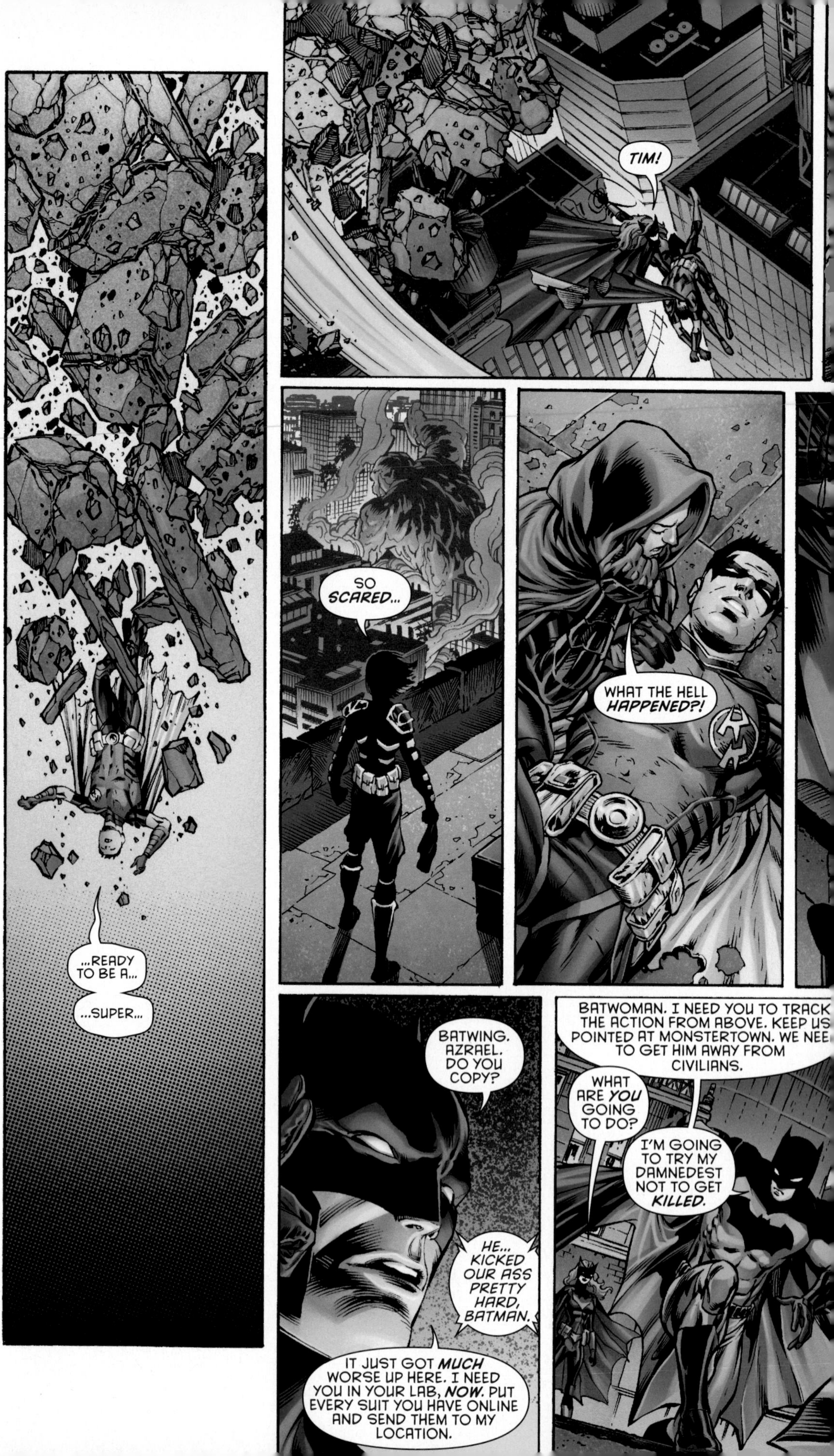
...READY TO BE A...
...SUPER...
TIM!
SO SCARED...
WHAT THE HELL HAPPENED?!
BATWING. AZRAEL. DO YOU COPY?
HE... KICKED OUR ASS PRETTY HARD, BATMAN.
IT JUST GOT MUCH WORSE UP HERE. I NEED YOU IN YOUR LAB, NOW. PUT EVERY SUIT YOU HAVE ONLINE AND SEND THEM TO MY LOCATION.
BATWOMAN. I NEED YOU TO TRACK THE ACTION FROM ABOVE. KEEP US POINTED AT MONSTERTOWN. WE NEE TO GET HIM AWAY FROM CIVILIANS.
WHAT ARE YOU GOING TO DO?
I'M GOING TO TRY MY DAMNEDEST NOT TO GET KILLED.

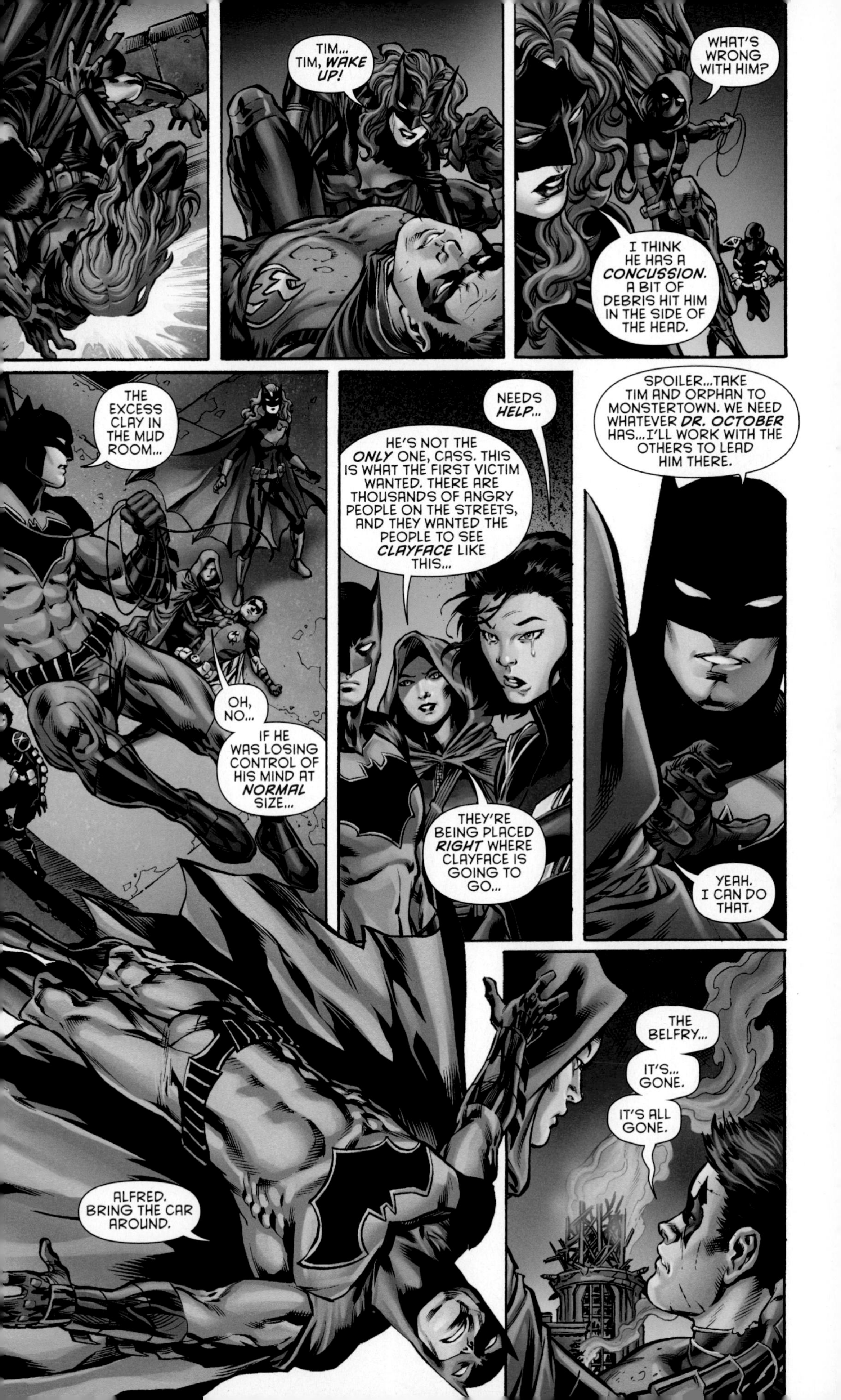
TIM... TIM, WAKE UP!
WHAT'S WRONG WITH HIM?
I THINK HE HAS A CONCUSSION. A BIT OF DEBRIS HIT HIM IN THE SIDE OF THE HEAD.
THE EXCESS CLAY IN THE MUD ROOM...
OH, NO...
IF HE WAS LOSING CONTROL OF HIS MIND AT NORMAL SIZE...
NEEDS HELP...
HE'S NOT THE ONLY ONE, CASS. THIS IS WHAT THE FIRST VICTIM WANTED. THERE ARE THOUSANDS OF ANGRY PEOPLE ON THE STREETS, AND THEY WANTED THE PEOPLE TO SEE CLAYFACE LIKE THIS...
THEY'RE BEING PLACED RIGHT WHERE CLAYFACE IS GOING TO GO...
SPOILER...TAKE TIM AND ORPHAN TO MONSTERTOWN. WE NEED WHATEVER DR. OCTOBER HAS...I'LL WORK WITH THE OTHERS TO LEAD HIM THERE.
YEAH. I CAN DO THAT.
ALFRED. BRING THE CAR AROUND.
THE BELFRY...
IT'S... GONE.
IT'S ALL GONE.

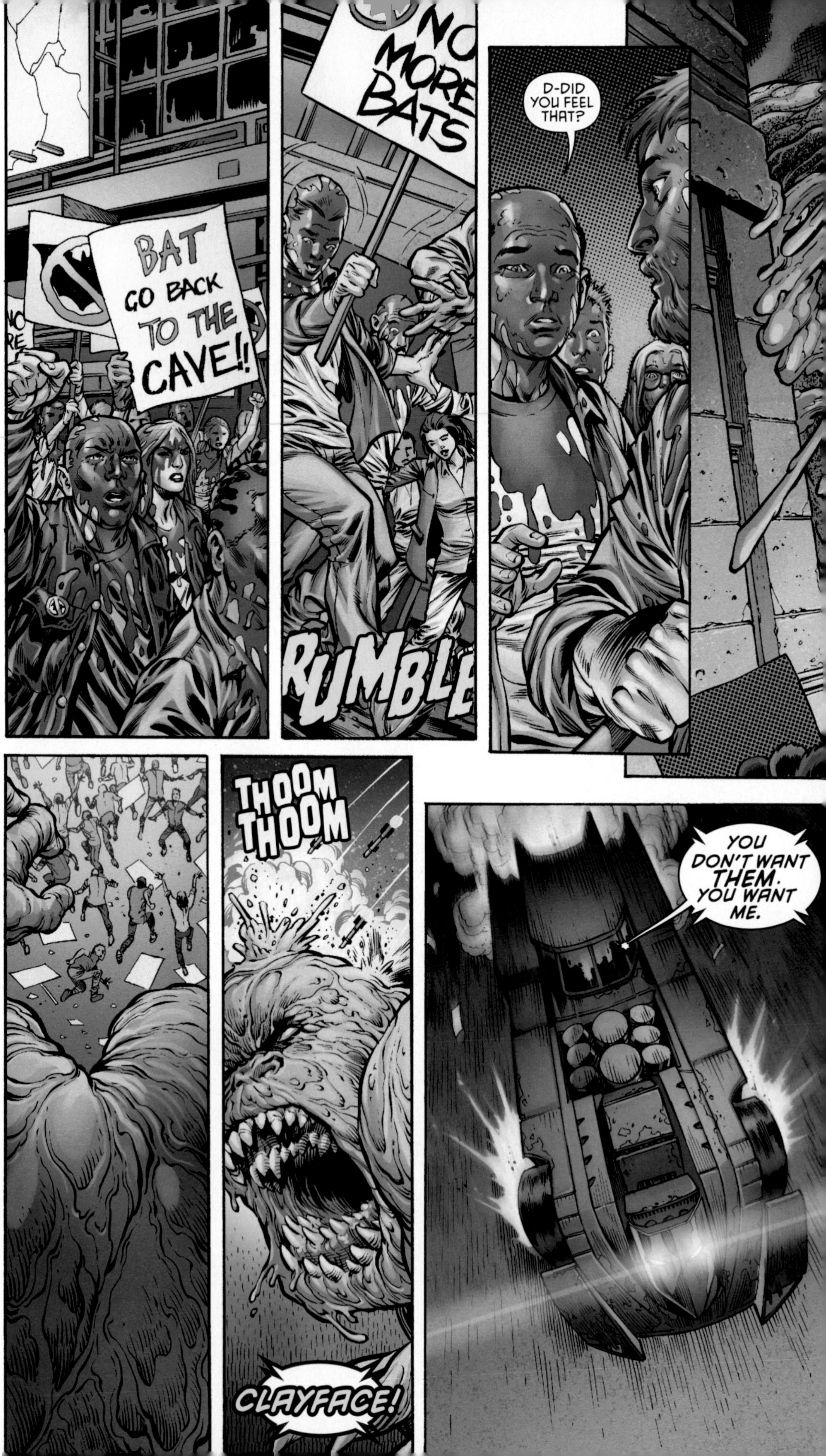
BAT GO BACK TO THE CAVE!!
NO MORE BATS
RUMBLE
D-DID YOU FEEL THAT?
THOOM THOOM
CLAYFACE!
YOU DON'T WANT THEM. YOU WANT ME.

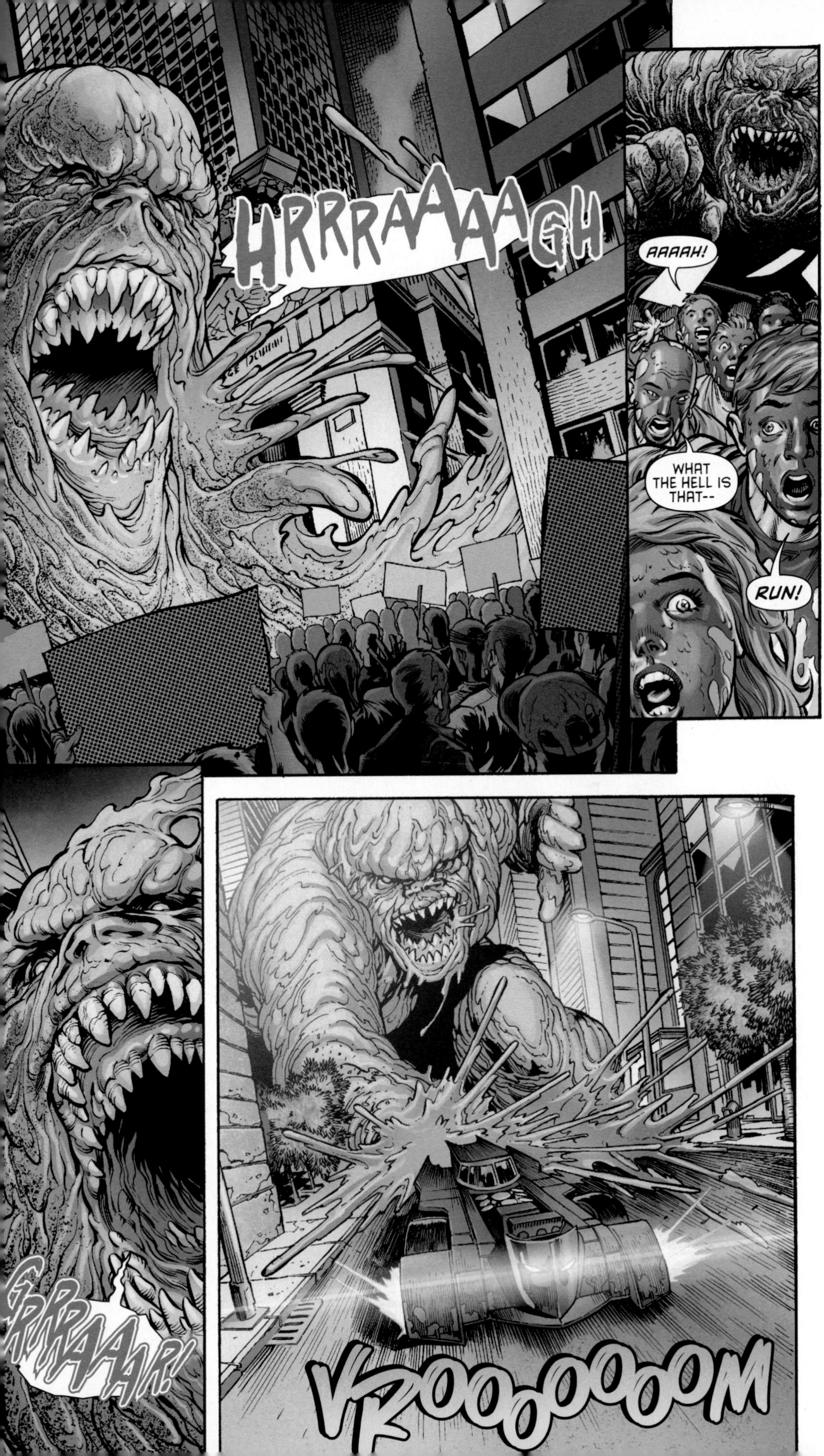
HRRRAAAAAGH
AAAAH!
WHAT THE HELL IS THAT--
RUN!
GRRRAAAAR!
VROOOOOOOOM

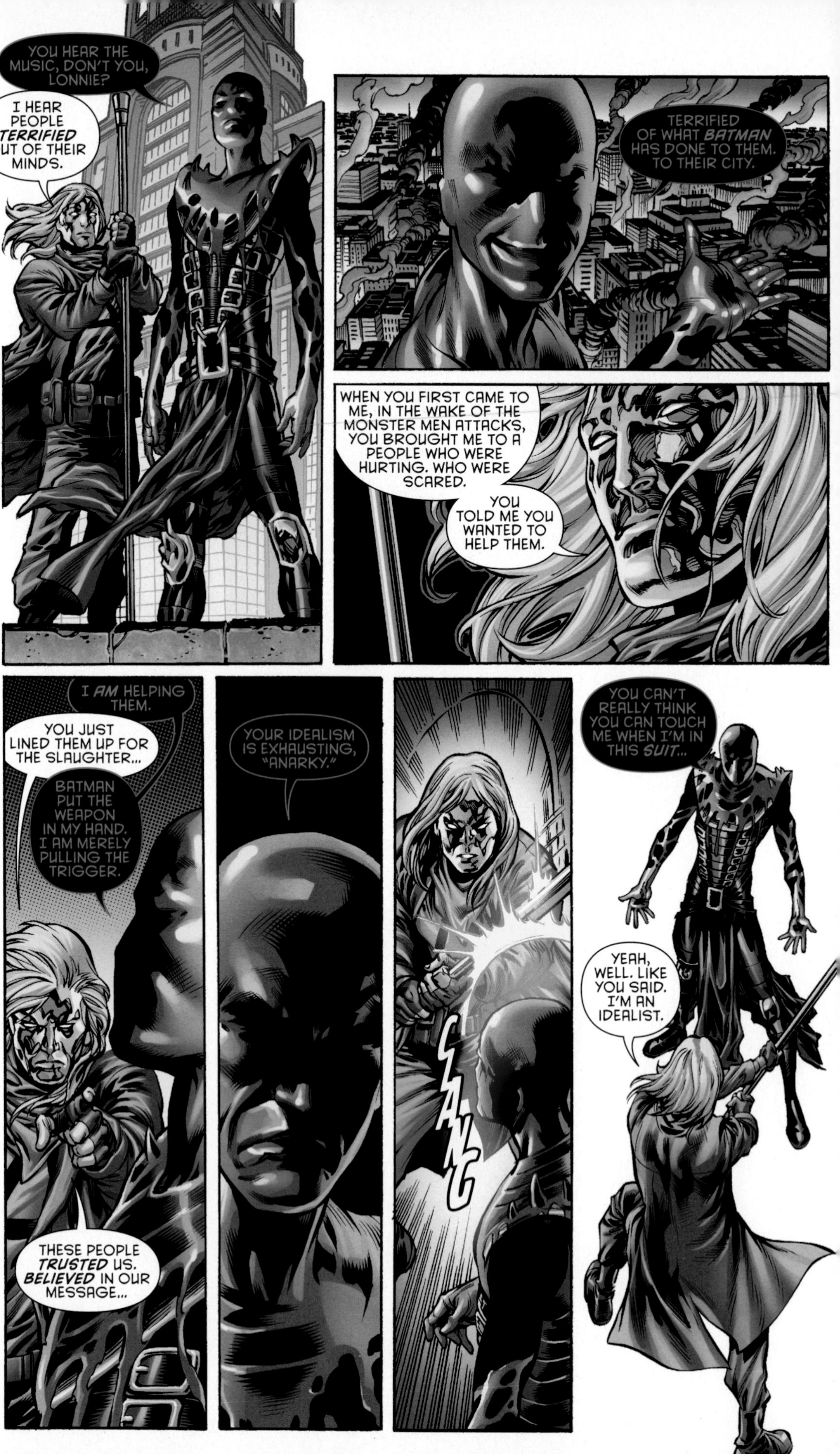
YOU HEAR THE MUSIC, DON'T YOU, LONNIE?
I HEAR PEOPLE TERRIFIED OUT OF THEIR MINDS.
TERRIFIED OF WHAT BATMAN HAS DONE TO THEM. TO THEIR CITY.
WHEN YOU FIRST CAME TO ME, IN THE WAKE OF THE MONSTER MEN ATTACKS, YOU BROUGHT ME TO A PEOPLE WHO WERE HURTING. WHO WERE SCARED.
YOU TOLD ME YOU WANTED TO HELP THEM.
I AM HELPING THEM.
YOU JUST LINED THEM UP FOR THE SLAUGHTER...
BATMAN PUT THE WEAPON IN MY HAND. I AM MERELY PULLING THE TRIGGER.
THESE PEOPLE TRUSTED US. BELIEVED IN OUR MESSAGE...
YOUR IDEALISM IS EXHAUSTING, "ANARKY."
CLANG
YOU CAN'T REALLY THINK YOU CAN TOUCH ME WHEN I'M IN THIS SUIT...
YEAH, WELL. LIKE YOU SAID. I'M AN IDEALIST.

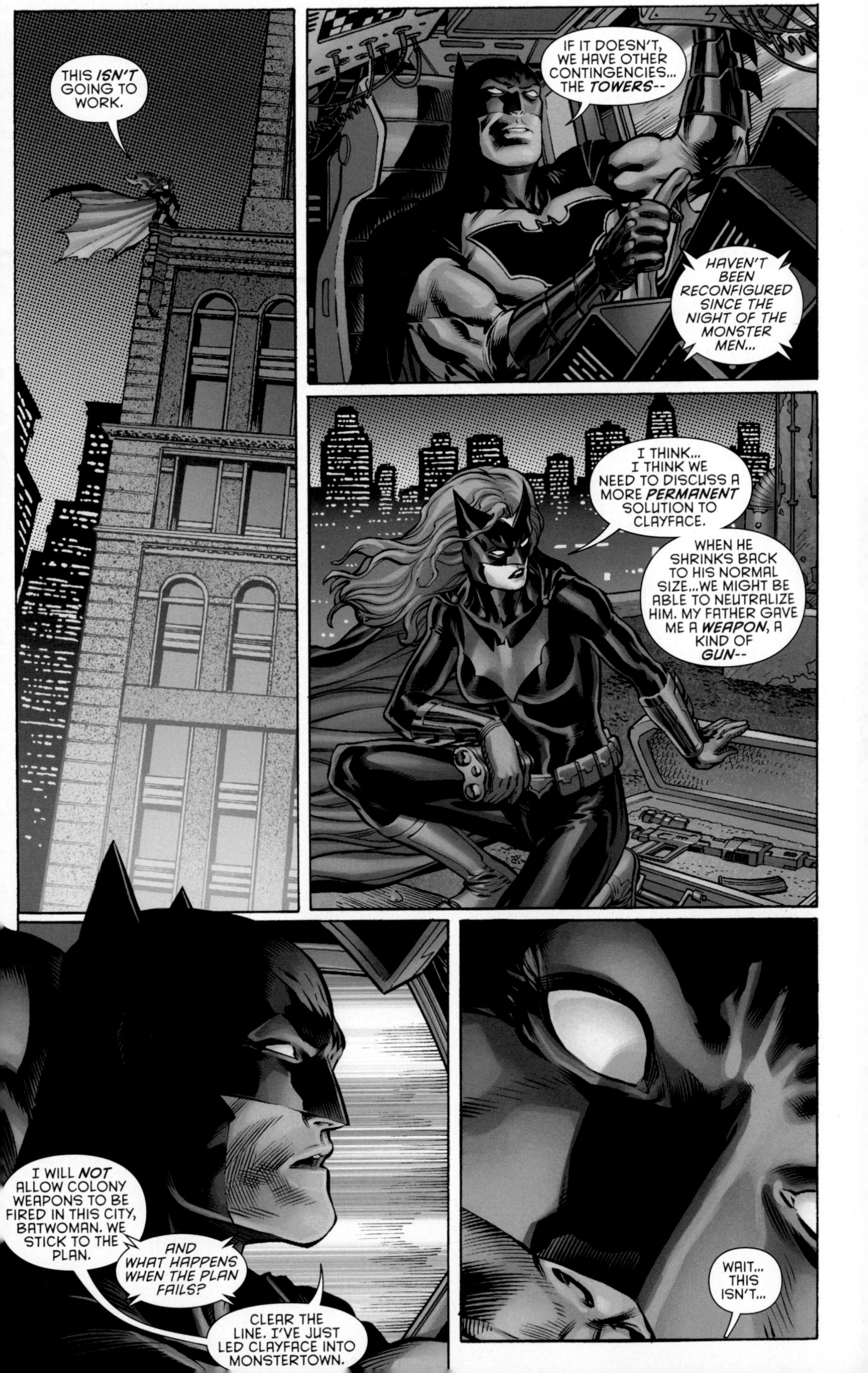
THIS ISN'T GOING TO WORK.
IF IT DOESN'T, WE HAVE OTHER CONTINGENCIES... THE TOWERS--
HAVEN'T BEEN RECONFIGURED SINCE THE NIGHT OF THE MONSTER MEN...
I THINK... I THINK WE NEED TO DISCUSS A MORE PERMANENT SOLUTION TO CLAYFACE.
WHEN HE SHRINKS BACK TO HIS NORMAL SIZE...WE MIGHT BE ABLE TO NEUTRALIZE HIM. MY FATHER GAVE ME A WEAPON, A KIND OF GUN--
I WILL NOT ALLOW COLONY WEAPONS TO BE FIRED IN THIS CITY, BATWOMAN. WE STICK TO THE PLAN.
AND WHAT HAPPENS WHEN THE PLAN FAILS?
CLEAR THE LINE. I'VE JUST LED CLAYFACE INTO MONSTERTOWN.
WAIT... THIS ISN'T...

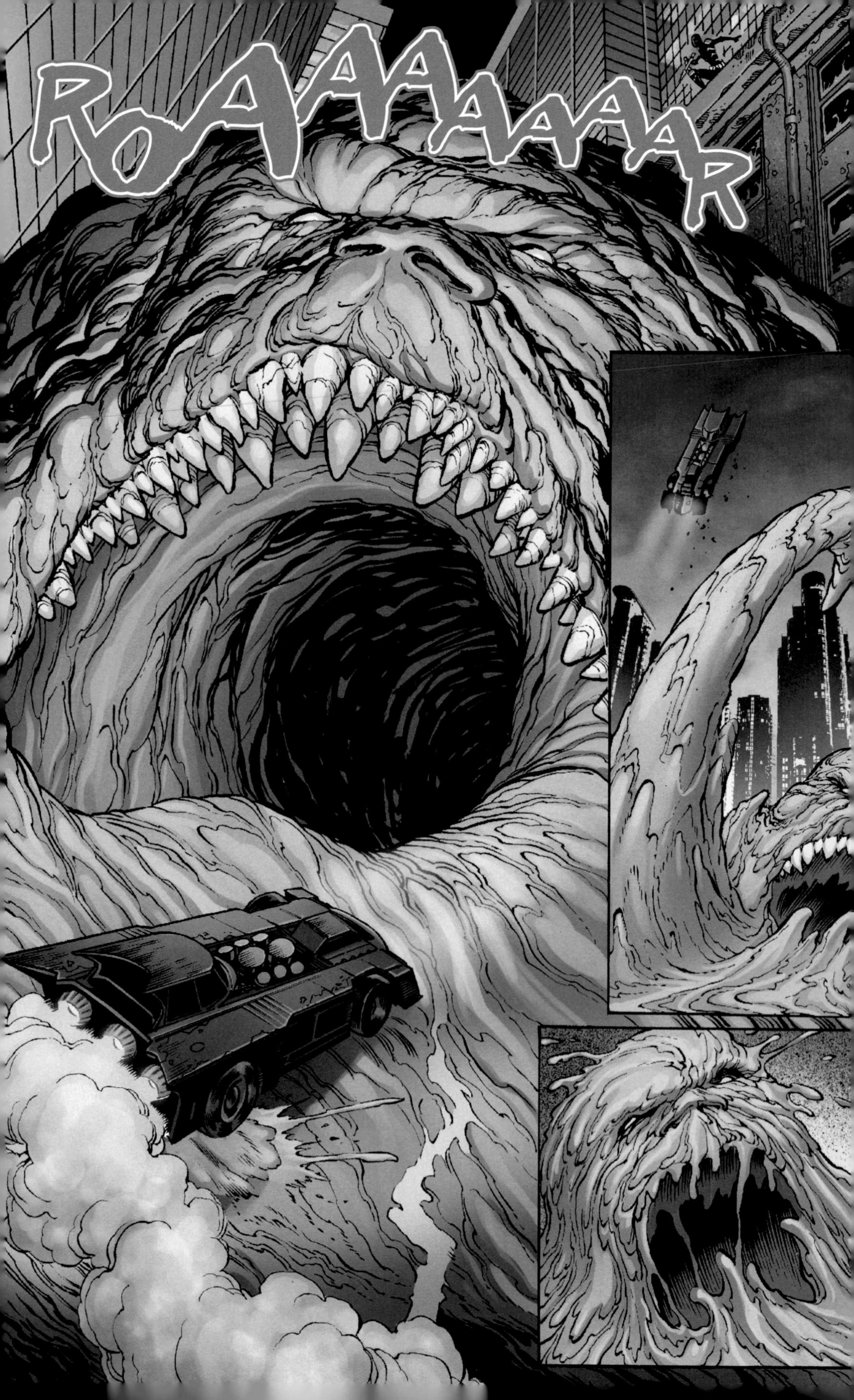
ROAAAAAAAR

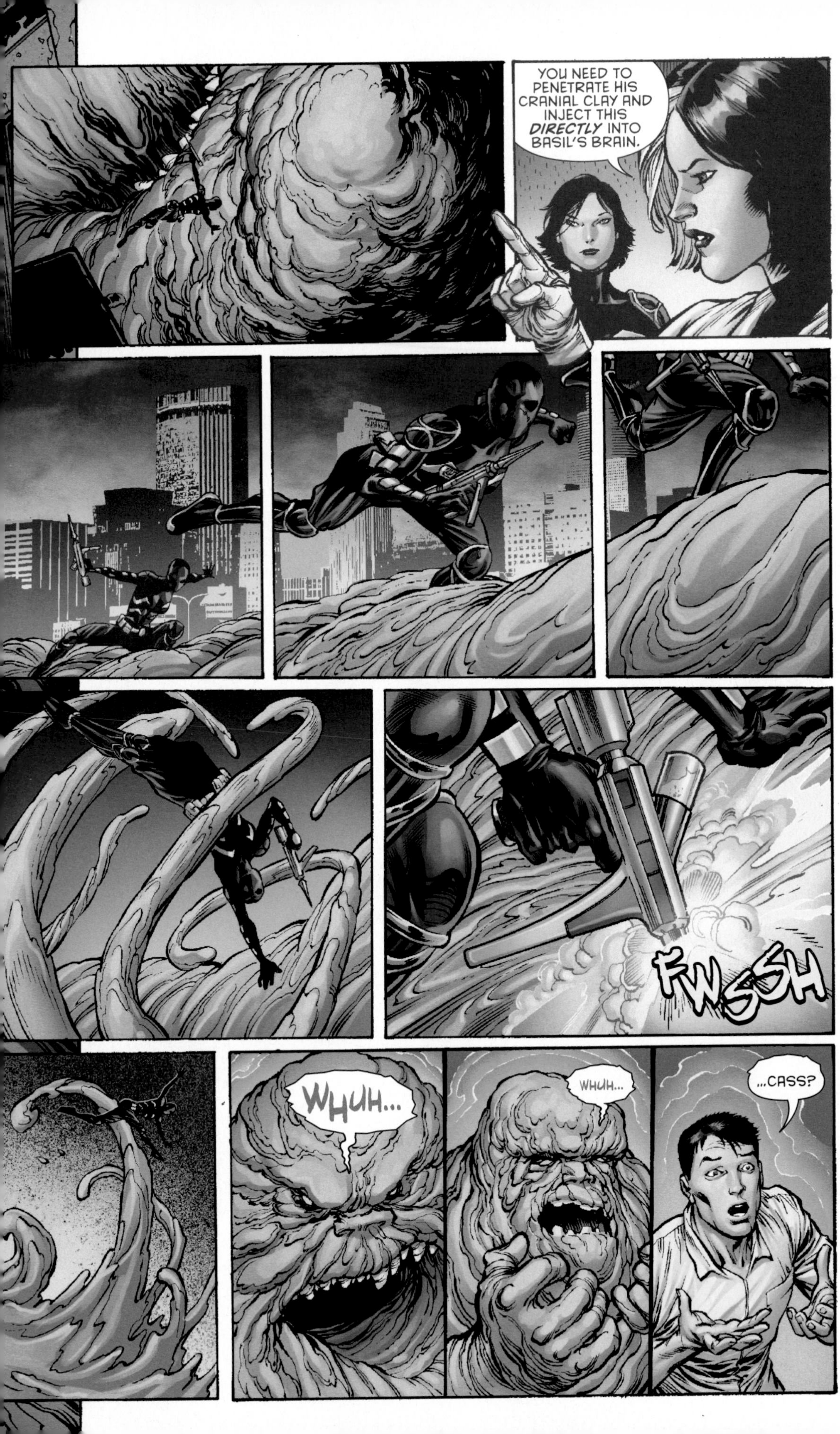
YOU NEED TO PENETRATE HIS CRANIAL CLAY AND INJECT THIS DIRECTLY INTO BASIL'S BRAIN.
FWSSH
WHUH...
WHUH...
...CASS?

WHERE... WHERE *AM* I? WHAT'S GOING ON?

OKAY. YOU'RE... OKAY.

YES.

DID I... DID *I* DO ALL THAT?

...PEOPLE *DIED* IN THERE, DIDN'T THEY?

IS IT *OVER*?

NO...YOU'LL TURN BACK. TOO...TOO MUCH CLAY.

NO. BAD GUYS DON'T *GET* HAPPY ENDINGS.

BUT RELEASE ME FROM MY BANDS, WITH THE HELP OF YOUR GOOD HANDS...GENTLE BREATH OF YOURS MY SAILS MUST FILL, OR ELSE MY PROJECT FAILS...

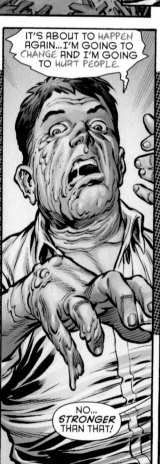

IT'S ABOUT TO *HAPPEN* AGAIN...I'M GOING TO *CHANGE* AND I'M GOING TO *HURT* PEOPLE.

NO... *STRONGER* THAN THAT!

AAHHHH...

NO... I'M NOT...

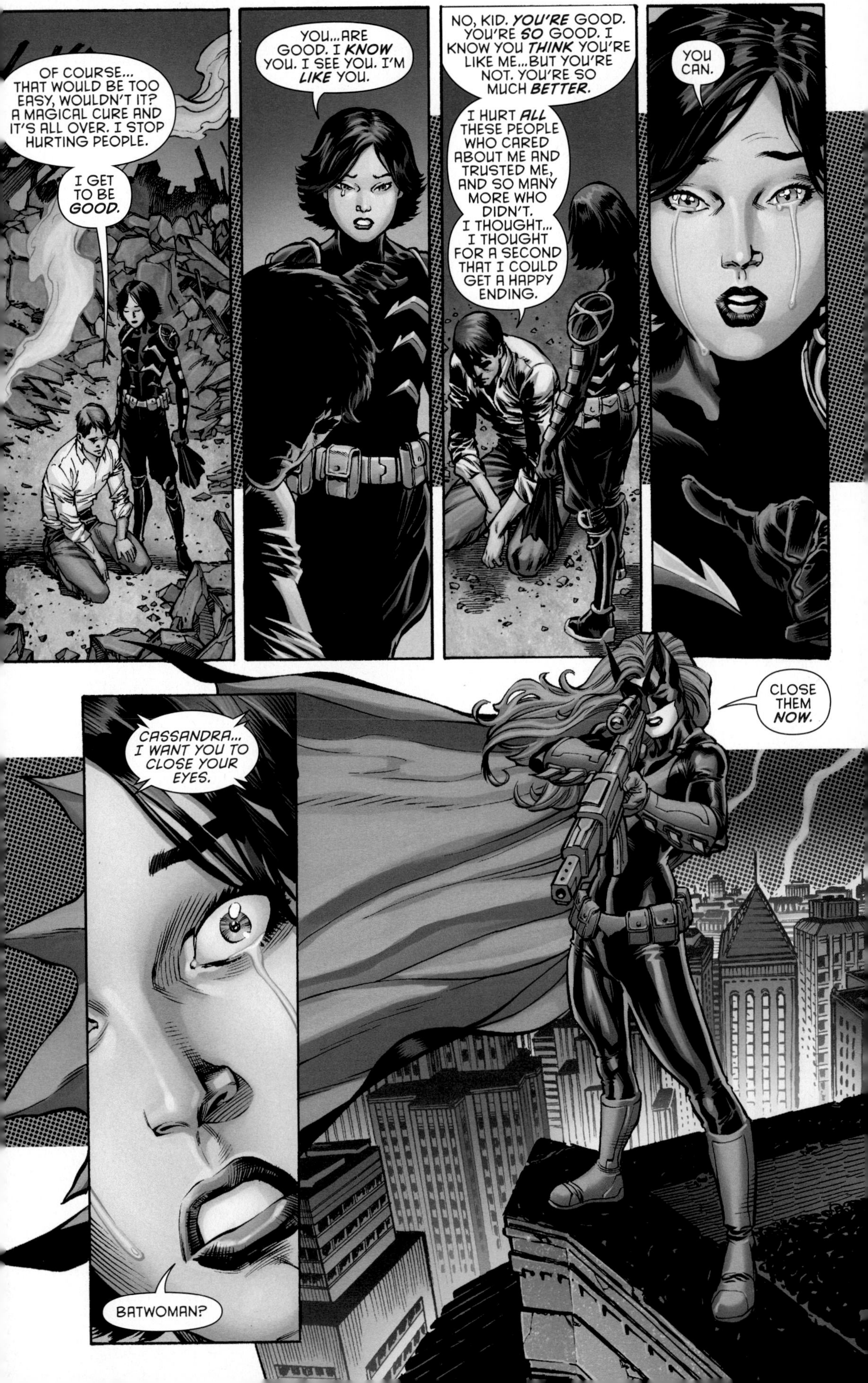
OF COURSE... THAT WOULD BE TOO EASY, WOULDN'T IT? A MAGICAL CURE AND IT'S ALL OVER. I STOP HURTING PEOPLE.
I GET TO BE GOOD.
YOU...ARE GOOD. I KNOW YOU. I SEE YOU. I'M LIKE YOU.
NO, KID. YOU'RE GOOD. YOU'RE SO GOOD. I KNOW YOU THINK YOU'RE LIKE ME...BUT YOU'RE NOT. YOU'RE SO MUCH BETTER.
I HURT ALL THESE PEOPLE WHO CARED ABOUT ME AND TRUSTED ME, AND SO MANY MORE WHO DIDN'T. I THOUGHT... I THOUGHT FOR A SECOND THAT I COULD GET A HAPPY ENDING.
YOU CAN.
CASSANDRA... I WANT YOU TO CLOSE YOUR EYES.
BATWOMAN?
CLOSE THEM NOW.

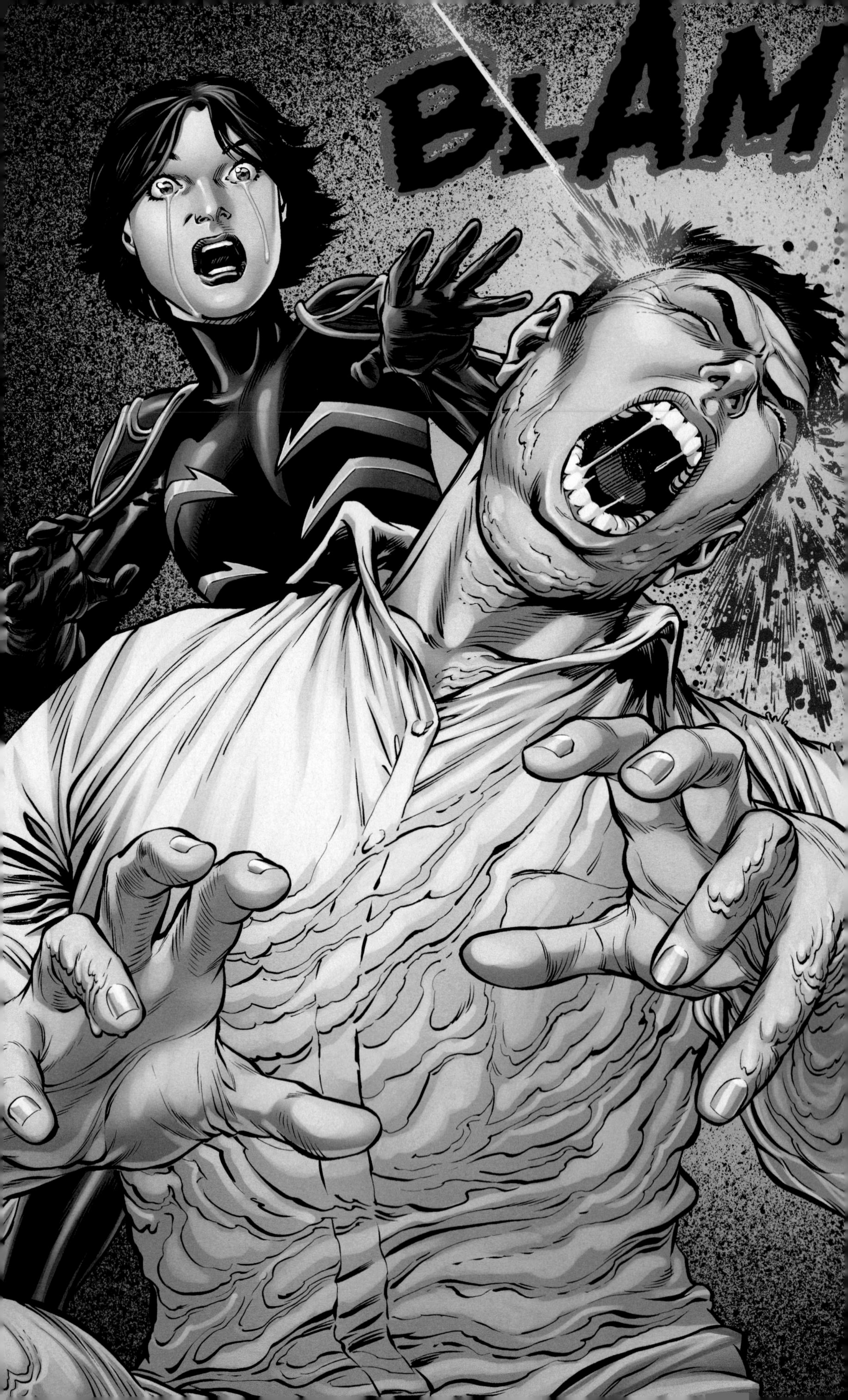
BLAM

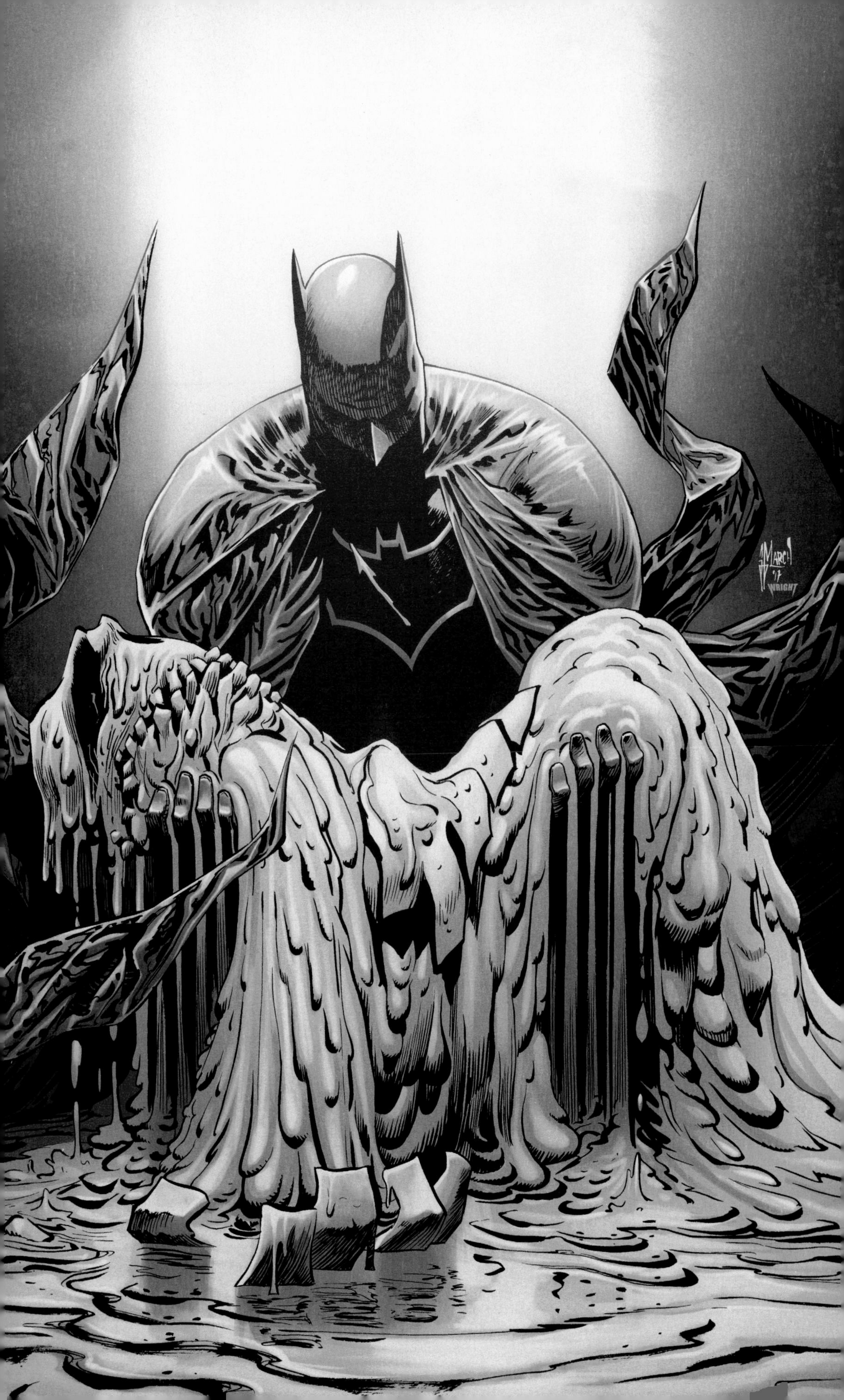

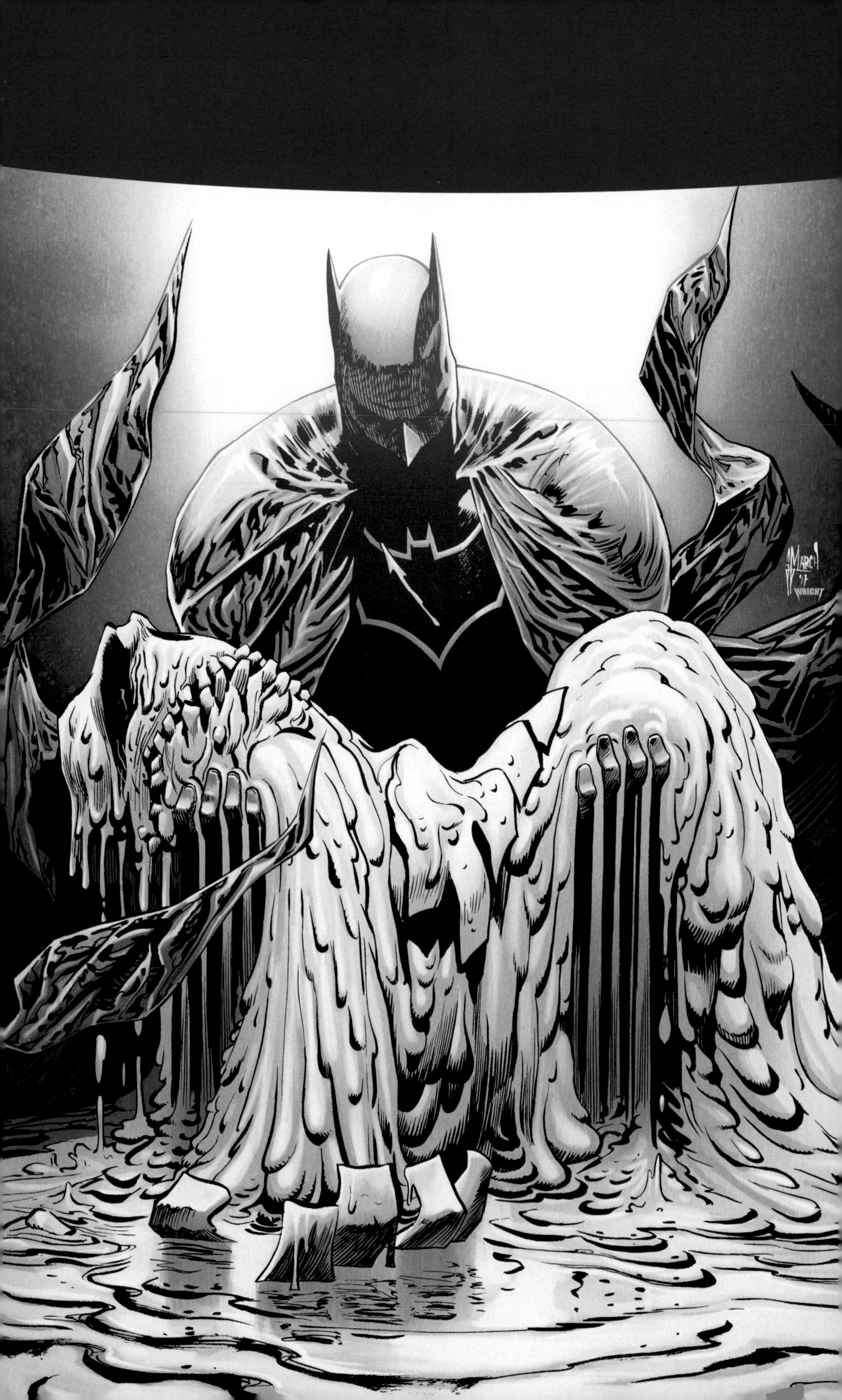
MARCH '17
WRIGHT

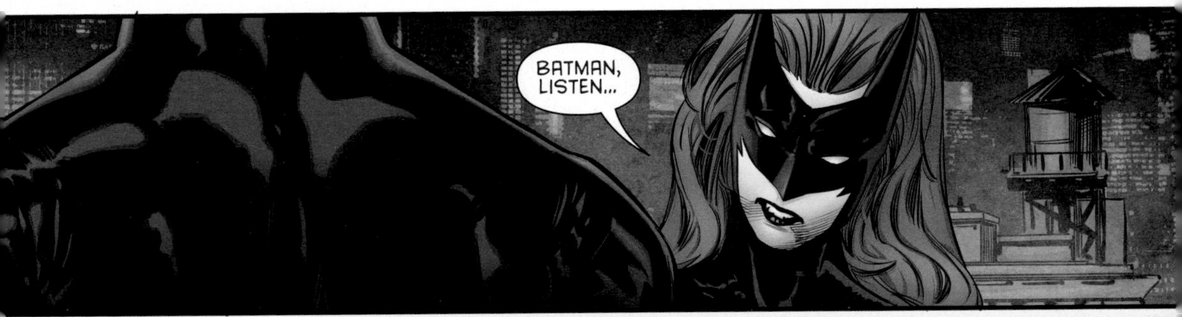
BATMAN, LISTEN...

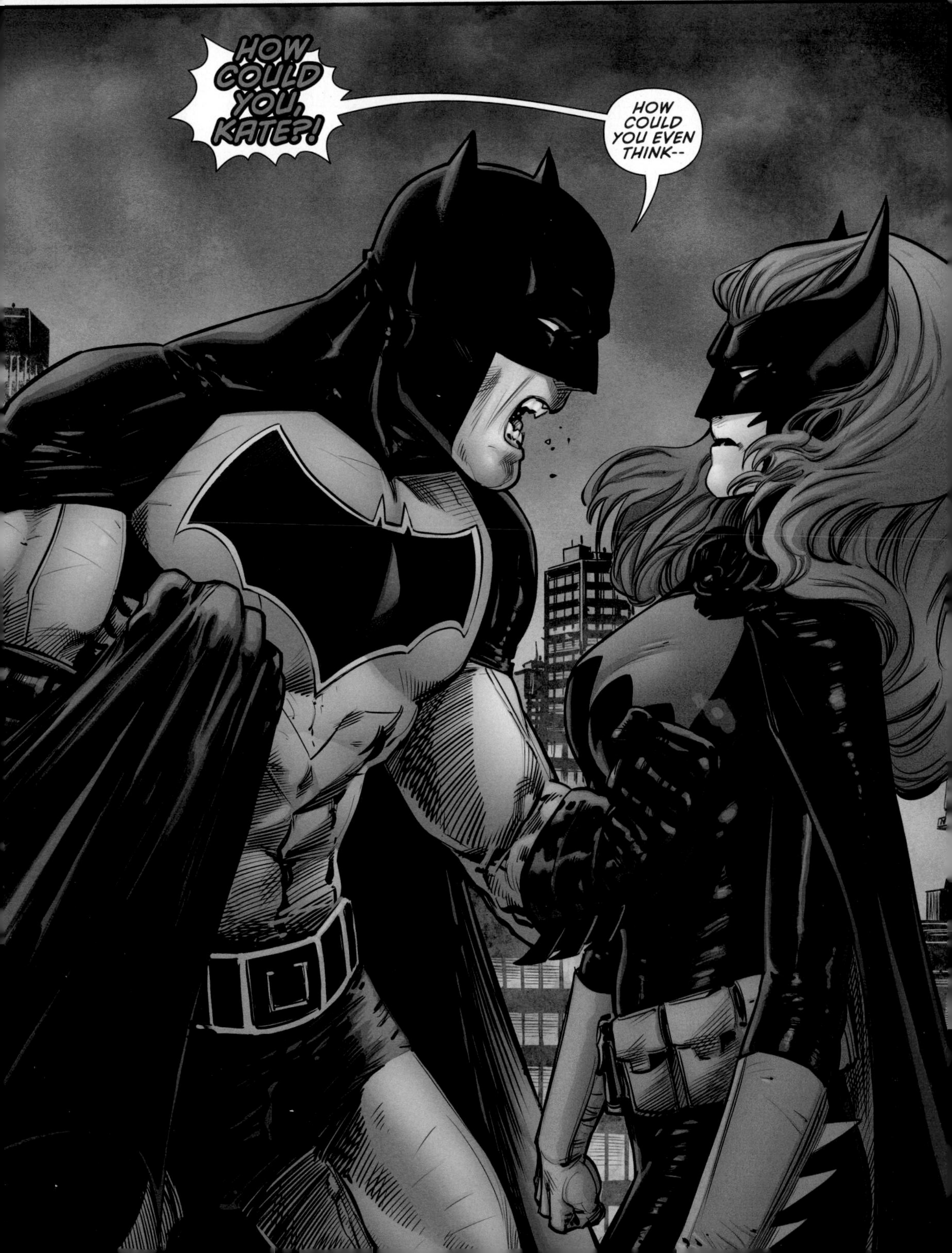
HOW COULD YOU, KATE?!
HOW COULD YOU EVEN THINK--

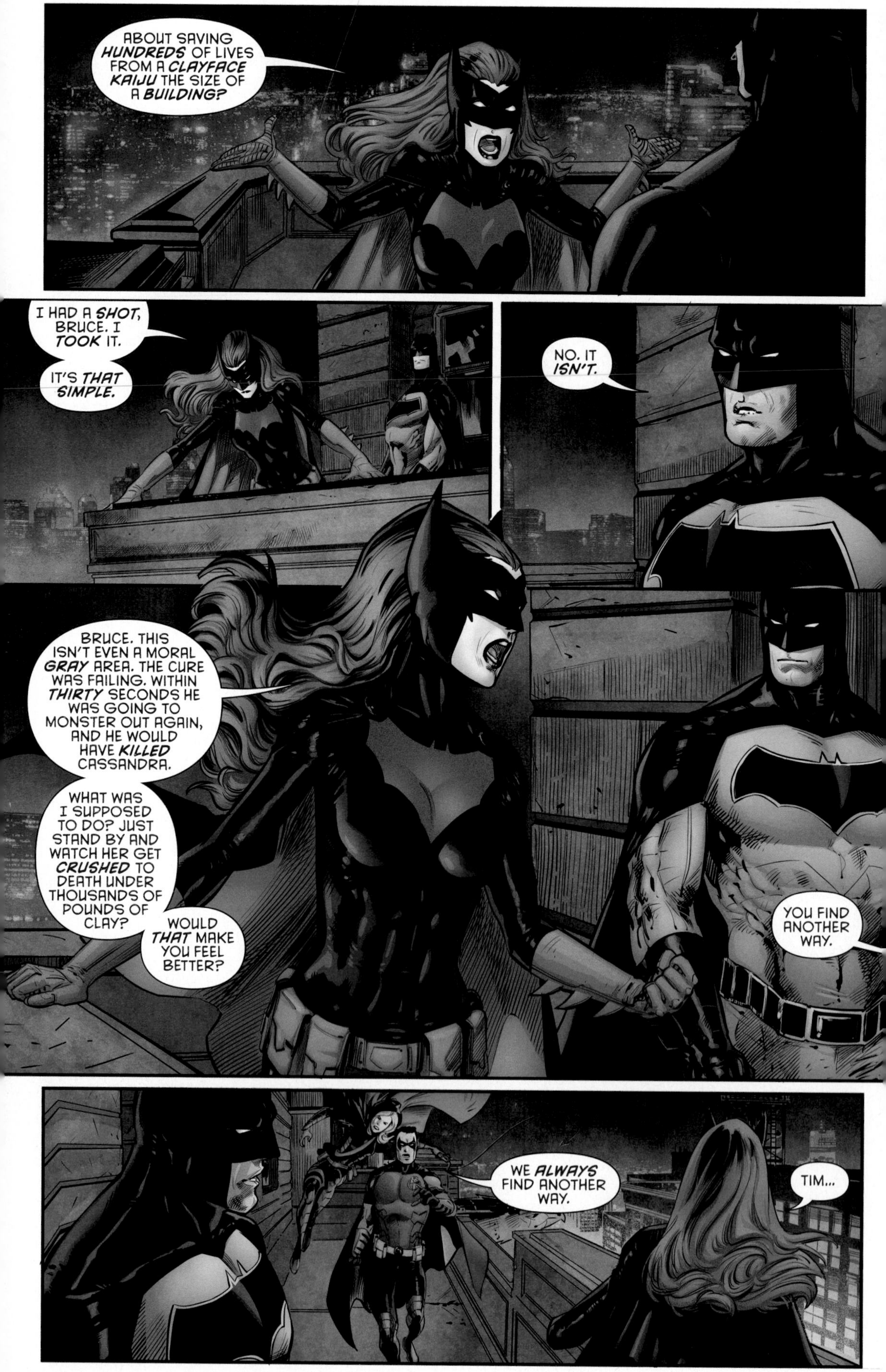
ABOUT SAVING HUNDREDS OF LIVES FROM A CLAYFACE KAIJU THE SIZE OF A BUILDING?
I HAD A SHOT, BRUCE. I TOOK IT.
IT'S THAT SIMPLE.
NO. IT ISN'T.
BRUCE. THIS ISN'T EVEN A MORAL GRAY AREA. THE CURE WAS FAILING. WITHIN THIRTY SECONDS HE WAS GOING TO MONSTER OUT AGAIN, AND HE WOULD HAVE KILLED CASSANDRA.
WHAT WAS I SUPPOSED TO DO? JUST STAND BY AND WATCH HER GET CRUSHED TO DEATH UNDER THOUSANDS OF POUNDS OF CLAY?
WOULD THAT MAKE YOU FEEL BETTER?
YOU FIND ANOTHER WAY.
WE ALWAYS FIND ANOTHER WAY.
TIM...

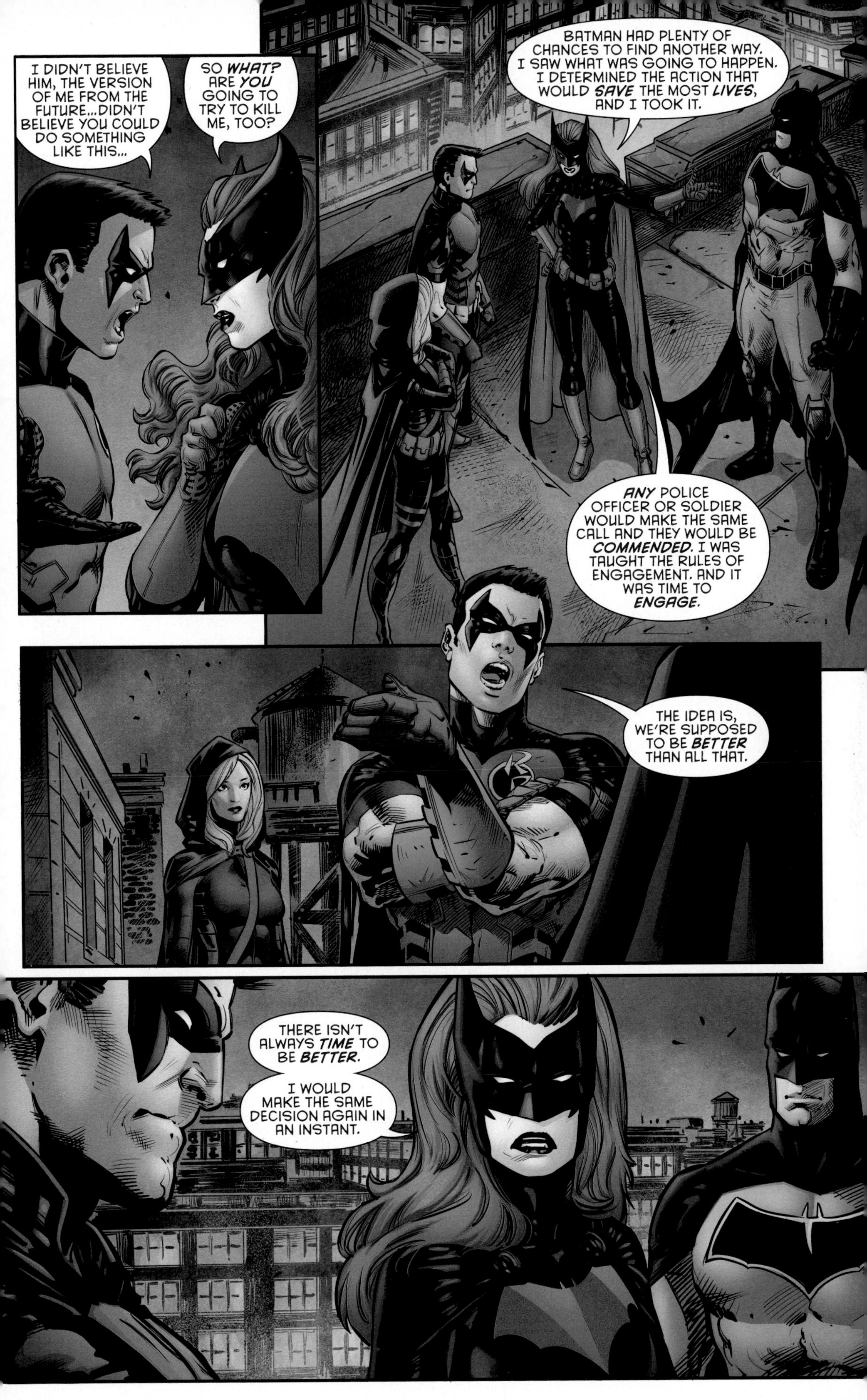
I DIDN'T BELIEVE HIM, THE VERSION OF ME FROM THE FUTURE...DIDN'T BELIEVE YOU COULD DO SOMETHING LIKE THIS...
SO *WHAT?* ARE *YOU* GOING TO TRY TO KILL ME, TOO?
BATMAN HAD PLENTY OF CHANCES TO FIND ANOTHER WAY. I SAW WHAT WAS GOING TO HAPPEN. I DETERMINED THE ACTION THAT WOULD *SAVE* THE MOST *LIVES*, AND I TOOK IT.
ANY POLICE OFFICER OR SOLDIER WOULD MAKE THE SAME CALL AND THEY WOULD BE *COMMENDED*. I WAS TAUGHT THE RULES OF ENGAGEMENT. AND IT WAS TIME TO *ENGAGE*.
THE IDEA IS, WE'RE SUPPOSED TO BE *BETTER* THAN ALL THAT.
THERE ISN'T ALWAYS *TIME* TO BE *BETTER*.
I WOULD MAKE THE SAME DECISION AGAIN IN AN INSTANT.

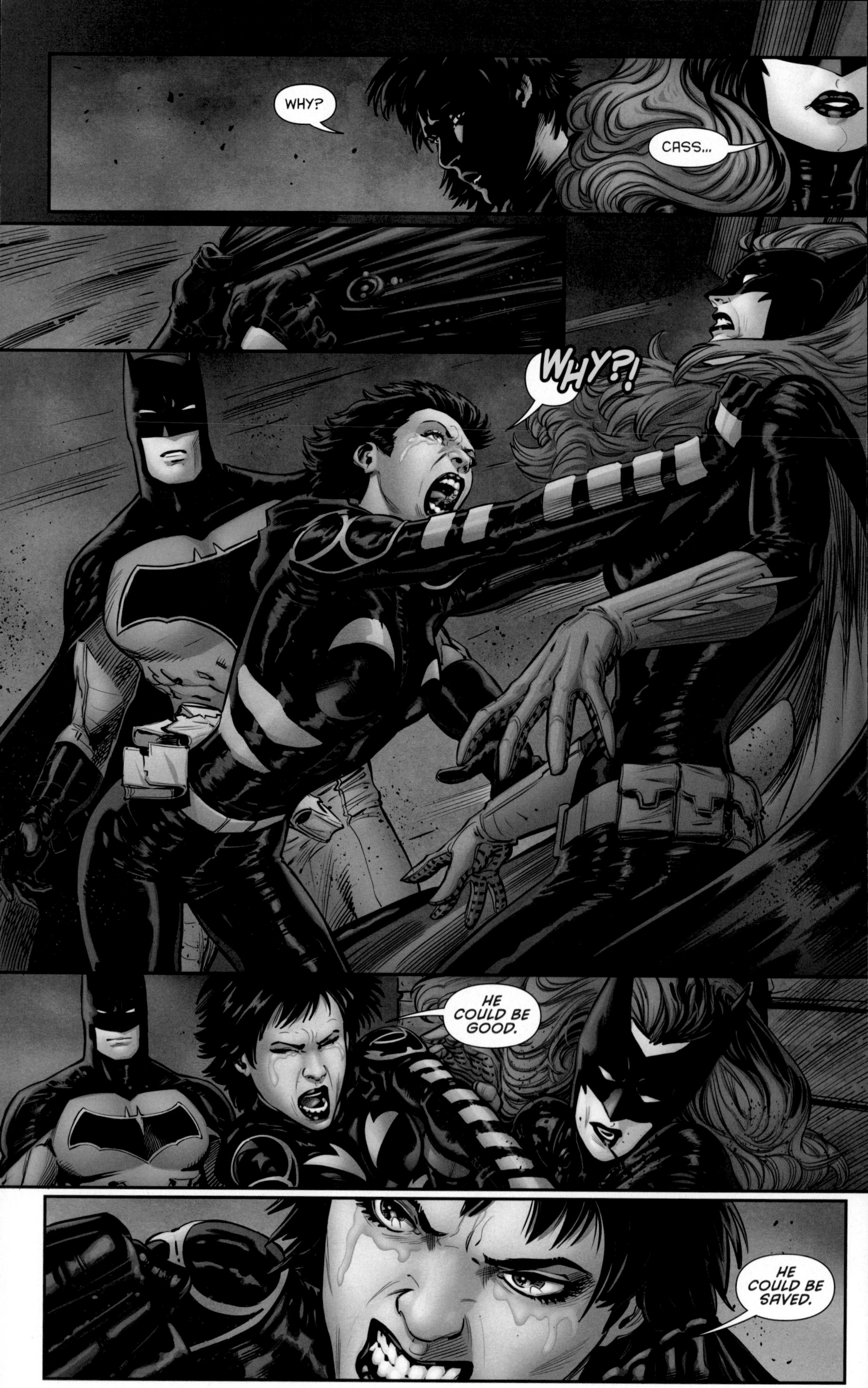
WHY?
CASS...
WHY?!
HE COULD BE GOOD.
HE COULD BE SAVED.

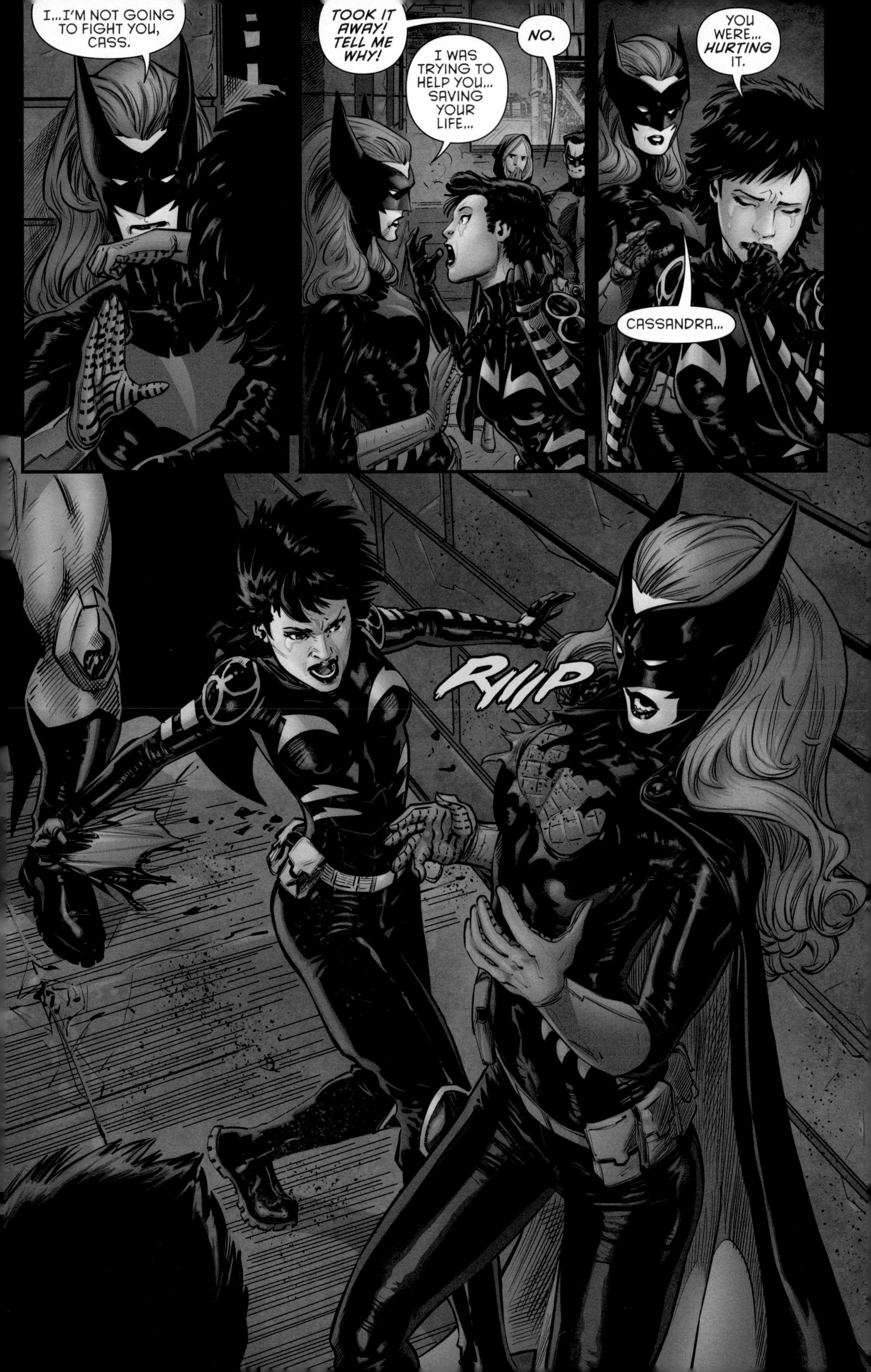
I...I'M NOT GOING TO FIGHT YOU, CASS.
TOOK IT AWAY! TELL ME WHY!
NO.
I WAS TRYING TO HELP YOU... SAVING YOUR LIFE...
YOU WERE... HURTING IT.
CASSANDRA...
RIIIP

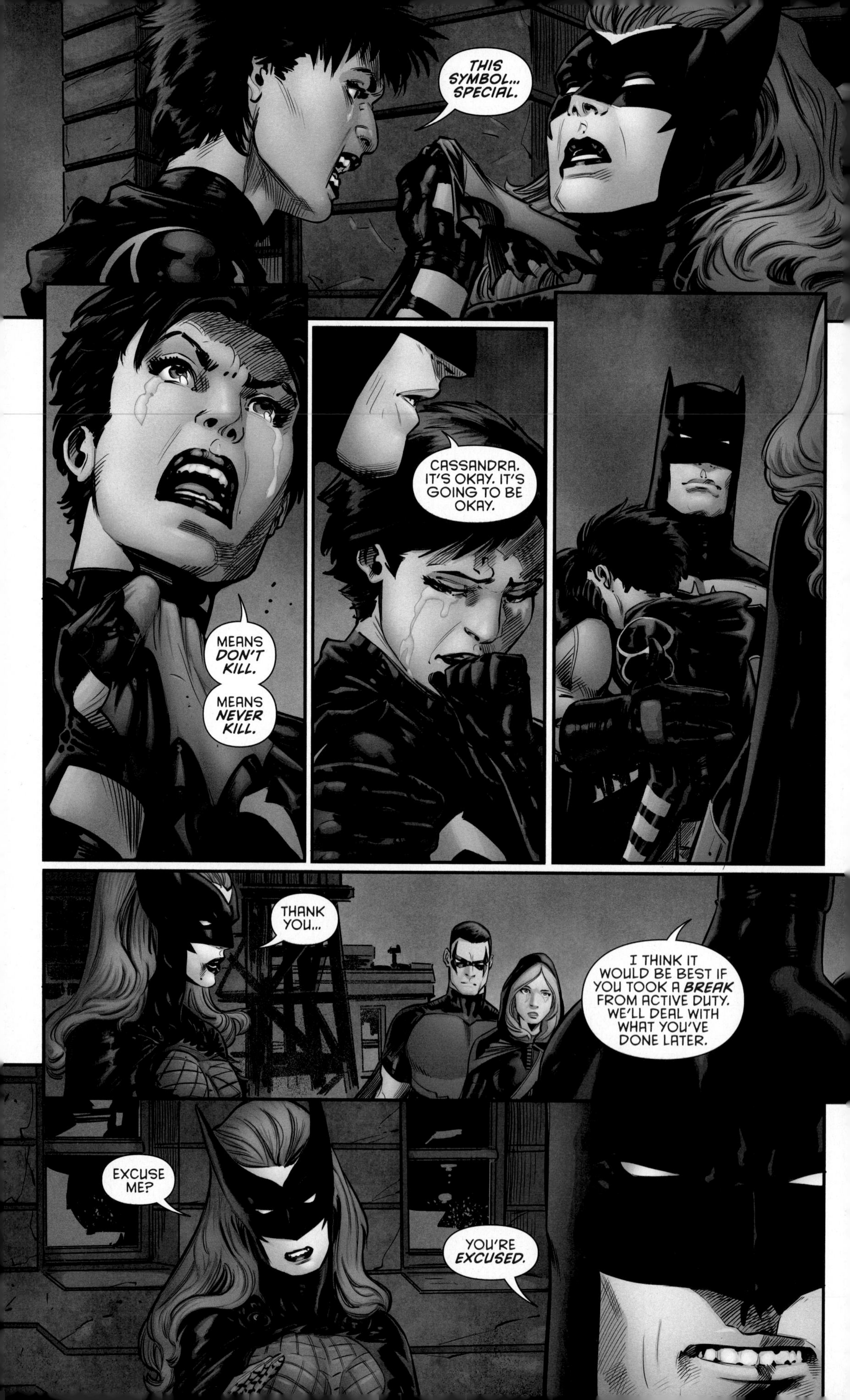
THIS SYMBOL... SPECIAL.
MEANS DON'T KILL.
MEANS NEVER KILL.
CASSANDRA. IT'S OKAY. IT'S GOING TO BE OKAY.
THANK YOU...
I THINK IT WOULD BE BEST IF YOU TOOK A BREAK FROM ACTIVE DUTY. WE'LL DEAL WITH WHAT YOU'VE DONE LATER.
EXCUSE ME?
YOU'RE EXCUSED.

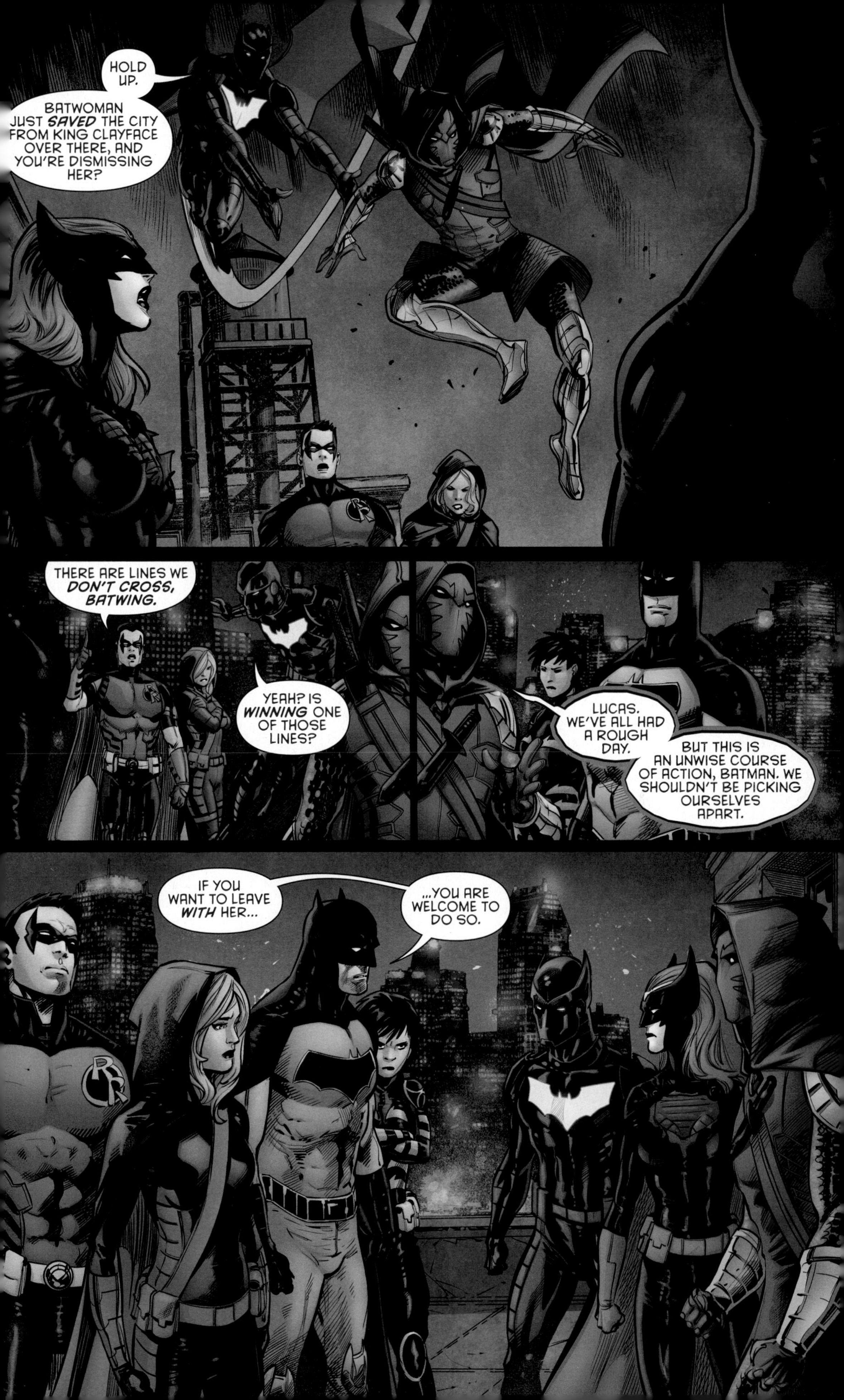
HOLD UP.
BATWOMAN JUST SAVED THE CITY FROM KING CLAYFACE OVER THERE, AND YOU'RE DISMISSING HER?
THERE ARE LINES WE DON'T CROSS, BATWING.
YEAH? IS WINNING ONE OF THOSE LINES?
LUCAS. WE'VE ALL HAD A ROUGH DAY.
BUT THIS IS AN UNWISE COURSE OF ACTION, BATMAN. WE SHOULDN'T BE PICKING OURSELVES APART.
IF YOU WANT TO LEAVE WITH HER...
...YOU ARE WELCOME TO DO SO.

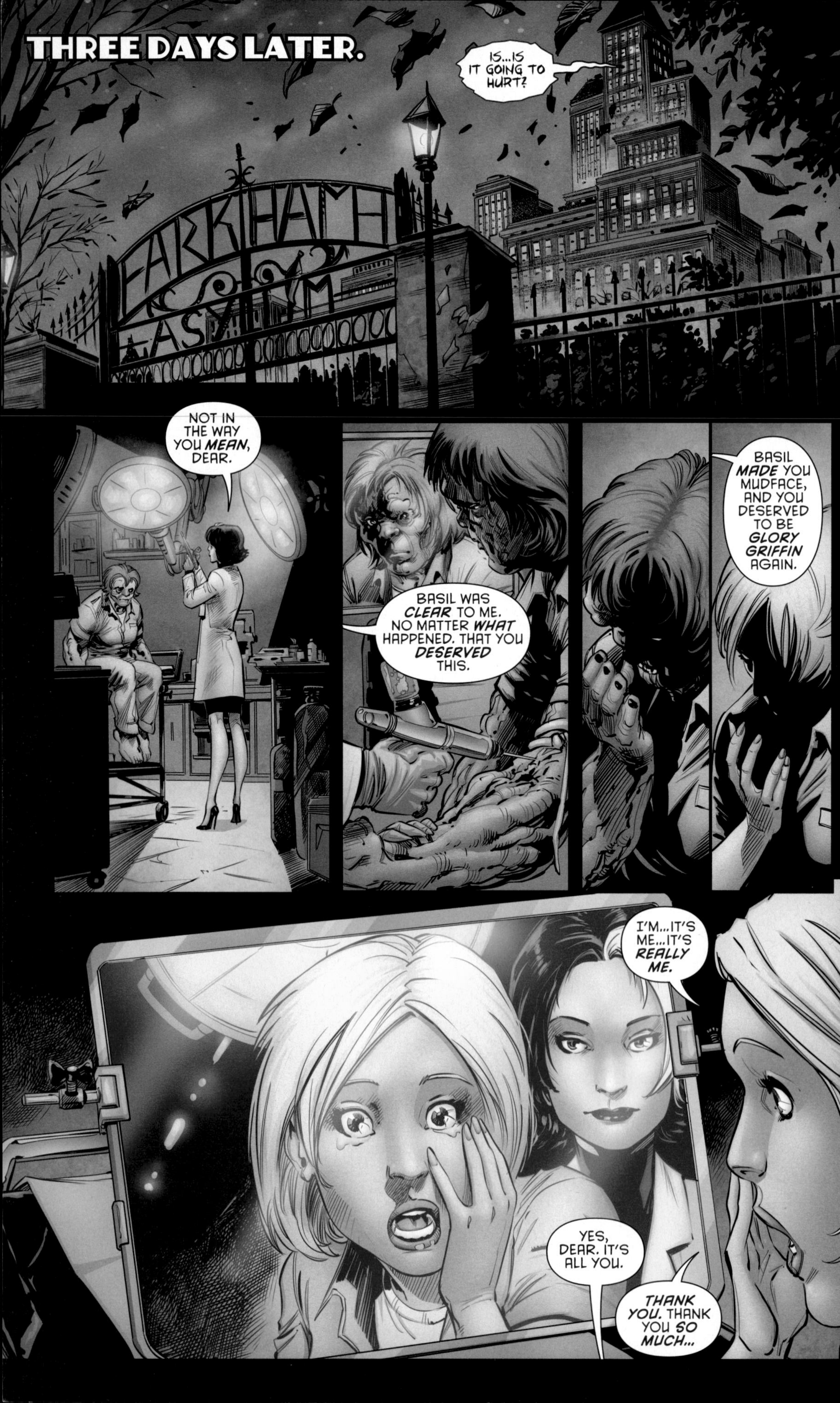
THREE DAYS LATER.
IS...IS IT GOING TO HURT?
ARKHAM ASYLUM
NOT IN THE WAY YOU MEAN, DEAR.
BASIL WAS CLEAR TO ME. NO MATTER WHAT HAPPENED. THAT YOU DESERVED THIS.
BASIL MADE YOU MUDFACE, AND YOU DESERVED TO BE GLORY GRIFFIN AGAIN.
I'M...IT'S ME...IT'S REALLY ME.
YES, DEAR. IT'S ALL YOU.
THANK YOU. THANK YOU SO MUCH...

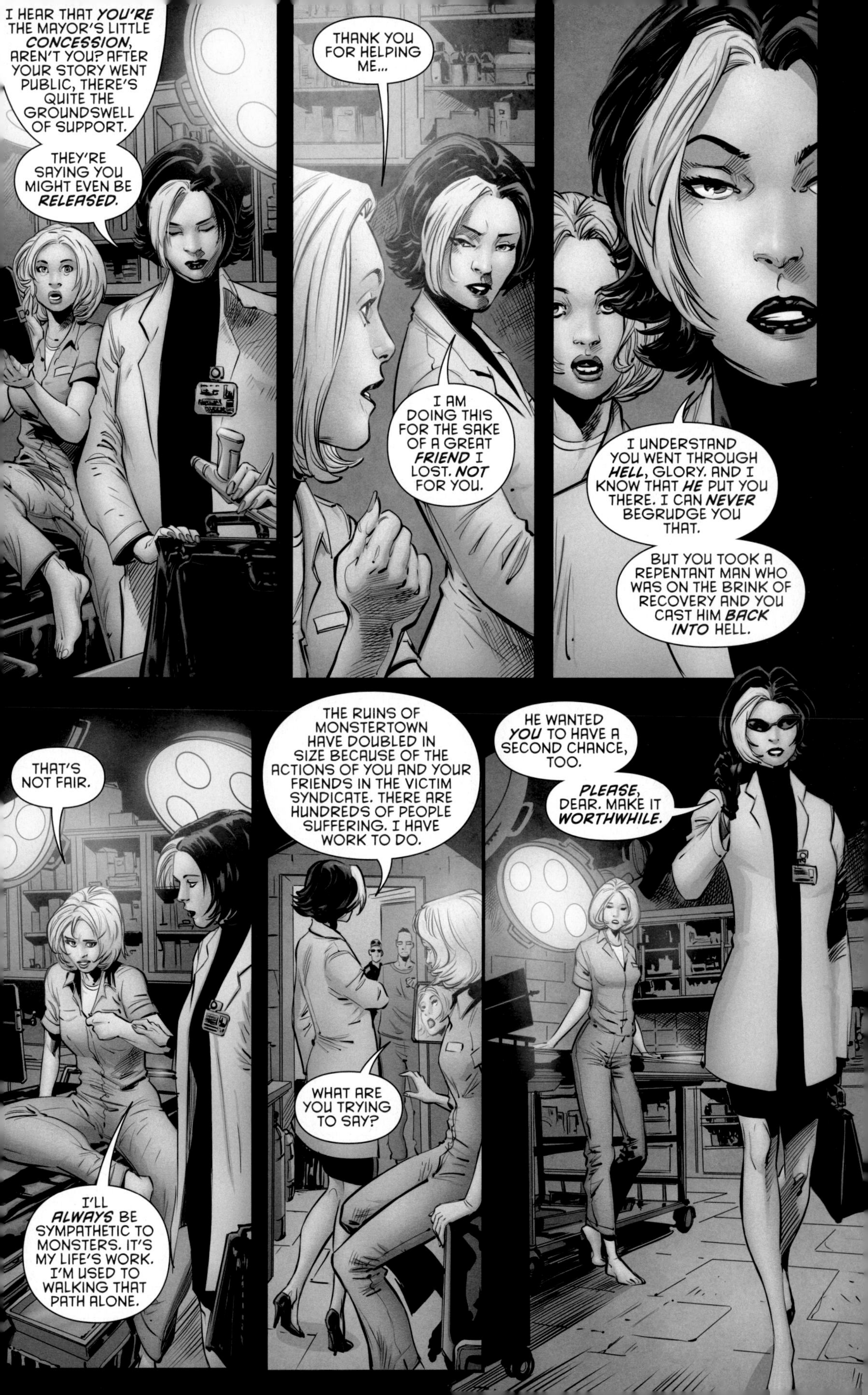
I HEAR THAT YOU'RE THE MAYOR'S LITTLE CONCESSION, AREN'T YOU? AFTER YOUR STORY WENT PUBLIC, THERE'S QUITE THE GROUNDSWELL OF SUPPORT.
THEY'RE SAYING YOU MIGHT EVEN BE RELEASED.
THANK YOU FOR HELPING ME...
I AM DOING THIS FOR THE SAKE OF A GREAT FRIEND I LOST. NOT FOR YOU.
I UNDERSTAND YOU WENT THROUGH HELL, GLORY. AND I KNOW THAT HE PUT YOU THERE. I CAN NEVER BEGRUDGE YOU THAT.
BUT YOU TOOK A REPENTANT MAN WHO WAS ON THE BRINK OF RECOVERY AND YOU CAST HIM BACK INTO HELL.
THAT'S NOT FAIR.
I'LL ALWAYS BE SYMPATHETIC TO MONSTERS. IT'S MY LIFE'S WORK. I'M USED TO WALKING THAT PATH ALONE.
THE RUINS OF MONSTERTOWN HAVE DOUBLED IN SIZE BECAUSE OF THE ACTIONS OF YOU AND YOUR FRIENDS IN THE VICTIM SYNDICATE. THERE ARE HUNDREDS OF PEOPLE SUFFERING. I HAVE WORK TO DO.
WHAT ARE YOU TRYING TO SAY?
HE WANTED YOU TO HAVE A SECOND CHANCE, TOO.
PLEASE, DEAR. MAKE IT WORTHWHILE.

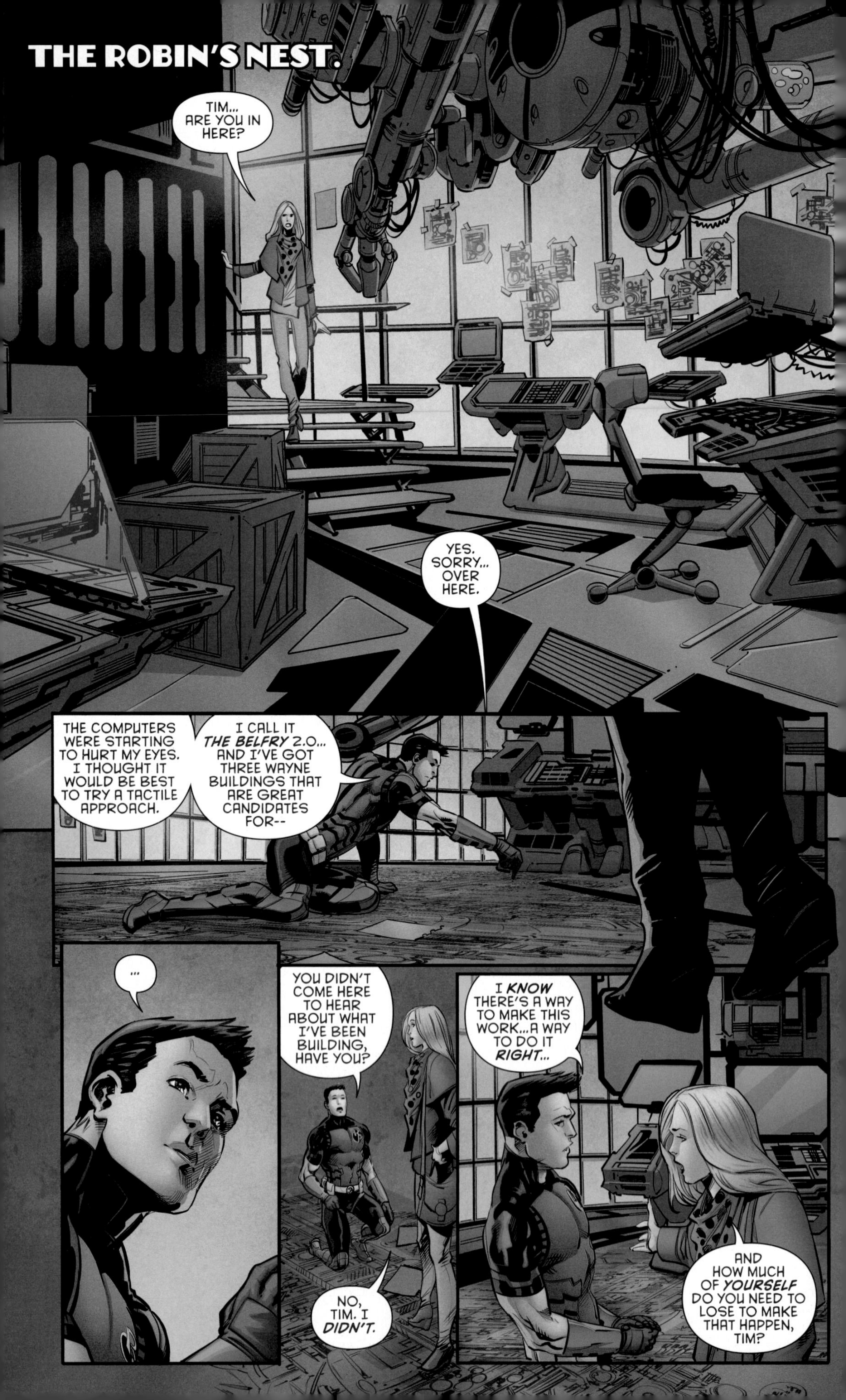
THE ROBIN'S NEST.
TIM... ARE YOU IN HERE?
YES. SORRY... OVER HERE.
THE COMPUTERS WERE STARTING TO HURT MY EYES. I THOUGHT IT WOULD BE BEST TO TRY A TACTILE APPROACH.
I CALL IT THE BELFRY 2.0... AND I'VE GOT THREE WAYNE BUILDINGS THAT ARE GREAT CANDIDATES FOR--
...
YOU DIDN'T COME HERE TO HEAR ABOUT WHAT I'VE BEEN BUILDING, HAVE YOU?
NO, TIM. I DIDN'T.
I KNOW THERE'S A WAY TO MAKE THIS WORK...A WAY TO DO IT RIGHT...
AND HOW MUCH OF YOURSELF DO YOU NEED TO LOSE TO MAKE THAT HAPPEN, TIM?

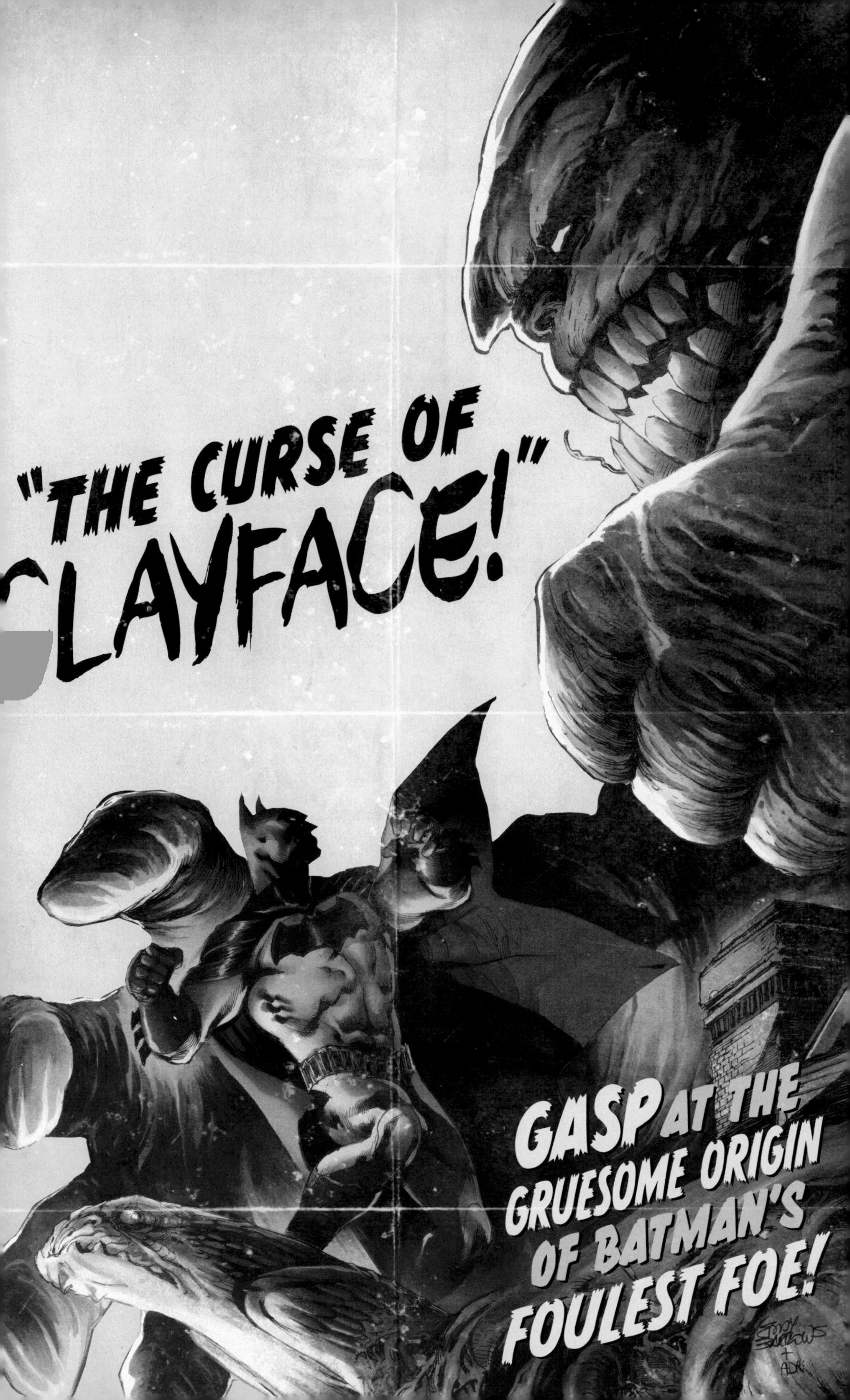
"THE CURSE OF
CLAYFACE!"
GASP AT THE
GRUESOME ORIGIN
OF BATMAN'S
FOULEST FOE!

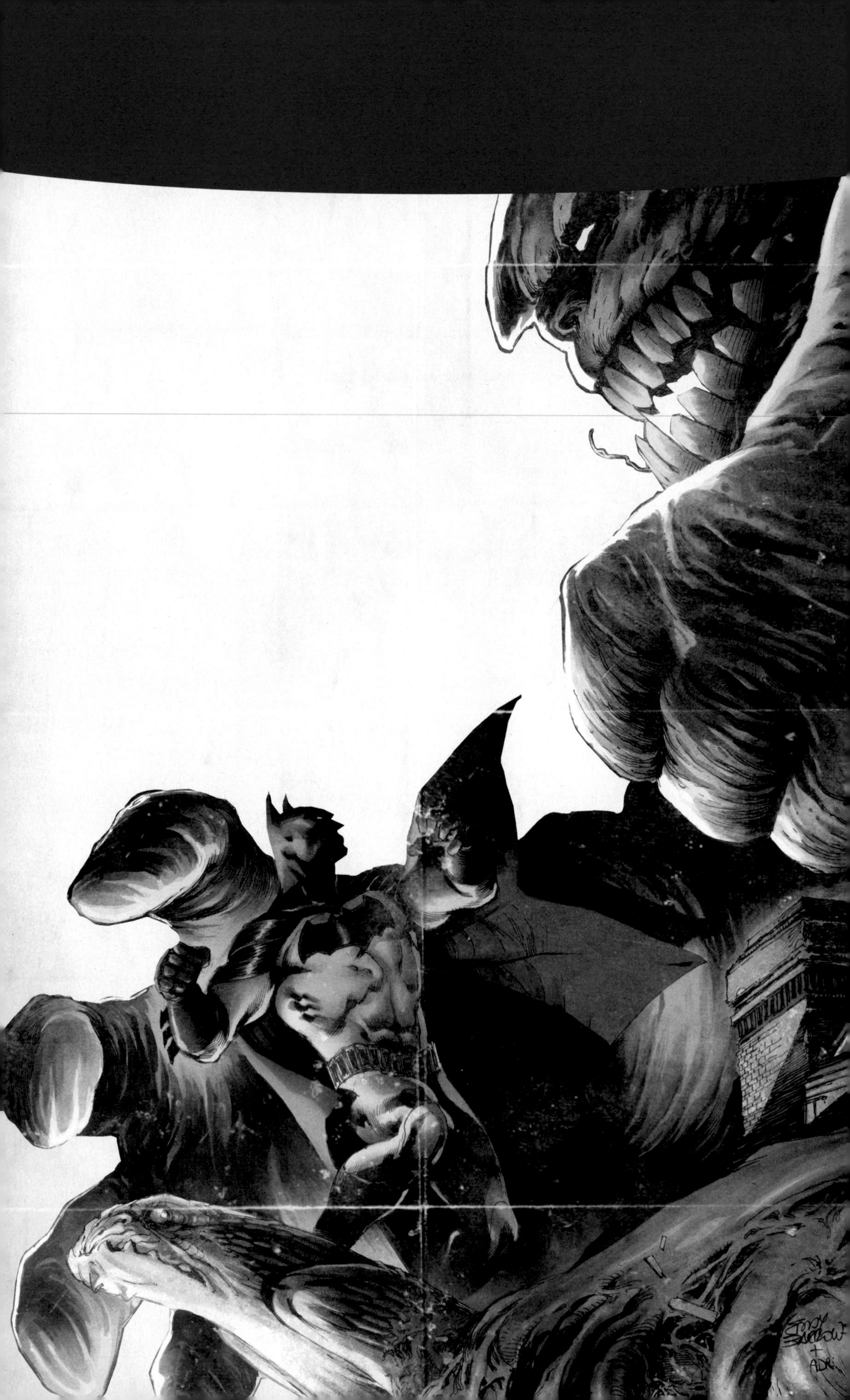

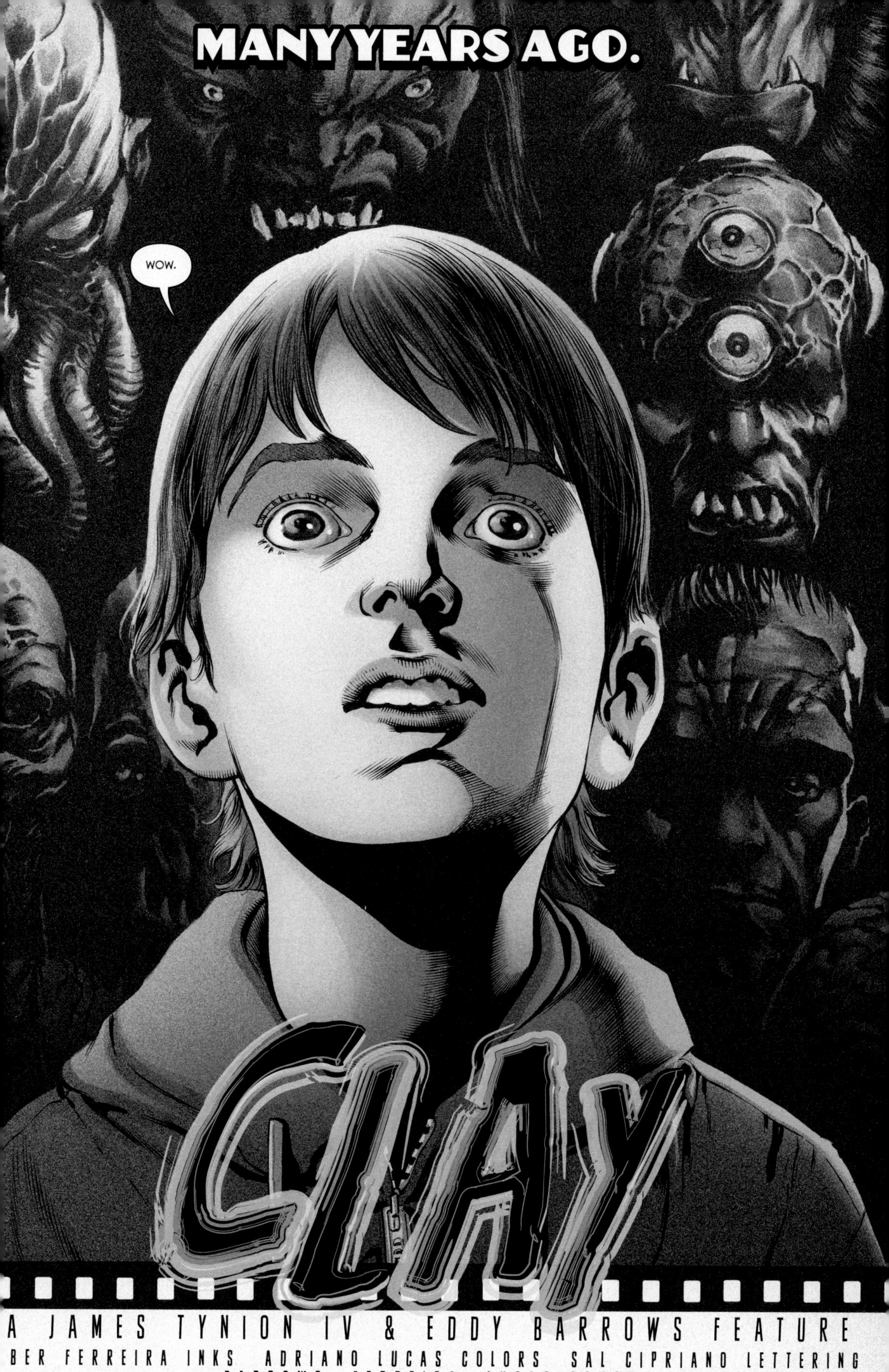
MANY YEARS AGO.
WOW.
CLAY

A JAMES TYNION IV & EDDY BARROWS FEATURE
BER FERREIRA INKS ADRIANO LUCAS COLORS SAL CIPRIANO LETTERING
BARROWS, FERREIRA, LUCAS COVER
DAVE WIELGOSZ ASST. EDITOR CHRIS CONROY EDITOR
JAMIE S. RICH GROUP EDITOR
BATMAN CREATED BY BOB KANE WITH BILL FINGER

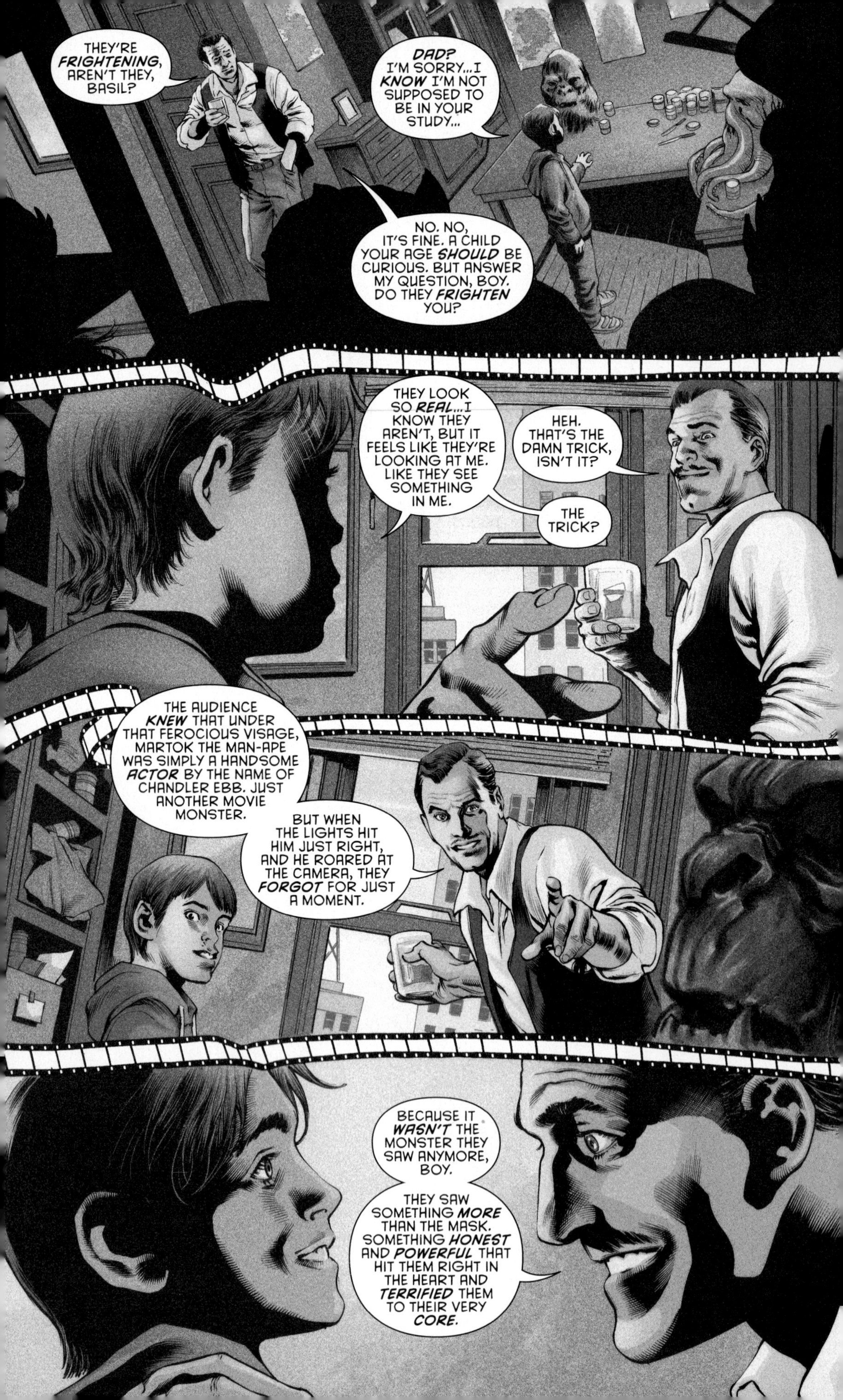

THEY'RE *FRIGHTENING*, AREN'T THEY, BASIL?
DAD? I'M SORRY...I *KNOW* I'M NOT SUPPOSED TO BE IN YOUR STUDY...
NO. NO, IT'S FINE. A CHILD YOUR AGE *SHOULD* BE CURIOUS. BUT ANSWER MY QUESTION, BOY. DO THEY *FRIGHTEN* YOU?
THEY LOOK SO *REAL*...I KNOW THEY AREN'T, BUT IT FEELS LIKE THEY'RE LOOKING AT ME. LIKE THEY SEE SOMETHING IN ME.
HEH. THAT'S THE DAMN TRICK, ISN'T IT?
THE TRICK?
THE AUDIENCE *KNEW* THAT UNDER THAT FEROCIOUS VISAGE, MARTOK THE MAN-APE WAS SIMPLY A HANDSOME *ACTOR* BY THE NAME OF CHANDLER EBB. JUST ANOTHER MOVIE MONSTER.
BUT WHEN THE LIGHTS HIT HIM JUST RIGHT, AND HE ROARED AT THE CAMERA, THEY *FORGOT* FOR JUST A MOMENT.
BECAUSE IT *WASN'T* THE MONSTER THEY SAW ANYMORE, BOY.
THEY SAW SOMETHING *MORE* THAN THE MASK. SOMETHING *HONEST* AND *POWERFUL* THAT HIT THEM RIGHT IN THE HEART AND *TERRIFIED* THEM TO THEIR VERY *CORE*.

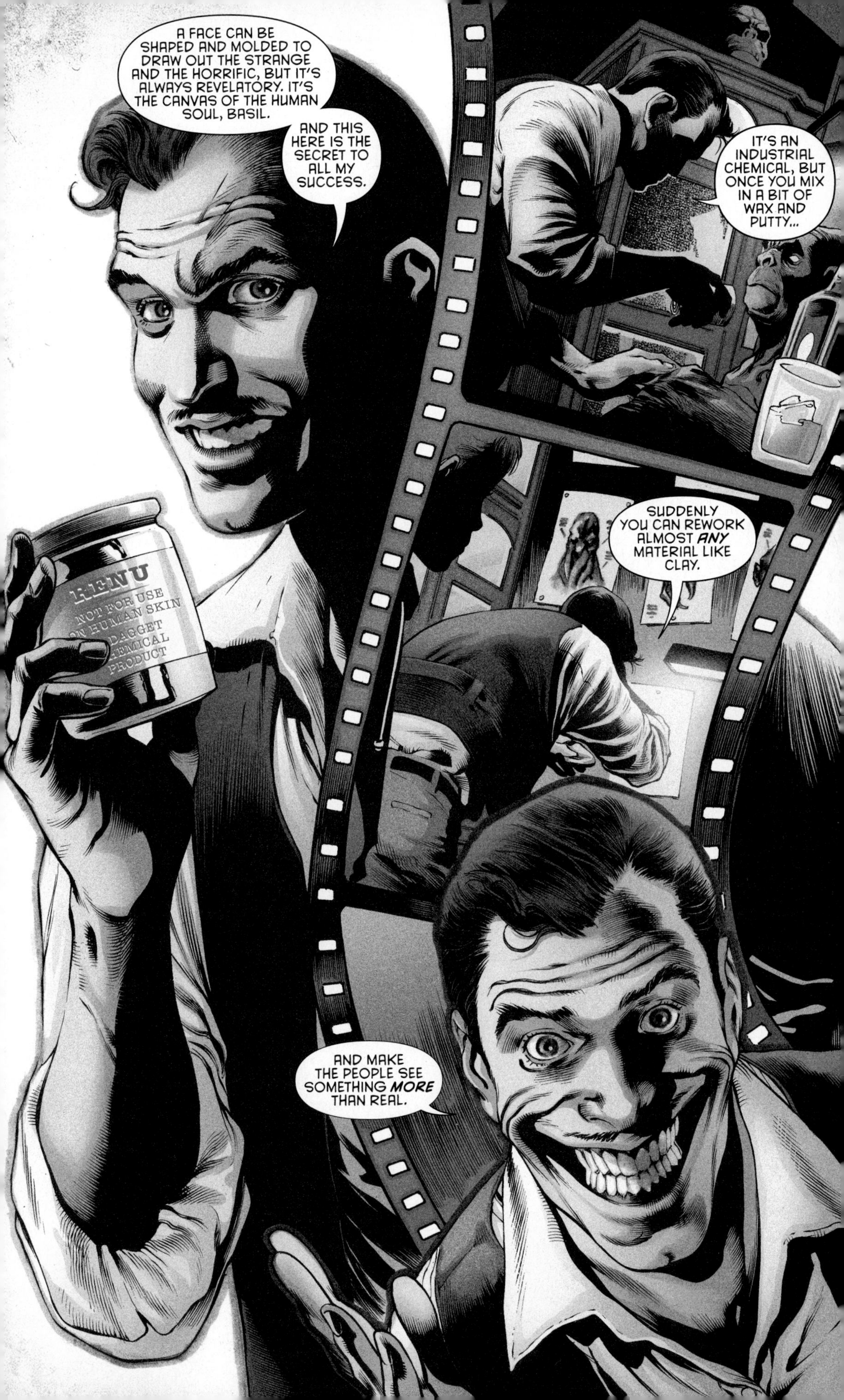
A FACE CAN BE SHAPED AND MOLDED TO DRAW OUT THE STRANGE AND THE HORRIFIC, BUT IT'S ALWAYS REVELATORY. IT'S THE CANVAS OF THE HUMAN SOUL, BASIL.
AND THIS HERE IS THE SECRET TO ALL MY SUCCESS.
IT'S AN INDUSTRIAL CHEMICAL, BUT ONCE YOU MIX IN A BIT OF WAX AND PUTTY...
RENU
NOT FOR USE ON HUMAN SKIN
DAGGET CHEMICAL PRODUCT
SUDDENLY YOU CAN REWORK ALMOST *ANY* MATERIAL LIKE CLAY.
AND MAKE THE PEOPLE SEE SOMETHING *MORE* THAN REAL.

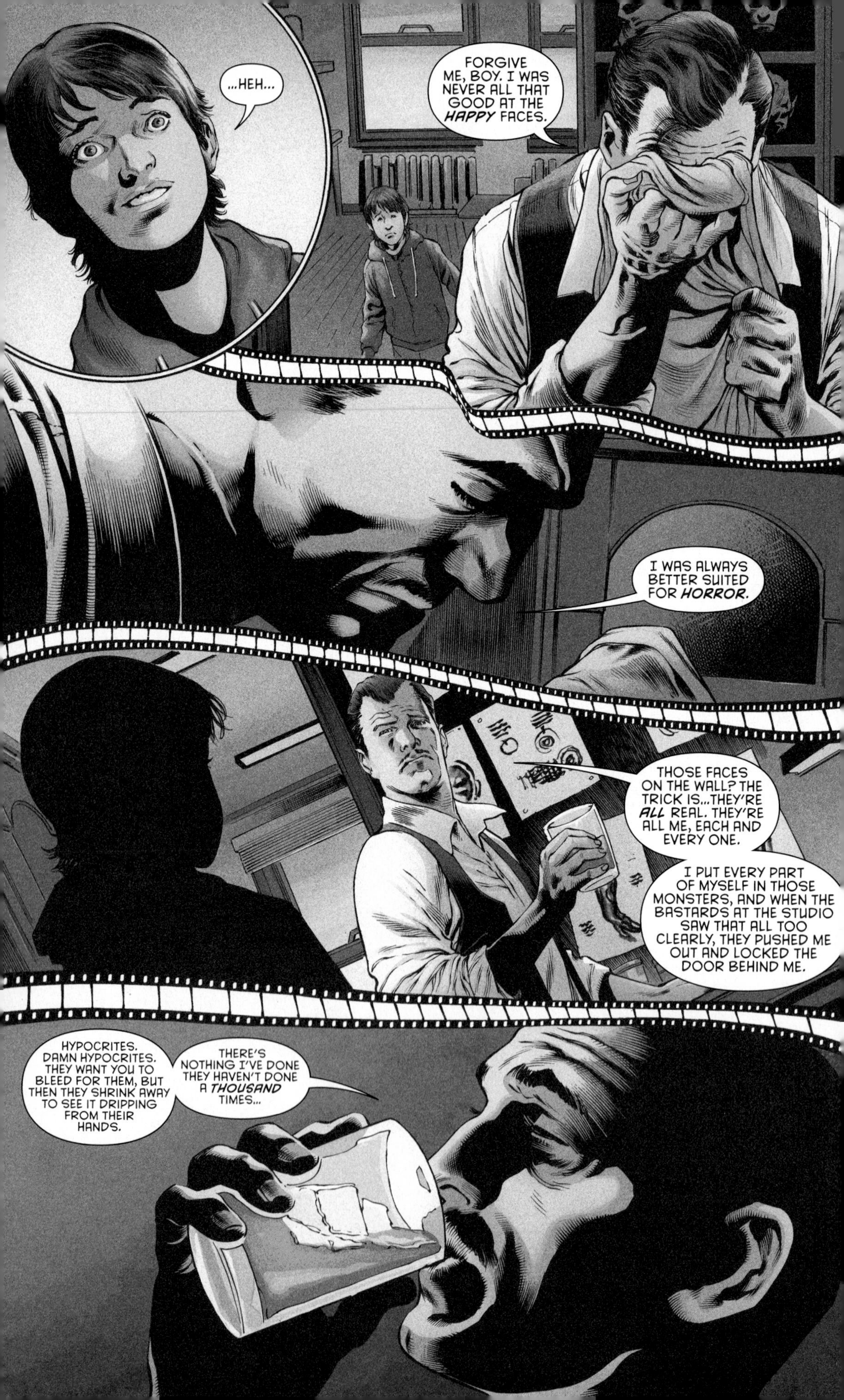
...HEH...
FORGIVE ME, BOY. I WAS NEVER ALL THAT GOOD AT THE HAPPY FACES.
I WAS ALWAYS BETTER SUITED FOR HORROR.
THOSE FACES ON THE WALL? THE TRICK IS...THEY'RE ALL REAL. THEY'RE ALL ME, EACH AND EVERY ONE.
I PUT EVERY PART OF MYSELF IN THOSE MONSTERS, AND WHEN THE BASTARDS AT THE STUDIO SAW THAT ALL TOO CLEARLY, THEY PUSHED ME OUT AND LOCKED THE DOOR BEHIND ME.
HYPOCRITES. DAMN HYPOCRITES. THEY WANT YOU TO BLEED FOR THEM, BUT THEN THEY SHRINK AWAY TO SEE IT DRIPPING FROM THEIR HANDS.
THERE'S NOTHING I'VE DONE THEY HAVEN'T DONE A THOUSAND TIMES...

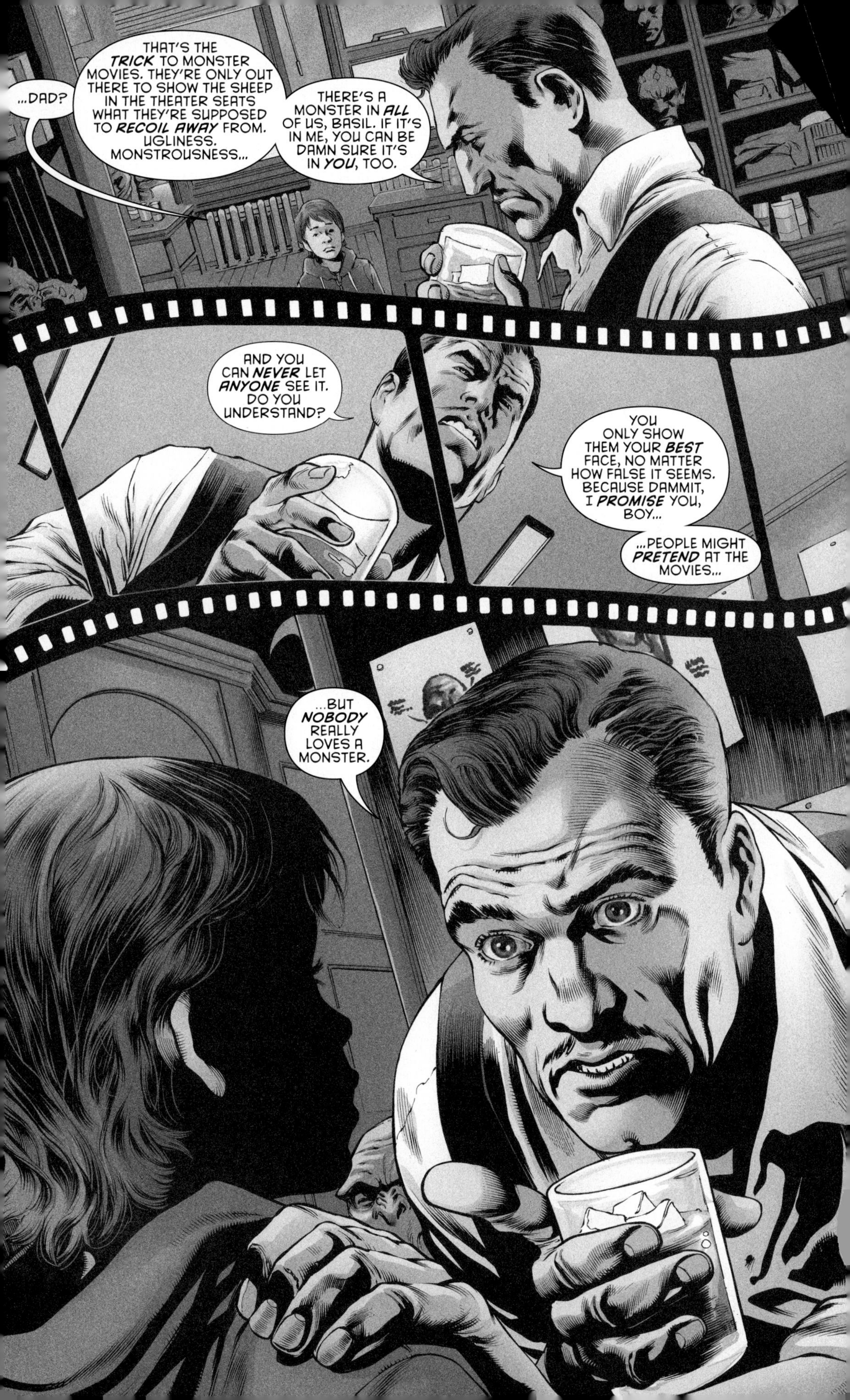
...DAD?
THAT'S THE TRICK TO MONSTER MOVIES. THEY'RE ONLY OUT THERE TO SHOW THE SHEEP IN THE THEATER SEATS WHAT THEY'RE SUPPOSED TO RECOIL AWAY FROM. UGLINESS. MONSTROUSNESS...
THERE'S A MONSTER IN ALL OF US, BASIL. IF IT'S IN ME, YOU CAN BE DAMN SURE IT'S IN YOU, TOO.
AND YOU CAN NEVER LET ANYONE SEE IT. DO YOU UNDERSTAND?
YOU ONLY SHOW THEM YOUR BEST FACE, NO MATTER HOW FALSE IT SEEMS. BECAUSE DAMMIT, I PROMISE YOU, BOY...
...PEOPLE MIGHT PRETEND AT THE MOVIES...
...BUT NOBODY REALLY LOVES A MONSTER.

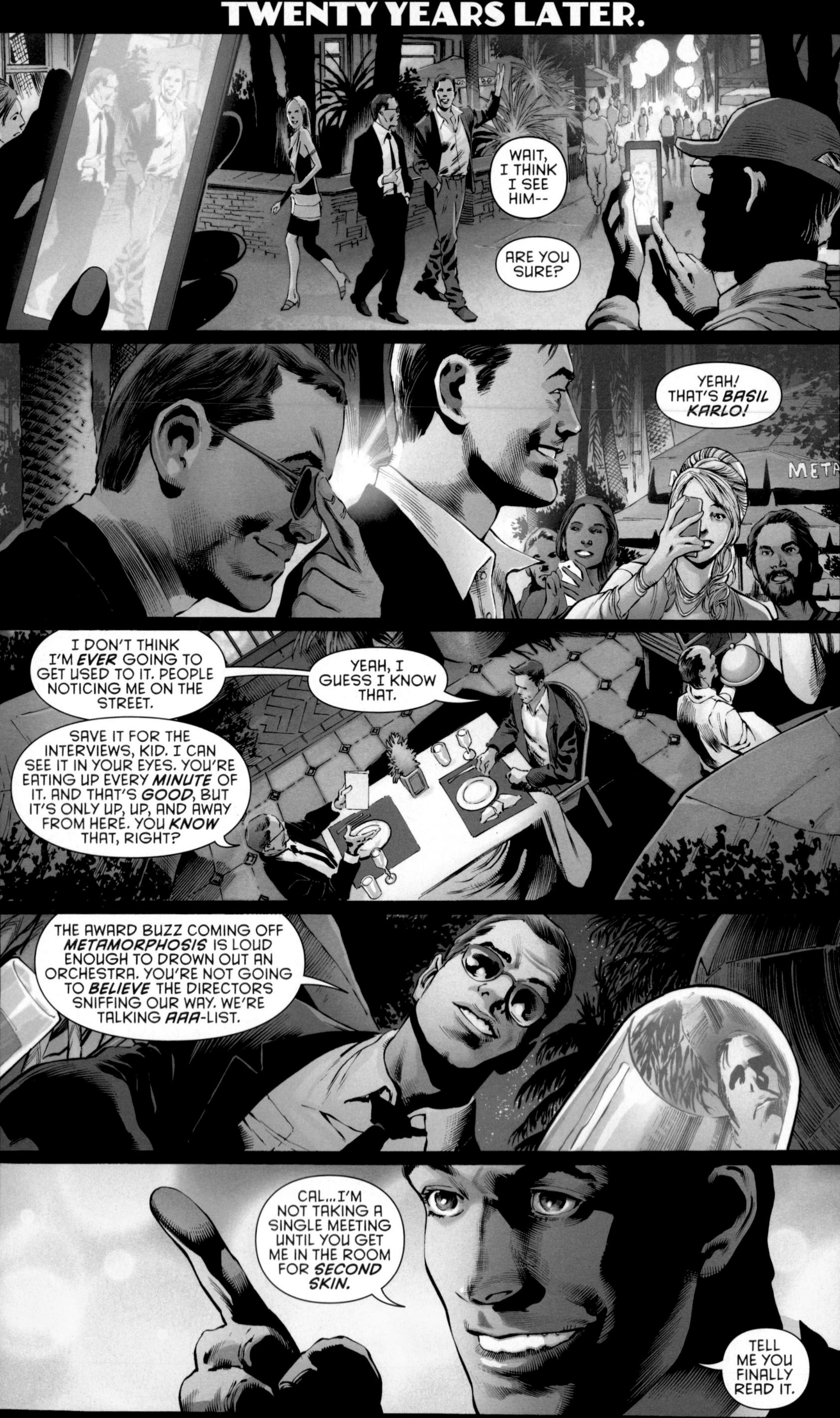
TWENTY YEARS LATER.
WAIT, I THINK I SEE HIM--
ARE YOU SURE?
YEAH! THAT'S BASIL KARLO!
I DON'T THINK I'M EVER GOING TO GET USED TO IT. PEOPLE NOTICING ME ON THE STREET.
YEAH, I GUESS I KNOW THAT.
SAVE IT FOR THE INTERVIEWS, KID. I CAN SEE IT IN YOUR EYES. YOU'RE EATING UP EVERY MINUTE OF IT. AND THAT'S GOOD, BUT IT'S ONLY UP, UP, AND AWAY FROM HERE. YOU KNOW THAT, RIGHT?
THE AWARD BUZZ COMING OFF METAMORPHOSIS IS LOUD ENOUGH TO DROWN OUT AN ORCHESTRA. YOU'RE NOT GOING TO BELIEVE THE DIRECTORS SNIFFING OUR WAY. WE'RE TALKING AAA-LIST.
CAL...I'M NOT TAKING A SINGLE MEETING UNTIL YOU GET ME IN THE ROOM FOR SECOND SKIN.
TELL ME YOU FINALLY READ IT.

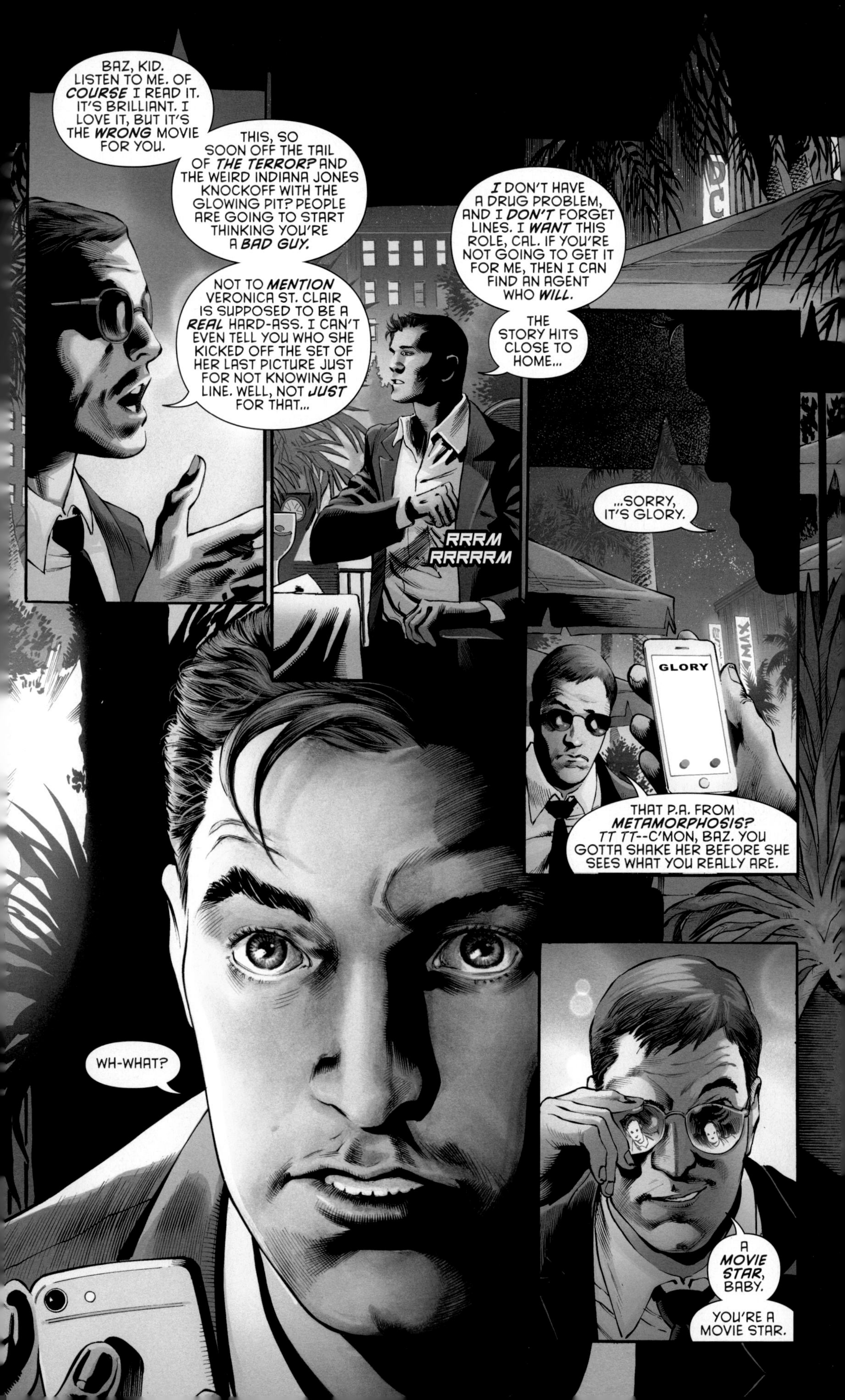

BAZ, KID. LISTEN TO ME. OF COURSE I READ IT. IT'S BRILLIANT. I LOVE IT, BUT IT'S THE WRONG MOVIE FOR YOU.
THIS, SO SOON OFF THE TAIL OF THE TERROR? AND THE WEIRD INDIANA JONES KNOCKOFF WITH THE GLOWING PIT? PEOPLE ARE GOING TO START THINKING YOU'RE A BAD GUY.
NOT TO MENTION VERONICA ST. CLAIR IS SUPPOSED TO BE A REAL HARD-ASS. I CAN'T EVEN TELL YOU WHO SHE KICKED OFF THE SET OF HER LAST PICTURE JUST FOR NOT KNOWING A LINE. WELL, NOT JUST FOR THAT...
I DON'T HAVE A DRUG PROBLEM, AND I DON'T FORGET LINES. I WANT THIS ROLE, CAL. IF YOU'RE NOT GOING TO GET IT FOR ME, THEN I CAN FIND AN AGENT WHO WILL.
THE STORY HITS CLOSE TO HOME...
RRRM RRRRRM
...SORRY, IT'S GLORY.
GLORY
THAT P.A. FROM METAMORPHOSIS? TT TT--C'MON, BAZ. YOU GOTTA SHAKE HER BEFORE SHE SEES WHAT YOU REALLY ARE.
WH-WHAT?
A MOVIE STAR, BABY.
YOU'RE A MOVIE STAR.

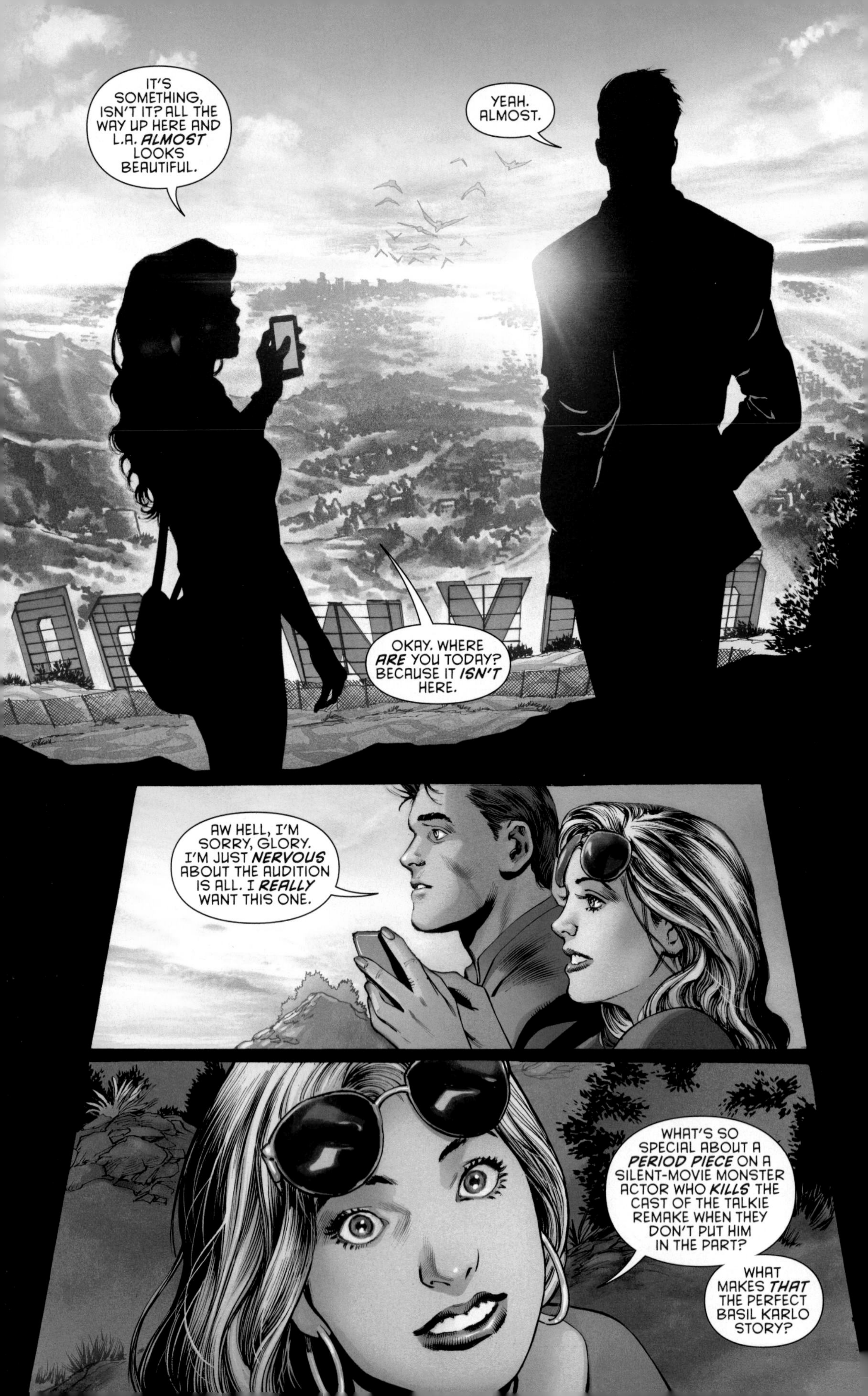

IT'S SOMETHING, ISN'T IT? ALL THE WAY UP HERE AND L.A. *ALMOST* LOOKS BEAUTIFUL.
YEAH. ALMOST.
OKAY. WHERE *ARE* YOU TODAY? BECAUSE IT *ISN'T* HERE.
AW HELL, I'M SORRY, GLORY. I'M JUST *NERVOUS* ABOUT THE AUDITION IS ALL. I *REALLY* WANT THIS ONE.
WHAT'S SO SPECIAL ABOUT A *PERIOD PIECE* ON A SILENT-MOVIE MONSTER ACTOR WHO *KILLS* THE CAST OF THE TALKIE REMAKE WHEN THEY DON'T PUT HIM IN THE PART?
WHAT MAKES *THAT* THE PERFECT BASIL KARLO STORY?

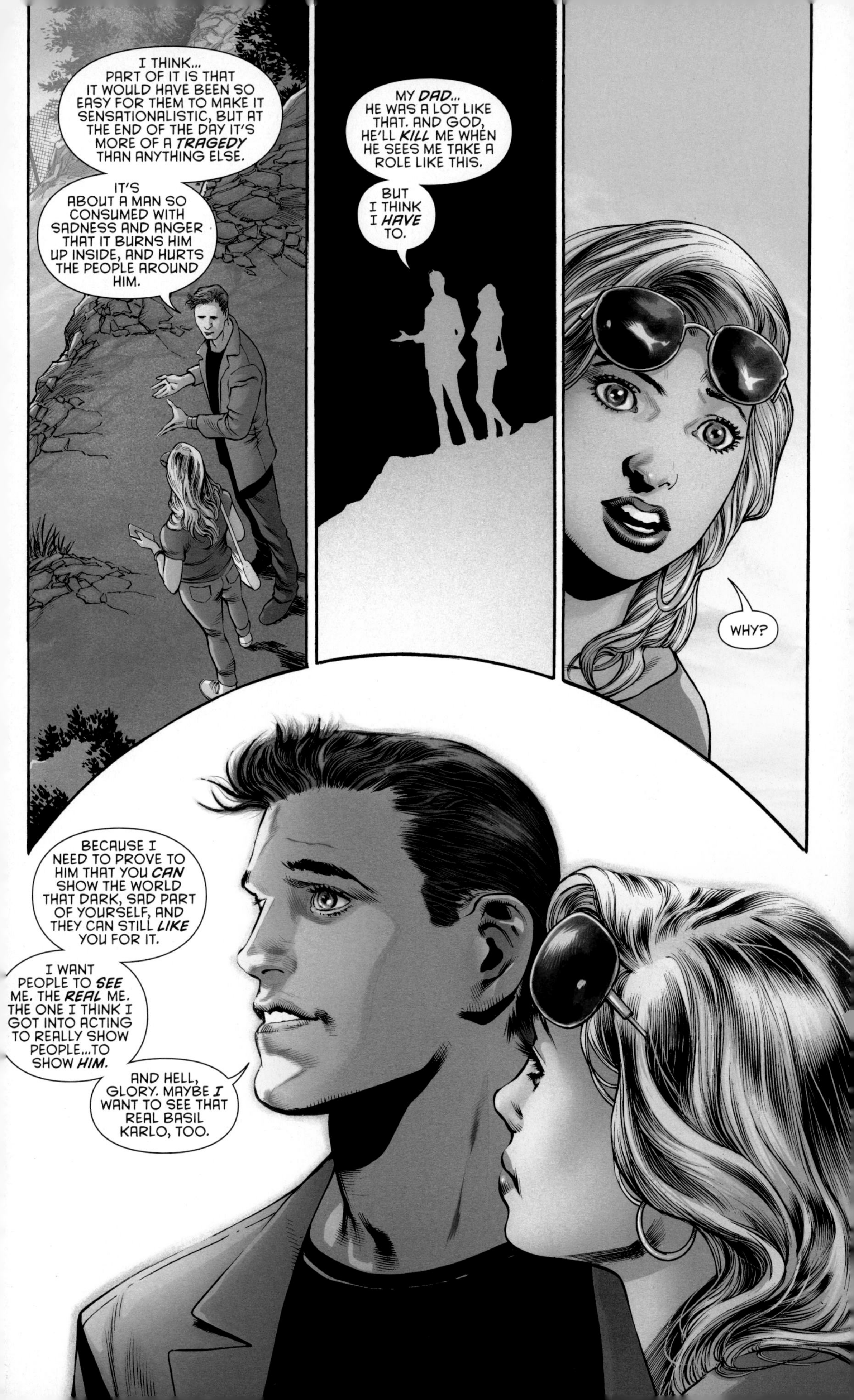
I THINK... PART OF IT IS THAT IT WOULD HAVE BEEN SO EASY FOR THEM TO MAKE IT SENSATIONALISTIC, BUT AT THE END OF THE DAY IT'S MORE OF A TRAGEDY THAN ANYTHING ELSE.
IT'S ABOUT A MAN SO CONSUMED WITH SADNESS AND ANGER THAT IT BURNS HIM UP INSIDE, AND HURTS THE PEOPLE AROUND HIM.
MY DAD... HE WAS A LOT LIKE THAT. AND GOD, HE'LL KILL ME WHEN HE SEES ME TAKE A ROLE LIKE THIS.
BUT I THINK I HAVE TO.
WHY?
BECAUSE I NEED TO PROVE TO HIM THAT YOU CAN SHOW THE WORLD THAT DARK, SAD PART OF YOURSELF, AND THEY CAN STILL LIKE YOU FOR IT.
I WANT PEOPLE TO SEE ME. THE REAL ME. THE ONE I THINK I GOT INTO ACTING TO REALLY SHOW PEOPLE...TO SHOW HIM.
AND HELL, GLORY. MAYBE I WANT TO SEE THAT REAL BASIL KARLO, TOO.

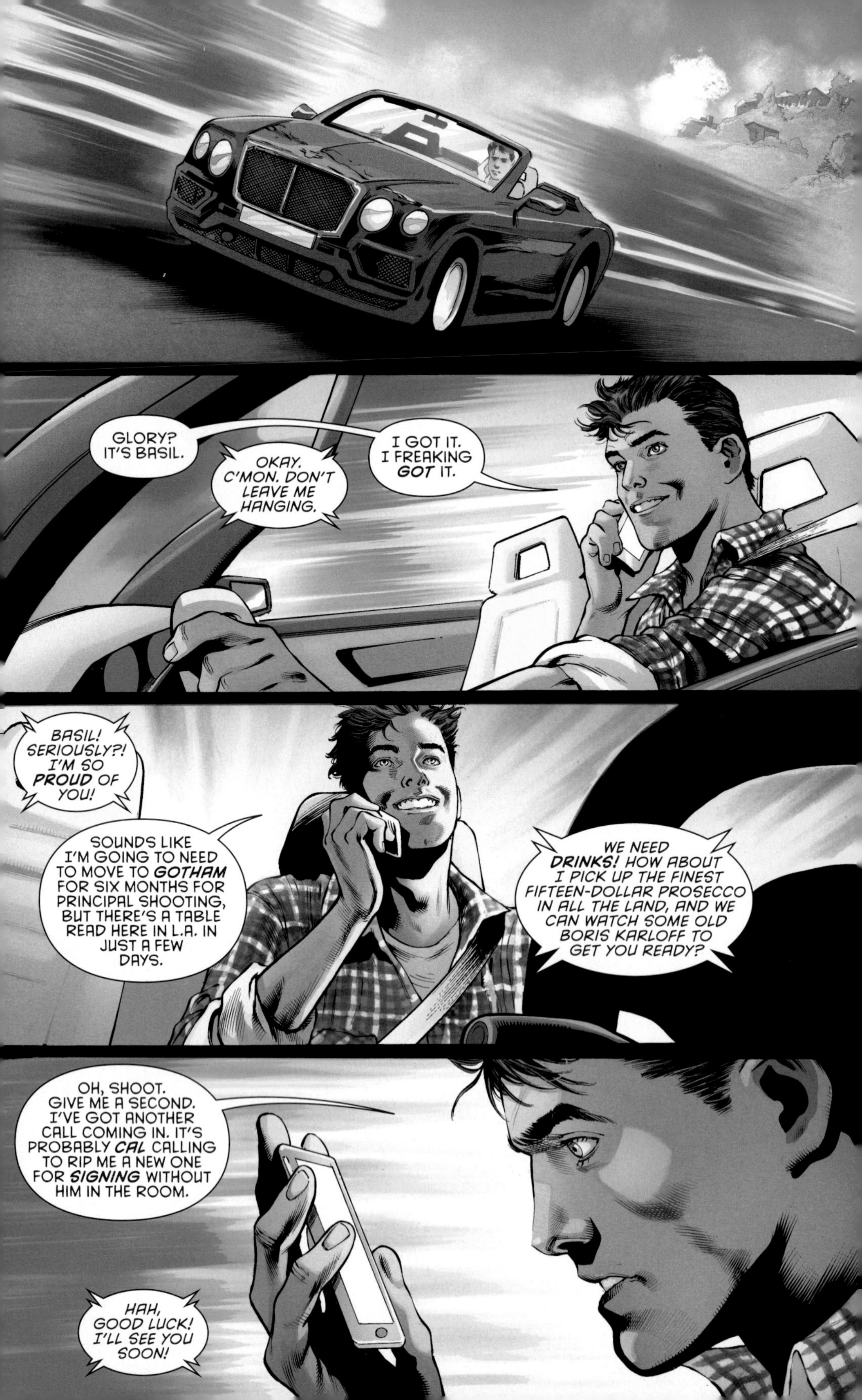
GLORY? IT'S BASIL.
OKAY. C'MON. DON'T LEAVE ME HANGING.
I GOT IT. I FREAKING GOT IT.
BASIL! SERIOUSLY?! I'M SO PROUD OF YOU!
SOUNDS LIKE I'M GOING TO NEED TO MOVE TO GOTHAM FOR SIX MONTHS FOR PRINCIPAL SHOOTING, BUT THERE'S A TABLE READ HERE IN L.A. IN JUST A FEW DAYS.
WE NEED DRINKS! HOW ABOUT I PICK UP THE FINEST FIFTEEN-DOLLAR PROSECCO IN ALL THE LAND, AND WE CAN WATCH SOME OLD BORIS KARLOFF TO GET YOU READY?
OH, SHOOT. GIVE ME A SECOND. I'VE GOT ANOTHER CALL COMING IN. IT'S PROBABLY CAL CALLING TO RIP ME A NEW ONE FOR SIGNING WITHOUT HIM IN THE ROOM.
HAH, GOOD LUCK! I'LL SEE YOU SOON!

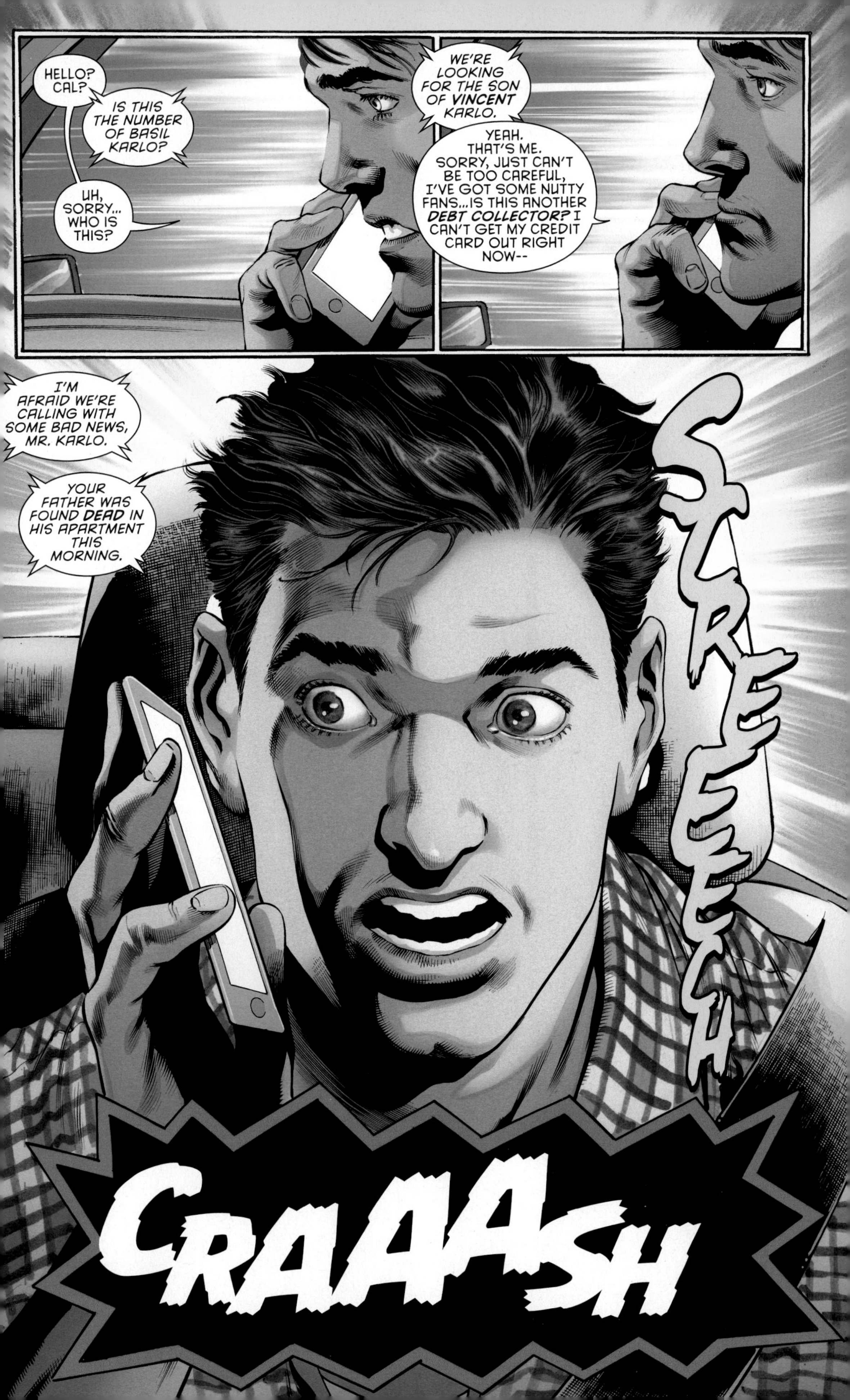
HELLO? CAL?
IS THIS THE NUMBER OF BASIL KARLO?
UH, SORRY... WHO IS THIS?
WE'RE LOOKING FOR THE SON OF VINCENT KARLO.
YEAH. THAT'S ME. SORRY, JUST CAN'T BE TOO CAREFUL, I'VE GOT SOME NUTTY FANS...IS THIS ANOTHER DEBT COLLECTOR? I CAN'T GET MY CREDIT CARD OUT RIGHT NOW--
I'M AFRAID WE'RE CALLING WITH SOME BAD NEWS, MR. KARLO.
YOUR FATHER WAS FOUND DEAD IN HIS APARTMENT THIS MORNING.
SCREEECH
CRAAASH

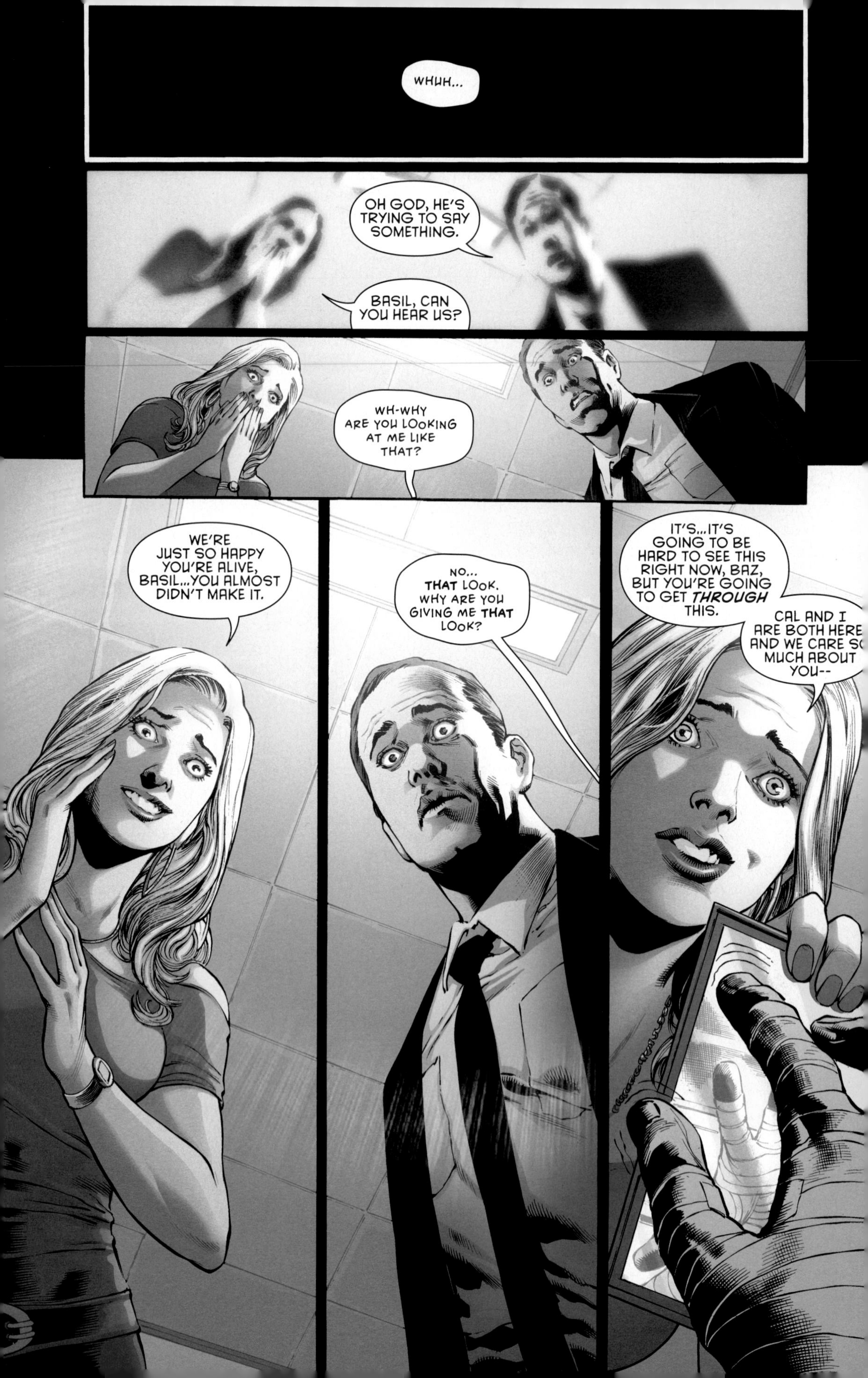
WHUH...
OH GOD, HE'S TRYING TO SAY SOMETHING.
BASIL, CAN YOU HEAR US?
WH-WHY ARE YOU LOOKING AT ME LIKE THAT?
WE'RE JUST SO HAPPY YOU'RE ALIVE, BASIL...YOU ALMOST DIDN'T MAKE IT.
NO... THAT LOOK. WHY ARE YOU GIVING ME THAT LOOK?
IT'S...IT'S GOING TO BE HARD TO SEE THIS RIGHT NOW, BAZ, BUT YOU'RE GOING TO GET THROUGH THIS.
CAL AND I ARE BOTH HERE AND WE CARE SO MUCH ABOUT YOU--

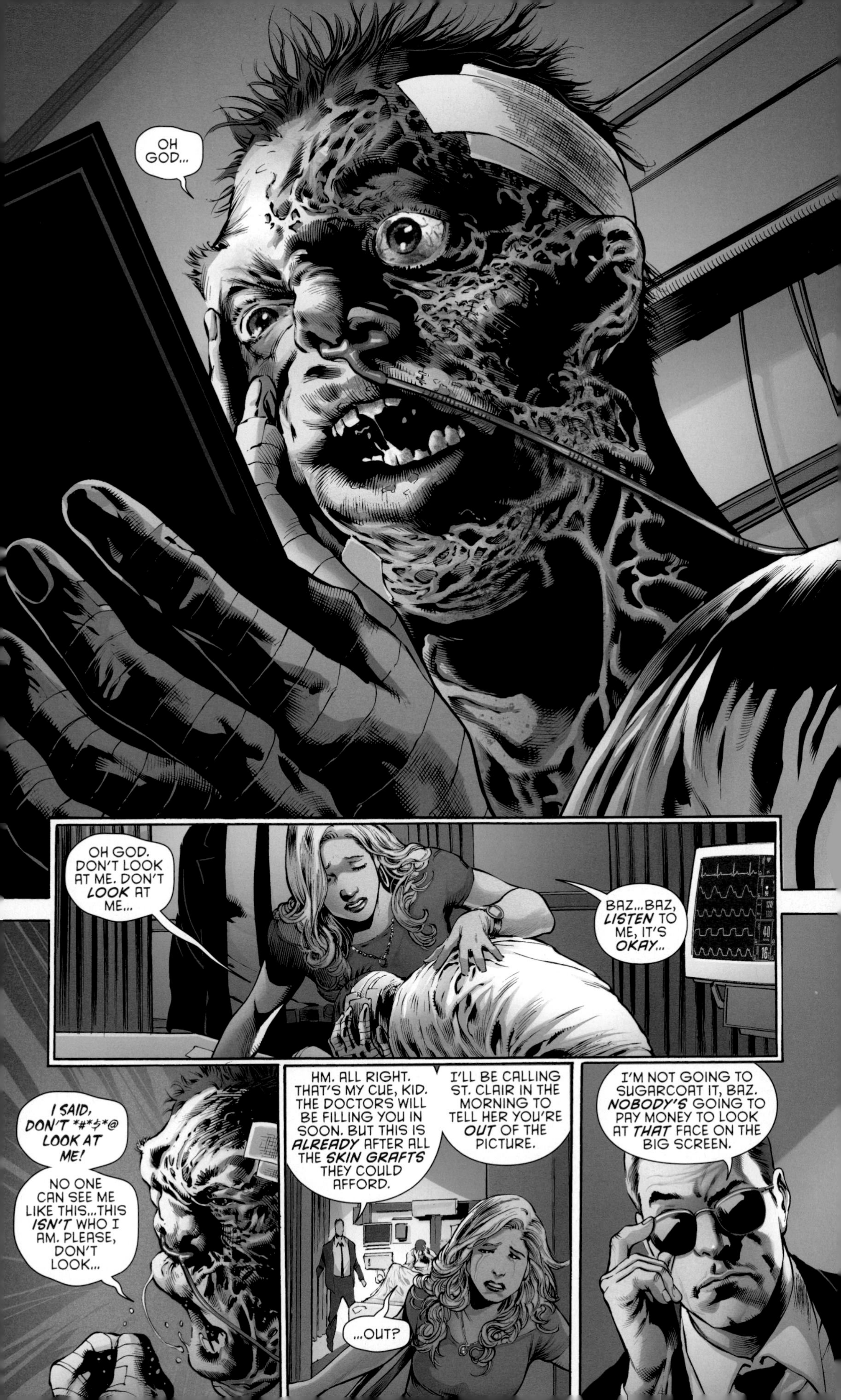

OH GOD...
OH GOD. DON'T LOOK AT ME. DON'T LOOK AT ME...
BAZ...BAZ, LISTEN TO ME, IT'S OKAY...
I SAID, DON'T *#*ఽ*@ LOOK AT ME!
NO ONE CAN SEE ME LIKE THIS...THIS ISN'T WHO I AM. PLEASE, DON'T LOOK...
HM. ALL RIGHT. THAT'S MY CUE, KID. THE DOCTORS WILL BE FILLING YOU IN SOON. BUT THIS IS ALREADY AFTER ALL THE SKIN GRAFTS THEY COULD AFFORD.
I'LL BE CALLING ST. CLAIR IN THE MORNING TO TELL HER YOU'RE OUT OF THE PICTURE.
...OUT?
I'M NOT GOING TO SUGARCOAT IT, BAZ. NOBODY'S GOING TO PAY MONEY TO LOOK AT THAT FACE ON THE BIG SCREEN.

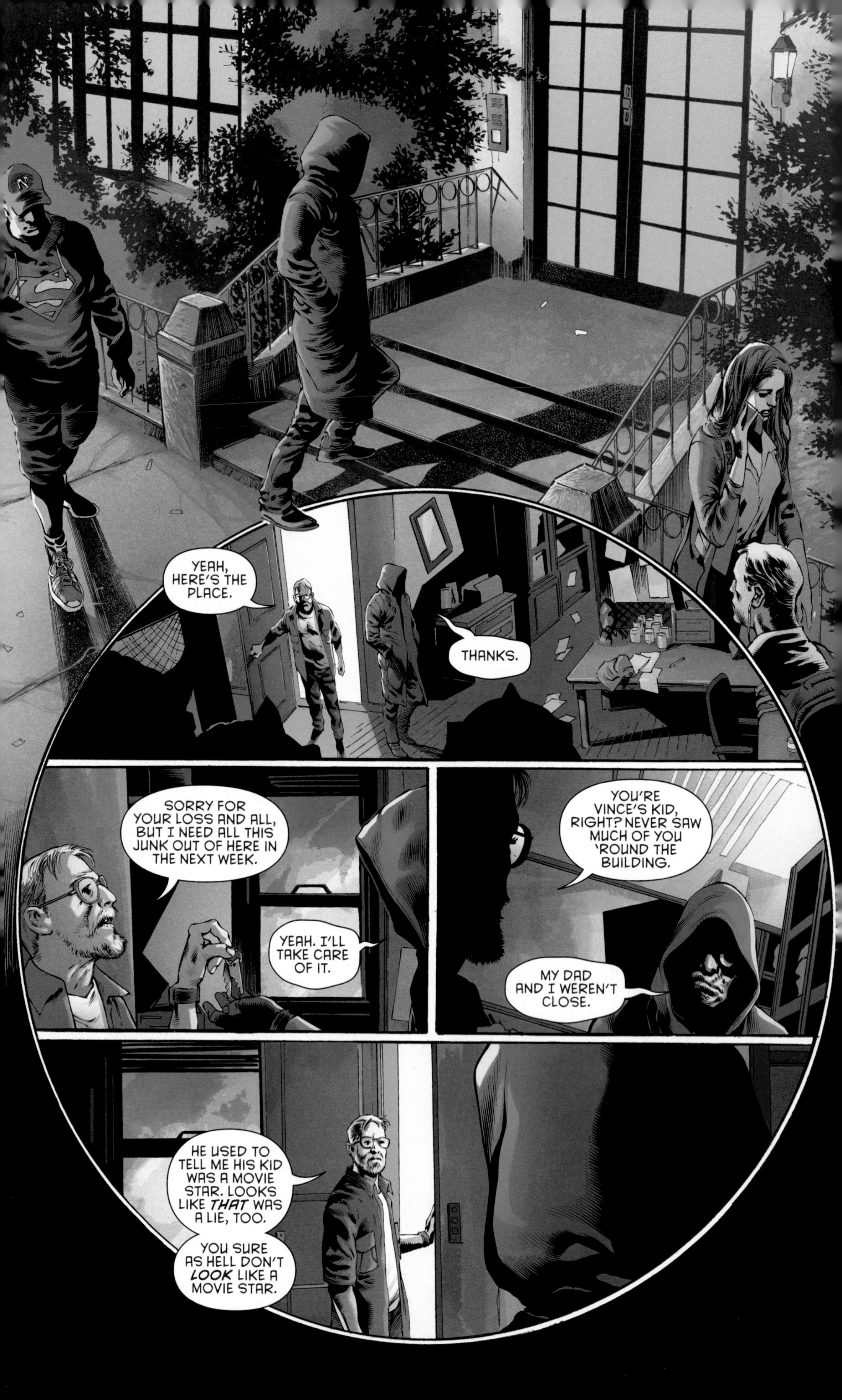
YEAH, HERE'S THE PLACE.
THANKS.
SORRY FOR YOUR LOSS AND ALL, BUT I NEED ALL THIS JUNK OUT OF HERE IN THE NEXT WEEK.
YEAH. I'LL TAKE CARE OF IT.
YOU'RE VINCE'S KID, RIGHT? NEVER SAW MUCH OF YOU 'ROUND THE BUILDING.
MY DAD AND I WEREN'T CLOSE.
HE USED TO TELL ME HIS KID WAS A MOVIE STAR. LOOKS LIKE *THAT* WAS A LIE, TOO.
YOU SURE AS HELL DON'T *LOOK* LIKE A MOVIE STAR.

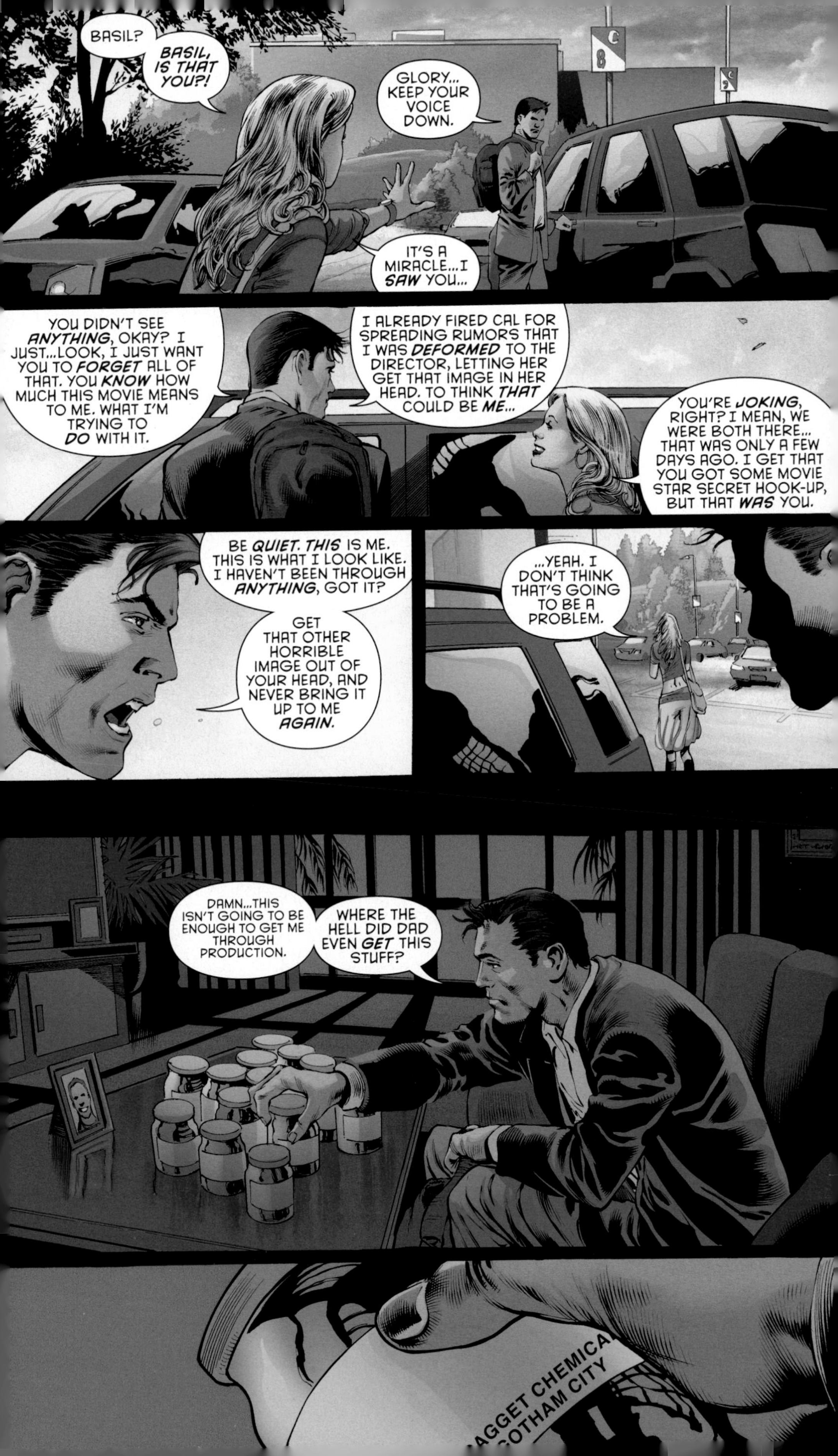
BASIL?
BASIL, IS THAT YOU?!
GLORY... KEEP YOUR VOICE DOWN.
IT'S A MIRACLE...I SAW YOU...
YOU DIDN'T SEE ANYTHING, OKAY? I JUST...LOOK, I JUST WANT YOU TO FORGET ALL OF THAT. YOU KNOW HOW MUCH THIS MOVIE MEANS TO ME. WHAT I'M TRYING TO DO WITH IT.
I ALREADY FIRED CAL FOR SPREADING RUMORS THAT I WAS DEFORMED TO THE DIRECTOR, LETTING HER GET THAT IMAGE IN HER HEAD. TO THINK THAT COULD BE ME...
YOU'RE JOKING, RIGHT? I MEAN, WE WERE BOTH THERE... THAT WAS ONLY A FEW DAYS AGO. I GET THAT YOU GOT SOME MOVIE STAR SECRET HOOK-UP, BUT THAT WAS YOU.
BE QUIET. THIS IS ME. THIS IS WHAT I LOOK LIKE. I HAVEN'T BEEN THROUGH ANYTHING, GOT IT?
GET THAT OTHER HORRIBLE IMAGE OUT OF YOUR HEAD, AND NEVER BRING IT UP TO ME AGAIN.
...YEAH. I DON'T THINK THAT'S GOING TO BE A PROBLEM.
DAMN...THIS ISN'T GOING TO BE ENOUGH TO GET ME THROUGH PRODUCTION.
WHERE THE HELL DID DAD EVEN GET THIS STUFF?
AGGET CHEMICA
GOTHAM CITY

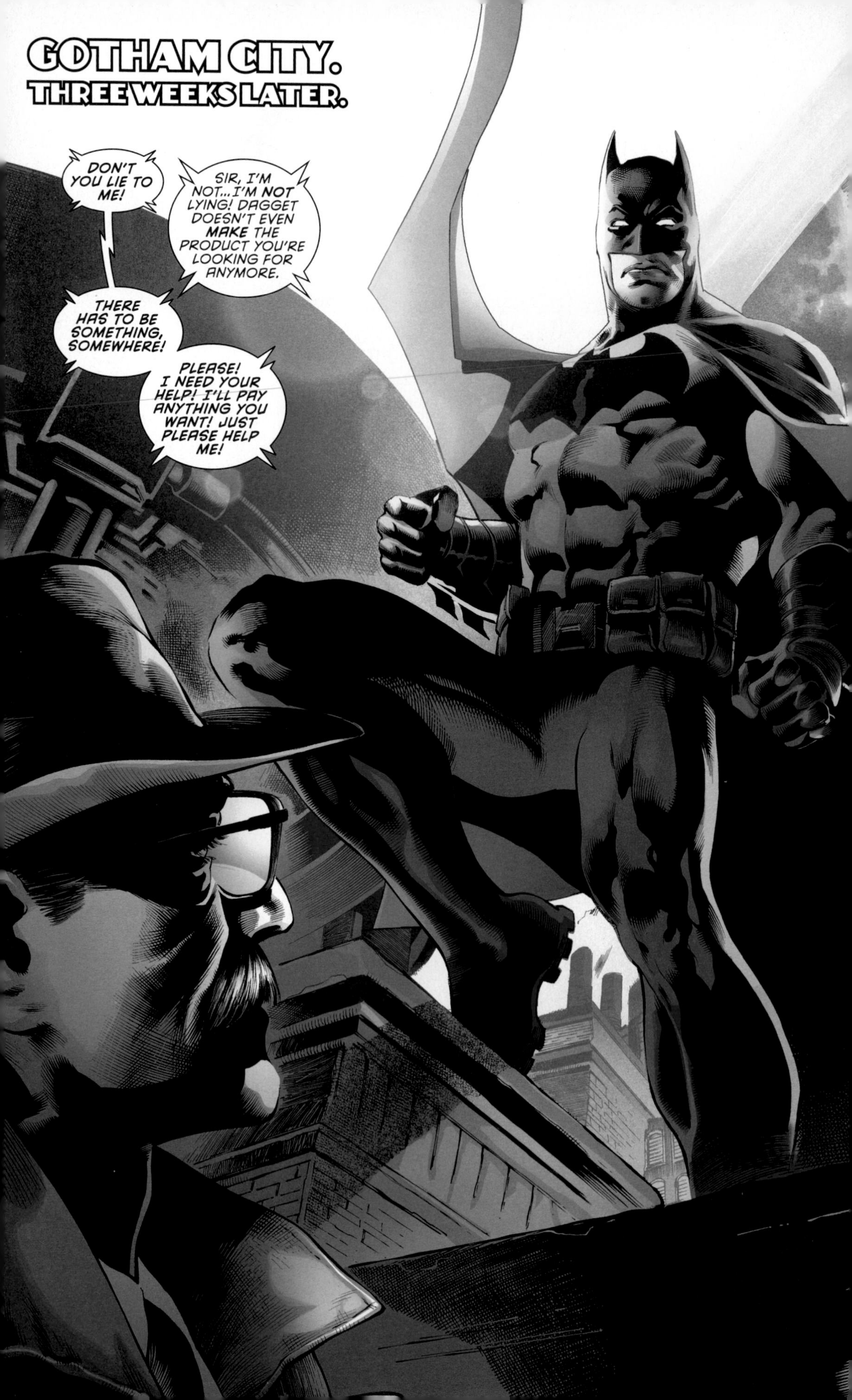
GOTHAM CITY.
THREE WEEKS LATER.
DON'T YOU LIE TO ME!
SIR, I'M NOT...I'M NOT LYING! DAGGET DOESN'T EVEN MAKE THE PRODUCT YOU'RE LOOKING FOR ANYMORE.
THERE HAS TO BE SOMETHING, SOMEWHERE!
PLEASE! I NEED YOUR HELP! I'LL PAY ANYTHING YOU WANT! JUST PLEASE HELP ME!

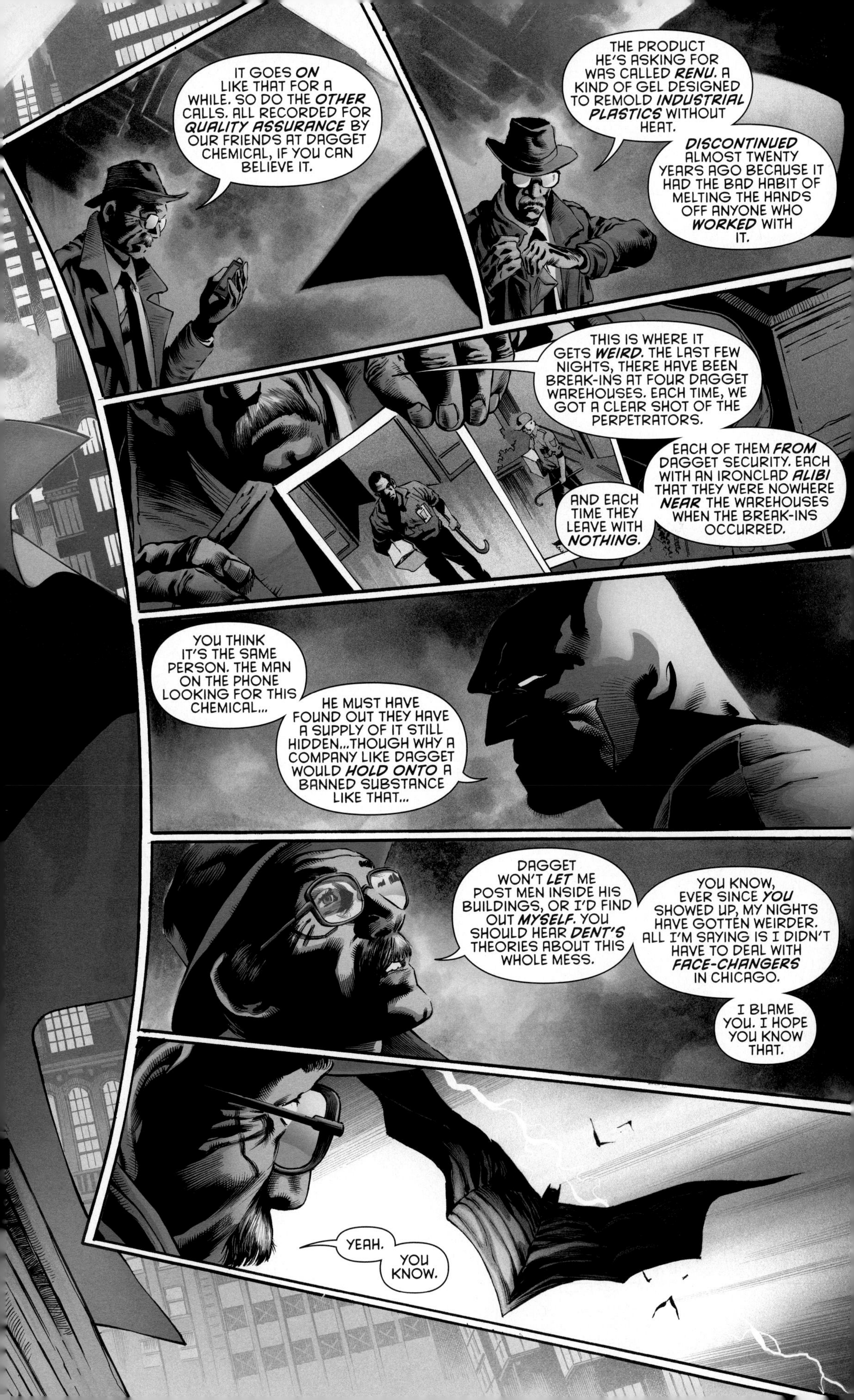
IT GOES ON LIKE THAT FOR A WHILE. SO DO THE OTHER CALLS. ALL RECORDED FOR QUALITY ASSURANCE BY OUR FRIENDS AT DAGGET CHEMICAL, IF YOU CAN BELIEVE IT.
THE PRODUCT HE'S ASKING FOR WAS CALLED RENU. A KIND OF GEL DESIGNED TO REMOLD INDUSTRIAL PLASTICS WITHOUT HEAT.
DISCONTINUED ALMOST TWENTY YEARS AGO BECAUSE IT HAD THE BAD HABIT OF MELTING THE HANDS OFF ANYONE WHO WORKED WITH IT.
THIS IS WHERE IT GETS WEIRD. THE LAST FEW NIGHTS, THERE HAVE BEEN BREAK-INS AT FOUR DAGGET WAREHOUSES. EACH TIME, WE GOT A CLEAR SHOT OF THE PERPETRATORS.
EACH OF THEM FROM DAGGET SECURITY. EACH WITH AN IRONCLAD ALIBI THAT THEY WERE NOWHERE NEAR THE WAREHOUSES WHEN THE BREAK-INS OCCURRED.
AND EACH TIME THEY LEAVE WITH NOTHING.
YOU THINK IT'S THE SAME PERSON. THE MAN ON THE PHONE LOOKING FOR THIS CHEMICAL...
HE MUST HAVE FOUND OUT THEY HAVE A SUPPLY OF IT STILL HIDDEN...THOUGH WHY A COMPANY LIKE DAGGET WOULD HOLD ONTO A BANNED SUBSTANCE LIKE THAT...
DAGGET WON'T LET ME POST MEN INSIDE HIS BUILDINGS, OR I'D FIND OUT MYSELF. YOU SHOULD HEAR DENT'S THEORIES ABOUT THIS WHOLE MESS.
YOU KNOW, EVER SINCE YOU SHOWED UP, MY NIGHTS HAVE GOTTEN WEIRDER. ALL I'M SAYING IS I DIDN'T HAVE TO DEAL WITH FACE-CHANGERS IN CHICAGO.
I BLAME YOU. I HOPE YOU KNOW THAT.
YEAH.
YOU KNOW.

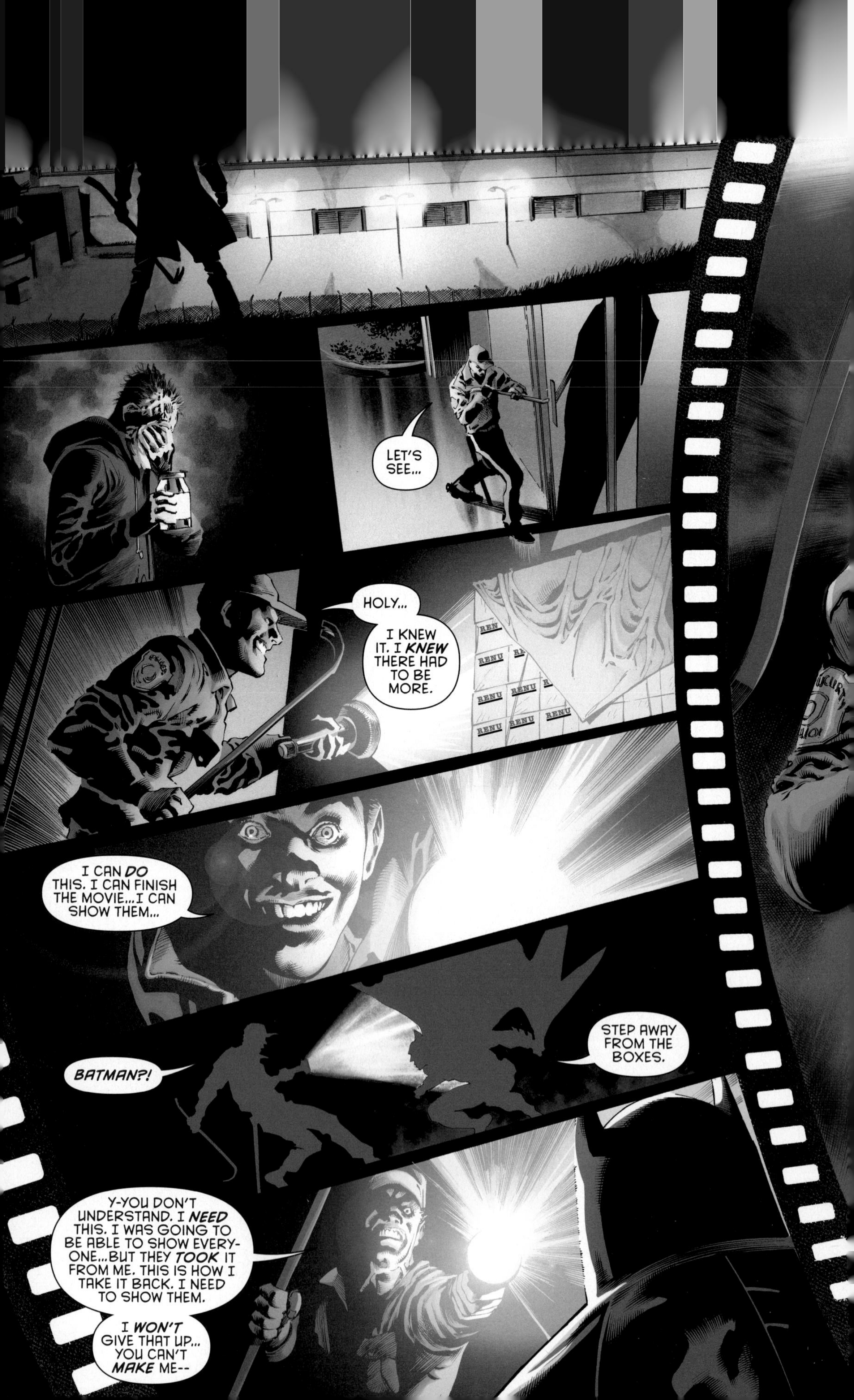
LET'S SEE...
HOLY...
I KNEW IT. I KNEW THERE HAD TO BE MORE.
RENU
I CAN DO THIS. I CAN FINISH THE MOVIE...I CAN SHOW THEM...
STEP AWAY FROM THE BOXES.
BATMAN?!
Y-YOU DON'T UNDERSTAND. I NEED THIS. I WAS GOING TO BE ABLE TO SHOW EVERY-ONE...BUT THEY TOOK IT FROM ME. THIS IS HOW I TAKE IT BACK. I NEED TO SHOW THEM.
I WON'T GIVE THAT UP... YOU CAN'T MAKE ME--

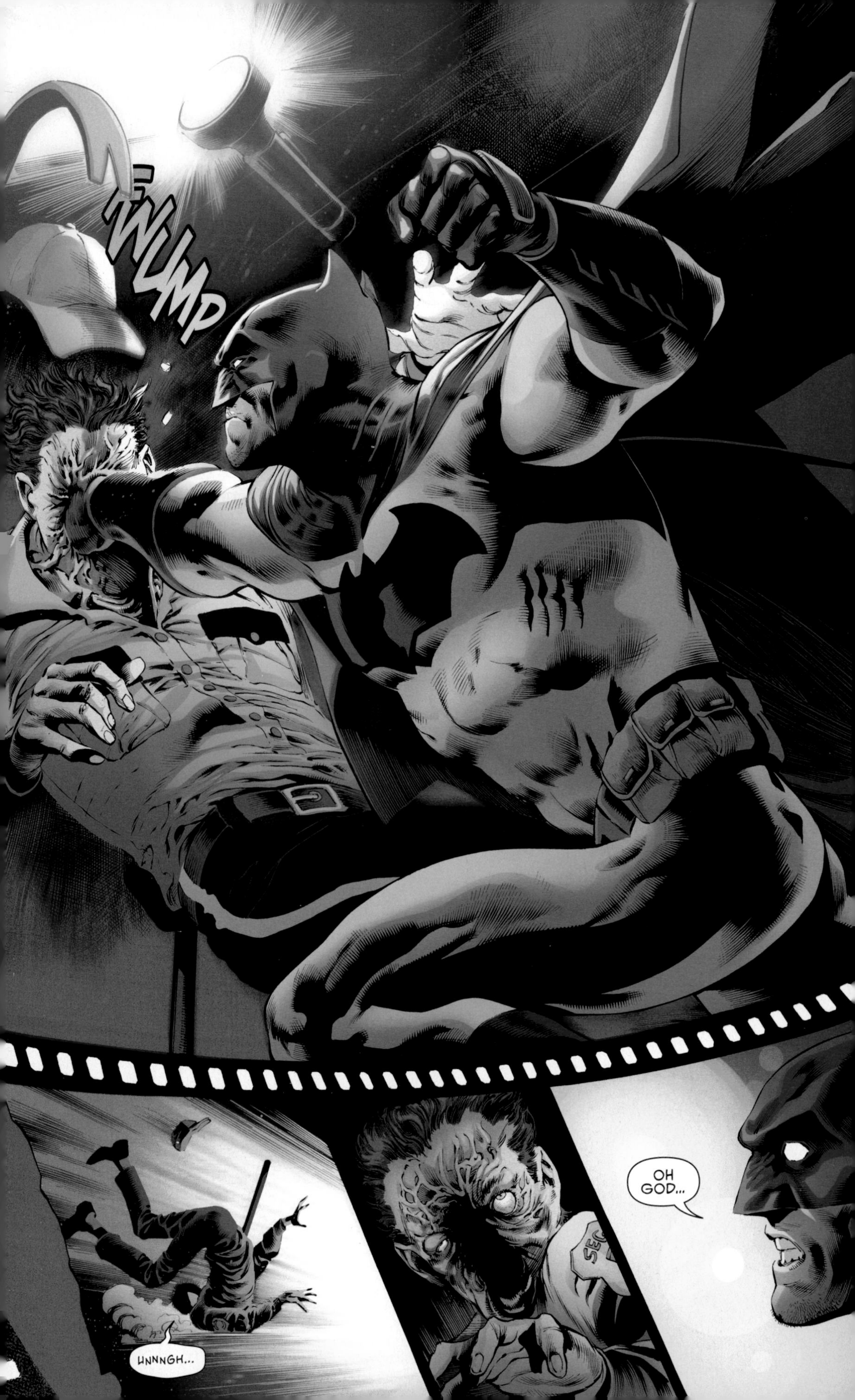
WUMP
UNNNGH...
OH GOD...

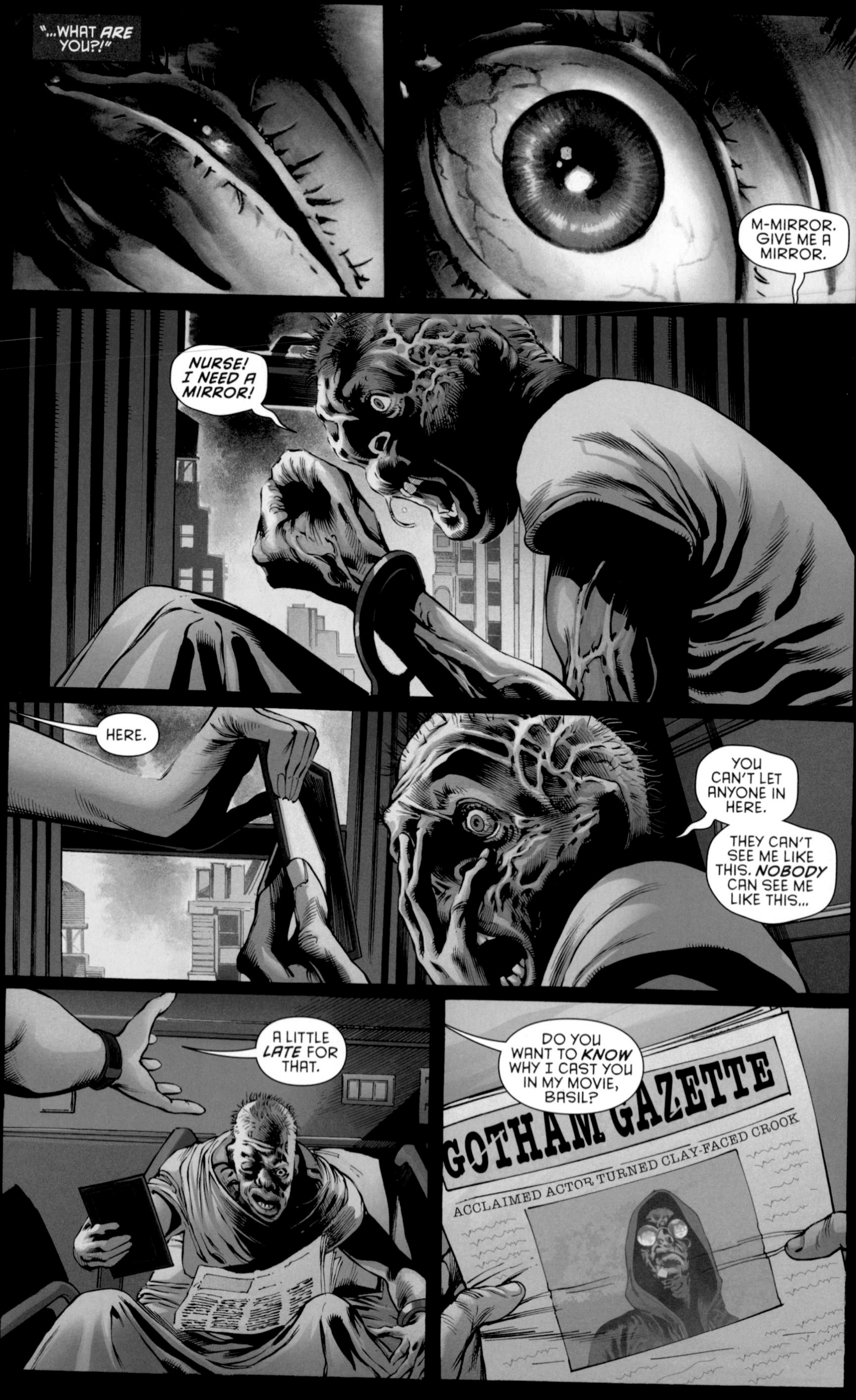
"...WHAT *ARE* YOU?!"
M-MIRROR. GIVE ME A MIRROR.
NURSE! I NEED A MIRROR!
HERE.
YOU CAN'T LET ANYONE IN HERE.
THEY CAN'T SEE ME LIKE THIS. ***NOBODY*** CAN SEE ME LIKE THIS...
A LITTLE *LATE* FOR THAT.
DO YOU WANT TO ***KNOW*** WHY I CAST YOU IN MY MOVIE, BASIL?
GOTHAM GAZETTE
ACCLAIMED ACTOR TURNED CLAY-FACED CROOK

V-VERONICA?

IT WAS YOUR *EYES*, BASIL. IT WAS THIS DARK SADNESS I SAW RIGHT BEHIND THE EYES. *THAT'S* WHAT GOT YOU THE PART.

OUR BUSINESS IS *UGLY*. IT'S *ALWAYS* BEEN UGLY. THAT'S THE WHOLE *POINT* OF THE MOVIE, TO PUT THAT UGLINESS ON SCREEN AND MAKE PEOPLE *SEE* WHAT IT CAN TURN A PERSON INTO.

AND THAT SORROW IN YOUR FACE WHEN YOU READ THE LINES--THAT QUIET AGONY--IT WAS GOING TO BE SOMETHING *SPECIAL*, BASIL. IT REALLY WAS.

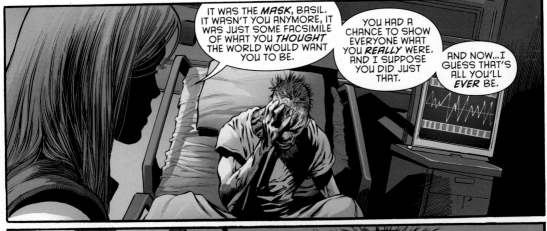

WHEN THAT P.A., GLORY GRIFFIN...WHEN SHE *TOLD* ME ABOUT THE *ACCIDENT*, AND THAT YOU WERE SAFE, BUT YOU MIGHT NOT RECOVER YOUR LOOKS, I *TRIED* TO COME SEE YOU IN THE HOSPITAL. I WANTED TO TELL YOU THAT NO MATTER WHAT HAPPENED, THE PART WAS *YOURS*. THAT I WOULD FIGHT THE STUDIO TOOTH AND NAIL IF I HAD TO.

I WAS RELIEVED FOR YOUR SAKE WHEN IT SEEMED LIKE GLORY HAD *EXAGGERATED* YOUR INJURIES...BUT THAT'S WHEN I NOTICED SOMETHING *CHANGE*. SOMETHING WRONG...BUT I COULDN'T PUT MY FINGER ON IT UNTIL TODAY.

IT WAS THE *MASK*, BASIL. IT WASN'T YOU ANYMORE, IT WAS JUST SOME FACSIMILE OF WHAT YOU *THOUGHT* THE WORLD WOULD WANT YOU TO BE.

YOU HAD A CHANCE TO SHOW EVERYONE WHAT YOU *REALLY* WERE. AND I SUPPOSE YOU DID JUST THAT.

AND NOW...I GUESS THAT'S ALL YOU'LL *EVER* BE.

I DON'T *CARE* IF THEY LET YOU WALK TODAY. YOU'RE *OUT* OF MY MOVIE.

AND I WANT YOU TO UNDERSTAND IT HAS *NOTHING* TO DO WITH WHAT YOU LOOK LIKE.

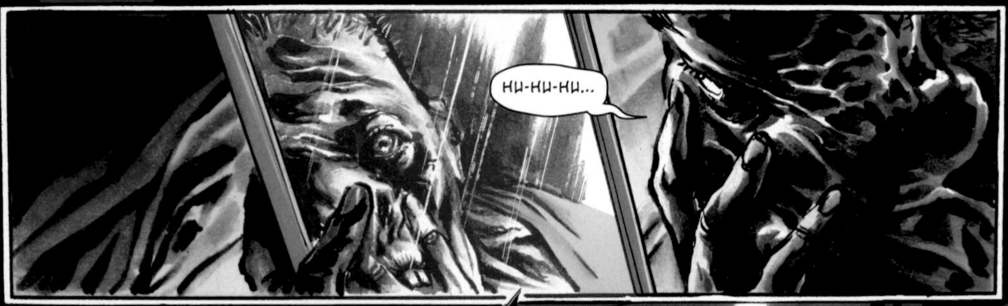
HU-HU-HU...

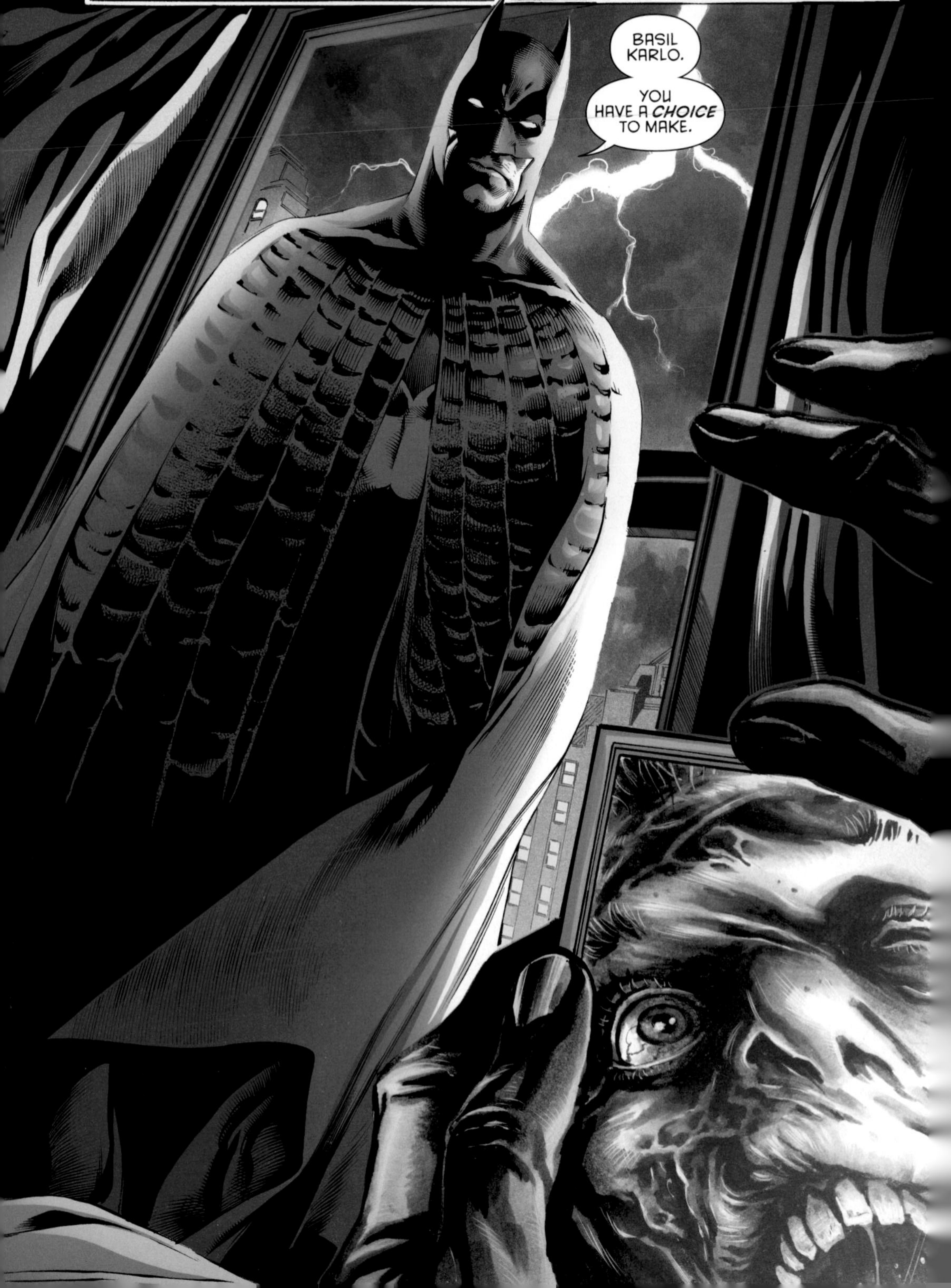
BASIL KARLO.
YOU HAVE A *CHOICE* TO MAKE.

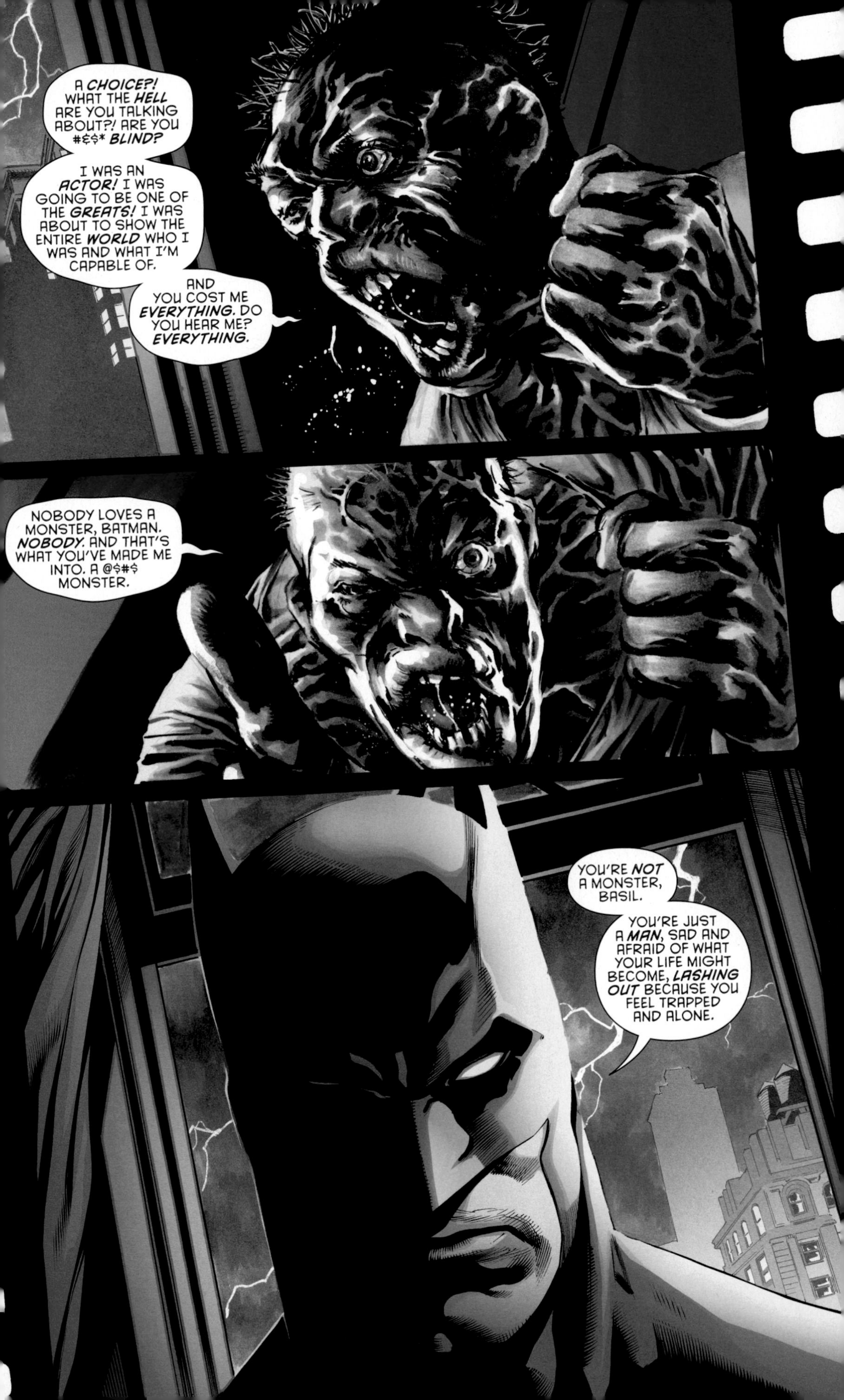
A CHOICE?! WHAT THE HELL ARE YOU TALKING ABOUT?! ARE YOU #$$* BLIND?
I WAS AN ACTOR! I WAS GOING TO BE ONE OF THE GREATS! I WAS ABOUT TO SHOW THE ENTIRE WORLD WHO I WAS AND WHAT I'M CAPABLE OF.
AND YOU COST ME EVERYTHING. DO YOU HEAR ME? EVERYTHING.
NOBODY LOVES A MONSTER, BATMAN. NOBODY. AND THAT'S WHAT YOU'VE MADE ME INTO. A @$#$ MONSTER.
YOU'RE NOT A MONSTER, BASIL.
YOU'RE JUST A MAN, SAD AND AFRAID OF WHAT YOUR LIFE MIGHT BECOME, LASHING OUT BECAUSE YOU FEEL TRAPPED AND ALONE.

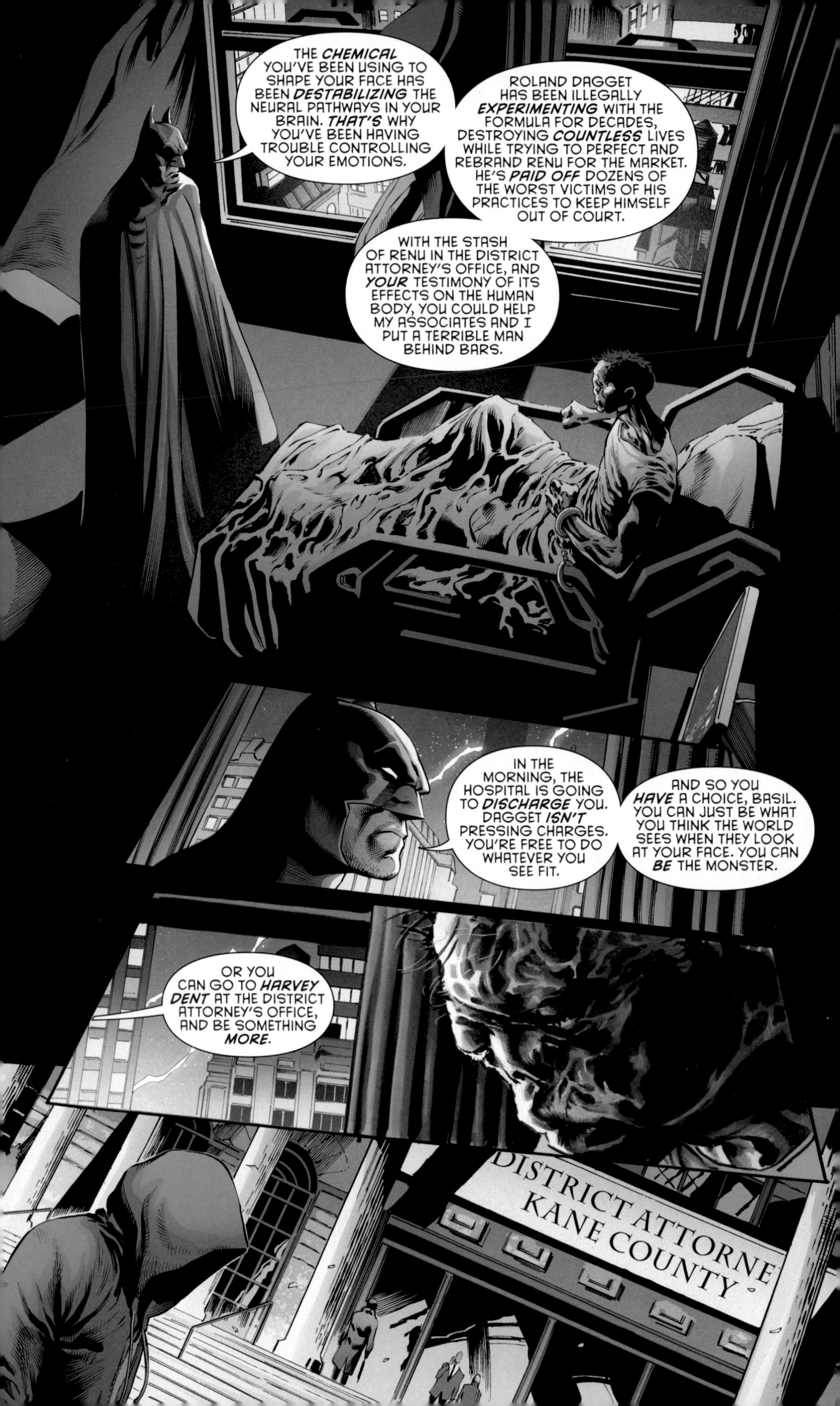
THE CHEMICAL YOU'VE BEEN USING TO SHAPE YOUR FACE HAS BEEN DESTABILIZING THE NEURAL PATHWAYS IN YOUR BRAIN. THAT'S WHY YOU'VE BEEN HAVING TROUBLE CONTROLLING YOUR EMOTIONS.
ROLAND DAGGET HAS BEEN ILLEGALLY EXPERIMENTING WITH THE FORMULA FOR DECADES, DESTROYING COUNTLESS LIVES WHILE TRYING TO PERFECT AND REBRAND RENU FOR THE MARKET. HE'S PAID OFF DOZENS OF THE WORST VICTIMS OF HIS PRACTICES TO KEEP HIMSELF OUT OF COURT.
WITH THE STASH OF RENU IN THE DISTRICT ATTORNEY'S OFFICE, AND YOUR TESTIMONY OF ITS EFFECTS ON THE HUMAN BODY, YOU COULD HELP MY ASSOCIATES AND I PUT A TERRIBLE MAN BEHIND BARS.
IN THE MORNING, THE HOSPITAL IS GOING TO DISCHARGE YOU. DAGGET ISN'T PRESSING CHARGES. YOU'RE FREE TO DO WHATEVER YOU SEE FIT.
AND SO YOU HAVE A CHOICE, BASIL. YOU CAN JUST BE WHAT YOU THINK THE WORLD SEES WHEN THEY LOOK AT YOUR FACE. YOU CAN BE THE MONSTER.
OR YOU CAN GO TO HARVEY DENT AT THE DISTRICT ATTORNEY'S OFFICE, AND BE SOMETHING MORE.
DISTRICT ATTORNE
KANE COUNTY

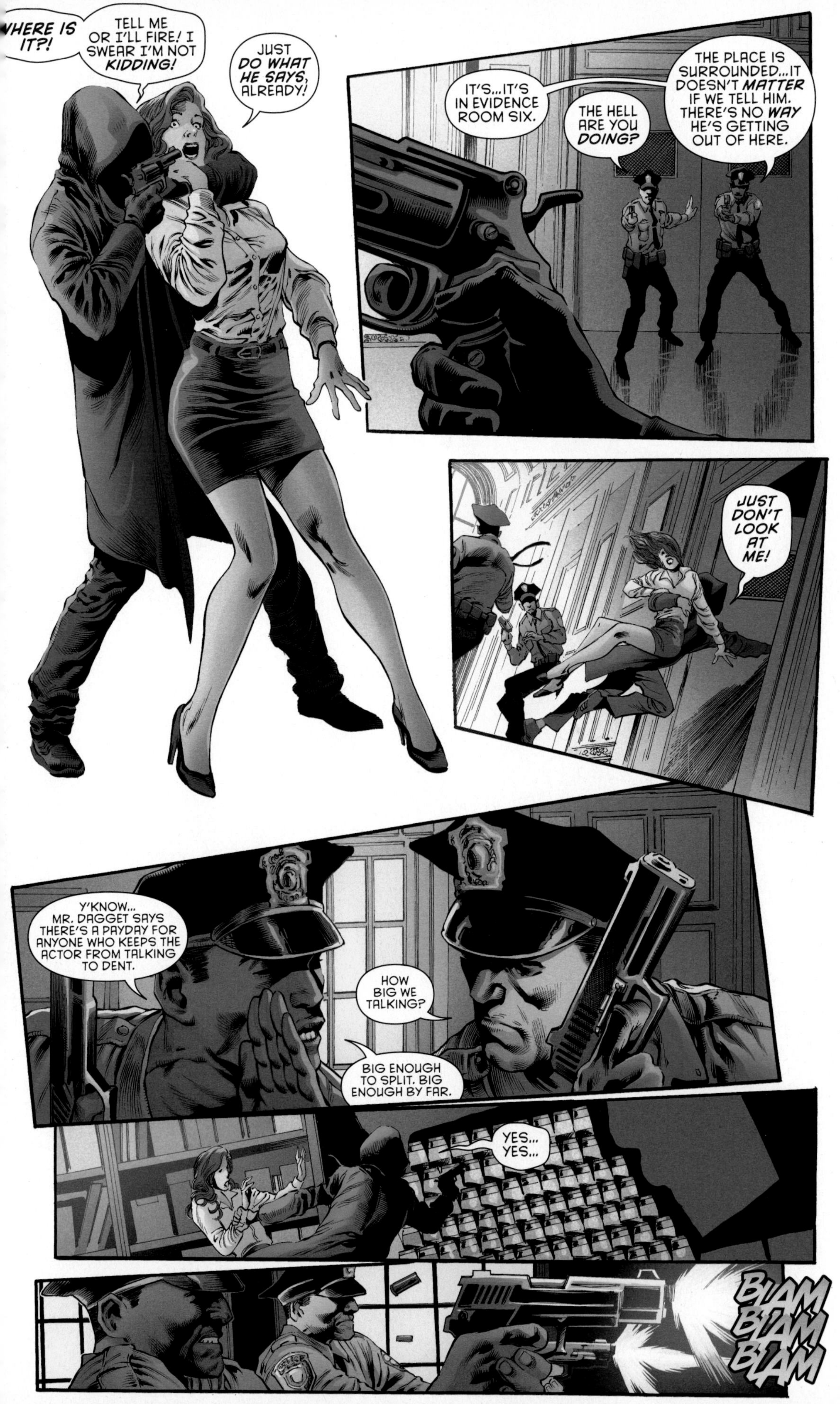
WHERE IS IT?!
TELL ME OR I'LL FIRE! I SWEAR I'M NOT KIDDING!
JUST DO WHAT HE SAYS, ALREADY!
IT'S...IT'S IN EVIDENCE ROOM SIX.
THE HELL ARE YOU DOING?
THE PLACE IS SURROUNDED...IT DOESN'T MATTER IF WE TELL HIM. THERE'S NO WAY HE'S GETTING OUT OF HERE.
JUST DON'T LOOK AT ME!
Y'KNOW... MR. DAGGET SAYS THERE'S A PAYDAY FOR ANYONE WHO KEEPS THE ACTOR FROM TALKING TO DENT.
HOW BIG WE TALKING?
BIG ENOUGH TO SPLIT. BIG ENOUGH BY FAR.
YES... YES...
BLAM BLAM BLAM

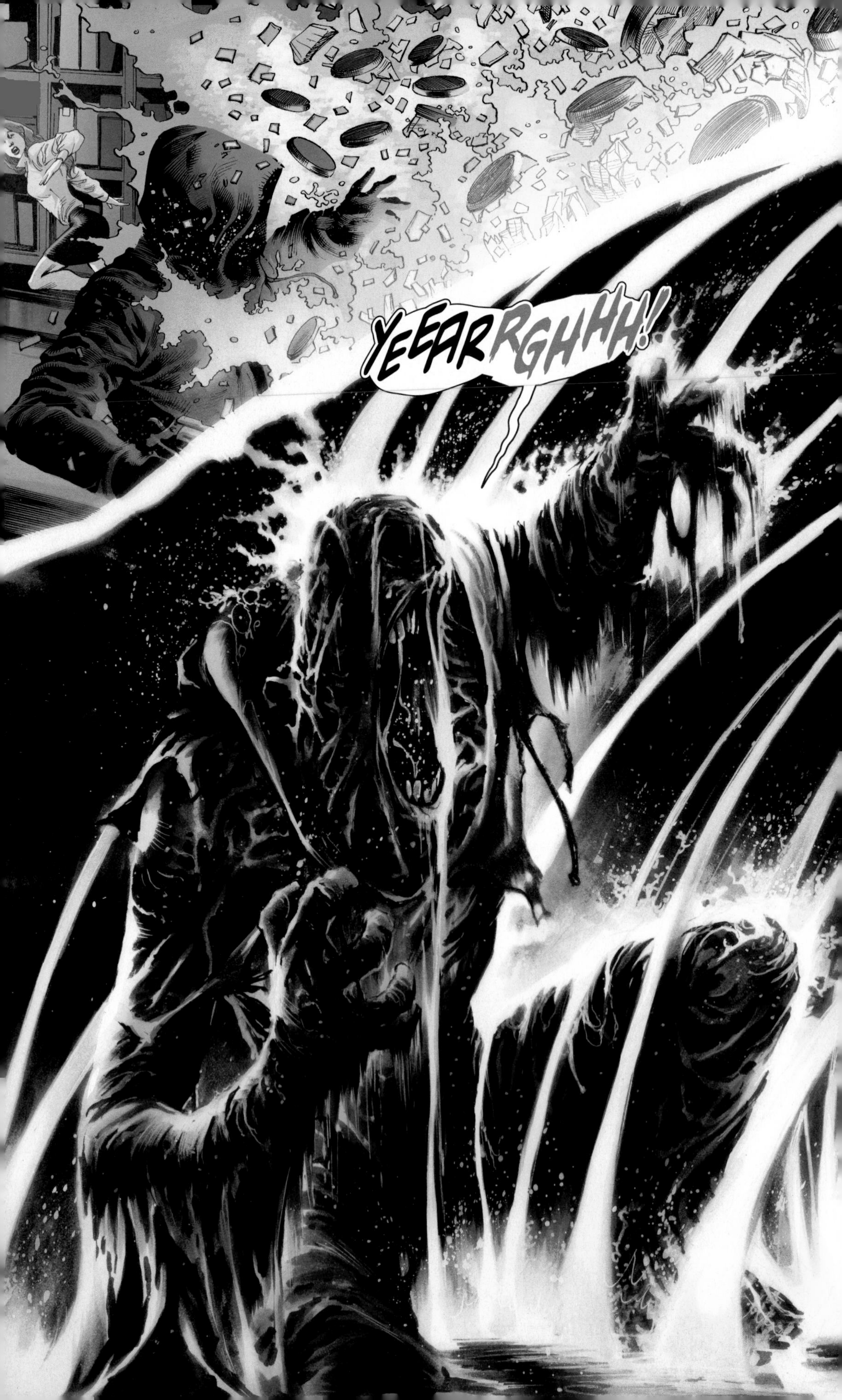
YEEARRGHHH!

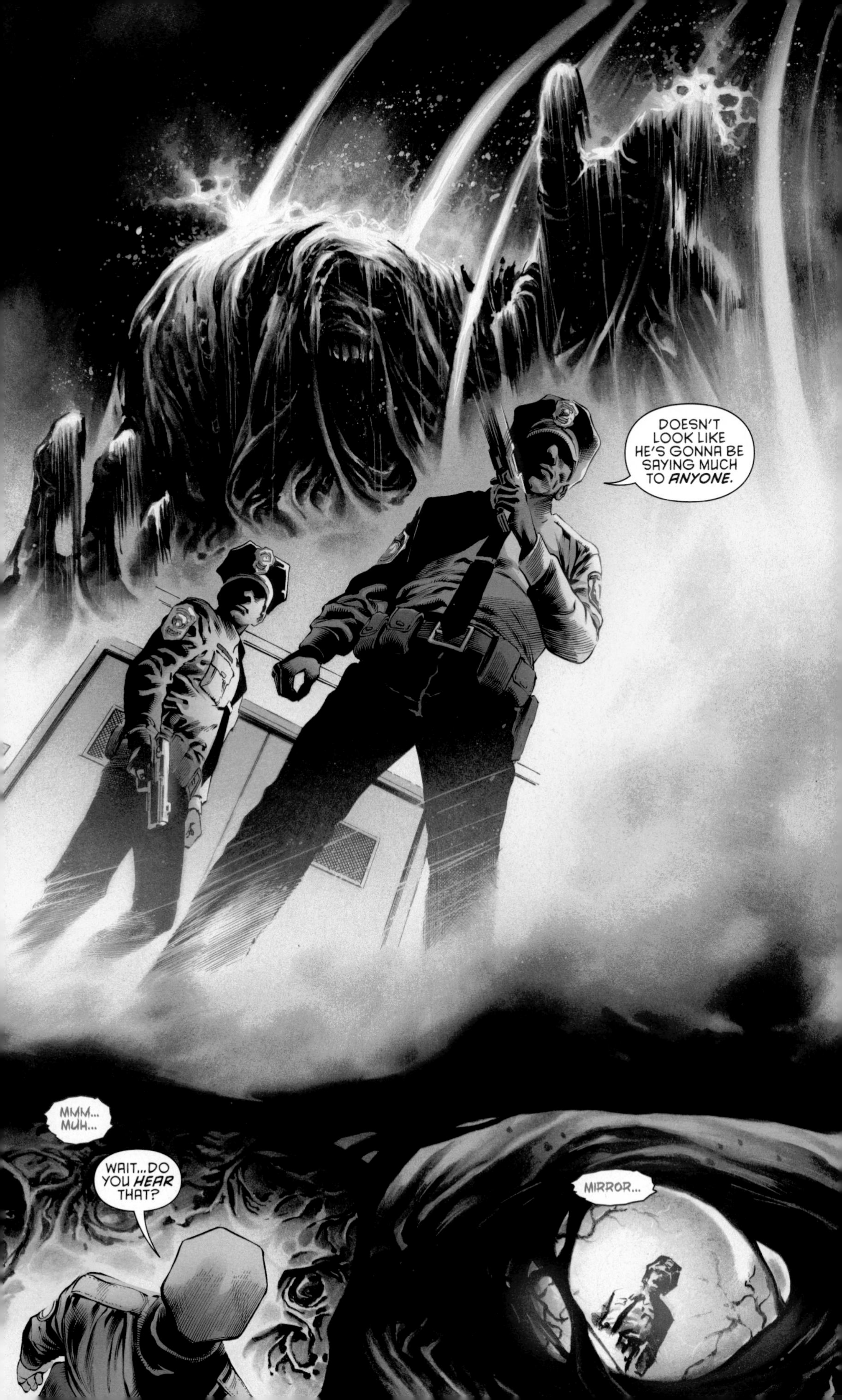
DOESN'T LOOK LIKE HE'S GONNA BE SAYING MUCH TO *ANYONE.*
MMM... MUH...
WAIT...DO YOU *HEAR* THAT?
MIRROR...

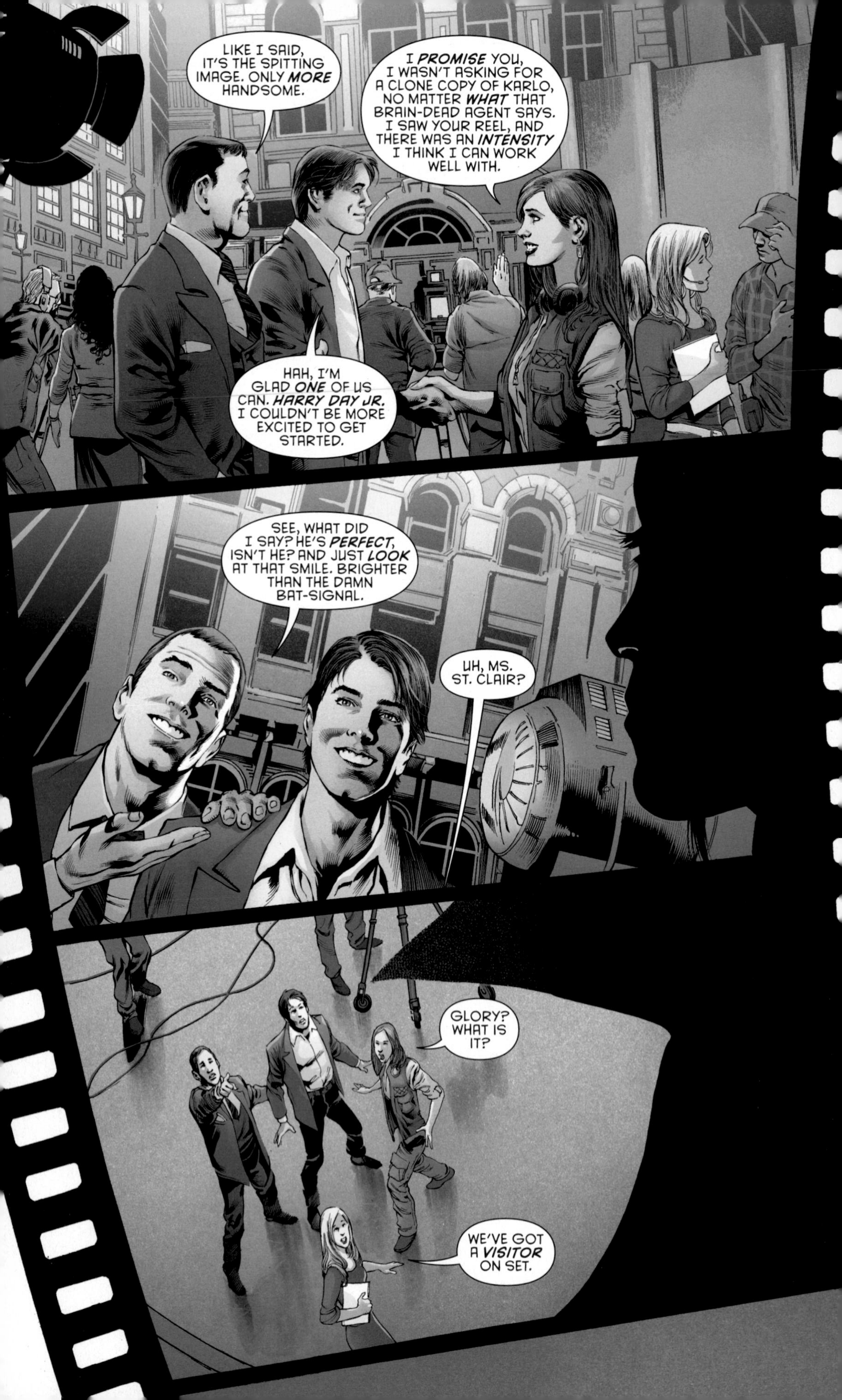
LIKE I SAID, IT'S THE SPITTING IMAGE. ONLY MORE HANDSOME.
I PROMISE YOU, I WASN'T ASKING FOR A CLONE COPY OF KARLO, NO MATTER WHAT THAT BRAIN-DEAD AGENT SAYS. I SAW YOUR REEL, AND THERE WAS AN INTENSITY I THINK I CAN WORK WELL WITH.
HAH, I'M GLAD ONE OF US CAN. HARRY DAY JR. I COULDN'T BE MORE EXCITED TO GET STARTED.
SEE, WHAT DID I SAY? HE'S PERFECT, ISN'T HE? AND JUST LOOK AT THAT SMILE. BRIGHTER THAN THE DAMN BAT-SIGNAL.
UH, MS. ST. CLAIR?
GLORY? WHAT IS IT?
WE'VE GOT A VISITOR ON SET.

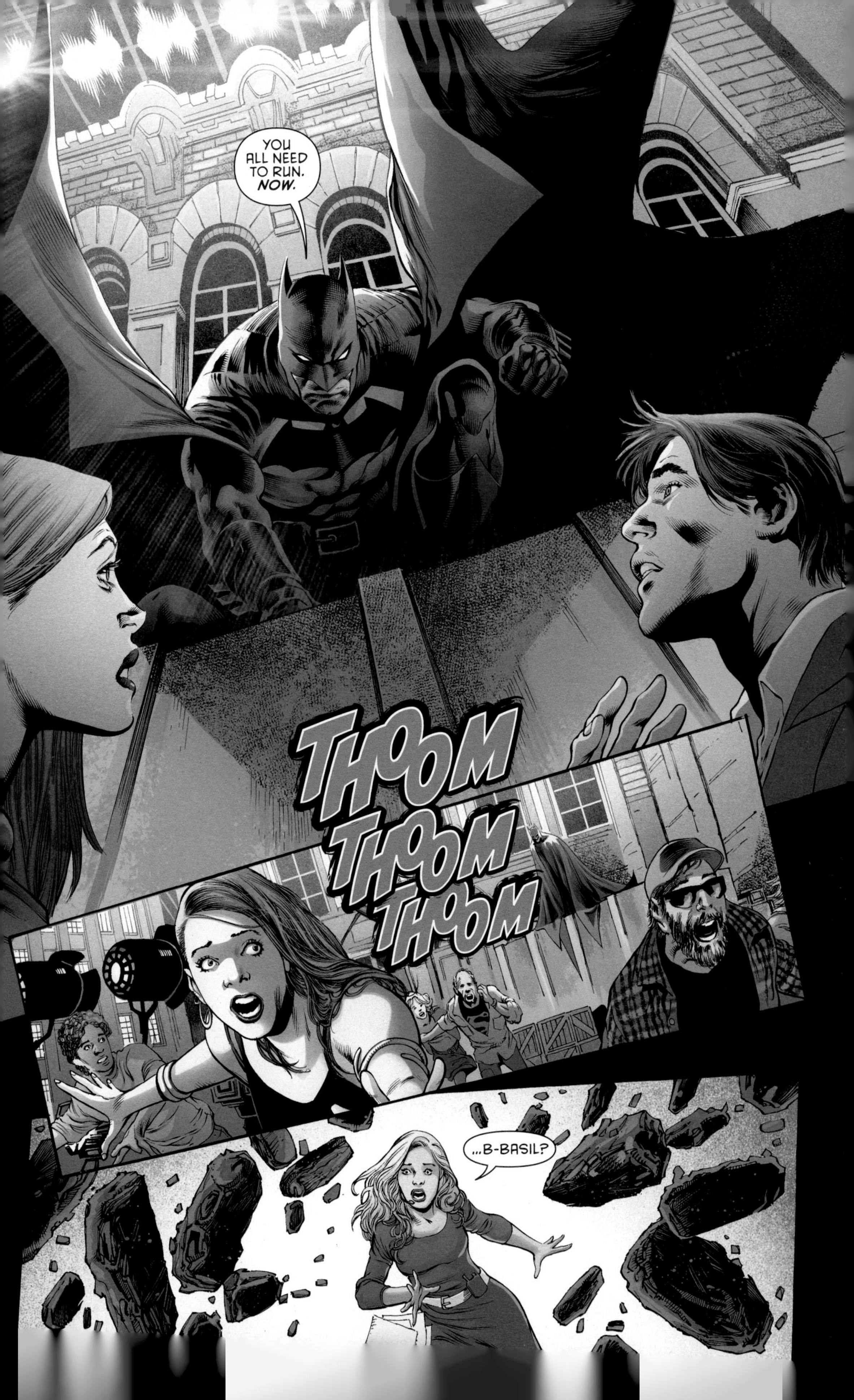
YOU ALL NEED TO RUN. NOW.
THOOM THOOM THOOM
...B-BASIL?

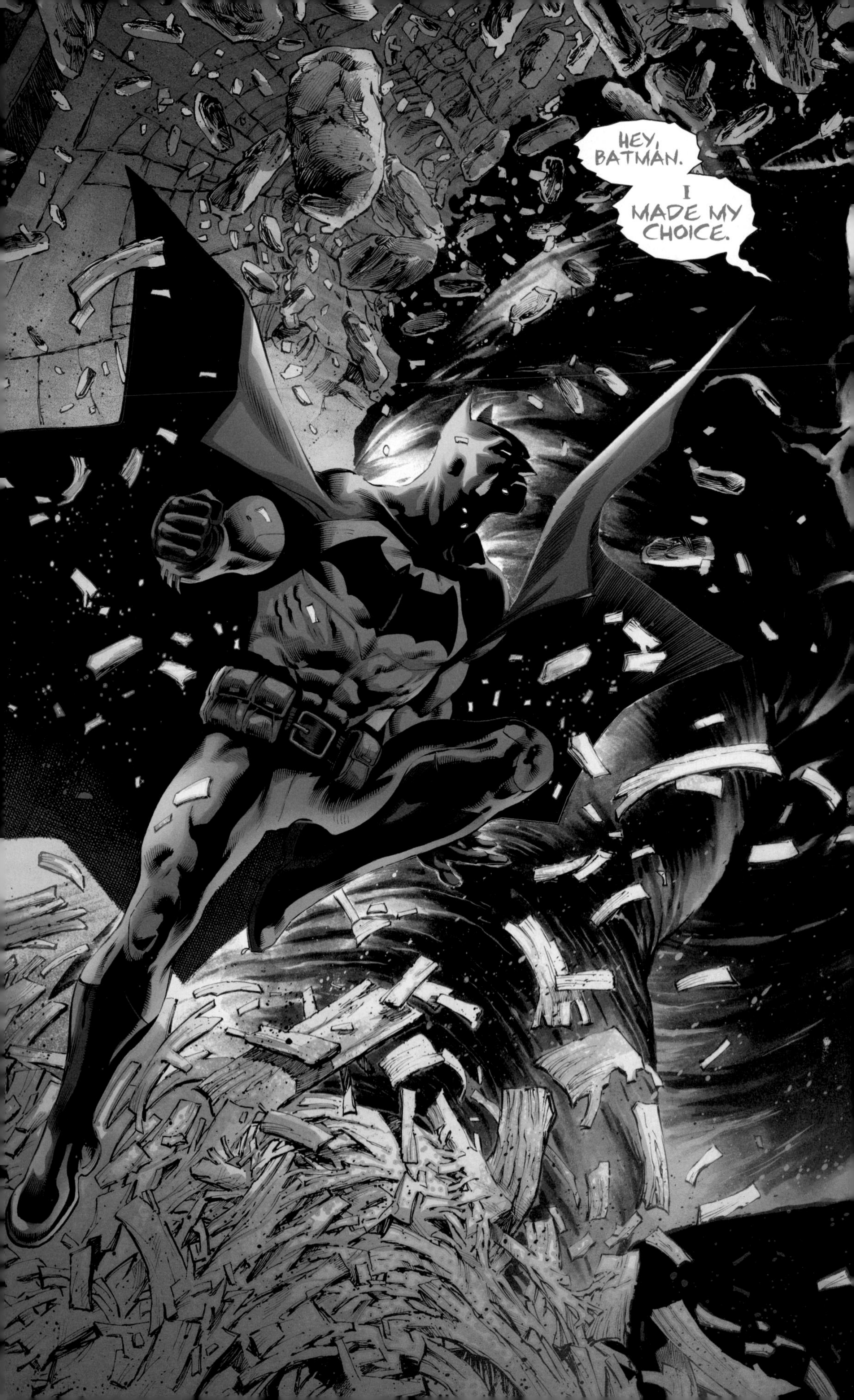
HEY, BATMAN.
I MADE MY CHOICE.

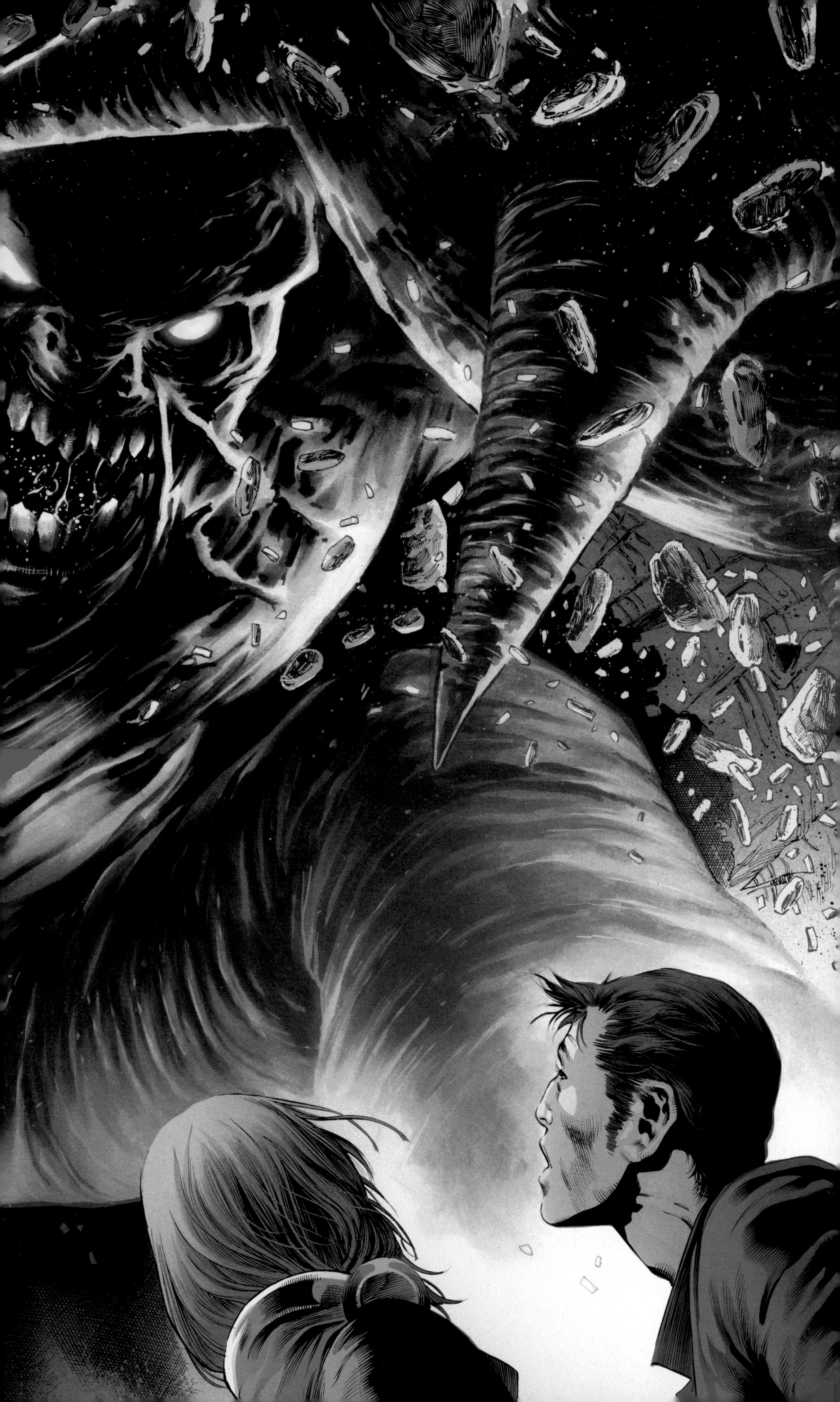

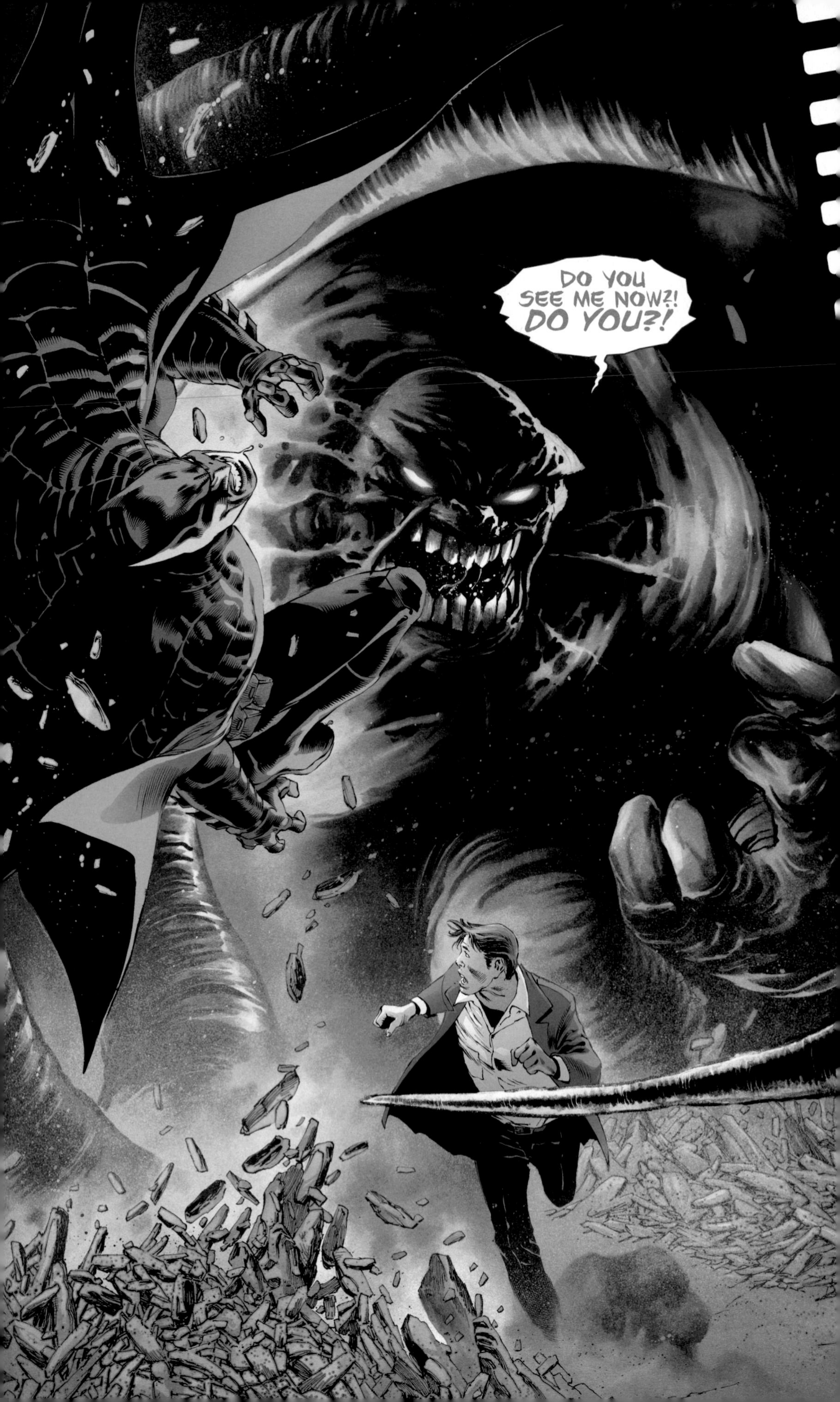
DO YOU SEE ME NOW?! DO YOU?!

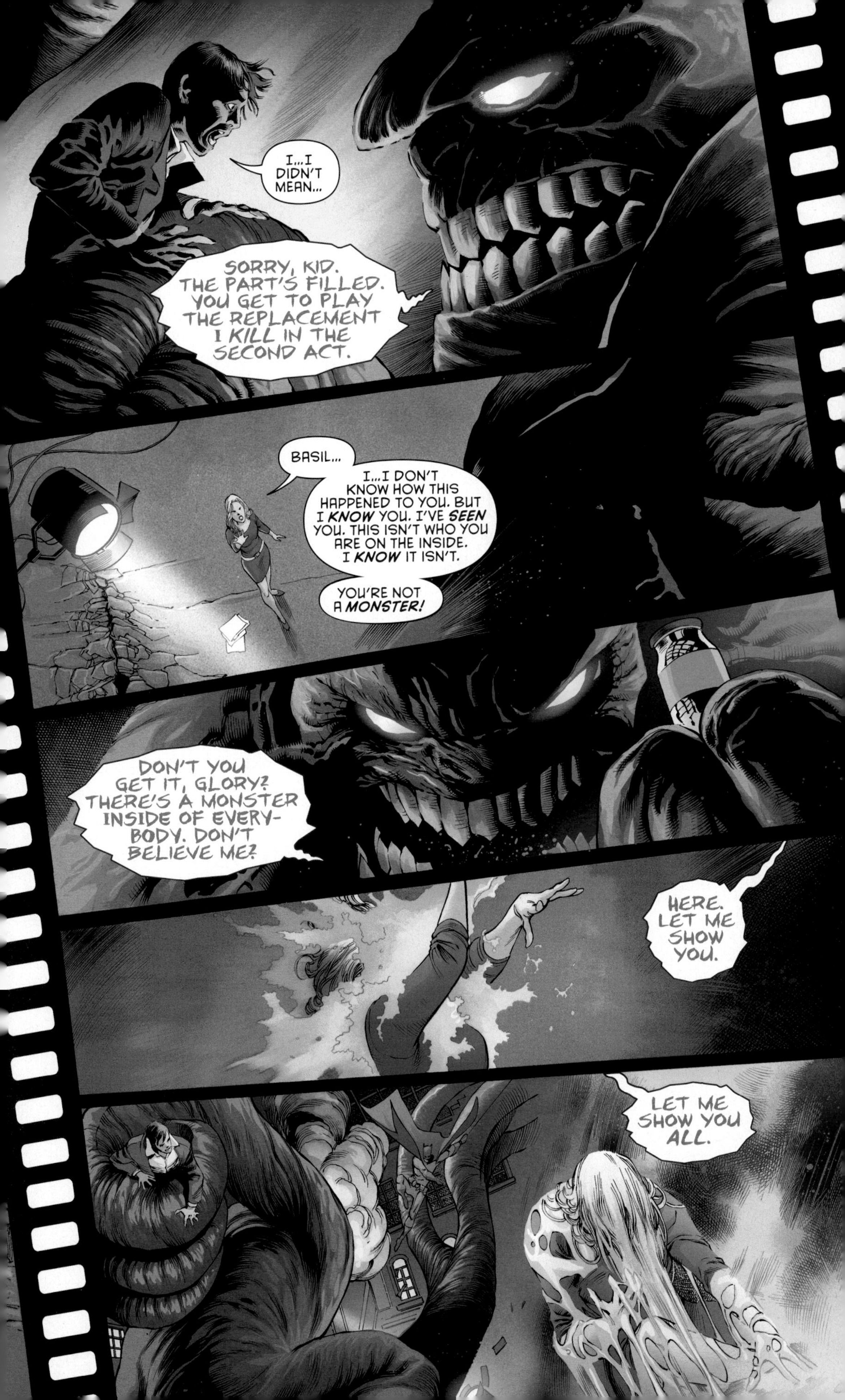
I...I DIDN'T MEAN...
SORRY, KID. THE PART'S FILLED. YOU GET TO PLAY THE REPLACEMENT I KILL IN THE SECOND ACT.
BASIL...
I...I DON'T KNOW HOW THIS HAPPENED TO YOU. BUT I KNOW YOU. I'VE SEEN YOU. THIS ISN'T WHO YOU ARE ON THE INSIDE. I KNOW IT ISN'T.
YOU'RE NOT A MONSTER!
DON'T YOU GET IT, GLORY? THERE'S A MONSTER INSIDE OF EVERY-BODY. DON'T BELIEVE ME?
HERE. LET ME SHOW YOU.
LET ME SHOW YOU ALL.

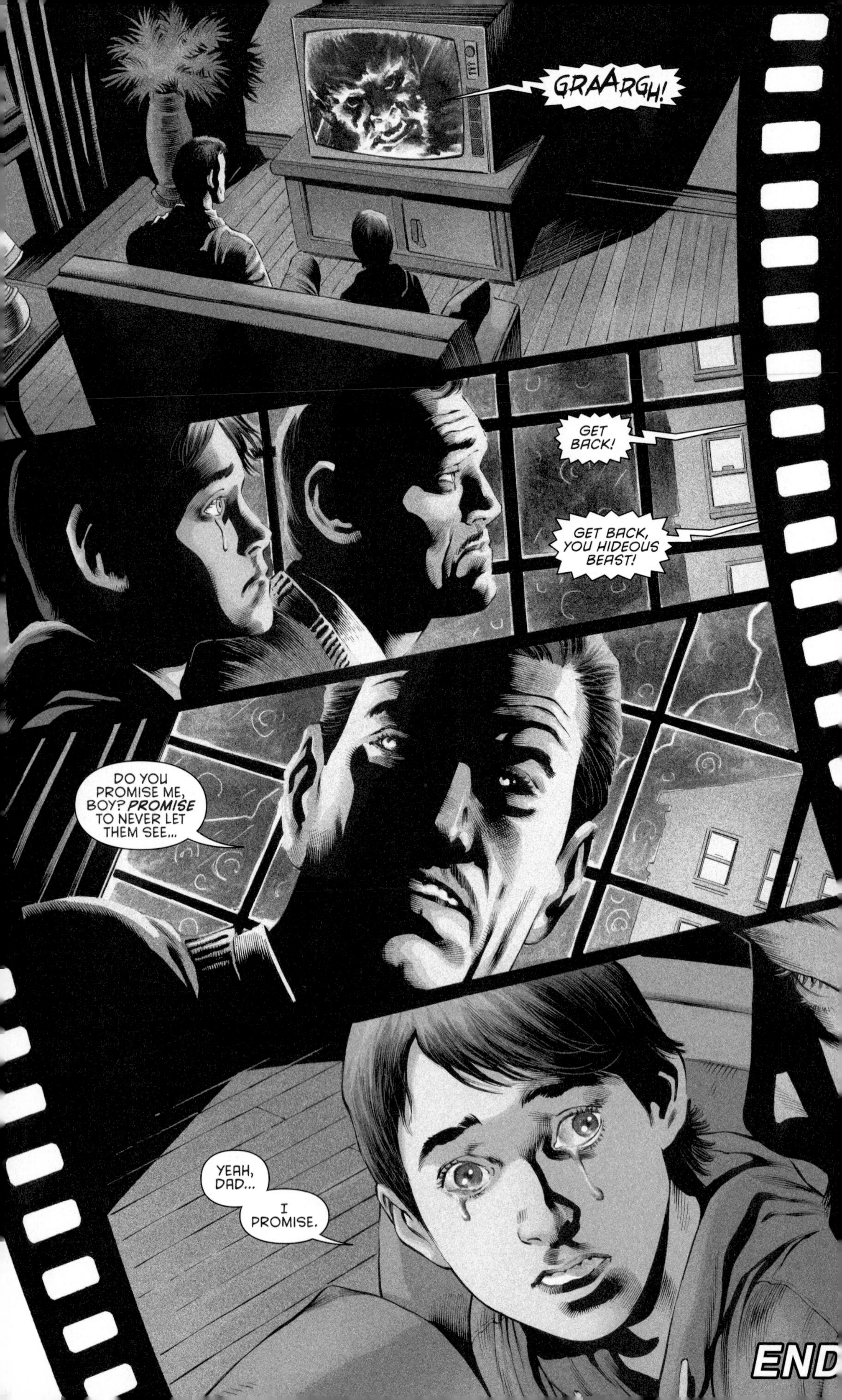
GRAARGH!
GET BACK!
GET BACK, YOU HIDEOUS BEAST!
DO YOU PROMISE ME, BOY? ***PROMISE*** TO NEVER LET THEM SEE...
YEAH, DAD...
I PROMISE.
END

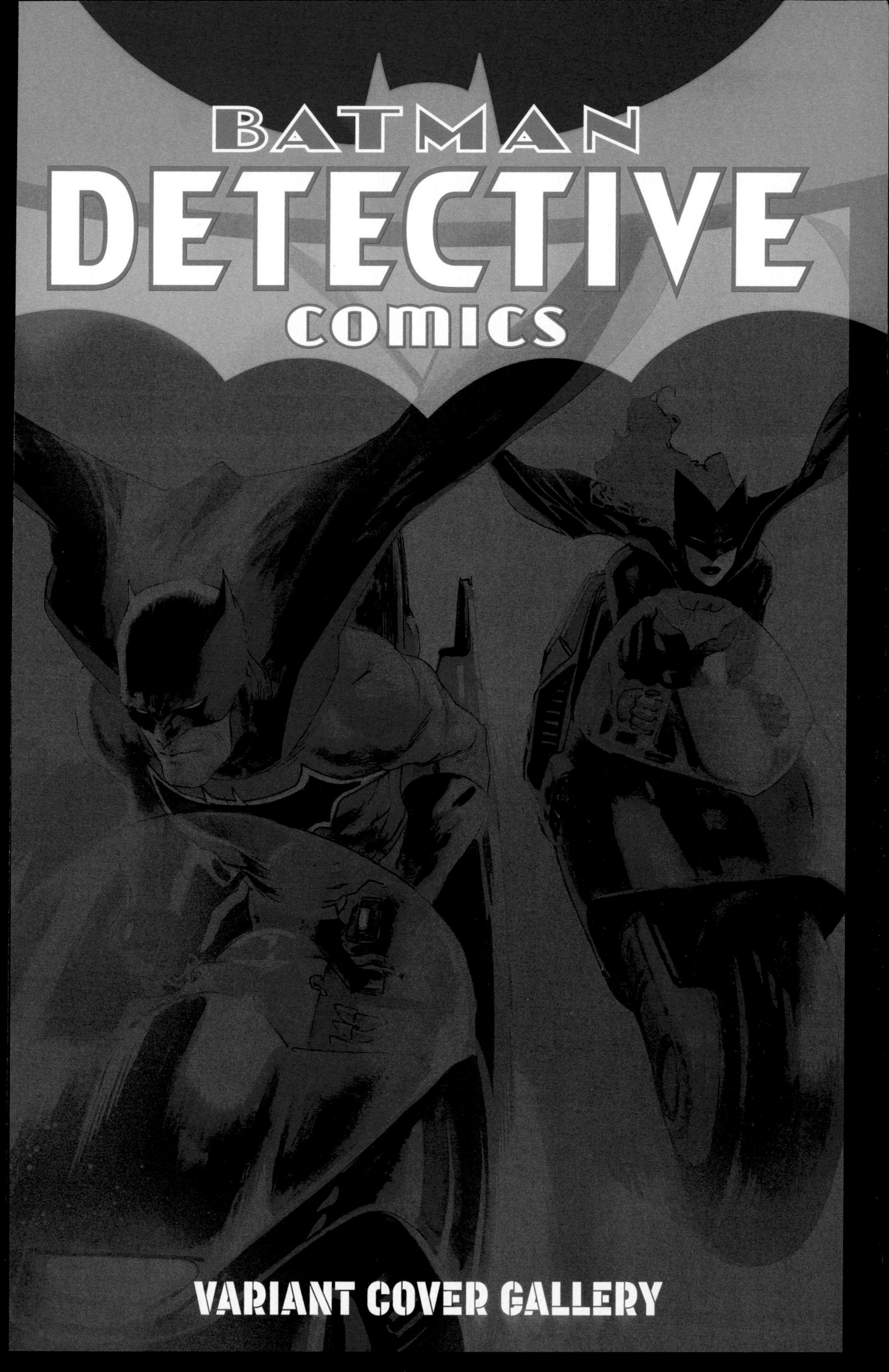
BATMAN
DETECTIVE
COMICS
VARIANT COVER GALLERY

DETECTIVE COMICS #969 variant cover by RAFAEL ALBUQUERQUE

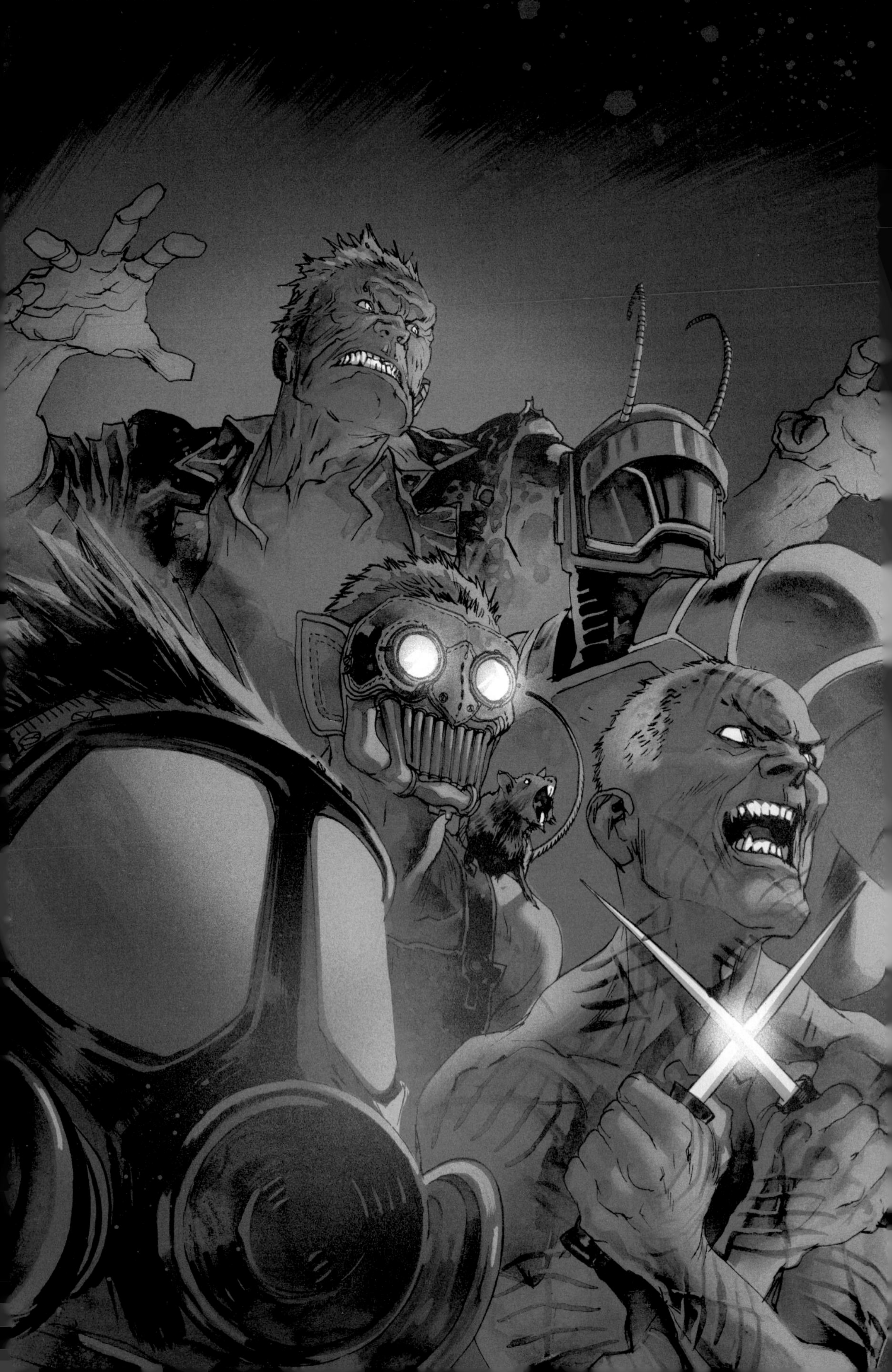

DETECTIVE COMICS #970 variant cover by RAFAEL ALBUQUERQUE

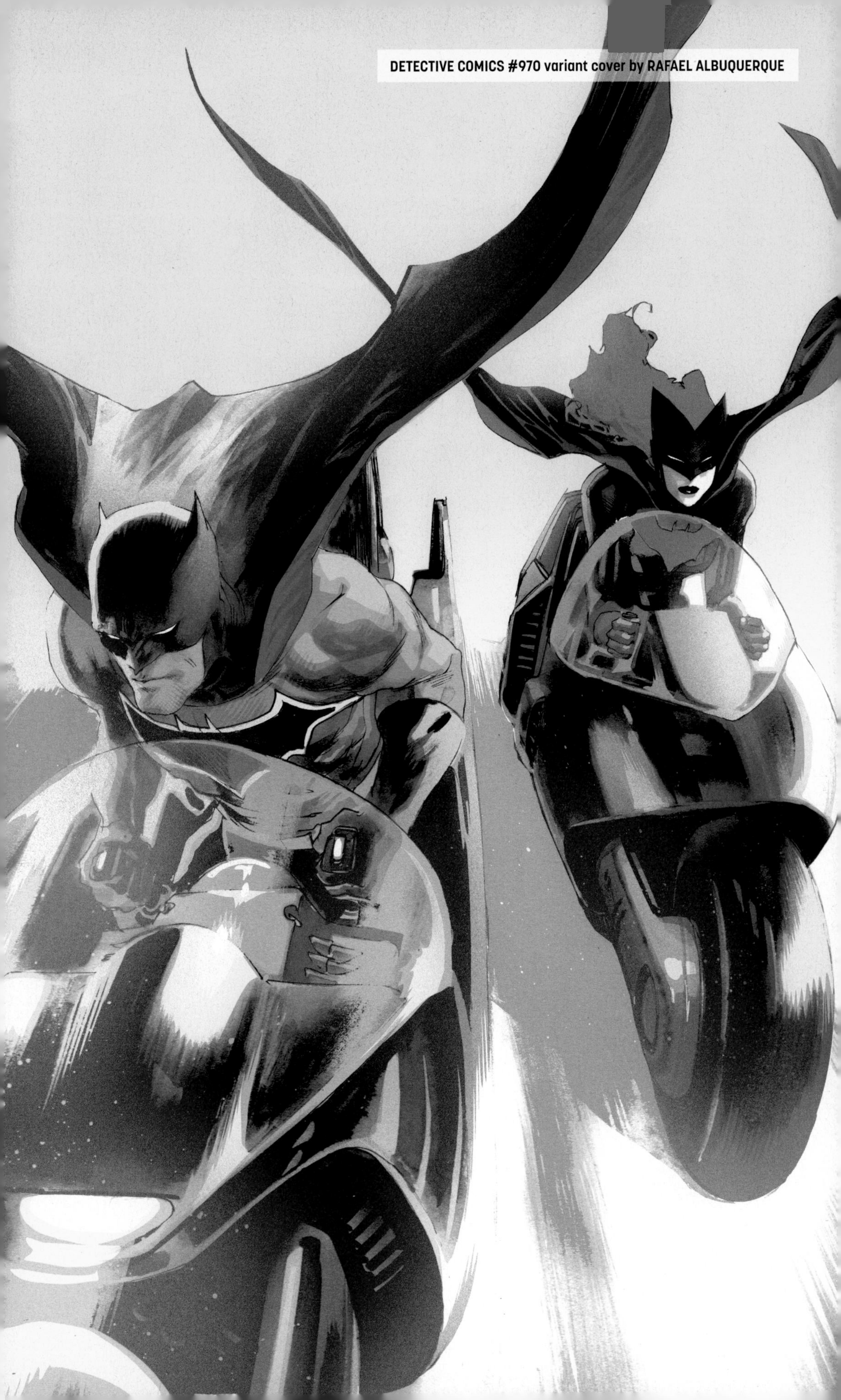

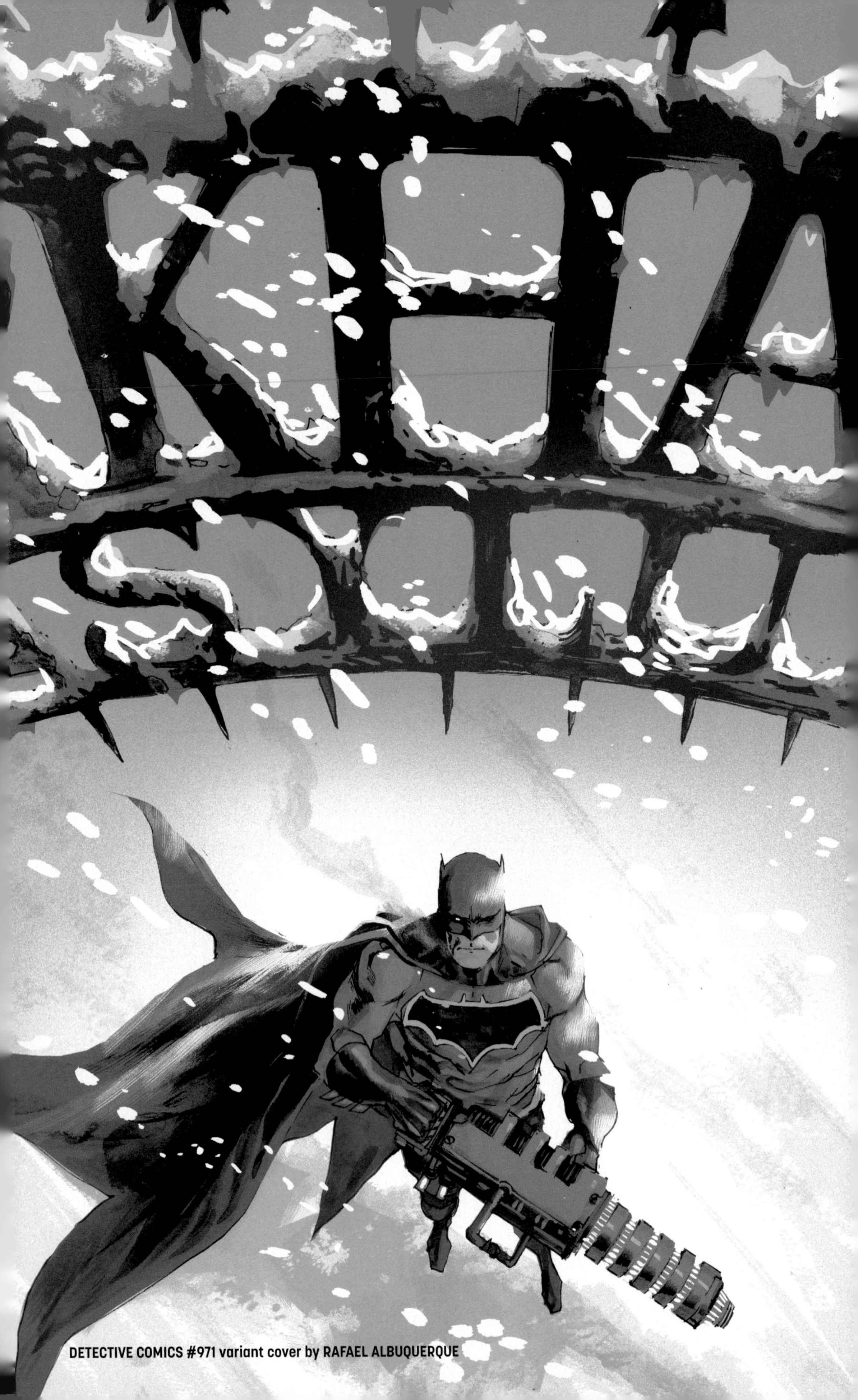

DETECTIVE COMICS #971 variant cover by RAFAEL ALBUQUERQUE

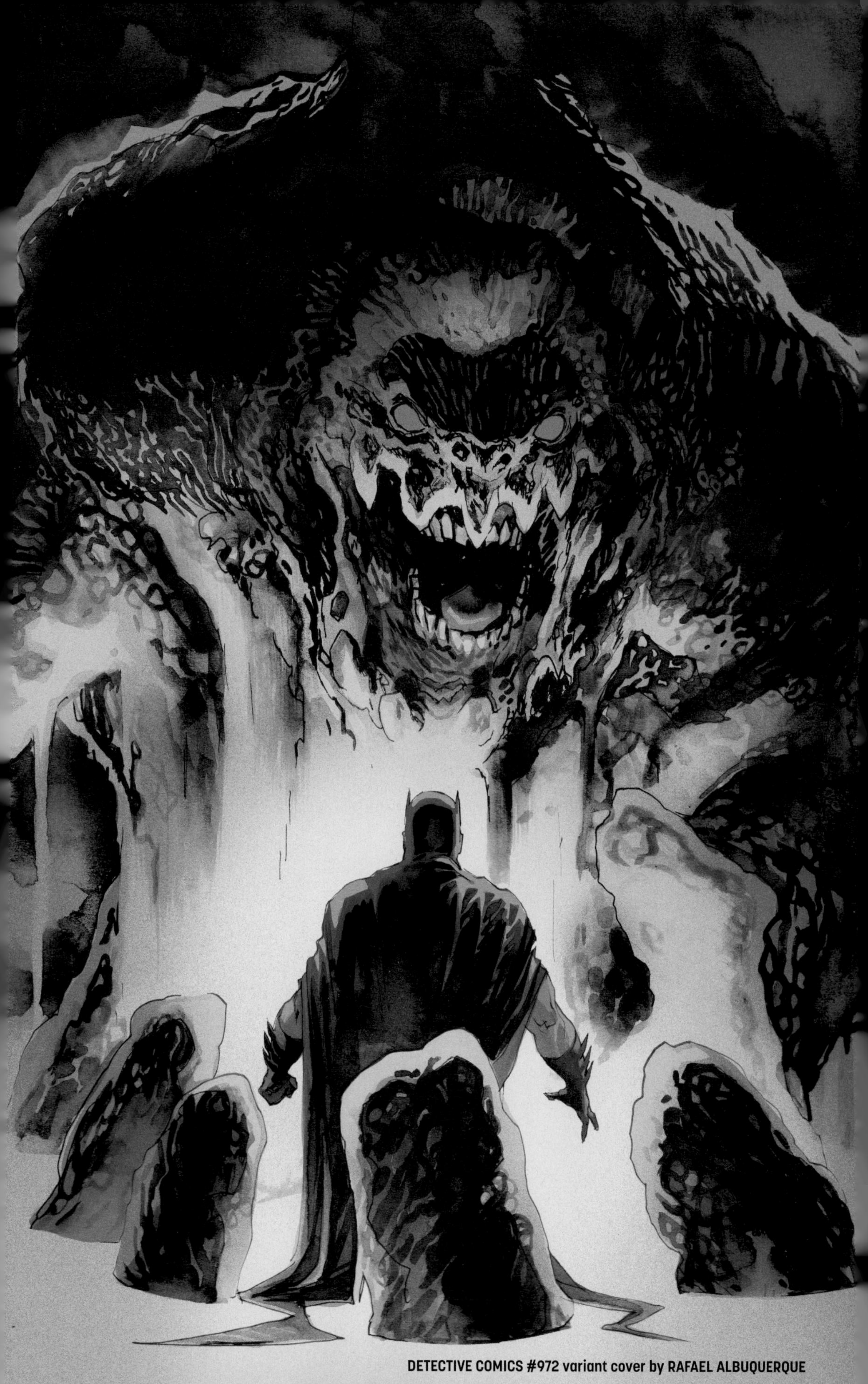

DETECTIVE COMICS #972 variant cover by RAFAEL ALBUQUERQUE

DETECTIVE COMICS #973 variant cover by RAFAEL ALBUQUERQUE

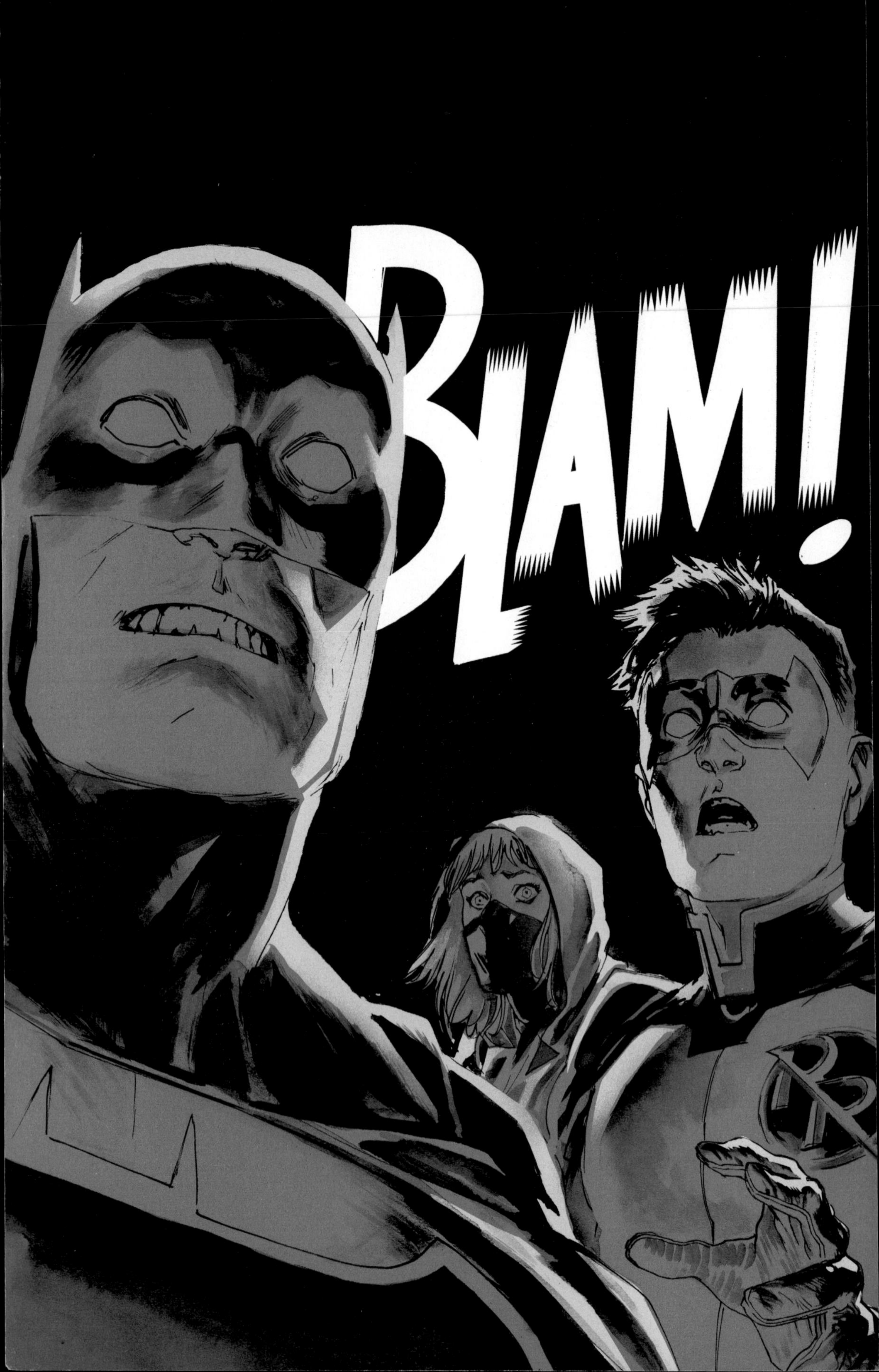
BLAM!

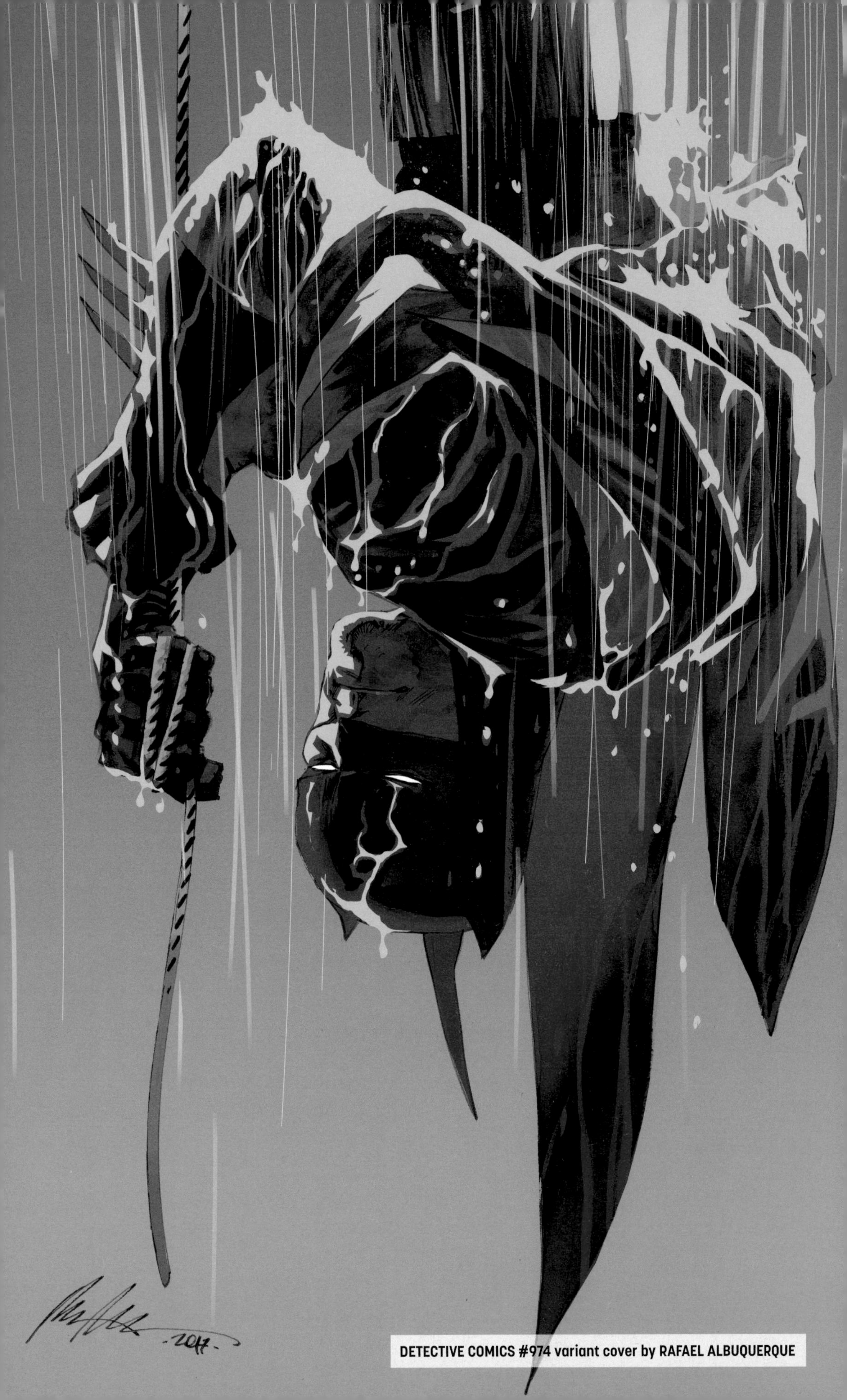

DETECTIVE COMICS #974 variant cover by RAFAEL ALBUQUERQUE

"Head-spinning spectacular from top to bottom."
— **MTV GEEK**

"This is your go-to book."
— **ENTERTAINMENT WEEKLY**

TONY S. DANIEL

BATMAN: DETECTIVE COMICS VOL. 1: FACES OF DEATH

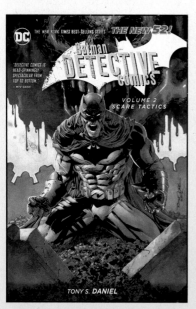

BATMAN: DETECTIVE COMICS VOL. 2: SCARE TACTICS

DEATHSTROKE VOL. 1: GODS OF WAR

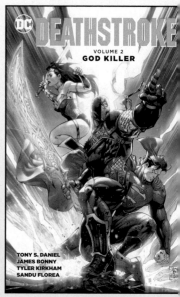

DEATHSTROKE VOL. 2: GOD KILLER